"*Sidewalk* will radically change the way we think about 'the public sphere.'"

—Robin D. G. Kelley, Professor of History and Africana Studies, New York University, and author of *Yo Mama's Disfunktional!*

"Duneier does more than simply provide a critique of racial and class stereotypes. He examines how people commonly stigmatized by and excluded from traditional society on the basis of their race and class struggle to define moral standards and to live according to those standards." —Charles Davis, *The Atlantic Unbound*

"A brilliant and meticulous description of a distinctly urban phenomenon: the life of the sidewalk and the people who live and work there." —Eve Claxton, *Time Out New York*

"A nuanced study of the lives of impoverished street vendors in New York's Greenwich Village . . . A work that adds much to our understanding of race, poverty, and our reactions to them."
—*Kirkus Reviews*

"*Sidewalk* is an important book . . . Duneier reaffirms the value and tradition of Chicago School symbolic interactionism [and also extends] this tradition by integrating new approaches and insights, particularly from feminist theory and conversation analysis. The result is an impressive blend of the past and present of our discipline." —Philip Manning, *Symbolic Interaction*

"Beyond its sensitive portrayal of black men living on the margins of society, *Sidewalk* is a testament to the survival skills of a people who from slavery to the present somehow have cobbled lives stunted by racial deprivation into a mostly unheralded affirmation of the human spirit."
—Derrick Bell, author of *Faces at the Bottom of the Well*

Acclaim for Mitchell Duneier's

SIDEWALK

"Duneier manages to cut through pie-in-the-sky idealism with convincing research married to a well-considered dialectic . . . Adding to the powerful text are hauntingly beautiful photographs by Ovie Carter."   —Andrew Jacobs, *The New York Times Book Review*

"[*Sidewalk*] is in the best traditions of participant observation. If I were still teaching, I would want all of my students to read this book."   —William Foote Whyte, author of *Street Corner Society*

"An inspired yet strategically conceived work that restores a sense of new possibility and passion to ethnography."
    —George E. Marcus, Rice University, author of
    Ethnography Through Thick and Thin

"*Sidewalk* brings us close to the hustle and bustle of urban street life—the book is a knowing, thoughtful exploration that will earn it a place among the classics of the documentary tradition."
    —Robert Coles

"That [Duneier] can be wry and in some instances condemnatory only makes more striking the sympathetic understanding that runs through his magnificent book, with luminous photographs by Ovie Carter, whose camera eye, held steady, records the humanity that ours avoids. Contrary to a periscope, *Sidewalk* refracts our vision downward, breaking through to what, for freshness, seems unnervingly like open sky underneath our feet."
    —Richard Eder, *The New York Times*

"Life on city sidewalks . . . is explored with novelistic nuance in this gritty, intimate study."
    —Megan Harlan, *Entertainment Weekly*

"The world of sidewalk vending [is] a highly complex socioeconomic sphere with its own rules, hierarchies and sense of order. In bringing that world to his readers with tremendous humility and integrity, Duneier has written what is sure to become a contemporary classic of urban sociology."   —Andrew O'Hehir, *Salon*

"No one has combined theory and intimate knowledge of city streets as successfully. A masterpiece of fieldwork."
—Howard S. Becker, author of *Outsiders*

"Always sympathetic to [the homeless'] struggles in a society whose reactions typically range from disapproval to fear, Duneier nonetheless avoids 'sociological romance' and doesn't fight shy of issues like criminality and drug abuse."   —*The New Yorker*

"Like [Jacob] Riis a century ago, Duneier—with the aid of Ovie Carter's excellent photographs of everyone concerned and all salient details—demonstrates the humanity and character of the city's forgotten, and enumerates the particulars of their oppression. I won't make any bets that politicians or cops will read this book, but perhaps the requisite shame and doubt will eventually trickle down to them the way the substance of Riis's *How the Other Half Lives* touched slumlords, if only for a little while."
—Luc Sante, *Voice Literary Supplement*

"Mitchell Duneier must be one of the outstanding ethnographers of our time: he renders visible what typically remains submerged as we take in the world at street level. This is a deep, complex, moving book that yanks you out of your own lived experiences of that world and draws you to another."
—Saskia Sassen, author of *The Global City*

"An eloquently persuasive argument . . . Duneier writes lucidly and sympathetically, with a minimum of jargon, and wisely lets incident and anecdote take the place—and do the work—of theory and abstraction . . . [Longtime vendor Hakim] Hasan's afterword completes the portrait that Duneier has so ably drawn."
—Francine Prose, *Los Angeles Times Book Review*

Mitchell Duneier is an associate professor of sociology at the University of Wisconsin–Madison and the University of California at Santa Barbara. His first book, *Slim's Table*, received the 1994 Distinguished Publication Award from the American Sociological Association.

Ovie Carter, a photographer for the *Chicago Tribune*, has received the Pulitzer Prize and multiple Awards of Excellence from the National Association of Black Journalists.

Also by Mitchell Duneier

SLIM'S TABLE

SIDEWALK

SIDE

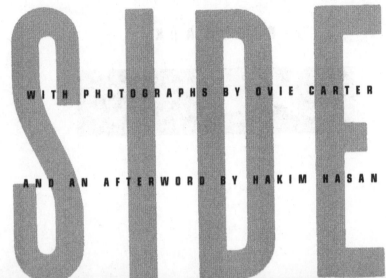

WITH PHOTOGRAPHS BY OVIE CARTER

AND AN AFTERWORD BY HAKIM HASAN

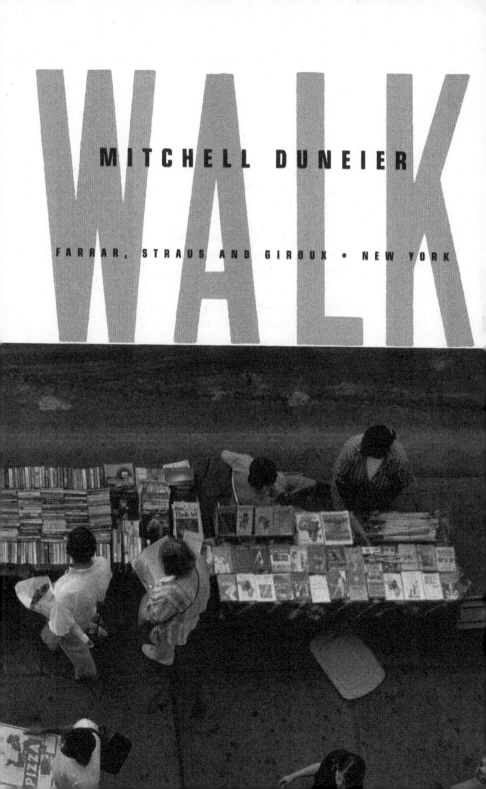

WALK

MITCHELL DUNEIER

FARRAR, STRAUS AND GIROUX • NEW YORK

Farrar, Straus and Giroux
18 West 18th Street, New York 10011

Distributed in Canada by Douglas & McIntyre Ltd.
Printed in the United States of America
Published in 1999 by Farrar, Straus and Giroux
First paperback edition, 2001

Library of Congress catalog card number: 98-73831
Paperback ISBN-13: 978-0-374-52725-9
Paperback ISBN-10: 0-374-52725-3

Cover and map concept by Penelope Hardy

www.fsgbooks.com

27 29 30 28

Contents

Who's Who on the Sidewalk

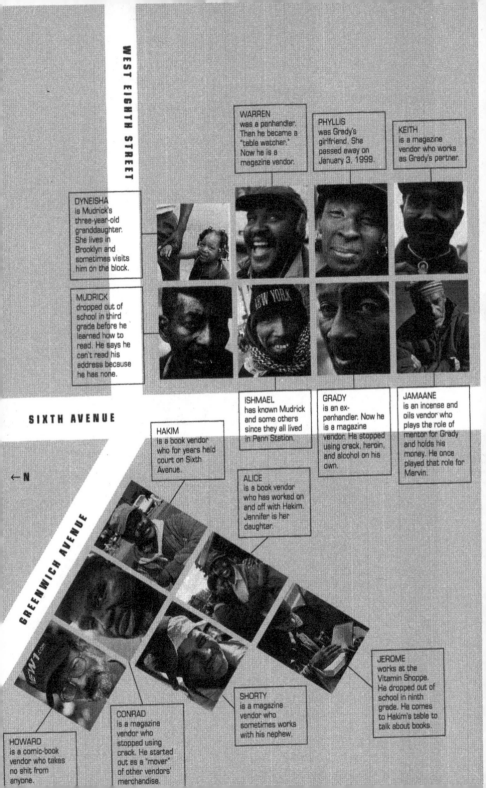

WEST EIGHTH STREET

WARREN
was a panhandler. Then he became a "table watcher." Now he is a magazine vendor.

PHYLLIS
was Grady's girlfriend. She passed away on January 3, 1999.

KEITH
is a magazine vendor who works as Grady's partner.

DYNEISHA
is Mudrick's three-year-old granddaughter. She lives in Brooklyn and sometimes visits him on the block.

MUDRICK
dropped out of school in third grade before he learned how to read. He says he can't read his address because he has none.

SIXTH AVENUE

ISHMAEL
has known Mudrick and some others since they all lived in Penn Station.

GRADY
is an ex-panhandler. Now he is a magazine vendor. He stopped using crack, heroin, and alcohol on his own.

JAMAANE
is an incense and oils vendor who plays the role of mentor for Grady and holds his money. He once played that role for Mervin.

HAKIM
is a book vendor who for years held court on Sixth Avenue.

ALICE
is a book vendor who has worked on and off with Hakim. Jennifer is her daughter.

← N

GREENWICH AVENUE

JEROME
works at the Vitamin Shoppe. He dropped out of school in ninth grade. He comes to Hakim's table to talk about books.

SHORTY
is a magazine vendor who sometimes works with his nephew.

CONRAD
is a magazine vendor who stopped using crack. He started out as a "mover" of other vendors' merchandise.

HOWARD
is a comic-book vendor who takes no shit from anyone.

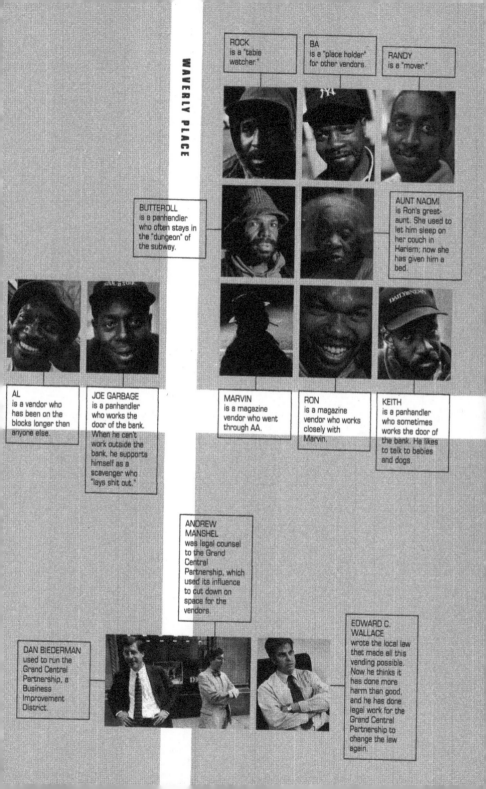

ROCK
is a "table watcher."

BA
is a "place holder" for other vendors.

RANDY
is a "mover."

BUTTEROLL
is a panhandler who often stays in the "dungeon" of the subway.

AUNT NAOMI
is Ron's great-aunt. She used to let him sleep on her couch in Harlem; now she has given him a bed.

AL
is a vendor who has been on the blocks longer than anyone else.

JOE GARBAGE
is a panhandler who works the door of the bank. When he can't work outside the bank, he supports himself as a scavenger who "lays shit out."

MARVIN
is a magazine vendor who went through AA.

RON
is a magazine vendor who works closely with Marvin.

KEITH
is a panhandler who sometimes works the door of the bank. He likes to talk to babies and dogs.

ANDREW MANSHEL
was legal counsel to the Grand Central Partnership, which used its influence to cut down on space for the vendors.

EDWARD C. WALLACE
wrote the local law that made all this vending possible. Now he thinks it has done more harm than good, and he has done legal work for the Grand Central Partnership to change the law again.

DAN BIEDERMAN
used to run the Grand Central Partnership, a Business Improvement District.

SIDEWALK

Introduction

Hakim Hasan is a book vendor and street intellectual at the busy intersection of Eighth Street, Greenwich Avenue, and the Avenue of the Americas—aka Sixth Avenue. He is a sturdy and stocky five-foot-seven African American, forty-two years old. In the winter, he wears Timberland boots, jeans, a hooded sweatshirt, a down vest, and a Banana Republic baseball cap.

One Thursday in February 1996, an African-American man in his mid-thirties came up to Hakim's table and asked for a copy of Alice Walker's book *The Same River Twice*, about her experiences in turning her novel *The Color Purple* into a movie. Hakim was all sold out, but said he would get some more in stock soon.

"When you get some, you let me know," said the man, who worked delivering groceries.

"I'll let you know."

"Because, you see, not only that," said the man, "I've got a friend that loves to read."

"Male or female?" asked Hakim.

"Female. She's like this: when she gets a book in her hand, in another hour it's finished. In other words—like, with me, I'll read maybe . . . five chapters, then I'll put it down 'cause I gotta do something, then maybe I'll come back to it. But with her, she gets into it and goes through the whole book like that. Boom. And she puts it on the shelf and it's just like brand-new. Like, when it's her birthday or what-have-you, I buy her books, because that's one of the things that she likes. I bought the book *Waiting to Exhale* in

paperback, right? Listen to this: when I approached her with the book, the movie was coming out and she said, 'You late! I been read that book!' "

Hakim laughed. "I think she had a point."

"I said, 'Better late than never.' I wish I read that book before I seen the movie. Now, you can tell me this, Hakim: is it the same thing in the paperback as the hardcover?"

"Yeah, it's just different print."

"Just different print? Okay. Well, when you get the other book by Alice Walker, you let me know."

The man made a motion to leave, but then he continued talking.

"Because, you see, what happens is that there are a lot of females . . . authors that are coming out that are making their voices heard. More so than ever black. Even Alice Walker says something about this. It goes deep, man."

"Yeah, I'm gonna read that book by Alice Walker," said Hakim. "I'm gonna read it today."

"Oh, you're gonna read it today?" the man asked, laughing.

"I just finished two books over the weekend. I read at least one book a week," said Hakim.

"I try to tell my son that," said the deliveryman. "If you read one book a week, man, you don't know how much knowledge you can get."

Hakim doesn't just name titles. He knows the contents. I have observed the range and depth of his erudition impress scholars, and have seen him show great patience with uneducated people who are struggling with basic ideas and don't know much about books. He might sit for hours without having a single customer step up to his table; other times the table becomes a social center where men and women debate into the night.

For two years, I lived around the corner from where Hakim sets up. Almost every day, whenever I had time to amble about on the block, I'd visit and listen to the conversations taking place at his table.

At first, Hakim sold what he called "black books," works exclusively by or about blacks. In later years, he became romantically involved with a Filipina book vendor named Alice, who carried used paperback classics and *New York Times* best-sellers, and they merged their vending tables. Now they are on their own again, working side by side. Alice is the only woman who works outside on Sixth Avenue every day, and she has practically raised her daughters and granddaughters there. Whereas Alice tends to be "about business," local residents, workers, and visitors come to Hakim to discuss topics of all kinds, from burning issues of the day to age-old questions.

•

Not long after we met, I asked Hakim how he saw his role.

"I'm a public character," he told me.

"A what?" I asked.

"Have you ever read Jane Jacobs's *The Death and Life of Great American Cities*?" he asked. "You'll find it in there."

I considered myself quite familiar with the book, a classic study of modern urban life published in 1961, and grounded in the author's observations of her own neighborhood, Greenwich Village. But I didn't recall the discussion of public characters. Nor did I realize that Hakim's insight would figure in a central way in the manner in which I would come to see the sidewalk life of this neighborhood. When I got home, I looked it up:

The social structure of sidewalk life hangs partly on what can be called self-appointed public characters. A public character is anyone who is in frequent contact with a wide circle of people and who is sufficiently interested to make himself a public character. A public character need have no special talents or wisdom to fulfill his function— although he often does. He just needs to be present, and there need to be enough of his counterparts. His main qualification is that he *is* public, that he talks to lots of different people. In this way, news travels that is of sidewalk interest.[1]

Jacobs had modeled her idea of the public character after the local shopkeepers with whom she and her Greenwich Village neighbors would leave their spare keys. These figures could be counted on to let her know if her children were getting out of hand on the street, or to call the police if a strange-looking person was hanging around for too long: "Storekeepers and other small businessmen are typically strong proponents of peace and order," Jacobs explained. "They hate broken windows and holdups."[2] She also modeled the public character after persons like herself, who distributed petitions on local political issues to neighborhood stores, spreading local news in the process.

Although the idea is meaningful to anyone who has lived in an urban

neighborhood where people do their errands on foot, Jacobs did not define her concept except to say, "A public character is anyone who is . . . sufficiently interested to make himself a public character." To clarify, we may consider her opening observation that the social structure "hangs partly" on the public characters. What Jacobs means is that the social context of the sidewalk is patterned in a particular way because of the presence of the public character: his or her actions have the effect of making street life safer, stabler, and more predictable. As she goes on to explain, this occurs because the public character has "eyes upon the street."

Following Jacobs, urban theorists have emphasized what city dwellers in pedestrian areas like Greenwich Village have always known: sidewalk life is crucial because the sidewalk is *the* site where a sense of mutual support must be felt *among strangers* if they are to go about their lives there together. Unlike most places in the United States, where people do their errands in cars, the people of Greenwich Village do many, if not most, of their errands by walking. The neighborhood's sidewalk life matters deeply to residents and visitors alike. Jacobs emphasized that social contact on the sidewalks must take place within a context of mutual respect for appropriate limits on interaction and intimacy. This made for interactive pleasantness, adding up to "an almost unconscious assumption of general street support when the chips are down."[3] The Village's "eyes upon the street," in Jacobs's famous dictum, indicated that residents and strangers were safe and consequently produced safety in fact.

•

Greenwich Village looked very different forty years ago, when Jane Jacobs was writing her classic book. Much of the architecture remains, and many people still live the way Jacobs's descriptions suggest; but there is another, more marginal population on these streets: poor black men who make their lives on the Village sidewalks. The presence of such people today means that pedestrians handle their social boundaries *in situ*, whereas, in the past, racial segregation and well-policed skid-row areas kept the marginal at bay.

In this book, I will offer a framework for understanding the changes that have taken place on the sidewalk over the past four decades. In asking *why* the sidewalk life has changed in this affluent neighborhood, I provide the context and point of departure for my research. It has changed because the concentration of poverty in high poverty zones has produced social problems of a magnitude that cannot be contained by even the most extreme forms of social control and exclusion. Many people living and/or working on Sixth Avenue come from such neighborhoods. Some were among the first generation of crack users, and so were affected by the war on those who use the drug and the failure of prisons to help them prepare for life after released. Some, under new workfare rules, have lost their benefits when they refused to show up to work as "the Mayor's slave."

In asking *how* the sidewalk life works today, I begin by looking at the lives of the poor (mainly) black men who work and/or live on the sidewalks of an upper-middle-class neighborhood. Unlike Hakim, who has an apartment in New Jersey, magazine vendors like Ishmael Walker are without a home; the police throw their merchandise, vending tables, clothes, and family photos in the back of a garbage truck when they leave the block to relieve themselves. Mudrick Hayes and Joe Garbage "lay shit out" on the ground (merchandise retrieved from the trash) to earn their subsistence wages. Keith Johnson sits in his wheelchair by the door of the automated teller machine and panhandles.

How do these persons live in a moral order? How do they have the ingenuity to do so in the face of exclusion and stigmatization on the basis of race and class? How does the way they do so affront the sensibilities of the working and middle classes? How do their acts intersect with a city's mechanisms to regulate its public spaces?

The people making lives on Sixth Avenue depend on one another for social support. The group life upon which their survival is contingent is crucial to those who do not rely on religious institutions or social service agencies. For some of these people, the informal economic life is a substitute for illegal ways of supporting excessive drug use. For others, informal modes of self-help enable them to do things most citizens seek to achieve by working: to support families, others in their community, or themselves. For still others, the informal economy provides a forum where they can advise, mentor, and encourage one another to strive to live in accordance with standards of moral worth.

Yet the stories of these sidewalks cannot ultimately serve as sociological romance, celebrating how people on the streets "resist" the larger structures of society. The social order these relationships carve out of what seems to be pure chaos, powerful as its effects are, still cannot control many acts that affront the sensibilities of local residents and passersby. How can we comprehend types of behavior such as sidewalk sleeping, urinating in public, selling stolen goods, and entangling passersby in unwanted conversations? What factors engender and sustain such behavior? How can we understand the processes that lead many people to regard those who engage in such acts as "indecent"? How do the quantity and quality of their "indecency" make them different from conventional passersby?

One of the greatest strengths of firsthand observation is also its greatest weakness. Through a careful involvement in people's lives, we can get a fix on how their world works and how they see it. But the details can be misleading if they distract us from the forces that are less visible to the people we observe but which influence and sustain the behaviors.[4] How do economic, cultural, and political factors contribute to make these blocks a habitat—a place where poor people can weave together complementary elements to organize themselves for subsistence? And how do such forces contribute to bringing these men to the sidewalk in the first place?

I look at all these aspects of sidewalk life in a setting where government retrenchment on welfare is keenly felt, as is the approbation of influential business groups. When government does assume responsibility in the lives of people like these, it attempts to eradicate them from the streets or to shape their behavior. These "social controls"—e.g., cutting down on the space for vending or throwing vendors' belongings in the back of garbage trucks—are the intended and unintended results of what has become the most influential contemporary idea about deviance and criminality: the "broken windows" theory, which holds that minor signs of disorder lead to serious crime. What are the consequences of this theory, its assumptions, and the formal social controls to which it has led?

In trying to understand the sidewalk life, I refer to an area of about three city blocks. Here we can see the confluence of many forces: some global (deindustrialization), some national (stratification of race and class and gender), some local (restrictive and punitive policies toward street vendors). Here, also, are blocks which can be studied in light of Jane Jacobs's earlier account and which contain the kinds of social problems that have become iconic in representations of the city's "quality of life" crisis. My visits to some other New York neighborhoods[5] and some other American cities suggest that they, too, have tensions surrounding inequalities and cultural differences in dense pedestrian areas. Across the country, liberals have voted to elect moderate, "law and order" mayors, some of them Republican. Whereas disorderly-conduct statutes were once enough, anti-panhandling statutes have been passed in Seattle, Atlanta, Cincinnati, Dallas, Washington, D.C., San Francisco, Santa Barbara, Long Beach, Philadelphia, New Haven, Raleigh, and Baltimore.

Yet New York City and Greenwich Village are unique in a multitude of ways. I certainly cannot hope to account for life in the majority of places, which have not seen severe sidewalk tensions in dense pedestrian districts; even many places that *have* seen such tensions are different from Greenwich Village.[6] Nor can I hope to show how the sidewalk works in low-income neighborhoods where the majority of tense sidewalk interactions occur among members of the same class or racial group. In the end, I must leave it to readers to test my observations against their own, and hope that the concepts I have developed to make sense of this neighborhood will prove useful in other venues.

•

I gained entrée to this social world when I became a browser and customer at Hakim's table in 1992. Through my relationship with him, I came to know others in the area. He introduced me to unhoused and formerly unhoused people who scavenge and sell on the street, as well as other vendors who compete with him for sidewalk space and access to customers. These relations then led me to panhandlers, some of whom also sometimes scavenge and vend.

Once I was in the network, contacts and introductions took place across the various spheres. Eventually, I worked as a general assistant—watching vendors' merchandise while they went on errands, buying up merchandise offered in their absence, assisting on scavenging missions through trash and recycling bins, and "going for coffee." Then I worked full-time as a magazine vendor and scavenger during the summer of 1996, again for three days a week during the summer of 1997 and during part of the fall of 1997. I also made daily visits to the blocks during the summer of 1998, often for hours at a time, and worked full-time as a vendor for two weeks in March 1999, when my research came to an end.

Although in race, class, and status I am very different from the men I write about, I was myself eventually treated by them as a fixture of the blocks, occasionally referred to as a "scholar" or "professor," which is my occupation. My designation was Mitch. This seemed to have a variety of changing meanings, including: a naïve white man who could himself be exploited for "loans" of small change and dollar bills; a Jew who was going to make a lot of money off the stories of people working the streets; a white writer who was trying to "state the truth about what was going on." More will be said about these and other perceptions in the pages that follow.

My continual presence as a vendor provided me with opportunities to observe life among the people working and/or living on the sidewalk, including their interactions with passersby. This enabled me to draw many of my conclusions about what happens on the sidewalk from incidents I myself witnessed, rather than deriving them from interviews. Often I simply asked questions while participating and observing.

Sometimes, when I wanted to understand how the local political system had shaped these blocks, I did my interviews at the offices of Business Improvement Districts, politicians, and influential attorneys. I also questioned police officers, pedestrians, local residents, and the like. I carried out more than twenty interviews with people working the sidewalk in which I explicitly asked them to tell me their "story." These sessions, held on street corners, in coffee shops, and on subway platforms, lasted between two and six hours. I paid the interviewees fifty dollars when their sessions were over, as compensation for time they could have spent selling or panhandling. Throughout the book, I try to be clear about the kind of research from which a quotation has been culled.

After I had been observing on the block for four years, Ovie Carter, an African-American photojournalist who has been taking pictures of the inner city for three decades, agreed to take photographs to illustrate the things I was writing about. He visited the blocks year-round and came to know the people in the book intimately. Ovie's photographs helped me to see things that I had not noticed, so that my work has now been influenced by his.

After three years passed, I believed I had a strong sense of the kinds of events and conversations that were typical on the blocks. In the next two years of this research, my field methods evolved to the point where intense use was made of a tape recorder. The tape recorder was on throughout my days on the block, usually kept in a milk crate under my vending table. People working and/or living on the sidewalk became accustomed to the machine and, after being exposed to it over a period of weeks, came to talk in ways that I determined to be like the talk I had heard before. Since the machine was taping on a public street, I hoped that I was not violating any expectation of privacy if it picked up the words of people who couldn't efficiently be informed that it was on. I have since received permission to quote almost all the people who were taped without their knowledge. When names are used, they are real ones, and I do so with consent. In those few cases when this is not possible (such as incidents involving police officers whose speech was recorded by my microphone without their knowing it), I have not used names at all or have indicated that a name is false.

I am committed to the idea that the voices of the people on Sixth Avenue need to be heard. To that end, my goal has been to assure the reader that what appears between quotation marks is a reasonably reliable record of what was said. (Some quotes have been edited slightly to make them more concise.) When the best I could do was rely on my memory or notes, quotation marks are not used. I have come to believe that this is perhaps especially necessary when a scholar is writing about people who occupy race and class positions widely divergent from his or her own, for the inner meanings and logics embodied in language that is distinctive to those positions can easily be misunderstood and misrepresented if not accurately reproduced. Furthermore, the increasingly popular practice of creating composite characters, and combining events and quotations sometimes occurring months or years apart, is *not* employed here. No characters have been combined. No events have been reordered.

Some of the people on the street volunteered to "manage" the taping by themselves, leaving the tape recorder on while wearing it in their pocket or resting it on their table when I was away from the scene or out of town. Such acts demonstrated the desire of persons in the book to ask their own questions, have their own topics addressed and recognized, and enable me to hear some things that went on when I could not be present. Sometimes they used the machine to interview one another and gave me the tapes. (In the pages that follow, I indicate when I rely upon such a source.) Given the knowledge Hakim had of both Jane Jacobs's work (which he inspired me to reread) and the life of these sidewalks, I asked him to respond to this book. He took time out of his daily grind as a vendor to write an afterword.

There was another way in which the vendors, scavengers, and panhandlers worked with me as collaborators. I invited some of them to classes to teach my students, in both Santa Barbara and Wisconsin. And I asked all of them to judge my own "theories" of the local scene when the book was complete, though always indicating that, while respecting their interpretations, I would not be bound by them. Throughout the book, it is I who have selected the material presented, and I take responsibility for the interpretations that go along with that material. For twenty-one people who figure prominently on the blocks, I have now made a commitment to return the advance and a share of any royalties or other forms of income that the book might yield.

Like all observers, I have my subjectivities. I know that scrupulous adherence to rules of method will not lead necessarily to objective truth. I believe that what is most important is that I try to help the reader recognize the lens through which the reality is refracted. I have written a statement on method to that end, and throughout the book I endeavor to explain my procedures for selecting data and my own biases and uncertainties about the inferences I draw.

Fieldwork is presumed to require trust. But one never can know for certain that he or she has gained such trust, given the absence of any agreed-upon indicator of what "full" trust would look like. In this case, I think, some level of trust was shown by people's readiness to provide access to information, settings, and activities of the most intimate sort. They sometimes revealed illegal activities or actions which, if others knew of them, might result in violent retribution.

But as I will explain, there were times when the trust I thought I had developed was nothing more than an illusion: deep suspicion lingered despite an appearance of trust. In some cases, perhaps it always will. Surely it takes more than goodwill to transcend distrust that comes out of a complex history. Though participant observers often remark on the rapport they achieve and how they are seen by the people they write about, in the end it is best to be humble about such things, because one never really knows.

Mitchell Duneier
March 1999

PART ONE

THE INFORMAL LIFE

OF THE SIDEWALK

The Book Vendor

It is not hard to understand why Hakim Hasan came to see himself as a public character. Early one July morning, a deliveryman pulled his truck up to the curb behind Hakim's vending table on Greenwich Avenue off the corner of Sixth Avenue and carried a large box of flowers over to him.

"Can you hold these until the flower shop opens up?" the deliveryman asked.

"No problem," responded Hakim as he continued to set up the books on his table. "Put them right under there."

When the store opened for business, he brought them inside and gave them to the owner.

"Why did that man trust you with the flowers?" I later asked.

"People like me are the eyes and ears of this street," he explained, echoing Jane Jacobs again. "Yes, I could take those flowers and sell them for a few hundred dollars. But that deliveryman sees me here every day. I'm as dependable as any store-owner."

A few days later, an elderly black man on his afternoon walk came up to the table. "Can I sit down?" he asked Hakim, who gave him a chair.

The man was panting and sweating, so Hakim went to the telephone on the corner and called 911.

As they waited for the paramedics to arrive, the man said he was going into the subway.

"It's too hot for you down there," Hakim replied. "You wait right here for the ambulance!"

Soon an ambulance arrived, and the crew carried away the old man. It turned out he had suffered an asthma attack.

Another day, I was present at the table when a traffic officer walked by to give out parking tickets.

"Are any of these your cars?" she asked Hakim.

"Yes, that one, and that one," said Hakim, pointing.

"What is that all about?" I asked.

"The day I met her, we got into an argument," he explained. "She was getting ready to give the guy across the street a ticket. I say, 'You can't do this!' She said, 'Why not?' I say, ' 'Cause I'm getting ready to put a quarter in.' She said, 'You can't do that.' I guess that, because of the way I made my argument, she didn't give out the ticket, and from that point onward we became friends. And when she comes on the block, she asks me, for every car on the block that has a violation sign, 'Is that your car?' Meaning, 'Is it someone you know?' And depending on whether I say yes or no, that's it—they get a ticket."

Once, a group of German tourists wearing Nikon cameras passed the table. Though the information booth run by the Village Alliance Business Improvement District was open on a little island across the street, they walked up to Hakim instead.

"How do we get to Greenwich Village?" one man asked.

"This *is* Greenwich Village," Hakim explained.

"Are these things part of your job description as a vendor?" I asked him once.

"Let me put it to you this way, Mitch," he replied. "I kind of see what I loosely call my work on the sidewalk as going far, far beyond just trying to make a living selling books. That sometimes even seems secondary. Over time, when people see you on the sidewalk, there is a kind of trust that starts. They've seen you so long that they walk up to you. There have been occasions when I've had to have directions translated out of Spanish into French to get somebody to go someplace!"

It is not only directions and assistance that I have seen Hakim give out. He also tells people a great deal about books—so much so that he once told me he was thinking of charging tuition to the people who stand in his space on the sidewalk.

I think he was only half joking. Indeed, Hakim seems to consider himself a person of some consequence out on the street, not merely a public character but a street intellectual of sorts as well. His self-image is sometimes reinforced by his customers. On a September afternoon, a middle-aged man walked up to his table. "Do you got the book *The Middle Passage*?"

"By Charles Johnson?" asked Hakim. "Is it a novel?"

"No. It's by Tom Feelings."

"Oh, it's a big, oversized black book with beautiful pictures! No, I do not have that. Yeah, I know the book. It's forty bucks."

"I know that if anyone knows, you know."

"Well, I'm one of the few who may know. There's a lot of people out here who know. I try to do my homework. I stay up late at night going through periodicals, newspapers, all kinds of stuff, to try to figure out what's published."

Hakim is one of many street book vendors throughout Greenwich Village and New York City generally. Most of these vendors specialize in one or more of the following: expensive art and photography books; dictionaries; *New York Times* best-sellers; "black books"; new quality mass-market and trade paperbacks of all varieties; used and out-of-print books; comic books; pornography; and discarded magazines.

On Sixth Avenue alone, among the vendors of new books, a passerby may encounter Muhammad and his family, who sell "black books" and an incense known as "the Sweet Smell of Success" at the corner of Sixth Avenue and Eighth Street. Down the block, an elderly white man sells best-sellers and high-quality hardcovers on the weekends. At Sixth and Greenwich (across the street), one encounters Howard, a comics vendor, also white, and Alice, a Filipina woman (Hakim's sometime business partner), who sells used paperbacks and current best-sellers.

These vendors take in anywhere from fifty to a couple of hundred dollars a day. By selling discounted books on the street (and I will discuss how these books get to the street in a later chapter), they serve an important function in the lives of their customers. Indeed, if all they did was to sell books at prices lower than those of the bookstores, this would be enough to explain why they are able to sustain themselves on the street. But to understand *how* Hakim functions as a public character, I thought it would be helpful to look more closely at the meaning the book table has in the minds of both the vendor and the customer who patronizes it.

It goes without saying, perhaps, that one good way to find out more about people is to get to know them at first hand, but this is more easily said than done. When I began, I knew that if I was to find out what was taking place on the sidewalk, I would have to bridge many gaps between myself and the people I hoped to understand. This involved thinking carefully about who they are and who I am.

I was uneasy.

One of the most notorious gaps in American society is the difference between people related to race and the discourse revolving around this volatile issue. Though there were also differences between our social classes (I was raised in a middle-class suburb, whereas most of them grew up in lower- and working-class urban neighborhoods), religions (I am Jewish and most of them are Muslim or Christian), levels of education (I hold a Ph.D. in sociology and attended two years of law school, whereas some of them did not graduate from high school), and occupations (I am a college professor of sociology and they are street vendors), none of these differences seemed to be as significant as that of race. Actually, the interaction between race and class differences very likely made me uneasy, though I was unaware of that at the time.

When I stood at Hakim's table, I felt that, as a white male, I stood out. In my mind, I had no place at his table, because he was selling so-called black books. I thought that his product formed the boundary of a sort of exclusionary black zone where African Americans were welcome but whites were not.

It is interesting that I felt this way. African Americans buy products every day from stores owned by whites, often having to travel to other neighborhoods to acquire the goods they need. They must shop among whites, and often speak of enduring slights and insults from the proprietors of these businesses.[1] I myself rarely have to go to neighborhoods not dominated by whites in search of goods or services. None of the book vendors ever insulted, offended, or threatened me. None of them told me I was not welcome at his table. None of them ever made anti-white or anti-Semitic remarks. Yet I felt unwelcome in ways I had not felt during previous studies that had brought me into contact with African Americans. This was because many of the conversations I heard were about so-called black books and because the people participating in them seemed to be defining themselves as a people. (Actually, there were also white customers at Hakim's table, though I didn't know it at the time.) I felt out of place. Also, I wanted the trust that would be necessary to write about the life of the street, and race differences seem a great obstacle to such trust.

One day, before I knew Hakim and after I had concluded that these tables were not an appropriate place for me to hang out, I walked by his book table on my way to an appointment. I was surprised to see for sale a copy of *Slim's Table*, my own first book.

"Where did you get this from?" I asked, wondering if it had been stolen.

"I have my sources," Hakim responded. "Do you have some interest in this book?"

"Well, I wrote it," I responded.

"Really? Do you live around here?"

"Yes. I live around the corner, on Mercer Street."

"Why don't you give me your address and telephone number for my Rolodex."

His Rolodex? I wondered. This unhoused man has a Rolodex? Why I assumed that Hakim was unhoused is difficult to know for certain. In part, it was due to the context in which he was working: many of the African-American men selling things on the block lived right there on the sidewalk. There was no way for me to distinguish easily between those vendors who were unhoused and those who were not, and I had never taken the time to think much about it. I gave him my telephone number and walked off to my appointment.

A few weeks later, I ran into an African-American man who had been in my first-year class at the New York University School of Law. Purely by coincidence, he told me that he was on his way to see a book vendor from whom he had been getting some of his reading material during the past year. It was Hakim.

I told my classmate about my interest in getting to know Hakim, and explained my reservations. He told me that he didn't think it would be as hard as I thought. Hakim had apparently gone through spells of sleeping in the parks during his time as a vendor, and sometimes stayed at my classmate's home with his wife and children.

A few days later my classmate brought him to meet me in the law-school lounge. When I told Hakim that I wanted to get to know him and the people at his vending table, he was circumspect, saying only that he would think about it. A few days later, he dropped off a brief but eloquent note at my

apartment, explaining that he didn't think it was a good idea. "My suspicion is couched in the collective memory of a people who have been academically slandered for generations," he wrote. "African Americans are at a point where we have to be suspicious of people who want to tell stories about us."

During the next couple of months, Hakim and I saw each other about once a week or so on our own. On a few occasions we met and talked at the Cozy Soup & Burger on Broadway. It seemed that we had decided to get to know each other better.

Early one morning a few months later, I approached his table as he was setting up and asked, What are you doing working on Sixth Avenue in the first place?

I think there are a number of black folks in these corporate environments that have to make this decision, he replied. Some are not as extreme as I am. Some take it out on themselves in other ways.

It had not occurred to me that Hakim had come to work on the street from a corporate environment. Learning this about him has been significant as I have worked to understand his life on the street. In the universities where I teach, I meet many African-American students who believe that it will be very difficult for them to maintain their integrity while working in corporate life. Many of them have come to this conclusion by hearing of the experiences of relatives and friends who have already had problems; others have themselves sensed racial intolerance on campus.[2] Yet, in choosing to work on the street, Hakim had clearly made what would be a radical, if not entirely incomprehensible, decision by the standards of my African-American students. Once we had discussed some of these issues in depth over the subsequent weeks, Hakim volunteered that he felt comfortable letting me observe his table with the purpose of writing about it, and I began to do so.

He told me he was born Anthony E. Francis in Brooklyn, New York, in 1957. His parents, Harriet E. and Ansley J. Francis, had come to Brooklyn from the U.S. Virgin Islands; they separated when he was in grade school. He joined the Nation of Islam as a high-school student. Later, he attended Rutgers University, his tuition paid by grants and loans for disadvantaged youth. He told me he had completed his coursework but never received a diploma, because at the end of his senior year he owed about five hundred dollars to the school.

During college, he wrote articles for *The Black Voice*, a school newspaper, as well as for a national magazine called *The Black Collegian*.[3] Hakim said that, two years after finishing at Rutgers, he ended his affiliation with the American Muslim Mission, although he retained his adopted Muslim name. In his own words, "I could no longer walk in lockstep. I needed my longitude and latitude." Even though he is no longer a practicing Muslim, he often says he still feels a special respect for people who have chosen that path.

After college, he told me, he aspired to enter publishing, but was turned down for every position for which he applied. He then began a series of jobs as a proofreader in law, accounting, and investment-banking firms, including Peat Marwick, Drexel Burnham Lambert, and Robinson, Silverman. During this period, he says, he read hundreds of books and magazines and spent most of his free time in bookstores throughout the city, including the Liberation Bookstore, the well-known African-American bookstore in Harlem. He told me he was dismissed from Robinson, Silverman in 1991, during an employee review, for alleged incompetence according to some unnamed attorney at the firm.[4]

He had observed the sidewalk book vendors in Greenwich Village and believed that they had discovered a way to subsist in New York without buying into the "corporate-employee mind-set." As a vendor of black books, he decided, he would have work that was meaningful—that sustained him economically and intellectually. He began by working for one of the other vendors for a few days, and then borrowed money from a former roommate to start his own table.

When Hakim and his customers use the term "black books," he says, they are using a kind of shorthand for works on a constellation of related subjects and issues. These books may be geared toward helping people of African descent understand where they fit in; codifying the achievements of people of African descent; uncovering the history of African Americans, and of white racism; or helping African Americans develop the knowledge and pride necessary to participate in the wider society.

The publishers of such books often signal their prospective readers by printing the label "African-American Studies" or "Black Studies" on the upper left-hand corner of the back cover. These labels refer to an academic discipline that began to be codified only as recently as the 1960s.[5] Responding to pressure from the first significant population of blacks to be admitted to college, around the time of the Vietnam War, a handful of universities began to offer instruction in the history, literature, and sociology of Americans of African origin. Though there was some debate about the ultimate purpose of this intellectual endeavor, it developed in response to a real demand for deeper understanding of African and African-American history and culture. Courses appropriate to enhancing such understanding came to be recognized as an academic discipline. Though African-American studies reached African-American college students through academic channels, the emerging discipline also had—and continues to have—a secondary impact among African Americans outside the universities, through the influence of alternative distributive networks among the greater African-American population.

As Hakim and I got to know each other over the course of many months, he often greeted me warmly when I came to his table. Standing by, I would note the great range in the educational backgrounds of customers who come to his table to talk about books, and the way this range testifies to this secondary impact of African-American studies. It also illustrates how the very presence of books on the street tends to prompt discussions about moral and intellectual issues. Of course, one might find such discussions taking place in churches, mosques, chess clubs, coffeehouses, reading groups, and colleges, though I don't know if the range in education among the participants is as great in any of those places. On any given day at Hakim's table, one might encounter a high-school dropout, a blue-collar worker, a film student, a law professor, a jazz critic, or a teacher in a Muslim high school. (The last of these figures, Shair Abdul-Mani, has studied and mastered over five languages.) I also discovered that I was wrong in my initial impression that this was an exclusively "black zone." A wide range of whites often stopped at the table to talk about books, including—among many others—a psychologist, a retired shoemaker, and a graduate student in English at Columbia. I think this variety gives a good sense of the wide-reaching impact a book vendor can have on the lives of many people on the street.

Over four years, I witnessed hundreds of these conversations, and Hakim suggested that if I was going to write accurately about them I might put a tape recorder in the milk crate underneath his vending table for a few weeks.

One such conversation took place on a Saturday morning in July, when a young African-American man came up to the table. Jerome Miller, who was twenty-two years old (as he told me later), was on a break from his job at the corner Vitamin Shoppe, where he earned $6.50 per hour as a part-time stock clerk. Approximately five feet eight inches tall, with a goatee and sideburns, he generally wears a pair of Italian-leather hightop shoes, black slacks, and a blue button-down shirt with a T-shirt underneath. I had seen him on previous occasions but was not present for this discussion. It represents a kind of relationship I have observed many times, perhaps once every few weeks over my years on the block.

"How you doing?" Hakim asked. "You off today?"

"No, I'm working," responded Jerome.

"So some Saturdays you on and some Saturdays you off," declared Hakim.

"Yeah. Like not last week, but the week before I worked on Saturday."

There was silence for a few seconds as a siren blared on Sixth Avenue.

"The next book I think you should read is this—*Makes Me Wanna Holler*, by Nathan McCall," Hakim told Jerome. "And one of these days this week I got to get you more information, because, like we were talking about the other day, I want to see if I can get you into that GED program to finish your high-school education. I'm more than certain you can do it. There's a man I know in the neighborhood, I mentioned it to him, and he's willing to help. He's a teacher, and he knows a lot about the examination. So we got to get some more information and see how we can fit it in. Once you pass that GED exam, then you on the way."

"That's what I'd like to do," Jerome responded.

"There's an article in yesterday's *New York Times*," Hakim continued. "Did you see the *Times* yesterday?"

"No," said Jerome.

"Well, the *Times* is something you need to read, and the Sunday *Times* has a wealth of information. It's thick and costs you about $2.50. In fact, what time you leave here on Saturday?"

"About 6:00 p.m."

"You can get it right here at the corner newsstand before you go home the night before. Because they have the bulldog edition the night before. They had an article in the business section about jobs, and the different kinds of preparation you need for these jobs. I think if you get the right kind of training you can do a lot better for yourself. You got to make that effort now to get that GED, and then probably get yourself into a junior college."

"The problem is that I used to go to this trade school in high school, but I didn't learn anything. It was bullshit. So I dropped out in ninth grade."

"How did your parents react?"

"It didn't matter. Nobody could tell me anything back then. I just got a job selling drugs for a while. Then I decided to get out of that."

"How old are you now?"

"Twenty-two."

"So how far do you think you can go, unless you plan on opening up a business of your own from scratch, with a ninth-grade education?"

Jerome stood silently.

"It's not that you dumb or anything," Hakim continued. "If you can read that book that I gave you last week, *Blacks in the White Establishment*,[6] and you did read it, and you did comprehend it, then you are clearly smart enough to do serious schoolwork. I think the problem before was that you might not have felt motivated due to the kind of classes you were taking."

"I need to have someone teach me something that I want to know about," responded Jerome.

"What is it that you want to know?" Hakim asked.

"Teach something that is interesting, I mean, I always say I'm gonna do it, but I end up straying away from it, you know what I mean?"

"Well, you didn't finish school, but you have managed to work and to read books on your own. How do you explain that?"

"I read books all the time, because they are interesting."

"What I'm trying to say is, you found school so nonmotivating when you were fourteen or fifteen years old, but you still managed to read. A lot of guys come down here who dropped out of high school in ninth grade but don't have a functional vocabulary like you definitely do have. Or their reading comprehension does not enable them to read the kind of books that I assign to you. I cannot assign these books to them."

"I just find myself wanting to know about things, and what goes on around me," said Jerome.

"So why don't you start thinking about converting wanting to know things into being able to sit in a class and get that work done?" Hakim asked.

"I can do that. And now I'm pretty sure it wouldn't be a problem. Another reason is that I got a little young one growing up."

"You got a little child? How old?"

"Two. A girl named Geneva. You want to give your kids the things you never had before."

"Are you still involved with the mother?"

"She's not up here right now."

"Where's she at?"

"Florida."

"So, obviously, your daughter is with her. So you don't see her that often."

"At first, you know what I'm saying, it was kind of hard. But I still didn't run away, 'cause I know I have to take care of my own. So I work and I send the money."

"What does your father do?"

"He used to be a carpenter the last time I talked to him, a year or two ago. He used to take care of us when we was younger, but everything changes. My parents haven't been together from when I was born. And my mother and I don't have a deep relationship. I mean, we talk, and I know she's my mother. I'm fortunate to just be alive, because she left me when I was a day old. And my father, I just don't know about it. We need to have a father-and-son discussion. I'm trying to have me and my daughter be close, so we can have discussions, because I don't want it to be like me and my father."

"Are your mom and dad still living here?"

"No. My father moved back to Jamaica, where he's from, and my mother moved down to Florida."

"Oh, she's in Florida as well? So how did you wind up staying up here by yourself? You got other relatives here?"

"You know how black families is. They don't really stick together."

"You think so?"

"Yeah. I mean, my family, they don't really stick together. If they would stick together they could have anything they want. But if they don't stick together there's nothing they could accomplish like that. My mom's got four of us, two boys and two girls. Put it like this—they claims I'm the bad one, or whatever."

"Well, are you?"

"I used to be. I mean, I don't think I'm a bad one. I didn't really follow the way, like natural, like everybody else. I've always been the rebellious type. Even when I was younger, I've been on my own. Even when my mom was there or whatever, I always depend on myself, buy my own self my clothes or whatever."

"You pay your own rent?"

"Yeah. I do."

"So, even though you didn't finish school, you still, to a large extent, responsible. What do you ultimately want to do?"

"I'd like to go into my own business."

"What kind of business?"

"I want to have a club and a restaurant. A place for recreation, where people can hang out."

"Yeah. As far as I'm concerned, you twenty-two years old. And what I'm advising you to do right now is think about trying to get yourself into a state of mind where you can divide your time in such a way that you have time to eat, work, and study for this GED exam. There's other men in this neighborhood who have repeatedly asked me about this, and I have helped them pass this exam. And I will continue to assign you books from my table that will help you bring your level of comprehension to another level."

"I'll get back with you. I have to go back to work," said Jerome.

"All right," Hakim responded.

•

A few weeks after this conversation, I saw Jerome through the window of The Vitamin Shoppe wiping down some shelves. It occurred to me that I might try to find out what he thought of his interactions with Hakim, and what role he thought books and reading played in his life. A couple of days later, when he was wandering through Greenwich Village on a day off from work, I introduced myself to him, and he said that he recognized me from the neighborhood. I explained my work and asked if we could sit down and talk. We went to the C3 Restaurant.

"I used to watch him through the window of The Vitamin Shoppe when I was working," he began. "A few times it was him and these people across the street having a conversation, and I knew I should be a part of the conversation, but I'm working. I know it's a deep conversation, because the people have been there for twenty or thirty minutes, so they have to be discussing something that's really deep. One day I was passing by and he was having a conversation with this older black guy who was saying that all black kids were bad, and I was trying to tell him that it ain't all of us that is the same way—that maybe you have two out of ten that was bad. Hakim didn't want to get into it, because he knew the guy was kind of ignorant. And I recognized that Hakim was selling black books, and I was very interested in black books, and I saw a book that I liked, so I picked it up. That's when we got started talking about how black youth was growing up today, and basically that's how it got started."

"What are black books?"

"Well, it teaches you about yourself and how white people look at you. It teaches you stuff that white people don't teach you. I didn't really know anything about myself, because they basically don't teach nothing like that in school. You know what I'm saying? Hakim doesn't only sell black books. He also sells white fictions or whatever. He gotta do what he gotta do to pay the bills."

"What books on his table were of interest to you?"

"The book by Haki Mahdabuti called *Black Men: Young, Dangerous, and Obsolete*, or something like that. I just liked the title and the picture on the cover, of a face of a man and a little girl. So I picked it up and I asked him what he thought about the book. I decided to get the book because of what he thought about it. 'Cause Hakim be about consciousness, and at this point in time you gotta be about consciousness. Then I brought it home and started reading it. And a lot of the stuff in there I could relate to. And it gives you reference to other books."

"Had you been reading a lot before you went to his table?"

"Not really. I think that was maybe the first book I started reading. I could talk to Hakim about the books. Because in the bookstore they have a lot of arrogance. They have their Ph.D. or whatever their title may be, and they arrogant in a certain way. But at his table we could talk about the books."

"You feel more comfortable with a street vendor than in a bookstore?"

"You can talk to the vendor, because he sits there and he sees what goes on. He sees all that. And people talk to him more and relate. A lot of people, they don't want to stop in no bookstore, because it's easier for them to conversate with a guy on the street and to see what he thinks about the book. That's why I would rather buy books from the guys on the street than in the stores."

"How many books have you read in your life?"

"I've only read the books I read since I met Hakim. He had a little influence on me. He told me to go back to school. He knows what he's talking about. He's been there. So I can relate to him, 'cause he's been through a lot of stuff. The way I see it is, a lot of the younger generation been through the same stuff like the older generation. That's the way you learn from them, because they've been there before."

"Is it hard for you to afford to buy books?"

"No. I would rather buy a book than buy clothes. Because I'm getting knowledge. I have this yearning for reading. I never really had it before. It's just something that came over me when I saw those books on the street. Because I know myself, but I don't really know much about myself. Reading a book, I could see what other people are talking about."

"When do you read?"

"I read on the train. Because I don't do anything else really than go to work and come home. So I read on the train."

"Do you talk to any other book vendors in the city?"

"There's this Muslim guy who sets up near my subway station in the Bronx, by the Number 5, Dyre Avenue stop. Yeah, we talked once. I got a book called *Malcolm Speaks* from him."

"What book did you buy next from Hakim?"

"He assigned me another book from his table called *Blacks in the White Establishment*. It's about inner-city kids going to prep schools and graduating. Tell you the truth, a lot of the kids in my neighborhood, even though they bad, if you give them a way to go forth, they will go forth. So that's what me and Hakim a lot of times talk about. He sees what goes on just like I see what goes on. That's why I try to listen to whatever he tells me. My parents would try to tell me what to do, but I never listen, so I end up in the predicament that I'm in. So I try to listen to what he has to say."

"What did you read next?"

"I read *Stolen Legacy*. It goes back to Aristotle and all these other people from back then. 'Cause it's, like—it's funny that a lot of the things that black people do never show up. It's like we never brought anything to the table.

And that's not right. Because we brought as much as anybody else ever brought to the table. We've been in America before a lot of people, and the way we get treated in America is not right. And it teaches you how Egypt got stolen from a part of Africa. 'Cause they consider Egypt not a part of Africa now. Which it *is* a part of Africa. It's like you taking a seed from an orange and you saying it's not a part of the orange. So that's a part of Africa.

"It teaches you about yourself. Like where you come from, way back. And it lets you know you have a self-worth in yourself. Once you start reading black books, you learn about yourself more. And not just following what everybody else thinks. Because, if you read what society says, then being black is like the sin of the earth, man."

"Who do you talk about books with, other than Hakim?"

"I have a roommate named Troy. Me and him live in a basement of this house in the Bronx. He works at Woolworth's. I bring books to him and I tell him to read them and he says he's gonna read them. I don't know, maybe he's not interested. But I have another friend who just got out of prison, and we talk a lot about books. He told me he was reading this book to his son. So then we got into a discussion about books. When I went to his house, I brought all my books with me. Then he said he got a lot of books, too. Because when he was in jail there was nothing better to do than read books. So he went up into his closet and was showing me his books. And I got this one from him, *From Superman to Man*, by J. A. Rogers.[7] And he had this other book I took from him called *Catch a Fire*, about Bob Marley and reggae music.[8] So after that we was talking about books. Because he was saying he has to teach his son about himself. Because a lot of our kids know nothing about themselves."

•

After my conversation with Jerome, I left New York for a few months. On my next trip back to the city, I asked Hakim how Jerome was doing, and used the conversation as an opportunity to find out how he saw his relationship with the young man.

"Jerome was here today. He stopped by during his brief break from The Vitamin Shoppe. From the very moment that we had our initial conversations, there was this level of trust being developed. And this is how relationships develop with many young black men. I started asking him questions about his life, what he hoped to accomplish in life, and he started to reflect on these things and open up and tell me a lot more about himself. I think what made him important to me was that I saw a significant level of genuineness in his discussion about himself that made me respect him. Furthermore, he seemed to be willing to work. He wasn't necessarily even saying to me, as some of these young kids say, that racism is the complete and total barrier, and that he therefore can't make progress. And furthermore, he was willing to listen to what I had to say."

"Were your discussions mainly about the books he bought?"

"No. After talking to him for a while, I came to the conclusion that I would help him in any way I could. On Friday, he and I were talking about what he should do if he encounters the police. And I was explaining to him that even in situations when you know you're right, you try to be respectful to these people and as calm as possible. That there's times when you realize that the reason you have to go through all of this is because you are a black man. But I told him that petitions and slogans will not bring you back to life. There's levels of common sense that I have to teach sometimes."

"What are black books, and how important are they to the intellectual development of men like Jerome?"

"They are books that emanate out of what is considered the black experience. With Jerome, I suspect they are very important. The other day he had a book called *Up from Slavery*.[9] For Jerome, what these books represent is a kind of history of navigation through the society. That's how I see these books. What went on and how did said person confront said situation, and in effect who were the victims and who were vanquished. No matter what these books really are, what they talk about, basically that is what these books for a lot of these guys represent, a point of black social navigation in the white society, be it history or economics or whatever the case may be. The first book Jerome bought was *Black Men*, by Haki Mahdabuti. That is what I think it means to him: How do I wake up in the morning and try to make progress, and how did other people do this? I think that's what they represent for a lot of these young guys that come here."

"Do you think that these books are in any sense counterproductive or dangerous for a kid that doesn't have a good grasp of history?"

"It's complicated, depending on how the individual chooses to reconcile what I consider to be a rather epic racial history in this country. There are a lot of black folk who come to these books hoping to find the kind of affirmative and in many cases mythic black self. I believe that, if the serious reading moves one to a point where he or she is able to make determinations of the difference between fact and propaganda, that's another thing. Jerome is not yet at that point. He is at the fundamental level, where he is trying to find out something about himself. It is very clear from my conversations with Jerome that he has not yet read a lot of what is considered to be the classic work in African-American literature or African-American thought. But that's okay. Because people gotta start where they are.

"Where I come in at is the ability to say, 'Okay, listen, that's fine, but now you gotta look at this and this and this.' That's why you got to be very careful and responsible about how you deal with people, particularly in this realm that I'm in. I could come down here and rant and rave and carry on and say, 'Well, listen, these books are just the greatest thing going on since people put pen to paper.' Like, some of these people might pick up some of these books and say, 'We're descendants of kings and queens.' And I might interject and say, 'Does that mean all of us were? Or maybe some of us? A few of us?' What this does is, it brings to bear a level of critical thinking, of critical evolution, so that we don't create a kind of mythic black history to act as a countervailing thrust to a white history that has basically made black folks into caricatures or a form of scholastic-appendix matter.

"People like Jerome come here and they're looking to find something that affirms what they perceive 'themselves' to be, or what they once were. So you got to work with them. But that is why I say to Jerome, 'You have to read as widely as possible, and, most importantly, you need to learn how to think and raise questions and ask yourself critical questions in order to arrive at conclusions about information and what you are reading and not to accept stuff.' There's so much I do not know. The reason that I know what I know is because there were folks up the road who were very patient and said, 'You need to read this book,' or 'You need to take a peek at this,' or 'You need to examine or re-examine this book.' "

"Whatever happened with the GED? Did he ever follow up on your suggestion that he get his high-school-equivalency degree?"

"On Saturday, we talked about the GED thing again. I said, 'I don't want to seem like I'm bugging you about this, but I have a [telephone] number here for a guy who teaches these classes to prepare you for the test.' I think that, when Jerome wants to take that step, he'll take it. I think it becomes a little counterproductive to proselytize. So I talk to him and prod him. And I also told him that I know it's tough. You not getting paid a lot of money. But if you can get in the program and if you have to buy books and stuff, I'll help you buy the books."

"He seems a little reluctant to do it."

"Very often people find themselves at a certain place in life and they figure there's no hope. There's nothing else out here you can do. Maybe nobody ever told him that 'Yes, you twenty-two years old, but you still *can* do this, and there's still light at the end of the tunnel.' I said, 'Listen, I know there's things that you going through with you family, things have been rough, but you still have time to do a lot of things. You a young man. You a lot younger than I am. And quite frankly, I think you have the intelligence to undertake this and do this. And if so, you can finish this GED thing and find yourself in a junior college, and who knows where you can go from there.' But from my end, I'm also mindful of not trying to push him. Because I don't want him to think that every time I come here that this guy's telling me what to do."

"How do you get young men to open up to you?"

"Well, you know, some days it is more easy than others. It could be by a smile or an inflection in your voice. Or the way in which you answer a question. Or, quite frankly, the way in which you induce conversation. As I have developed a relationship with men like Jerome, they start to talk to me about their father and mother and the chasm between them. And I identify with that, because, when I was growing up, my father and mother didn't make it, and it was my mother who raised all of us. So I can identify very, very deeply with him."

. .

When Hakim tries to let Jerome know, "You twenty-two years old, but you still *can* do this," he is providing a level of personal support and encouragement at present found in few or none of the family relations and institutions in Jerome's life. At the same time, it is possible that, by defying certain social norms and working outside the institutions of the formal economy, Hakim affects young black men like Jerome less significantly than he otherwise might: if he took a job as a schoolteacher, he might be able to affect the lives of many more children. But Hakim believes that he cannot work within those institutions. In any case, he contributes to social cohesion by giving needed support to men like Jerome.

Jerome is an "at-risk youth," facing substantial needs that are not being met by the institutions of American society. For young black men who have not completed high school, the prospects are especially bleak (less than 60 percent are employed in the formal economy),[10] and the numbers in prison, on parole, or on probation are high (higher than 40 percent for males between 18 and 24 years old).[11]

The extent to which young people who grow up in single-parent families are particularly at risk is a politically charged issue, because many scholars are uncomfortable with the idea that men are necessary to raise healthy children.[12] Sara McLanahan and Gary Sandefur indicate in *Growing Up with a Single Parent* that low income is the most important factor in the problems of children who grow up without a father, giving some support to these feminist scholars.[13] They also report that the remainder of the disadvantage from such an upbringing stems from "inadequate parental guidance and attention."[14] This may simply be a matter of having less parenting (another finding not necessarily in conflict with those who wish to rethink the family). Much of the effect they note comes from the fact that having one parent "reduce[s] a child's access to social capital outside the family by weakening connections to other adults and institutions in the community that would have been available to the child had the relationship with the father remained intact."[15]

Such developmental risks are not new, and as a result informal relationships between older men and children and young adults have traditionally been important in African-American communities, where formal ties between fathers and their children have historically been weak. Though this is not necessarily a uniquely African-American tradition, in African-American communities such informal mentors are known as "old heads." In his firsthand study of the Philadelphia African-American residential areas, *Streetwise*, Elijah Anderson explains, "The male old head's role is to teach, support, encourage, and in effect, socialize young men to meet their responsibilities with regard to the work ethic, family life, the law, and decency," and this can also apply to the socialization of young women.[16] Here on the sidewalk of Greenwich Village, Hakim was assuming the recognizable old-head role by telling Jerome not to give up.

Though sociologists have long referred to role models, old heads, and mentoring, they have always provided evidence for these relationships with nostalgic stories and reminiscences. Through this present-day documentary account, we can better understand the nature of the old-head/young-man relationship. It is not necessarily one of authority or domination: commands are not given, and obedience is not expected. The special nature of this relationship is better understood as an example of what the German sociologist Max Weber called "the exercise of 'influence' over other persons."[17] If the young boy complies with the old head's suggestions, he does so voluntarily. His decision to do so may be based on a rational calculation of the advantage to his own life, but not on a calculation related to the power of the old head to make him suffer in any way if he does not comply. In his old-head role, Hakim is not shy about reprimanding a younger person for failing to live up to high standards; he is not afraid to give advice based on the wisdom of experience or learning. For Jerome, Hakim is a symbol of precisely those values necessary to live in accordance with ideals of self-worth.

One aspect of such "influence" as it is developed on the sidewalk is that specific advice need not be followed for the relationship to maintain itself through repeated visits to the table. The continuing discussion between Hakim and Jerome regarding the GED has not led Jerome to take a GED course. The old head's specific advice may be less important to the young man than the very fact that he has a conversation about his life with an older man who is willing to listen. Likewise, though Hakim would like to see Jerome take the test and improve the material circumstances of his life, he also feels satisfied that Jerome wants to listen and talk. The relationship serves an important purpose in a world where, according to Hakim's testimony, many young persons do not want to listen to him.

In fact, the expectation of continued discussion, rather than compliance with authoritative commands, seems to be the marker of many stable relationships between Hakim and young persons on the sidewalk. Advice is usually easier to give than to take; in order for such relationships to be stable, it may be necessary for Hakim to demonstrate a certain tolerance when his advice goes untaken. Besides, even if Jerome does ultimately follow Hakim's advice, it is likely that a long period of apparent inactivity would precede any visible action. For Jerome to accept Hakim's advice on the GED, he would have to change his work schedule in a manner that might not be acceptable to his bosses. And even if Hakim helps him with some of his expenses, the GED course would likely result in other costs.

What is the basis of Hakim's influence? The old head has knowledge deriving from experience—i.e., wisdom. Jerome says about Hakim, "He knows what he's talking about. He's been there," indicating that he is willing to listen to the older man because of some fundamental experience Hakim can draw upon in legitimating his worldview. But this experience does not always, in and of itself, serve as the final source of legitimacy. Rather, in many cases, the old head makes arguments that can be legitimized by rational means. When Hakim tells Jerome to read the *Times*, for example, he is not doing so merely out of a general claim based on his experience. He goes on to legitimize the claim by explaining how a particular article provides information about the job market that is relevant to the young man's life. In fact, such advice demonstrates that Hakim is not simply relying on his own experience in the job market, or that of his generation, but is giving advice based on some of the best data about the structure of contemporary American society.

Finally, Hakim's influence seems also to derive from the fact that, to use Jerome's words, he is "about consciousness." The young man's statement derives from inferences he makes about Hakim based on conversations about "black books." He believes that Hakim is a man who sees the advancement of African Americans as a value *per se*.

In writing *Streetwise*, Anderson discovered that, "as economic and social circumstances of the urban ghetto have changed, the traditional old head has been losing prestige and credibility as a role model." This is because it is difficult for old heads who learned their lessons about life in a manufacturing economy to legitimize their claims to authority when the street economy poses a more attractive alternative, given the decline in manufacturing jobs: Young men do not possess the alternatives they once did. And it is difficult for young men to believe in the lessons of the old head when the institutional paths to fulfill those lessons have been eroded. As one young man quoted by Anderson says of the old heads, "They don't understand the way the world really is."

In recent years, other analysts have described in detail the decline of community institutions like churches and YMCAs within high-poverty areas as the working- and middle-class old heads described by Anderson have moved out of these districts. In his influential study *When Work Disappears*, the sociologist William Julius Wilson describes the devastation of those institutional infrastructures that he and his staff found in the highest-poverty neighborhoods, such as the Bronx area Jerome comes from. When those institutions go, the developmental hazards associated with the absence of relations between fathers and children are certainly exacerbated. Wilson emphasizes that major structural transformations in the economic and political order will be required if these problems are to be solved.

Anderson reports that one place young people do turn within the context of the current vacuum is what he calls the "new old head"—a person who derives his legitimacy from the "influx of the drug culture. . . . The emerging old head is younger and may be the product of a street gang, making money fast and scorning the law and traditional values."[18]

The image of urban social change as a movement from the old head of the formal economy to the old head of the underground economy leaves open the question of what other kinds of mentoring relationships between older and younger men have emerged in the face of the decline of the industrial economy and the rise of the "new urban poor." In his contribution to the life of the sidewalk, Hakim is an old head who is located squarely in the new urban economy, imparting lessons about life that seem to have direct meaning and application for a young man from a high-poverty area. Though the exact meaning of Hakim's life is not necessarily clear, his presence emphasizes that gang leaders and drug dealers are not the only alternatives to the traditional old head. With that in mind, I asked Hakim what lessons he thinks his life as a street vendor can teach to a young man like Jerome who is working in the formal economy.

"I don't necessarily know if my life is a model for him, depending on what it is he thinks he has to do. I came to this sidewalk by choice, not by force. If I was walking up the street nonchalantly, and let's say I was a black lawyer at one of these high-priced law firms in New York City, the same question could be posed: how is the existence of that lawyer a model for Jerome? He might not be able to relate to the lawyer. So I think that the fact that I'm on the sidewalk may not be the model. What is the model is what I try to explain to him. There were times when people who worked for GM, in the factory, might have been good models. But those factory jobs are gone. So what you have to impart to a young guy is that they have to have diverse skills and flexibility. My own experience is that I had to confront a very painful need to figure out how to exist economically without having to go and apply for what is considered a 'job.' And I think part of the answer for these young people lies there. They have to muster up creative ideas and find ways to finance these ideas to create small little entrepreneurial enclaves so that they can have some kind of economic futures."

"But how can Jerome have faith in what you are telling him to do? Even if he never took any of your advice about finishing high school, he could still do what you do—work on the sidewalk."

"I've had the luxury—if you want to call it the luxury—of working in the formal economy, and of working at certain companies that required a certain level of training, however rudimentary, and a certain level of education. And if I decided right now to leave these sidewalks, throw on a suit, and have to go and talk to people at one of these office buildings in the formal economy, I'm capable of doing that. What I'm trying to explain to Jerome is, you make choices in life, but at the same time what you try to do in spite of certain set-backs is prepare yourself for the next step, no matter how arduous it might seem. I'm telling him that, even if I was a crack addict sitting on the side-walk, there are possibilities for you. I'm not necessarily the barometer for your possibilities, but the fact is that you have a certain level of potential if you go and use it.

"When I think about very successful black folk, some of these people are very important academics, bankers, lawyers, and journalists. In many cases these persons are so busy just trying to sustain themselves and do what they have to do, they don't have time for people like me, and forget about a guy like Jerome. I have problems with this idea of a role model, because 'role model' generally has meant, at least by the media's definition, some of these very high-profile people, but the truth of the matter is that the little people who really have proved catalytic to a lot of very successful people hardly ever get talked about, or even make it into the sweep of history."

Hakim could not have been unaware of his own importance to young men like Jerome when he made reference to the influence of those "little peo-ple." He also knows that sidewalk contacts of the kind depicted here cannot substitute for the larger transformations and rebuilding of family, institu-tions, and neighborhoods.[19] But just as there is no substitute for wholesome institutional structures, so there is no substitute for the power of the informal social relations that constitute a wholesome sidewalk life and society. Indeed, it is important to recognize the importance of the informal activity of public characters like Hakim. As Jane Jacobs wrote in *The Death and Life of Great American Cities*, the "first fundamental lesson of successful city life . . . [is] that people must take a modicum of public responsibility for each other even if they have no ties to each other. . . . The essence of this responsibility is that you do it without being hired."

The Magazine Vendors

Jane Jacobs saw the public character as a person whose presence probably makes the sidewalks safer and more vital for pedestrians. But on the very street where Hakim came to be known as a public character, there are other men, also poor and black, who make those streets feel *less safe* and *less vital* to many pedestrians. There are unhoused people who (to use their jargon) "lay shit out," placing miscellaneous items on pieces of corrugated cardboard or directly on the sidewalk. They might be trying to sell anything, including (on one particular evening) a pair of used tennis shoes, an extension cord, leather gloves, a lightbulb, some candles, unmarked VCR tapes, a tape recorder, a straw hat, and some shirts—all retrieved from local trash. Once, at night, I saw them lay pornographic pictures on the sidewalk and try to sell these. And there are other men who panhandle, standing by the doors to the automated-teller machines, shaking their cups as people come and go.

In such a context, I had been surprised to hear anyone working on Sixth Avenue define himself as a public character. But after spending five years on the blocks, I would propose that the role of the public character need not be filled by conventionally respectable people. Not only do the vendors and scavengers, often unhoused, abide by codes and norms; but mostly their presence on the street enhances the social order. They keep their eyes upon the street, and the structure of sidewalk life encourages them to support one another. Moreover, many citizens enjoy the presence of the vendors on the sidewalk.

Consider the case of the magazine vendors. When you walk up and down Sixth Avenue between Eighth Street and Waverly Place, it is not uncommon to see on tables or the sidewalks old and current copies of *Architectural Digest, Artforum, Hustler, Town & Country, Penthouse, Interview, Communication Arts, National Geographic, Forbes, Vanity Fair, Paris Vogue, Marie Claire, Time, GQ, Esquire, Wired,* and *Playboy,* and catalogues from L.L. Bean and Lands' End, Victoria's Secret, Christie's and Sotheby's, as well as used books. These items have been retrieved from recycled trash by Marvin and Ron and six or so other vendors of scavenged printed matter.

All of the magazine vendors are black males. Most spent time in jail for crimes committed during the first wave of crack use in the 1980s. They range in age from their mid-thirties to their late fifties. About a third are Vietnam veterans. A few say they are HIV-positive; others state that they would rather not know. All except one are or have been addicted to drugs; at least six came off their addictions while working on the block.

About half of them work every day, the rest a few days a week. Three of the men currently admit to receiving public assistance and Medicare. Like many welfare recipients, they do not live on welfare alone,[1] and vending scavenged written matter helps them with their extra expenses, including nonessential items like drugs (which welfare payments would hardly be enough to subsidize). Although only three of the men say they are on welfare at the current time, seven have indicated that they have been on welfare while working on these blocks during the past five years. Two men showed me papers indicating that they lost their public assistance and medical assistance (but not food stamps) after failing to participate in a workfare program; others have reported such experiences as well.[2]

A few days before Christmas in 1995, Hakim introduced me to Marvin Martin, suggesting that he would be a good person to talk to about the magazine and book vendors who get their materials from recycling. Marvin has been out on the sidewalk for twelve years, and he has taught the trade to many of the other men out there.

"I am the overseer of all the men who sell used magazines and books," Marvin jokingly told me when I asked him if he could give me an introduction to the world of the magazine vendor. "I'll put you under my wing out here." We kept in touch, and it was through working for Marvin on and off

for a year, including two three-month summers—the first without a day off—
that I came to know all of the men on the blocks, including Ron.

Marvin, an African American in his late forties, is one of the magazine
vendors who are no longer unhoused. After serving in Vietnam, he says, he
spent seventeen months in the Ohio state-prison system for an armed robbery he did not commit; he worked for the Dana Corporation before going
to prison, he says, and after he got out he tried to find work in the automobile industry, with no luck. So he learned to support himself as a brick
scavenger, recovering bricks from demolished buildings and selling them
for ten cents apiece. After moving from Toledo to New York to help his
cousin sell leather belts, he lived on the streets as an alcoholic for a few
years, and finally enrolled in a substance-abuse program at the Veterans Ad-
ministration (VA) Medical Center. Through the program at the VA, he went
into a shelter, then found his own apartment as he made his way off drugs
and alcohol.

Today, seven years later, he is (according to his addiction therapist,
Nona Lynch, who met with me after Marvin signed a release) one of the VA's
success stories. He still attends the VA's one-hour support-group meetings
twice a week, and weekly meetings of Alcoholics Anonymous. Because of
his alcoholism, he has been certified as unable to work, so he is eligible for a
biweekly public-assistance grant of $167, plus $120 in food stamps.

Marvin says that his partner, Ron, "is one of the best book and magazine
vendors in New York City. He has a charm about how he sells books and
magazines to customers, and he knows how to get a good price. That's why I
always want to work with him."

Ron came to this country from Jamaica at the age of eleven, when his
mother (whom he hadn't known since he was a baby) sent for him. Unlike
Marvin, Ron still uses alcohol and drugs. He can be charming, but he has
gone through periods in the past when he was feared by both local residents
and other people working the streets, especially when drunk. He has served
time in jail for drug possession. Once, he went to jail after slashing the face
of an unhoused man who tried to pick on him, which he explained to me
like this:

"The guy demanded money from me. Then he grabbed Leo [another
magazine vendor working on the block], threw him down, and the next thing

he was sitting on top of [him]. . . . The guy wouldn't let Leo go, so I took my box cutter out and I slashed him. For some reason I just couldn't stop. I just kept going. The police car came up on the sidewalk and drove along and almost run me over. This was a real vicious slashing. I think the guy is still sick, to be honest. But he never pressed charges."

When I first started working for Marvin, I found Ron gentle, sharp, and insightful. Nevertheless, Hakim, Alice, and others had warned me that Ron could be dangerous. Alice had a pending lawsuit against him for assault and battery, and a restraining order making it illegal for him to go within twenty feet of her. Marvin thought that Ron might get jealous of my working at the table, seeing me as a threat to his livelihood (even though I was returning all of the money I made). When Marvin left us alone so he could go place bets on the horse races at the OTB (a common occurrence), Ron ran the transactions and I charged whatever prices he told me. Ron would always hold all the money.

I came to understand that, unless Ron was intoxicated, he could be a charming and honest person. When he was drunk, he was even more honest, which meant that he was no longer charming. At such moments, it was important to go somewhere else, which I always did.

After I had been working the table for two weeks, Ron gradually began to tell me bits and pieces about his life. He said that in the tenth grade he had been expelled for truancy from Erasmus Hall High School in Brooklyn because he was afraid to go to school when so many of his classmates were carrying guns.[3] His father and mother were both alcoholics. The children would come home from school and see their mother passed out. He said that he is now thirty-six years old and has been on Sixth Avenue for the past seven years. Over the course of the summer, I got to know his brother-in-law and spoke with his sister, who gave me independent accounts that confirmed these details about his life.

Before coming to Sixth Avenue in 1989, he says, he was working as a timekeeper at J. A. Jones Construction Company. He got paid twice a week for keeping track of the time of five hundred workers, but he would get so high on crack that he couldn't make it to work. "I'd go home and I would be depressed because I couldn't pay the rent and I had no food. . . . I called and said, 'I quit because I got a drug problem.' And I just decided I wasn't gonna

go home. I left my apartment, my clothes, television, everything. I just left it there!"

"You just left it there?"

"I just left it there!"

.

When Ron says he "just left it there," he implies that he made a choice to live on the streets. It is instructive to compare the kind of "choice" Ron speaks of making with the kind of choice Hakim talks about. When Hakim said that he could put on a suit immediately and work in the formal economy, he gave the impression that he has made a clear choice between two different kinds of lives, what some people call a "lifestyle choice." He says that his experiences working at the law firm had led him to believe there was no place for him in corporate America and, perhaps, in mainstream society. I don't think he means by this, however, that he could not obtain such a job. Rather, perceiving that the institutional racism of corporate environments would continue to cause him psychological trauma, he saw working as a street vendor to be among the reasonable alternatives that were open to him at the time. He imagined the freedom and self-direction of working as a street vendor, and his life has largely followed the expectations.

In Ron's case, and that of other unhoused men on Sixth Avenue, the use of the term "choice" means accepting something that seems inevitable. At first, he says, he stayed out on 42nd Street and panhandled. "It was cold, it was freezing, I remember I was in a state of depression, and I went over there to the East Side, to the shelter over there, and I got a bed. I used to come out in the daytime and panhandle here on Sixth Avenue, by the PATH train, and there was a guy who used to pretend like he's crippled so people would give him money. He was panhandling and he was complaining that that was *his* spot, his location, and that he didn't want me to be there. Old ladies would come up to me and say, 'He's crippled and you want to take his spot?!' One day the guy comes up and says, 'Yo, man, you trying to take my spot? Here's a bunch of magazines. Take these and try to sell them.' And that's how I started.

"I never went back to the shelter. I was out making a hundred dollars every single day! And that's when I started sleeping over here. Being that I was a crack addict and an alcoholic when I first came out here, the hundred dollars a day went by like that, every day. I stored my stuff in the corner over there, by the bank, where I eventually started living, 'cause I had to watch my stuff."

"So what happened to your apartment?"

"During all this time I had my apartment that I could've always gone home to, but I refused to go back there, you understand? For some reason I refused to, because, the way I saw my life, I saw the way it was going, was hard times, I was going down, I seen hardship, you know? I was always scared of living on the street, I was always scared that I was gonna walk the streets looking like all those bums, all dirty and grungy like a mad person, you know? And I got to the point where I said to myself, If it's gonna happen I want it to happen now."[4]

It is not uncommon for people on Sixth Avenue to talk about having played an active part in becoming unhoused. Most, like Marvin, report coming to the street after they were put out of their houses by their families. Some say that nothing they could have done would have mattered; others clearly believe they were in control at all times.[5] Since the number of people who spoke to me of actively participating in the decision to become unhoused is higher than that reported by other researchers,[6] and since most of the people on Sixth Avenue do not make this claim, we cannot conclude that this aspect of Ron's story is typical of unhoused street people. It is also important to distinguish between the idea of playing an active part in being unhoused and making a voluntary choice to be that way. There is no evidence that Ron chose to be unhoused in the sense that we usually use the concept of choice. He did not appear to me to have had any idea what he was getting into, as Hakim did when he began vending, or ever to have said to himself, "I want to live the life of an unhoused person," whatever that would have meant to him.

Yet, in going beyond the biographical roots of being unhoused to the social-psychological condition of the people on Sixth Avenue, I *do* find representative value in Ron's story. In the discussions I eventually conducted with the men I met, I discovered that almost every one of them spoke of a time when he had essentially given up and said, "I don't care anymore." Even men who had been put out of their houses, coming close to lacking any control at that moment, had a moment when they gave up and said (to use the vernacular of the streets), "Fuck it!"

"When I say, 'Fuck it!' I don't care anymore," a magazine vendor named Warren explained to me. "When I got put out my house and I went to all my friends and nobody would do nothing for me, I said, 'Well, fuck everybody. Fuck it.'" For these persons, the combination of knowing that their addictions have had a role in their having become unhoused (many of them behaved in ways that hurt family members before they were "put out") and the sense of having finally said, "I don't care," leads to their descriptions of active participation. It is in this frame of mind that each of them reports arriving on the street, gradually giving up on some of the most basic culturally prescribed goals and means for living, and entering the informal written-matter economy.

A couple of other thorny issues are suggested by these stories. Ron speaks of his drift to vending as a kind of destiny ordained by the pharmacological effect of crack on his life. Marvin, by contrast, attributes his movement into the informal economy to his inability to find work in the automobile industry in Ohio. It is, of course, difficult to rigorously project individual cases onto the template of societal processes, so we speculate here with caution. Although both these stories may be true for the men who tell them, there is a great deal at stake in our thinking of them as representative accounts.

If we take Ron's life story as representative, we may gain the impression that people who use crack end up in the informal economy because the effects of the drug make it impossible for them to keep a job in the formal economy. If we take Marvin's story as representative, we may infer that many drug users on the street move into the informal economy because of a lack of opportunity, rather than because of drug or alcohol use. Is either of these stories helpful?

Over the past ten years, a great deal has been learned about crack users, contradicting earlier assumptions made by scholars and the media. As Craig Reinarman and his co-authors have shown, "What was most telling . . . is not so much that their extreme use disrupted their lives in various ways, but rather that such disruption almost always remained within the bounds . . . of their lives. . . . Most of our respondents were gainfully employed and had otherwise conventional lives and attachments."[7] Likewise, John P. Morgan and Lynn Zimmer have concluded that "many crack users take the drug occasionally, do not engage in prolonged binges, and do not become dysfunctional."[8] In other words, it was not inevitable or "destined" that a crack user like Ron would give up a job in the formal economy. Yet about half of the persons currently working out on Sixth Avenue tell such stories.

Though none of the men on Sixth Avenue were "destined" for the informal economy, broader economic and social factors probably did limit their chances in the formal economy. Like Marvin, about a third speak of ending up on the streets when they could not find work in manufacturing or new computer technologies and took to using drugs and alcohol. Such men speak of turning to drugs and/or crime after they became discouraged by their economic prospects.[9] In most cases, their failure to make it in the formal economy and their use of drugs led to some combination of their (a) no longer looking for employment; (b) becoming disconnected from family and friends; and (c) having some interaction with the criminal-justice system—leading to a period spent in prison with eventual release to the sidewalk.

A Night at the Tables

A heavy summer rainstorm had emptied the sidewalks of Greenwich Village. The vendors selling books from tables set up by the curb had put their goods away when the rain started in the late afternoon, or were huddling under the awnings of the stores along Sixth Avenue. In the doorway of Blockbuster Video, Marvin and Ron sat on milk crates, waiting for the storm to pass.

Shortly after 8:00 p.m., the dark rain clouds gave way to a faint image of the twin towers of the World Trade Center. "I thought it was gonna quit," Ron said. The emulsion of gasoline fumes, soot, and dust that had built up over the past few days had also disappeared with the rain. "And now it's a brand-new type of day." Soon the residents of the Village would emerge, followed by shoppers and tourists. "People will want to get a breath of fresh air for their own selves," Marvin said. "They'll also browse over the tables."

Then, interrupting his own thought, he turned to his partner and asked, "Ron, now, when we gonna work again?"

This was the way Marvin and Ron ended many of their nights together, with Marvin trying to find out whether Ron expected to be too drunk to work the next morning. The alertness and paranoia caused by crack use, as well as the depression that follows the high, leads some users to "come off" their runs by drinking many bottles of beer or malt liquor.[10] If Marvin arrived on the block and Ron was drunk, screaming at pedestrians and making a scene, he knew from experience that the day would be as good as lost.

Ron sat, quietly pondering Marvin's question. Then he said, "Tomorrow's gonna be a nice day. We gotta get in as many days as we can up till July 4." That was the answer Ron would often give, substituting whatever holiday was coming up next, whether Memorial Day, Labor Day, Thanksgiving, or Christmas. It was Ron's way of telling Marvin that he wouldn't be intoxicated in the morning; this actually wasn't considered a definite contract until the moment arrived and Ron was sober.

Ron called me over to help him lift the industrial-plastic drop cloth, taking care that no water seeped onto the top row of their *Vogues*. As we did so, Mudrick, an unhoused man who sometimes assisted the others, came over and talked to Marvin. Mudrick is fifty-seven years old, six feet four inches tall, two hundred pounds, and known for getting tourists to pay him for directions. "It costs money to talk to me," he says. Once he put a sign by his table that read, "Information 25 Cents Correct Information: 50 cents." Whenever people asked him for directions, he answered their questions and then pointed to the sign. Whether out of fear, respect, amuse-

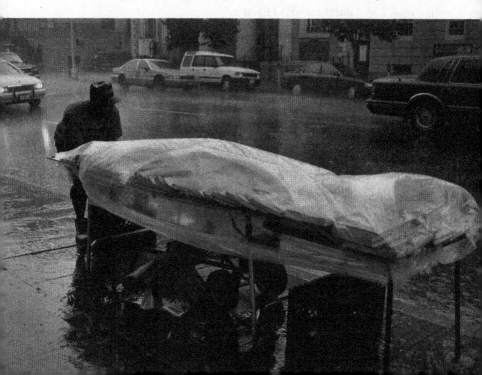

ment, sympathy, or some other motive, most people gave fifty cents or more.

Mudrick is an alcoholic who gets paid in cash for working as a carpenter and tradesman for many building superintendents in the Village. He also takes out the trash for one building every day, and he does major and minor repairs when the need arises. These jobs take only a few hours, so that he has time on his hands to spend on the block. He is another man who claims that he is unhoused by choice.

The ensuing conversation between Marvin and Mudrick (which I discovered months later, when I listened to the tape, and quote now with their permission) told me a bit about how some of the men saw what I was doing, as well as about the relationship between Marvin and Ron that I had begun to witness.

"He's trying to understand the people in the street," Mudrick told Marvin, referring to me, as I worked with Ron to lift the plastic sheeting off the magazines.

"People don't understand what we're about," said Marvin. "They already think negative about us."

"I don't give a fuck about what nobody else thinks," said Mudrick. "I like what I do. I did it because I liked it."

"But the point is, what I'm saying, what other people is looking upon you as, you not doing anything wrong," responded Marvin.

"I don't give a fuck about nobody else," said Mudrick.

"I'm not saying that," responded Marvin. "I'm trying to say these other people looking at you like you're doing wrong."

"Fuck the other people!" said Mudrick.

"You talking to me wrong!" exclaimed Marvin.

"All we trying to do is make ourselves a couple of dollars," said Mudrick.

"Yeah, but you talking to me wrong!" said Marvin.

"Why you say something like that?" asked Mudrick.

"Because you said you don't give a fuck about other people," said Marvin.

"I don't!" said Mudrick.

"So that means you don't give a fuck about me, too?" asked Marvin.

"You 'other people'?" asked Mudrick.

"Yeah! I'm 'other people,' " said Marvin.

"What's your name? Marvin?"

"Yes."

"Marvin, right?" said Mudrick. "I said 'other people.' Marvin is here. 'Other people' don't mean Marvin."

The two men laughed.

"So that means Ron's 'other people' because he's over there?" asked Marvin.

"Ron's 'other people.' " Mudrick laughed.

Marvin laughed with him.

"That doesn't mean you," Mudrick continued. "He's over there, right? I don't give a fuck about him. He's 'other people.' I'm talking to you. You is Marvin."

Marvin stopped laughing as he stood silent for a moment.

"That's my *partner* over there," he went on. "You *gotta* care about him!"

A thirtyish black woman on a bicycle who sells crack cocaine passed by and stopped near the table. Ron handed Marvin fifty dollars and told him not to give it back to him if he asked for it later on. Then Ron walked over to the lady on the bicycle, and together they made their way down the block. This was a bad sign, Marvin explained. It meant that Ron was about to go on a "mission" to buy crack and get high. It also meant that Marvin might not be able to set up the next morning. I asked Marvin why he seemed to sacrifice his own well-being and put up with Ron.

"He's like the little brother I always wanted," Marvin explained. "I care kind of daily for him, 'cause I trust him. It's like a blinded love I have for another human being. His goodness is there, but it is blocked by his drug use. He still can be a good man, and I'm trying to teach him how to be good. There is a lot he doesn't want to go along with.

"He still doesn't believe I'm cured. He says he thinks I'll go back to it after a while. He can't do it. I've been sober for over six years. I didn't know him well until four years ago. My closeness to him began then. He was selling magazines in the bus-station block. I was here on the Blockbuster Video block. He was fighting on the other block and he came down to work here.

"I said, 'Hey, let's hook up. If you want to work together, all I want is honesty.' I saw his honesty and his integrity about himself. Because, believe it or not, honesty is the main quality about Ron or anybody that I can desire

about. I can go away from the table and come back and Ron has got my money. Or he's taking care of my stuff."

In talking about both Ron and himself, Marvin often used the terminology of "recovery," which I had sometimes heard from friends who were in Alcoholics Anonymous. This was the language he seemed to draw upon as he provided support for Ron and Mudrick and others on the block. "I say everyone finds a way if they have any kind of spirituality of dealing with the higher power," he continued. "I have a good way that I feel comfortable with of relating to God. Because I know I make mistakes and I'm six years sober now and I'm forty-seven and I'm a baby when it comes to this world of sobriety.

"I came out of the service when I was twenty-two. And then I got married at twenty-four. I thought I had it made; I had a wonderful wife and everything. But the way I carried on after that, I wasn't thinking. And everything started hitting me the wrong way because I wasn't doing things right. And that's when the stress started hitting me. And that's when I started drinking more. But I didn't necessarily make them things happen. Because, for one, my wife lost a baby and I started drinking more. And then she had cancer of the uterine. And then I kind of like flipped the lid."

"And what happened?"

"Well, the cancer vanished, but I was slowly drinking more and more," he explained. "The shit hit the fan. We loved each other very much. And everything was great, except my alcoholism.

"I had lost my family and all that stuff. I was burning bridges left and right through my alcoholism. And when I came to New York something like twelve years ago, I saw you could drink and do everything and I went crazy drinking and drugging. And in the last part of my drinking I was selling books and stuff and getting money the best way I could."

"How did you stop?"

"I went to the VA for messing up my leg. I have a tendency when I'm drinking of always kicking my leg. And it got infected and I had to go to the hospital and get penicillin because I kicked it and a little scar come on it that became infected.

"I said, 'Fuck it!' I was drinking on top of the penicillin. Next time I saw the doctor I said, 'Doc, what's gonna happen next time?' He said, 'I don't think there is going to be a next time.' I said, 'Doc, what are you talking about?' He said, 'Quite frankly, I think you gonna be dead.' I just saw the light from then on. And believe it or not, just like I am Ron's sponsor, Jamaane [a sober oils and incense vendor who once worked on the block] was my sponsor. He let me live with him. He always gave me good advice. He said, 'Marvin, I'll be with you all the way if you decide to get help.'

"I almost ruined my life. If it wasn't for Jamaane's support and for me and God, I mean me getting back with God, I wouldn't have been here right today. My mentality would have still said, 'Fuck it!' That's two words I don't even say anymore: 'Fuck it.' Because that mentality is like saying, 'The hell with you or whatever's right.' And that's saying, 'The hell with things. Fuck it.' Rather than saying, 'Okay, that's the way it is. And I'll go ahead on living the way I got to live for myself.' "

It is midnight, and we have been on Sixth Avenue since 9:00 a.m. Ron doesn't return. Marvin infers that he'll be up drinking and smoking all night. He may cause so many disturbances in the morning that there will be no way to set up. Marvin says he is frustrated, but he accepts that this is how things are.

We pack the crates in silence and walk eight long blocks to the Manhattan Mini Storage on Varick Street, where he and other vendors rent storage spaces for forty-five dollars per month. Marvin insists on pushing his four crates on a hand truck, weaving in and out of the heavy traffic on Sixth Avenue. I stay on the sidewalk. Once there, as we stand on a steel ladder and unload the crates into his locker, Marvin makes a firm decision about when to set up next. "Ron's gonna be making a scene. Meet me at 8:00 a.m. the day after tomorrow."

The next morning, I set out to find Jamaane, to see whether and how he sees himself as Marvin's "sponsor." I had heard about the support Jamaane gave to a number of other men on Sixth Avenue, including a former heroin-and-crack addict named Grady who sells magazines by the bus shelter and often slept next to the subway trains in an area known as the Bat Cave.

Jamaane was selling oils and incense on the corner of Broadway and Houston Street. "I believe highly in role models and trying to set examples," he told me, and described his relationship with Marvin: "He's another one I brought in my house who doesn't drink anymore. There's a number of them. I stayed behind them to the point where we would sit down and we would

talk. Grady would be crying, and crying, and crying, and telling me to stay on him. His exact words would always be, 'Jamaane, stay on my ass.' "

They were there for him, too, Jamaane explained. "My two children was raised out here with me, and I had to carry them on my back. They used to sleep under my table while I worked. And while I was arrested with my merchandise [for vending where vending was not permitted], the police confiscated my oils. I said I had two kids on the block and didn't know where they were. Could he wait? He arrested me and said, 'The hell with your two kids.' " While Jamaane went to the police station, Grady and Marvin looked after his children.

The "Fuck It!" Mentality

Before finding a "mentor" or a "sponsor" working the streets, each of these men reached a moment of personal emotional crisis. Despite the vulgarity, it is best described in the terms the men themselves use for it: it is the moment when a person says, "Fuck it!"

In telling how they reached this point, the men invariably referred to depression, to feeling "down in the dumps," to lacking an interest in anything. Although giving up was a choice of sorts—no one forced them to do it—it was not a choice they made at a time of rational stability; it was not a choice that a person wanted to make. Ron's choice between, say, buying a vial of crack and keeping his money for rent was not the choice a healthy, well-functioning person who is short on money makes between buying a cup of coffee and buying a newspaper. Furthermore, a person who is depressed may perceive a fifty-fifty chance that he will be evicted as a nine-to-one chance (given that depression alters perceptions of future life chances).[11] It is also important to distinguish between the moment a person makes a choice that leads him to be on the street, and the choices he makes after he is without a home, when he has a rather different set of possibilities.[12]

For Ron, as well as others on the sidewalks, using crack became initially a way to feel much better, "out of the dumps," energized. Unlike the middle classes, who are accustomed to seeing psychiatrists when they are clinically depressed, many poor black men like Ron do not have access to drugs like Prozac and often try to help themselves.[13] Ron spoke of using crack as a self-medicating process—a way of treating depression and feeling better in the short run. Yet daily withdrawal from crack can lead to even more severe depression. A person feels so depressed that he begins to take more drugs to alleviate the bad feeling of withdrawal.[14] What is most important about these stories is the representative moment of lethargic resignation, leading to a moment when a person gives up on culturally prescribed goals and means for living.[15]

My fieldwork suggests that the form of retreatism whereby a person says "Fuck it!" or "I don't give a fuck" has at least four distinct characteristics. First, it is pervasive in that it affects most major aspects of his life. Second, he becomes indifferent to behavior that he once thought of as basic, necessary, and natural, such as sleeping in a bed or defecating in a toilet. Third, he feels extreme embarrassment and/or shame for having hurt loved ones who paid a high price for his drug or alcohol use. This leads him to become distant from family, friends, and loved ones, who he hopes will not see him in his new state. Fourth, he feels the freedom that comes from having given up all responsibilities to others. Together, these characteristics make the "Fuck it!" mind-set an extreme form of retreatism, rather than a form of resignation, such as when people say "What the hell" and give up on a diet or a workout regime.[16] It enables a person to give up an apartment and sleep in his own or others' urine and feces on the street or among rats in the Bat Cave of the subway. It often involves a fundamental resocialization of the body. As we shall see, some aspects of this extreme "I don't care" mentality have an explicit political justification, especially when a person believes that his attitude is the result of an indifferent society rather than of his own addictions and personal weaknesses.

There is another, even more extreme form of "Fuck it!," in which we observe the loss of sense for fellow human beings that makes it possible to break into cars, rob deliverymen, or commit physical violence in order to get money to achieve the self-medicating crack high. "They can start robbing, stealing, whatever," Warren explained. "This 'Fuck it!' is a very severe level!"

Indeed, this most extreme mentality of the streets usually manifests itself in what the sociologist Stanley Cohen, in another context, calls "acquisitive vandalism, damage done in order to acquire money or property," rather than in "tactical vandalism," where "the damage done is a conscious tactic used to advance some end other than acquiring money or property." Rare among the men I studied are what Cohen calls "vindictive vandalism" (property destruction as a form of revenge) and "malicious vandalism" (which "carries the implication not just of hatred but of action enjoyed for its own sake").[17]

Whereas the "Fuck it!" mentality is a kind of retreatism with pervasive effects on a person's life, and its most "severe level" reflects an indifference to basic standards that will be destructive to others, it is not a wholesale retreatism from society itself, nor does it eradicate every social emotion. I saw this illustrated one afternoon when Conrad, a magazine vendor working on Greenwich Avenue, brought the relatives of Butteroll, a forty-two-year-old panhandler who lives by the tracks of the Sixth Avenue subway, to see him on the sidewalk. A few days later, when I reminded Butteroll of their visit, he interrupted, with pain on his face and in his voice:

"I know! I got mad. That was my cousin he brought. I didn't want him to do that! I didn't want Conrad to bring them out here to see me in the situation I look like. It was embarrassing. I can't describe it. Conrad knows better."

"Were those your kids?"

"No, my cousins. I saw [knew] them as kids. Conrad knows what I was talking about. That hurt my feelings. Those are my first cousins."

Even if the "Fuck it!" mentality is pervasive in its impact on a person's life, all of the men on Sixth Avenue do "give a fuck" about certain things. This is illustrated by their sense of shame and embarrassment, emotions most firmly rooted in how they believe they look in the eyes of family members.[18]

Even if each of these men was a retreatist at some point in time, and if it was the retreatist mode that facilitated heavy drug use in the first place,[19] the extreme "I don't care" mentality is not a natural or automatic result of excessive drug use. It is a particular subsequent form of retreatism, an attribute of the individual interacting with a particular situation.

The Rehabilitative Forces of the Sidewalk

The sidewalk is a social structure that may encourage or discourage retreatist behavior. Here a person may be pressured to continue to say, "Fuck it!" or to say instead, "It's never too late to turn your life around," and "I'm gonna live a better life." The "Fuck it!" option is likely on a city sidewalk that provides little opportunity for a person like Marvin or Ron to "make it." In a city that permits scavenging, vending, and panhandling, Marvin and Ron are more likely to find opportunities to take control of a small part of their lives, and support themselves as they try to do so. At the very least, like Butteroll, they can make a living through panhandling without hurting others. In other cases, vending becomes a way for a person to devise new goals and exercise control in a limited domain, which through a process of generalization can affect other aspects of his life. In the same way that the "Fuck it!" mentality can have a generalized effect, so can limited economic opportunities for self-direction and positive interpersonal relations, like scavenging and vending, lead to a more far-reaching positive transformation of his personal life.

I found strong evidence for the rehabilitative forces of sidewalk life in the self-respect these men maintained as they sold their scavenged magazines and did complex work, and in the interactions with customers that I observed. This was also apparent through the lens of Marvin's deep and caring relationships with Ron, Mudrick, and others as a "mentor" in the structure of sidewalk life. These effects are not surprising when seen in the framework of a long-standing tradition of research on the relationship between work and personality, and specifically job conditions and psychological functioning. This research demonstrates the importance of opportunities for self-direction in psychological well-being.[20]

.

Two mornings later, as agreed, Marvin and I meet on a quiet Sixth Avenue at 8:00 a.m. to claim a choice spot in front of Blockbuster Video. Many of the magazine vendors and panhandlers are still asleep on lounge chairs and corrugated cardboard pressed flat on the sidewalk.

Mudrick wanders over from the steps of St. Joseph's Church, where he has slept all night.

"Hey," Marvin tells him. "You wasn't supposed to be here today. You were supposed to be with Dyneisha [his granddaughter]."

"She's going to Woolworth's to have pictures taken," he explains.

"The same pictures you always have in your pocket?"

"Yeah, but we got them this big." He holds his hands six inches apart. "It costs seventy-five fucking dollars. I gave them all my money."

"That was good," Marvin tells him.

Then he gives the key to his storage space to Mudrick—a rare occurrence. Mudrick will get Marvin's four crates and move them out to the block in exchange for money to buy a few cans of St. Ides malt liquor. As we sit waiting for Mudrick to return, Marvin looks over the *Daily Racing Form* and drinks a cup of black coffee mixed with two sugars.

"When you first start off in the morning, the best thing you should do is handicap. And you have your figuration on what you think is the best horse to win the race. Looking at the form, you can get a general futuristic idea of what's getting ready to go on with this race."

As I get a lesson in handicapping, Ron appears.

"Marvin, you got my money?"

"Oh, you don't have any money?" he joked. "Here's your fifty dollars. How you doing this morning?"

"Good."

"Yeah, you look good," Marvin says, and resumes. He has been having bad luck betting on the races at the Belmont track. He has been doing much better with those at Aqueduct.

When Mudrick arrives with the crates, he sees Ron.

"You-all working together today?" asks Mudrick.

"You know that's my partner," Marvin responds. "You ought to know that when Ron's straight we work together. He looks good today. I like the way he is today. He's *Ron* now. That's the kind of Ron I like to see."

"He's had a beer this morning," Mudrick says.

"It don't matter. He's straight enough to work. That's the point, Mudrick. Even *you* look straight enough to work. You look good. You ain't looking sick. You got some money in your pocket. That's what it's about. That's what I be talking about. If you do that on a daily basis, you ain't gonna be worrying about nothing. Just keep yourself together."

"You need another load of crates?" asked Mudrick.

"I got enough," Marvin tells him, as Ron walks over and begins to unpack the magazines.

Mudrick takes his payment from Marvin and goes off for his St. Ides, which he refers to as his coffee or his medicine.

BEING IN CHARGE

A fiftyish white man in a tweed jacket picks up a copy of *GQ* and holds it up in the air without saying anything.

"Okay, two dollars," says Marvin.

The man pays without a word.

"Thank you, sir."

A twenty-fiveish black woman riffles through a number of magazines and puts a few aside.

"These are two dollars apiece," Marvin explains. "Three for five."

She picks up three magazines and hands him a ten.

"You got anything smaller?" he asks.

She hands him a five.

"Thank you," he says.

"Do you have a bag?"

"Sorry, I ran out," says Marvin.

"That's okay."

"Thank you."

The money is starting to roll in—two dollars here, five dollars there. But not all of the sales are so easy, and I begin to see a bargaining process that is infused with a sense of what is "right." The bargaining itself is a means for these men to maintain their self-respect.

"How much?" asks a black woman of about forty as she holds up a hardcover book called *Lenin's Tomb* by David Remnick.

"Five dollars," says Marvin.

"That's bad," responds the woman. "Sixty-nine cents."

"Bad?" says Marvin. "How do you think we're gonna live?"

"I don't know," responds the woman.

"You don't know, huh?" says Marvin. "Well, I know! We're charging three, four, five dollars for a good book."

"They're selling those in the used shops for sixty-nine cents," responds the woman.

"Well, that's where you have to go to get it," Marvin tells her as she walks away.

Much of the discussion between the magazine vendors refers to the morality of prices. If you ask any man, he will say that making a sale is mainly about making money, but observing the men at the tables shows that in sidewalk vending it is also important to confirm the respect one person (the customer) should give another (the vendor). As the magazine vendor Ishmael once said to Marvin, "I think it is an insult for someone to want to pay me fifty cents for a magazine they would have to pay five dollars for at the newsstand."

The respect dimension of any sale is crucial to the vocabulary that is used to explain it, but the magazine vendor also feels a need to educate buyers about the appropriate price. These vendors don't try to undersell one another; they believe this would lead prices to spiral downward.

They do not want customers to expect to pay anything less than two dollars for a good domestic magazine. Though they might make more money in the short run by accepting every offer for a sale, it is not clear that this would work to their benefit if the prices of magazines did plummet. Though there is a generous supply of magazines, there is a relatively limited supply of salable magazines, and a limited number of prospective buyers. Plus, there are costs to the men in time and effort to retrieve the magazines from the trash, even if they are free.

"How much?" a customer asks Ron as she holds up a current issue of *Paris Vogue*.

"Four dollars."

"Four dollars?"

"Give me three dollars," Ron responds.

She hands over the money and walks away with the magazine.

By saying, "*Give me* three," Ron is saying, "I'm accepting it, but I'm in charge," even if he's doing so on the terms the customer suggested. In these transactions, he insists on maintaining the respect of his customer as well as his own self-respect.

When Ron and Marvin started working together, Marvin says, he didn't know how to bargain. Ron had "the professionalism to let the customers know that this is a business and this is how it is," Marvin explains. "Knowing me, and how soft I was, I might have given in to a customer. I was gullible. Ron taught me to be 'strictly business.' "

What he had learned from Ron was "good hustling," the need to take control of an exchange in the face of uncertainty about how much money they would otherwise make from day to day. What marks the transaction as a "hustle" is not its status as legal or illegal activity ("hustling" can fall into either category) but precisely the ability to use one's "ingenuity" and "re-siliency" to maintain self-respect while engaging in an "economics of make-shifts."[21]

A defining characteristic of hustling's challenge in the minds of Marvin and Ron is the uncertainty that comes from not knowing what is going to happen from day to day. "If regardless of the weather or how hard you work, you are going to get paid, as in a nine-to-five job, where you *just have to be there* [emphasis mine], then you are not hustling," Marvin explained. "A vendor is a hustler. He doesn't know what he is going to get every day."

For Marvin and Ron, essential to maintaining self-respect and overcoming the uncertainty built into the hustle is the need to take control of the exchange. "Ron taught me to let the customer know that he's not getting away with anything," says Marvin. "*Give me* three dollars means, 'I'm accepting the three dollars,' not because I *needs* it, almost like I'm doing you a favor."

Central to the ethos of the hustle Ron taught Marvin is "getting over," which, Marvin explains, means "getting a good transaction out of what you pursued." From that perspective, in every transaction Ron and Marvin either "get over" on the customer or the customer "gets over" on them. When Ron accepts a customer's offer of three dollars by saying "Give me three," he is saying, "You think you got over, but you really didn't." His self-worth is at stake as he haggles over the price.

The magazine vendor's ability to charge any price he wishes helps illustrate that, though his work may place him at the bottom of the American class hierarchy, he nevertheless feels a satisfaction more usually associated with jobs that are higher in the hierarchy.[22] The vendor is not subject to supervision, is not engaged in routine, repetitive tasks, and is completely self-directed in his work. There is a substantive complexity to his work: finding the magazines, taking them in and out of storage, setting them up, knowing what kind of magazines to carry, how to price them, and what to charge.

All of the vendors on Sixth Avenue have a baseline amount of money they want to make before they go home. This is called "quota." Today, the money has been flowing in steadily, and Marvin and Ron have each made $120, twenty dollars above quota. (Between eighty and a hundred dollars is common on any twelve-hour day.) The money is not steady, and Marvin and Ron generally work four days per week when the weather permits.

RELATIONS WITH CUSTOMERS

Another way the informal social structure of sidewalk life discourages re-treatist behavior on Sixth Avenue is through the many friendly relations that develop between magazine vendors and their customers. When I started working with Marvin and Ron, it was difficult for me to comprehend what kind of person would actually buy the magazines on their tables. As a resident of the Village, I knew that cockroaches were a problem in local apartments. I was personally so vigilant about not allowing my own apartment to become infested that I usually threw away paper bags or cartons immediately after my trips to the grocery store. It was inconceivable to me that I might bring home magazines that had been retrieved from trash. As I worked at their tables each day, though, I noticed that the people buying these magazines represented a mix of all kinds of New Yorkers, most of whom were dwellers in local apartments. (I also discovered that magazines tend to be very clean. Storing stacks of them in my apartment never led to any problem with roaches.)

Some regular customers are poor, but many are upper-middle-class people. In the vendors' dealings with customers, I noted an ease of interaction on both sides. And a shared knowledge of their customer base was integral to Marvin and Ron's sense of themselves as engaging in an enterprise together.

"Oh, here comes Jack," Marvin says. "He's back."

Ron looks down the block at a sixty-year-old man dressed in black.

"Oh yeah!" Marvin continues. "Jack's here. We got the Christie's catalogues."

"Oh yeah!" says Ron. "Let him see them."

"Hey, Jack!" says Marvin.

"Hey, Jack. How you doing?" asks Ron.

"Okay," says Jack.

"We thought you was going away," says Ron.

"We thought you were on vacation," says Marvin.

"I *am* on vacation," says Jack. "A big vacation. I'm on my 'I don't have to go to school' vacation!"

"When are you going to Europe?" asks Marvin.

"On the third of next month," says Jack.

"Okay, how long you going to stay?" Marvin asks. "Two weeks?"

"Two months," says Jack.

"Oh no, Jack. You gonna be gone!" says Marvin.

"Two months," repeats Jack. "I'll come back very *greedy*," says Jack. "Needy and greedy I'll come back!"

"We got a few Christie's catalogues," says Marvin. "Sit down here on this crate. You know how to look."

"Uh-huh," says Jack.

"A couple of interesting things," says Marvin as Jack holds a catalogue from an exhibit of Fabergé clocks.

Jack will be at the table for the next fifteen minutes, while other customers make quick two-, three-, and five-dollar purchases. Then, after he puts together a stack of eight catalogues, Jack hands Ron a twenty-dollar bill and Ron puts it in his pocket. At two catalogues for five dollars (a special price for a very good customer), no change is due.

"I'll be seeing you again," says Jack.

"Yeah, but you gonna be gone for two months!"

"I'll be back!" says Jack.

"Two months, though!" says Marvin. "Damn! We gotta wait to see our favorite customer!"

"See ya-all," says Jack.

As he turns away, Marvin takes a ten-dollar bill from Ron and announces, "Okay, I want to go to OTB."

Before he leaves, I ask Marvin and Ron about Jack.

"He's an art teacher," says Marvin.

"A professor, actually," says Ron. "At a college."

"A professor, yeah," says Marvin. "He used to do a column on something. He made a lot of money on something he did."

I remark on how interesting and diverse the clientele is, and Marvin explains, "You learn a little something from each and every one of these people. And you can get advice from some of them. And you can learn a pattern about how people are in general. The peoples that live around here—you can see a diversity of all different kinds of people."

Two months later, Jack returned from Europe and agreed to be interviewed at the local Starbucks. He told me that for the past thirty years he has taught at the School of Visual Arts, a private college. "I know all kinds of people and I love all kinds of people. They like all of us because we're different, and that's why I like them. I like to go get the magazines because I like *them*. I kind of miss Marvin and Ron sometimes. When I'm in my apartment [three blocks away], I'll say, 'Let's have a break.' So I go out and I see my magazine men. It's a joy for me to be outside, and I get some nice little juicy things that I can work with and I cut them up and make scrapbooks with them. That stuff I get from them is really my own education. Because look at the incredible, vast differences of things they have at the table."

Marvin and Ron develop relations with an extraordinarily diverse customer base. In *The Global City*, Saskia Sassen argues that cities like New York, London, and Tokyo have a distinctive consumption structure as a result of distinctive economies and vast disparities in income.[23] Marvin and Ron's table is a site for interaction that weakens the social barriers between persons otherwise separated by vast social and economic inequalities.[24] Many of these customers spend ten or twenty dollars in single purchases. They are people with disposable income and a desire for catalogues from auction houses or current issues of fine-art, architecture, or graphic-arts magazines. Some of them are collecting advertisements, and immediately turn the magazine over to see what is on the back cover, or start looking through an issue for a specific page. Many such customers walk up to the table with a typed list in hand, trying to find advertisements they need for their collections.

Two ad campaigns in particular seemed to attract collectors to the table: "Milk Mustache" and Absolut Vodka. The Milk Mustache ads, produced by the American Milk Processors in an effort to dispel negative attitudes about milk, consist of Annie Leibovitz photographs of celebrities wearing milk mustaches. Those that generated the most interest during my first summer on the block featured TV stars Jennifer Aniston and Lisa Kudrow, film director Spike Lee, and news anchor Joan Lunden.

Unlike the Milk Mustache ads, which tend to be printed inside magazines (thus requiring customers to turn the pages to find them), the Absolut Vodka ads generally appear on back covers. Once, a boy walking with a woman who appeared to be his mother (dressed in a Chanel-looking suit), came up to the table and asked, "How much are the *Wireds*?"

"The *Wireds* are two dollars. Three for five dollars," said Marvin.

It was surprising to me that such a young person would want a magazine

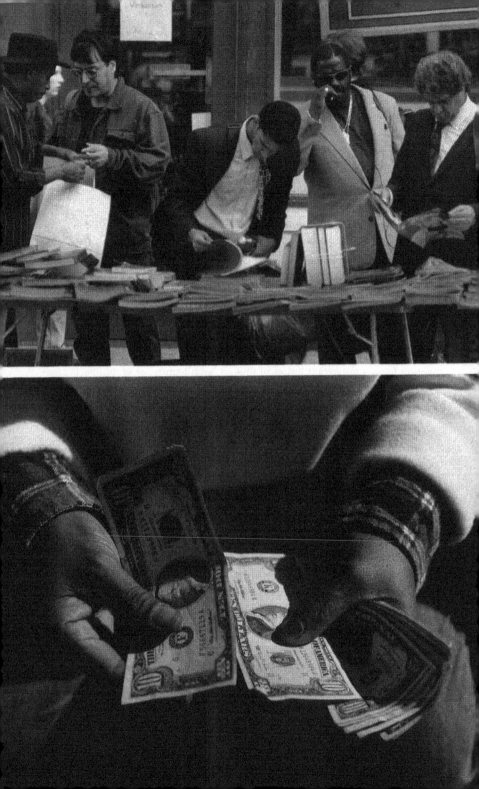

clearly aimed at an adult market. When I mentioned this to Hakim, who was standing by the table, he asked some questions of the boy to help explain what was going on.

"Do you collect those for the Absolut ads?" he asked.

"Uh-huh," said the boy. "It's sort of like a collection. Like baseball cards."

"So you don't even read the magazine?" said Hakim.

"Well, sometimes I read the magazine."

"Do you read *Wired*?" asked Hakim.

"Yeah."

"Oh, you do! How old are you?"

"Eleven."

•

When I first saw Marvin and Ron displaying catalogues from Victoria's Secret, Lands' End, and L.L. Bean, I wondered what manner of man would expect someone to pay money for a catalogue that was originally sent out by the company free of charge and now has been picked out of a bundle of trash. The answer, it turns out, is simple: a man who knows his market. The vendor who sells a free catalogue, usually for a dollar, is actually redistributing written matter to people who don't have ready access to it in their neighborhoods. Some of the customers who patronize these tables come from Harlem, the outer boroughs of New York City, and certain parts of New Jersey, ZIP codes in which L.L. Bean and Lands' End do not ordinarily solicit much business.

Back at the upper extreme of buyers, who spend a lot of money, are men and women looking for fashion magazines from France, Spain, Australia, Germany, Italy, and Great Britain (French *Marie Claire*, *Paris Vogue*, and British *GQ* are among the most popular). These imported magazines sell for ten to fifteen dollars on the newsstand; an issue in good condition can bring five dollars for Marvin and Ron, with both parties believing they are "getting over."

"I'm looking for something with Naomi Campbell on the cover," says an African-American woman of about thirty.

"Yeah, I got something right here," says Ron.

"Everything she's done, I collect," says the woman. "That's the only one you got?"

"Two dollars," says Ron.

The woman pays, while a twenty-fiveish white woman picks up a *Paris Vogue.* "How much is this?"

"Give me three," says Ron.

"And this?" she asks, picking up another *Paris Vogue.*

"Give me six altogether."

As she hands over the money, Ron says, "Where you from? Your accent is . . ."

"You guess," she responds.

"Italy?" Ron asks.

"Close. Very close. Try again!"

Ron laughs.

"Try again," she urges. "You have to try again."

"That's the only one I can think of," says Ron. "Spain?"

"Very close. Mediterranean. That's right."

"I don't know," says Ron.

"Israel," reveals the customer.

"Israel!" exclaims Ron. "Okay!"

"Have a nice day!" she tells him.

"All right, you, too."

Through all of these otherwise banal interactions, I came to learn who the customers were and see the ease with which Marvin and Ron interacted with them. I also came to believe that in this entrepreneurial activity Marvin and Ron maintained a connection to the larger society.

SOCIAL SUPPORT AND MENTORING

Ron's capacity to do so would have been limited were it not for Marvin's support and tolerance. It was possible to see these men motivating one another to try to live "better" lives. Though their drug addictions had the capacity to reduce any of them to the extreme "Fuck it!" mind-set, the friendships on the street were crucial in crystallizing the importance of a life devoted to some moral ideals, even if only the ideal of not saying, "Fuck it!"

An incident that illustrates this point occurred during the Christmas season. Rather than sleeping outside, Ron had been spending more and more time on a couch in the Harlem apartment of his elderly great-aunt. When I arrived on the block one Saturday in the middle of December, Marvin was try-

ing to convince Mudrick to watch a table while he went away for a while.
Ron had promised his aunt he would check on her, but he had just realized
that it was essential he go back right away because he had left the stove on
and there was no phone in the house with which to warn her. Mudrick was
saying he couldn't watch the table, when I showed up. Marvin said, "Mitch,
I'm glad you're here. I need you to do me a favor. Ron gotta go home. He *got*
to go home, to check on his aunt. I need you to watch one of the tables until
he gets back."

"No problem," I said.

"You want me to go now?" Ron asked.

"You gonna be longer than an hour or two?" asked Marvin.

"An hour and a half, maybe," said Ron. "The time it take to go and come
back. On the train!"

"Yeah, but you might get there and be stuck," said Marvin.

"I'm not gonna be stuck, because I know what I'm gonna do. I'm going
home to check on her to make sure she's all right."

Ron's decision to get on the subway and go all the way up to Harlem was
an example of his not saying, "Fuck it." A person who had given up on family and responsibility would have taken his chances that his aunt would
discover the hot stove on her own. He wouldn't have cared.

After Ron went down into the subway, Marvin said, "See, his aunt is living by herself now. She really wants him to stay home. It's that season where
old people ain't got nobody there."

"His cousin is living there," said Mudrick.

"No, he's not there," said Marvin. "That's what I was telling him. I said,
'Regardless of what you do, you got somebody in your life that needs you, so
it's time for you to do it doggone right!' "

"Yeah," said Mudrick. "Do the right thing."

"It's just like you," said Marvin. "When your granddaughter wasn't here,
you were running around with the guys and blowing all your money. Soon as
your granddaughter was born, you know you love your little granddaughter,
you have a little responsibility for her, and you give her everything. He's supposed to give his aunt everything that he can."

"All he can right now," agreed Mudrick. "That's what I'm doing with
Dyneisha. I give her all I can get."

" 'Cause can you imagine if he would go home every time he get paid and at least fill the refrigerator and go buy her something once in a while?" said Marvin. "She would put him in her will! He had been sitting up there wondering why he don't be in the will."

About an hour later, Ron emerged from the subway and took a seat on his milk crate.

"What happened with your aunt?" Marvin asked.

"Oh, it was a good thing I went home. She didn't want me to leave at all."

"Is it because she's lonely?" asked Marvin.

"She was begging me to stay," said Ron.

"Yeah, that's what I was telling Mitch and Mudrick. Do your little bull-shit thing. It's getting ready to get cold and you gonna have a place to lay and you got someone who wants you."

"Oh, she was begging me," replied Ron, and then, imitating her: " 'Please don't go back to work.' "

"And she's telling you she's gonna give you money to stay! You can't beat that!" said Marvin.

"And I left the stove on this morning with the pot overheated," exclaimed Ron. "Could have burned down the house. It's a good thing she checked. And I called my cousin, the guy who moved out, right? I called him this morning, when I got downtown, 'cause I didn't want to go back. I figured it's probably too late now. It probably started to catch. I called him up and said, 'Yo, call the lady in the building that has a key to the apartment. She'll go downstairs and check.' He said, 'I'm not calling that woman at this time of morning.' I said, 'This is an *emergency*. The house could be burning down. It's not like you calling her for some kind of fun or game. If the place catch fire, she gonna wake up anyway!' He says, 'I'm not calling her at this time of the morning. I'll give *you* her number.' He gave me a wrong number! I told my aunt about it. She said, 'Don't tell him nothing no more.' "

"You know why your aunt wants you there?" asked Marvin. "Because you are sincere when you're sober. And she know your cousin don't even drink or drug and she knows he's a bunch of bullshit. She knows you a good person, but you drink and drug. Come on. Stop that dumb shit, man. Come on, you have to promise me you gonna do something better, Ron!"

This discussion illustrates the kind of support I witnessed regularly between Marvin and Ron on the street. It did not urge adherence to particularly strict codes of conduct, but instead encouraged Ron to be responsible, not to do drugs, not to drink, not to say, "Fuck it."

The conversation between Marvin and Ron might have gone on longer, but one of their regular customers, a gay white man in his forties, walked past the table.

"He didn't see us," Ron said to Marvin.

"Hey, we got some more of them magazines right here!" Ron called out, referring to the stack of gay pornography kept beneath the table. (Magazine vendors on Sixth Avenue tend not to display pornography during the day, out of respect, they say, for passing children.)

The man seemed not to hear.

"Did he see the gay books?" Marvin asked.

"I don't know."

Mudrick was across the street with a plate, and the topic changed again.

"What food are they giving away at the church today?" Ron asked.

"Chicken," Marvin responded.

"Oh yeah?" said Ron. "I made my own chicken. I told you I cooked at four o'clock this morning. I got up at four o'clock this morning and cooked for my aunt."

"Yeah?" said Marvin. "That was good, Ron! You see, that's what I'm talking about. A few days out of the month doing that, your aunt will fall in love with you. She may want to marry you!"

•

Six months later, when I was back in New York working on the street, Ron looked very different to me. Whereas once he'd had the disheveled appearance of a man who never shaved or showered, now he was clean-cut. He explained that he was still living with his Aunt Naomi, and had continued taking good care of her. Now that his cousin was gone, she had given him the spare bedroom.

The photographer Ovie Carter and I asked if we could meet Aunt Naomi, and on a Wednesday morning in June, Ron invited us up to the apartment. She was a frail ninety-two years old. Ovie took a number of photographs of Ron and his aunt together, then left. As we waited for the elevator, we heard Ron yell to her: "Do you want your boiled milk now?"

Ovie went back inside, and before they noticed him he made the accompanying photo of Ron serving the boiled milk. It illustrates, perhaps better than any interview might, the positive changes that Ron was making with the support of Marvin on the street.

One morning the following December, Ovie and I were in Harlem again and stopped by Aunt Naomi's to bring her flowers for Christmas. A shopping cart full of recycled books and magazines was by the front door. We found Ron in the kitchen, cooking a meal of fried bananas and a boiled egg. A cup of hot chocolate was already on the table with a slice of bread.

"I don't want the bread," Aunt Naomi called out.

"You sure?" Ron called back. "Take a little piece of bread. You don't have to eat it all."

•

I began this book by saying that I know a scrupulous adherence to rules of method will not lead to objective truth. Surely this is in part because being a social scientist does not preclude having strong opinions, values, or feelings. But here it demands a willingness to be public about the way they affect

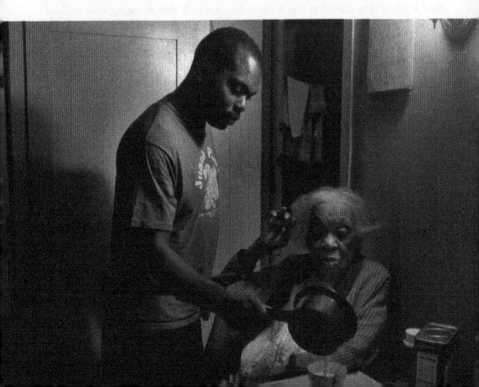

one's standards and the claims one makes. One of the greatest barriers to maintaining standards is the strong attachments one develops with one's subjects, which can lead to emotions that make the idea of social *science* less than realistic. Riding downtown on the subway with Ovie that morning, I was full of passion for the vendors and their sidewalk life. But I tried, with both success and failure during my ride, to remain detached.

Here on the sidewalk, men are able to engage in legal entrepreneurial activity that helps them maintain respect for others and for themselves. Although the act of picking through recycled trash and setting up tables on the street appears to create disorder, which might lead to crime, I have rarely seen any crime spring from this environment. I wonder how Ron would get the money for his drugs if he could not earn it; selling magazines seems to provide a way for Ron to avoid committing crimes. Furthermore, many other Village residents appreciate having these men on the sidewalk, which enables them to stay in business.

I thought about how far Marvin has come since the days when he said, "Fuck it!" The work has provided a structure that exerts a pressure not to give up. His behavior, like Ron's, indicates that they care about society and wish to be a part of it.

Just as the "Fuck it!" mentality has a pervasive effect on a person's life, so can the opportunity to take control and earn respect within a limited domain. Whereas Marvin and Ron had once said, "The hell with you and whatever's right," now they have used the opportunity provided by the sidewalk to become innovators—earning a living, striving for self-respect, establishing good relations with fellow citizens, providing support for each other. For Ron, panhandling led to scavenging and vending, which have given him a trade of sorts and a mentor, who in turn encouraged him to take care of Aunt Naomi.

When alcohol and drugs, once central to a person's life, are no longer a part of that life, what does the recovering person substitute for them? He may not be ready to enter the formal economy. What might he put in place to become a self-respecting, productive member of society? It seems to me that the entrepreneurial activity Marvin is engaging in on the sidewalk a few days a week fills that void.

Moreover, Marvin has taken on the role of mentor or sponsor or "old head." He learned how to do it by watching Jamaane do it for him. He is acting as sponsor for both Ron and Mudrick in a way that no government or social-service agency, religous institution, or charity can. The task of the sponsor is to encourage responsible behavior. And the essence of this effort—to invoke Jane Jacobs again—is that Marvin does it "without being hired."

I am also thinking about Jerome. It might only be a short step between his life as a young father with a ninth-grade education and that of Marvin and Ron on the sidewalk. Jerome is undoubtedly experiencing great pressures. Thank goodness for whatever encouragement he has received from Hakim and the others.

I am thinking about the sidewalk. Thank goodness for the sidewalk.

The Men without Accounts

Until 1996, the local bank had four doormen who divided among them a twenty-four-hour shift. They received no paychecks from the bank and no benefits. But when you entered the automated-teller-machine vestibule adjoining the Sixth Avenue branch, they would hold the door for you and wish you a nice day.

"Hello," said Joe with a broad smile, shaking a Starbucks cup as he held the door for a middle-aged white woman, who did not return the warm greeting or look pleased to see him. He is a heroin addict with a gentle manner who has been in and out of jail for petty crimes associated with drug use. He never asks directly for money when he holds the door open, and leaves it up to the bank's customers to infer that in performing this "service" he is soliciting a donation from them.

Leo, another ex-convict, addicted to crack cocaine, left little room for interpretation. "Good afternoon. How you doing? A little help on the way out if you can, please," he said. He showed off his operatic voice, singing love songs while opening and closing the door with one hand and holding a blue-and-white Acropolis coffee cup with the other.

Keith Johnson, also an ex-convict, was perfectly sincere. "Hi, welcome to Chemical Bank. Change you can spare or any contributions you choose to give me will be put to good use, such as beer, food, or clothing. Thank you and have a nice day."

Unlike some panhandlers, who got contributions by purposefully instilling fear in pedestrians, these particular men tended to be polite and gregari-

ous and, in return for their opening the door, they hoped you would put money in their cups.

I came to call them and others working the door of the automated-teller vestibule "the men without accounts," though any one of them could make regular deposits in the machine with the seventy dollars he could make on an average day. Saturdays and Sundays were particularly good: it was not unusual for a person to make that much money in a few hours.

In 1996, Mayor Rudolph Giuliani worked with fifteen City Council members to gain passage of a bill banning certain forms of solicitation, including panhandling near automated-teller machines. After the law had been in effect for about a year, I noticed that panhandlers were back begging at many of the ATMs around the city. In the Sixth Precinct, however, the police have remained strict. While some men can sometimes be seen working the door, it is now much riskier in that location. Most of the men who worked the door before the law was passed now earn their money in the written-matter economy.

The law notwithstanding, soliciting donations at the door of the ATM vestibule or at a subway entrance in Greenwich Village can yield enough money to create stiff competition for good spots. Every man must be prepared to share the door or stairwell with others who have established themselves as members of the current regime. The amount of time these men can spend in a spot is thus limited. So a number of men augment their panhandling and pass some of their time on the street by serving as assistants to the book vendors and magazine scavengers.

In theory, any panhandler can set up his own table on the street if space is available. So what distinguishes the men without accounts from the magazine scavengers they work for? The men without accounts often say that they are unable to maintain the kind of normal, routine life necessary to have a regular table and stock of magazines, or that they lack the patience to sit at a table all day. The magazine scavengers are less generous in explaining the difference. They say that the panhandlers lack ambition, or that they aren't willing to work as hard as you have to work to be a magazine vendor.

Both panhandlers and magazine vendors have told me, on occasion, that they have too much pride to engage in each other's activity, and each knows that the other looks down on what he does. While he shakes his cup at the Chemical Bank (now Chase), Leo sees Ron go by, pushing a crate of magazines on a hand truck. "Ron does not panhandle," he says. "You would never catch him with a cup."

"Why?"

"Pride, I guess. He would rather sell trash. He figures it's degrading to himself to panhandle," he says. "I think it is degrading to look through trash. I would never go that low."

Though Leo knows that magazine vendors like Ron look down on panhandling, he sees no shame in it. "You got to be versatile when you in the streets. You got to find a way to make money without putting a pistol in your hand or going around busting somebody up the head, or snatching some woman's pocketbook." The men without accounts take satisfaction in what they do by comparing panhandling with the way of life that once sent them to prison. They think of themselves now as having not given up on what is right. Rather than saying, "Fuck it, the hell with you and whatever is right," Leo can say, "Whatever I do with my money, at least I can say I earned it. That I have a reason to hold my head up."

Many panhandlers derive self-respect from the way they conduct themselves *as panhandlers*. "I've never found it to be degrading to ask for what you need," says Keith Johnson, who is forty years old. "Everybody gotta eat, you know. But before the night is out, you'll see a couple of panhandlers go over to that outdoor café and ask people for money while they are eating. How would I feel if someone came to me at my table and said, 'I'm hungry, too. I want to eat. Can I have the money that you was gonna leave for a tip?' [Imitating the diner:] 'Get the fuck out of here! I'm with my wife and my kid and you're breathing all over their food.' "

"But you don't do that," I say to Keith.

"I refuse to. I never have and I never will. I'm not gonna do something to anybody that I don't want done to me."

Some men see the difference between panhandling and selling scavenged magazines as reflecting personal rather than objective standards. Warren used to panhandle alongside Keith, but now he is selling magazines. "I chose to move on," he explains. "That's not something I wanted to keep doing, shaking a cup. That's something that he prefers to do."

The panhandling population resembles that of the magazine vendors in age, race, prison experience, and drug use. The panhandlers, too, came to the sidewalk after they had been released from prison or "put out" by relatives, or had been evicted from or had "given up" apartments. They, too, have found it hard to enter the formal economy, and consider their begging an honest living. Although they rarely display the strong pride and self-respect that I see in Ron when he demands his price as a magazine vendor, I do see in the constant references to the trade-off between stealing and begging their sense that they have chosen to engage in a worthy enterprise, rather than an unworthy one.

"I'd rather ask for what I need than take it," Keith says.

"Is that the choice?" I ask.

"I'd take it if I wanted to. I mean, if I really wanted to be nasty, I don't have to be in the situation that I'm in. See, there's a dark side in me that's been buried for years, that I've been trying to bury since I was a kid. And that's the don't-give-a-fuck side."

As support staff of sorts to the written-matter vendors, the men without accounts are part of a working system of complementary elements. I came to know all of them while I was working with Marvin and Ron. The economy of book vendors and magazine scavengers doubtless could survive without them, but these men have made places for themselves on the street, becoming part of the lifeline, the web of interactions that constitutes the ongoing life of the sidewalk. They perform a number of distinct and recognized roles: the place holder, the table watcher, the mover, and the person who "lays shit out." The range of roles demonstrates the many ways that the sidewalk's informal written-matter economy can support a life on the street, and the many ways a person can make something for himself out of nothing. In this process, the men have created roles for themselves by adapting to the distinctive logic of the sidewalk. These economic roles also show how the informal system of mentoring is part of a larger system of informal social organization and social control, which makes the sidewalk safer by providing an outlet for men to earn money to support drug habits by means other than stealing or themselves selling drugs.

The Place Holder

An informal system governs property rights on the street. Vending space is scarce, and some locations are more remunerative than others. Some men support themselves by acting as place holders for the magazine scavengers and vendors. In effect, they hold a spot of public sidewalk overnight and sell it to a vendor or scavenger in the morning.[1]

Take Leo, at the door of the ATM vestibule. One day I asked him to explain what he does on the sidewalk when he is not working the door of the bank.

"There's not enough room for [all the vendors] to set up. Everyone wants their own specific spot. They will pay me twenty dollars per spot to hold a place for them. I will put a table there all night. Sometimes I've had as many as eleven tables out."

"How does this get arranged?"

"They come to me. It is at their request. They all pay me."

Though Leo says there have been periods when he made a couple of hundred dollars a day holding places, I have only seen him paid forty dollars for holding a couple of spots. At any given time, there are several panhandlers competing to hold places for the scavengers and vendors.

"How do you establish your ownership right to a piece of sidewalk that belongs to the City of New York?"

"A lot of people fear me. My psychiatrist told me that when I feel stressed out to scream and holler. Just let it out. So I will run up and down Sixth Avenue screaming and hollering at anybody because I am so angry with myself. I got a fairly strong voice. And some people will take my screaming and hollering as intimidation. But actually it is not. It is just my way to release some of my anxiety, and people look up to me because they see I don't fear police or no man. And then, when I use some intellect along with brutal strength, it has a tendency to work."

Another man who works as a place holder is B.A., who has been on these blocks on and off for ten years. He explained his work routine to me on a Friday afternoon, as he was getting ready to secure a space for an elderly white book vendor.

"Explain to me how that system works."

"He gives me fifty dollars in the morning to hold a spot down for him. Because he knows how it is out here. People try to get out here early and get a spot. He can't sell from the van, 'cause he get a ticket. But he make enough to pay me that. I be out here all night to watch his spot. I set up a table right there at 3:00 a.m. Then I wait for him to come at 5:00 a.m."

"What happens if someone else puts a table there?"

"They gotta move!"

"Do you have the force to make them move?"

"Yeah! Me."

"You're a little guy."

"That's all right." B.A. laughed. "They gonna move! I'm stepping to my business! If they don't move, I'm gonna move it. And the people on the block know this. Friday night, after they pack up, they don't even think about coming there. They move down. I get my little respect. I respect them for that, too."

"How long have you been saving that space for the old man?"

"Three years. One day he came there and couldn't find a space. I was saving a spot for this other guy I was working for. He was paying me forty dollars a space. Eighty dollars for two spaces on Friday and Saturday, $160 for a weekend's work. Then the old man came up to me and said, 'Could you move down a little bit? I'll give you twenty-five dollars for a space.' So I said, 'Sure.' Then he said, 'Could you do this every week? Then I'll pay you for two spaces.' So I made eighty dollars from the other guy and fifty dollars from the old man. That was $130 that was guaranteed for each day, $260 for the weekend." (This has been verified by others on the block, but I have never observed the money change hands.)

"What is an appropriate amount of money to charge for a spot?"

"It depends on how much a man is making. Twenty-five to thirty dollars is not really enough to stand out all night to watch a spot. If he is a good vendor, he is entitled to pay you forty to fifty dollars to be out there all night."

"What is the minimum you will accept for being out there all night?"

"I'd say fifty dollars."

"And you can get this money for selling space that belongs to the public?"

"Yeah. You right. You right. But this is something that they want, not that I created. Because the fifty dollars don't mean nothing to him if his books is still up in the van. Because he can't make no money. He would rather pay me the fifty dollars than lose money and not have a spot. He paid it for his own benefit."

"But this shows a certain creativity on your part."

"Sure! It ain't nothing nobody else can't do. I was always like that. I could make nothing into something. Where there is a will there's a way. That's what the street is about: survival."

The Table Watcher

The Administrative Code of the City of New York states that no street vendor may occupy more than eight by three linear feet of sidewalk space parallel to the curb. Since most tables are six to eight feet long, generally no vendor can have more than one table on the street. So those vendors who wish to use more than one table pay some of the men without accounts to stand behind or "watch" their second and third tables. A vendor or magazine scavenger may also hire a table watcher if he needs to urinate or defecate, eat, go on a "hunt" for used magazines in the recycled trash, or go on a "mission" to find crack or heroin and then use it away from Sixth Avenue. Otherwise, the police may confiscate his table as "unattended."

There are different kinds of table watching, and these differences determine how much a person will make for a day's work. At one extreme are the men who merely sit on a crate near the vendors, perhaps leaning up against the side of a building or in the shade across the street. They receive no guarantee of money, but if they are around when the police come by, a vendor operating several tables will call on one of them to stand by a table. Once the police leave, the vendor will pay the table watcher five or ten dollars.

More common is the table watcher who sits by a table for several hours or all day. For such work he can expect to share in the profits from all books and magazines sold from that table (his cut is usually 50 percent). Some of them stand by when the vendor does the selling; others do the selling themselves. When the table watcher makes a sale, he usually holds the money for a little while, then gives the vendor his share. The time that passes between the sale and the transfer indicates respect and trust between the vendor and the watcher.

Sometimes, a vendor will leave his table for long periods of time. When Conrad was offered a job selling watermelons in Brooklyn on Saturdays during the summer, he arranged to set up his table of magazines in the morning

and have Baby Face watch it for him all day. The two men kept to this arrangement all through the summer I worked on the block.

Most table watchers are familiar with the prices of magazines, and each has been trained over the years to "get his price." But the vendor usually tells the watcher about special prices on the table, and apprises him of magazines or books that might have an unusual value. For example, when Marvin found a special issue of Italian fashion collections that sold on the newsstand for more than seventy dollars, he told Mudrick not to sell it for less than twenty dollars. The vendor normally has a good idea of what was on his table when he went away, and he expects the watcher to have gotten his price if the merchandise is gone when he returns. Sometimes, though, the table watcher uses his own discretion and sells a magazine for less than what he has been told it is worth. One day, for example, Keith and Warren were jointly watching Shorty's table while he was away from the block. After making a sale, Keith said to Warren, "I took a dollar off that book and sold it for three dollars. That way I get a dollar, you get a dollar, and Shorty gets a dollar." This happens often.

Working as a table watcher gives a man a place to sit during the day and a way to occupy himself. Sometimes he will sit quietly and look at the magazines on his table, commenting to men nearby on pictures or articles that strike his fancy. When Keith came upon an ad for an automobile in one of the magazines, he said, "I wouldn't mind having this car right here."

"What kind of car is that?" asked Warren.

"A Mercury Custom. Twenty-two thousand dollars. And there's my truck right there," Keith said, pointing to another picture.

"Oh, that's it?"

"That's the one I want," said Keith.

"Oh, you want a really big one?" said Warren.

"It's the same thing as the smaller one, except that it comes as a full van. I take that over any of these cars, even this Lamborghini."

"Oh, that's the fucking thing I saw here in the street!"

"It's ugly," said Keith.

"Yeah, it *is* ugly," Warren agreed. "That looks like Darth Vader invented it. That's the one that costs $270,000?"

"No. That's one of these," said Keith, pointing to a different car. "I can't see paying that kind of money! And look at this: Porsche wristwatches. Fifty-five hundred dollars."

"In gold?" asked Warren.

"No. Steel or titanium."

"Fifty-five hundred dollars for a fucking steel watch? You got to be crazy!" said Warren.

"You paying for the name," said Keith.

"It's made by the same people that made the car? It don't even look that nice," said Warren.

"There's another car in here I'm in love with, man," said Keith. "I wouldn't mind having this."

"What the fuck is that?" asked Warren.

"It's amphibious," said Keith.

"Oh, my God! What is that? From World War II or something?"

"Look at this one here," said Keith.

"What's that? A Thunderbird?"

"A Chevy," said Keith. "That's for when you want to just hang out with your friends at the beach. And look at this one: it has a bar and TV/VCR built into it. It's a dream machine. If I had money, I would spend money on that. That would be my play car. See, my dreams are small! I don't want to own the World Trade Center. For what? So they can try to blow it up again? So my insurance premiums can go up higher? I don't need that kind of headache! Let me take care of my grandmother and my aunt. And I would have a 'going out with my girl' car. Or 'a going out to get a girl' car!"

It is during downtime at the tables that a great deal of mentoring and personal support takes place. Once, when Warren was watching Ishmael's table, he saw Rock, who he thought had stolen his Walkman.

"Why do you do this shit, man?" Warren called out to him.

"What the fuck's wrong?" asked Rock.

"Why do you think you can just take shit from people and you can walk by them the next day without getting your fucking ass kicked? You do something to me, next time I'm gonna fuck you up. I'm gonna try to kill you or you're gonna fuck me up. I'm tired of you taking my shit."

Rock sat down and started telling Warren what had happened to him in his life. One day he came home from work to find that his wife had taken all his stuff out of the house. "Took everything. I like flipped, I bugged out."

"Okay, fine," said Warren. "That happened. That was adversity in your life. What? You gonna say this is what you're gonna accept, this is what you're gonna be now? Then in turn you're gonna hurt other people? That's why you say, 'Fuck it!' 'Cause what happened to you? It's never too late to turn your life around."

Unlike Keith, who sat daydreaming as he watched Shorty's table, or Warren, who tried to give guidance to another man while he sat at his table, many of the table watchers will not work at a table for very long without spending the money they have made on crack or alcohol. If he is working with such a person, Marvin will usually try to hold the man's money all through the day and pay him a lump sum when he is taking down his tables that night. "Okay, Marvin, come over here. We have some business to talk about," a table watcher nicknamed T. says in an effort to get Marvin to give him some money so he can leave the table toward the end of the day.

Marvin does not want him to go. "Come on, now. Sit tight! Damn."

The table watcher persists, and finally Marvin gives him a couple of dollars—less than he has earned, and not enough for him to buy much more than a soda pop or a pack of cigarettes.

"I'll be right back," says T.

"Come back, now," says Marvin. "One time you didn't."

"Didn't what?" says T.

"You didn't come back," says Marvin.

"When?"

"I forget when it was. You want me to tell you an exact date? Come on, T. Just come back, please!"

Many a table watcher with a pocketful of money has been known to disappear into Washington Square Park to buy crack, not to return until after the police have come and confiscated the table he was supposed to be watching.

The Mover

Most of the men who sell new and high-quality used books on Sixth Avenue have their own apartments, to which they return each night. Some, like Marvin, keep their merchandise at the Manhattan Mini Storage some blocks distant. Book vendors like Hakim and Alice and comic-book vendors like Howard keep their goods in a space at the parking garage around the corner, paying two hundred dollars per month to do so. A few men on the block—

B.A., Randy, and Conrad among them—have earned a steady income by moving the vendors' goods in and out of these storage spaces.

Because there is competition among the movers for this business, they have come to a tacit agreement as to who will work when. B.A. calls himself the "morning man" for Hakim, Alice, and Howard; Randy calls himself the "night man."

"I'm in my own moving-and-storage business now," Randy explains to me with genuine pride. He is around five feet eight and has a prominent scar on his face, which he got when he was robbed two years ago in the 125th Street subway station. "I'm like a company. I started when someone asked me to help move them in. Then someone else saw me helping and they asked me. So I said, 'Damn! I can make money off of this! I can move them in and bring 'em out.' Sometimes I even get their stuff and bring it out before they get here! I call them my clients. I even have a thing called the clients of the month and the clients of the year. They get a little award, a little drawing, or I might move them in free once in a while. Because that's how you're supposed to be when you in business."

"How much do you charge them?"

"My normal fee is five dollars for around the corner."

"What about for the walk to the Manhattan Mini Storage? That's ten blocks."

"That's five dollars, too. But I might have to up my prices, because the cost of living is really going up!"

The Storage Provider

Most men who sleep on the sidewalks, like Ron and Marvin, eventually find their way to a housed existence. When this occurs, they usually do not have the credit or financial wherewithal to get a storage space for their goods. They must find someplace to keep their written matter.

This need is filled by men who earn a subsistence income by working as storage providers. When Grady and Keith White take their tables down, they call Butteroll to come up from the "dungeon" of the subway to store their goods. He carries their tables and crates down two flights of stairs and then brings them beneath the platform to the space by the side of the tracks where he sleeps. For this, he gets paid ten dollars. In the morning, the men can go get their goods, or ask him to carry them upstairs for an additional fee.

Some nights, Mudrick stores Ron's books in the storage room of the building on Bleecker Street where he works taking out the trash. After Ron packs up all the crates, he summons a man who needs extra money to work as a "mover." Then Mudrick will hail two separate cabs, filling each one with crates, and send the "mover" in the other taxi to meet him at the building. There the "mover" is responsible for carrying the crates up two flights of stairs. For this, he gets paid five dollars. Mudrick will get anywhere from seven to ten dollars for providing the storage space.

There is one local resident, beloved by the men, who also provides storage for Ron's tables, which will not fit in Mudrick's cabs. Known on the street as "the Mighty Whitey" or "Mighty," he is a white superintendent in his sixties who resides in the basement of a nearby building. When Ron is finished at the end of the day, he will hire one of the "movers" to carry his tables (no merchandise) to the man's apartment. The Mighty Whitey responds within moments of hearing his name yelled from the street, taking hold of the tables as they are passed over his iron fence. He usually gets about five dollars for performing this service, though he never asks for money and often gets nothing if Ron has had a bad day.

"Laying Shit Out"

Half a dozen men come to Sixth Avenue with a few miscellaneous items from local trash baskets and put them on a blanket, or corrugated cardboard, or on the sidewalk. Joe Garbage, who got his name for trying to sell whatever he finds, comes to the block with a shopping cart full of items. Others, such as Mudrick, might come with nothing in their pockets and nothing to sell. If Mudrick gets a job working as a table watcher for one of the magazine scavengers, fine; if not, that's fine, too; but either way, he has no expectation of panhandling. The men who "lay shit out" can sometimes leave the block at the end of the day with their pockets as full as anyone else's.

The written-matter vendors on the block believe that the act of "laying shit out" poses the biggest threat to their livelihood. As they see it, the police tend to crack down on all the vendors when some get out of hand by failing to put their stock on tables, as the law demands. When some men on the block endanger everyone, the "old heads" or mentors often try to exert social control, before the police come and make life difficult for everyone. Once, for example, when Butteroll and Al, his sometime co-worker, had a number of pornographic photographs laid out by the bus shelter, Ishmael called Marvin to see what was going on.

"They got porno and other stuff sitting all over the sidewalk right by the bus stop," Ishmael said. "Someone gonna call the cops and they gonna roll up in here if we don't take care of this."

"Is that Al's shit?"

"You been down there yet?" asked Ishmael. "Go take a look at that shit, Marvin!"

Marvin asked me to stay at his table while he went down the block. A few minutes later, the pornographic photos were off the sidewalk. Although on most occasions the vendors are self-regulating, there are times when men "laying shit out" will get careless and the police will appear, often enforcing the letter of the law, including the number of tables that can be on the block, and whether they are the proper distance from doorways. This provides a further incentive for the vendors to be self-regulating. Usually, the vendors

who "lay shit out" show a constant awareness that they must watch out for the police.

.

On a Sunday in late August, I arrived on the block around 10:00 a.m. Only a few vendors and magazine scavengers were set up. Because many of them work late into the night on Saturdays to benefit from the throngs of people who trek to Greenwich Village on weekends, it is common for the sidewalk to be pretty bare on Sundays until after noon. Furthermore, Marvin had indicated that he would take this particular day off to escort his girlfriend to church. Outside Store 24 (now Go Sushi), Hakim and Alice, who never use a place holder, had already claimed their usual space and were setting up their books. Ishmael was set up in his regular spot on the southeast corner of Sixth Avenue and Eighth Street, and Shorty had taken advantage of the extra space by setting up two tables (rather than his usual one) outside Blockbuster Video.

After me, the next person to arrive on the block was Mudrick, who had slept in the park the night before and awakened to find his wallet gone.

Without sentimentalizing our relationship, I think it is fair to say that Mudrick and I had grown fairly close since his and Marvin's discussion of whether Ron was "other people." In those three months, Mudrick had done a great deal to "watch my back" from day to day. I knew his bargaining techniques, as well as whom he trusted on the street. In recent weeks, I had spent more and more time with his granddaughter, Dyneisha.

When he arrived on this particular Sunday, Mudrick told me that he needed to make some money for breakfast. This implied that he wanted a twenty-two-ounce black-and-silver can of St. Ides Premium Malt Liquor, his "coffee." He fully expected that some money would come his way during the next few hours. If you asked him how exactly this might happen, he would not know, though the fact that Shorty had two tables set up indicated that Mudrick might begin his day by working as a table watcher.

Not five minutes after Mudrick arrived, Shorty asked him and me to watch his two tables while he went away. Mudrick now had a place to sit, a milk crate next to the table. When Shorty came back a few minutes later, he said that Mudrick and I could watch the other table and keep half the profits.

We positioned our milk crates next to each other at one end of the table.

"How much is the *New York* magazine?" a woman asked.

"All of these magazines are New York magazines," Mudrick responded. "This is New York City! Point to the magazine you want."

Playing along with what she took to be Mudrick's joke, the woman pointed to the only *New York* magazine on the table. Later, when I asked him why he always asked people to point to the magazine they wanted, he said:

"I can't read that good."

"Can you read any magazine on this table?"

"No, I can't."

"But you seem to be able to read some things."

"I can read some things."

I point to the sign across the street that says RESTAURANT.

"Can you read that sign?"

"No. I can't make it out."

"Can you read your name?"

"I could read my name."

"Could you read your address?"

"My address? No. 'Cause I don't got one! Mitch, listen to me. You a professor, right? No need to lie to you. I can read some things. But it outside my jurisdiction to try to read anything! Because I don't care about reading. I lived fifty-six years and I don't care about it. If I had that kind of education like you got, I'd be on top of the world. Certain things I can read and certain things I can't. This sign over there, I don't know what it stands for. I'm not ashamed of my game. Because, if you come from where I come from, you would understand what I'm talking about."[2]

As we talked, an African-American man about fifty years old was pushing a canvas mail cart marked U.S. POSTAL SERVICE down the street. He was back from what appeared to have been a successful hunt through local trash. Inside the mail cart were three dressing mirrors, each of them about four feet by six feet. He said he had found them outside a building in the West Village. To judge from the backs of them, the mirrors had been removed from a wall. Other than that, they seemed to be in mint condition. When I later went into a mirror store to get an estimate of their value, I determined that each of them would sell for about $250.

The man pushed the mail cart to Shorty's table, but Shorty said he didn't want them. As he rolled the mirrors away, Mudrick yelled out, "Lis-

ten, I don't have no money right now. You know me for a long time. I'm trying to make some money. Let me have the mirrors, and when you get back,
I'll have you some money. How much you want for them?"

"I want ten dollars."

"Give 'em to me, then."

"All right, I'll leave the mirrors with you. When I come back, give me
some kind of money."

I had never seen this man selling on the street, and Mudrick didn't know
who he was, either. It is common for people to come down the sidewalk with
mail carts or shopping carts full of things that might be sold on the sidewalk.
Local residents suspect that some of these items do not come from the trash
but have been stolen, usually out of cars. I have accompanied every scavenger working these blocks on hunts and seen items such as mirrors moved
from a Dumpster to the sidewalk market. Though there is doubtless a good
deal of stolen merchandise on some sidewalks, this tends to occur in notorious thieves' markets, such as the one at the corner of Second Avenue and
Twelfth Street after eight o'clock at night. I think that most scavenged items
on Sixth Avenue have not been stolen, though some no doubt have.

·

Mudrick carefully removes two mirrors from the cart and leans them
against the side of the Blockbuster Video building. He balances the third mirror against a small tree planted near the curb. In the language of Sixth Avenue, Mudrick, who apparently came to the block with no particular plan, is
now "laying shit out."

The presence of these mirrors on the street initiates a series of little dra-
mas. As pedestrians walk by, they fix their hair, put on lipstick, or simply
stop and stare at themselves. A minute after the mirrors are placed on the
street, a conventionally attractive white woman in her early twenties walks
up to one, starts looking at herself, and asks Mudrick how much he wants
for it.

"You can have it for free!" he jokes.

"All right! But I don't know how I'm gonna get it back to Detroit!"

"I'll take it back to Detroit for you!" says Mudrick. "How you want to
travel? On the bus? I'm not flying in no planes!"

"You gotta go on the plane," she teases.

"I can't go with you, then," says Mudrick.

Next, three middle-aged black women stop and look in the mirrors.

"That's all right, ladies," Mudrick tells them. "Take a look at yourself. See how nice you look!"

The women walk on. The mirrors have been on the street for less than three minutes, but Mudrick is already impatient: "Let's go, New York," he yells. "I've got some mirrors. Wake up and smell the coffee!"

Three minutes later, an elderly black man walks up, pushing a shopping cart. He is one of the unhoused people who walk by every day with something to sell, providing a kind of supplier function. Today, it's a computer. As he takes the unit out of his shopping cart, he almost drops it on the side of a mirror.

"Hey, come on! Come on!" Mudrick yells. "You gotta stay away from the mirrors."

"I brought the computer I was telling you about," the man says.

Mudrick ignores him as he tries to set it down on the sidewalk next to the mirrors.

"He's gonna break the mirrors," I say.

"He won't break my fucking mirror or I'll break his ass. Nobody fucks me over here. They understand me. They know I'm crazy already, Mitch."

The man leaves his computer without receiving any further acknowledgment from Mudrick. It is understood that, if the computer isn't there in a few hours, Mudrick will give him "some kind of money."

The sidewalk is quiet for about five minutes. A young woman comes up to the table and buys three children's books from the table Mudrick and I are covering. Mudrick negotiates with her. The total sale is seven dollars.

"I might give you my credit card," she says in jest.

"We take credit cards," I joke back.

"But you'd rather have cash! You have a bag? Books are wonderful, aren't they?"

As she walks away, another woman interrupts, asking, "Are you selling the mirrors?"

"Yes, we are," says Mudrick.

"How much are they?"

"Twenty each," says Mudrick.

She walks on without responding.

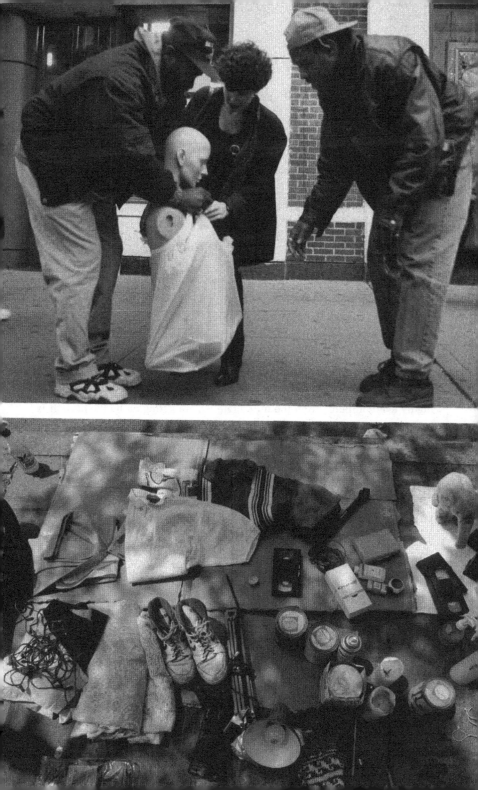

"You want them?" Mudrick calls out.

She ignores him.

"Come here a minute. Listen, miss. Listen, talk to me."

But the woman is out of earshot.

"She don't want to spend no money. She just wants to fuck around!" Mudrick explains.

Another group of three middle-aged black women pass by. "Hi, ladies. Look in the mirror at yourself. You-all look nice today. Fifteen dollars apiece," Mudrick calls out.

They all walk on.

"We gotta sell them for more than fifteen dollars," I tell him.

"I know they is worth more," he responds. "But I gotta get rid of these motherfuckers before 911 [the police] get here. They took Joe Garbage's stuff already. They take everything. They don't like to see nobody make no money." Under the municipal laws, which are discussed in the next chapter, it is legal to sell written matter on the streets without a license, but nothing else.

The avenue is beginning to get crowded; about twenty people are walking by every minute. From the milk crate we are sitting on by the curb, it is impossible to talk to all of the people looking at the mirrors against the wall of the video store, twenty feet away. After a time, Butteroll, whom Mudrick has known for over twenty years, comes down the street.

Butteroll lives by the side of the tracks on the bottom level of the Sixth Avenue subway, in a place known on the street as the dungeon. To the police he is known as John Smith and Kenny. Lore on the block (confirmed to me by Conrad, another magazine vendor, who was married to Butteroll's cousin) is that his real name is Robert F. Kennedy, Jr. A few years ago, when he was arrested for disorderly conduct, the officer asked him his name, and upon hearing Butteroll's reply, decided to bring him to Bellevue Hospital. After he returned to the street, he began using the names "John Smith" and "Kenny" to make things easier.

Butteroll is on his way to the area he refers to as "my office," across the street, near the subway entrance. There he often sits against the brick wall for hours, panhandling with a cup from McDonald's or Starbucks. On this occasion, though, he won't make it to his office.

"Butter! Sit down there 'side that mirror. Twenty dollars apiece. I'll give you a cut!"

"How much will you give him?" I ask.

"I'll give him four dollars," Mudrick says.

"For each mirror?" I ask.

"I'll give him four dollars for *all* the mirrors he sells!"

Butteroll protests, saying that's not enough.

"Shut up!" Mudrick says, "I'm talking! Those are my mirrors! What the fuck you talking about?"

Without responding, Butteroll sits down on the ground next to one of the mirrors. This means the commission has been established. He tries to move the mirror as he situates himself.

"Hey, watch it," Mudrick tells him. "Easy with it! Nice and easy!"

A Puerto Rican woman and her daughter walk up to Butteroll and ask how much the mirrors are. He motions to Mudrick, who said, "I want twenty dollars apiece for them."

"Twenty dollars for all of them?"

"No. Twenty dollars apiece! You know how much this cost in a store? A hundred dollars apiece. You getting it cheap. We got one more over there!"

"Are you gonna be here later on? Because I gotta go eat."

"We gonna be here later on, but the mirrors might not be here."

"We're gonna come back at six o'clock."

"The first one to come is the first one to get 'em. We can't hold 'em."

As the women walk away, Mudrick turns to Butteroll: "You may have just made yourself four dollars." Then he hands him a piece of chicken from the pan of food he got for free from a truck that passes by sometimes, distributing food to unhoused people.

In an amused, raspy voice, Butteroll exclaims, "What you mean, four dollars? They twenty dollars each."

"I'm giving you four dollars for selling all the motherfuckers," Mudrick says, laughing. "You know I'm a slick motherfucker, right?"

Butteroll laughs. "A dollar each? Damn!"

"You got fucked on the deal," Mudrick continues, rubbing it in.

"No. I didn't! Four dollars is better than nothing!"

"You know you can't fuck with me when I'm trying to make a deal," says Mudrick. "You know I'm the wrong fucking motherfucker to fuck with."

"I'll settle for four dollars."

"I'm getting *twenty* dollars apiece and I'm only giving you four dollars for selling them. You understand English? If you don't understand English, you get the fuck up and get the fuck out of here!"

"I'm going anyway. After they come back! When they get back, I'll go!" Butteroll laughs.

"I'm feeding you, motherfucker," Mudrick shouts back. "I'm feeding you beer. What the fuck else do you want from me? This chicken cost me $6.50."

"Six dollars for that?"

"Yeah, I paid six dollars for this. You want the receipt?"

"No. I want the food!"

Mudrick laughs, talking to me. "He want the food. I can't understand him. He's eating my food, talking shit, every kind of thing."

"She's gonna pay you twenty dollars per mirror."

"You know me, Butteroll. I've been here thirty-five years. A lot of that shit is for real, a lot of my shit is a fucking game."

"That's sixty dollars!"

"I know it's sixty. I'm going to Brooklyn with it, too. Give it to my granddaughter, Dyneisha." Mudrick laughs again. "She might need it for medicine for her chicken pox."

"Everyone have chicken pox," says Butteroll. "You got have it once. If you don't get it in childhood it's a problem."

Mudrick's comments to Butteroll express the ethos of "good hustling"—the need to take control of an exchange. Even though they are joking, for the most part, Mudrick is always letting those around him know that they are not getting away with anything.

·

An African-American man in a suit walks over to the mirrors and asks Mudrick how much he wants for them.

"I want twenty dollars apiece. I got three of them. If you want all of them, I'll make you a package deal."

"What kind of deal you making?"

"I'll give you five dollars off for each one."

The man looks silently in the mirror as Mudrick continues. "I sold seven of them already," he says with a straight face.

"Twenty dollars for each one?" the man exclaims. "Never mind. You ain't gonna tell me that. Where did you get 'em from?"

"I said I'll give you five dollars off each one," Mudrick responds. "That way you only have to pay fifteen dollars apiece."

"Where did you get 'em from?" the man asks again, perhaps wondering if they are stolen. As he turns and walks over to the mirror against the wall of Blockbuster Video, Mudrick mumbles to me, "Listen to his bullshit. Where did I get them from? That's outside of his jurisdiction!"

After preening in front of the mirrors a few minutes, the man returns to Mudrick: "I'll take my chances that you'll be here when I get back."

As the man walks away, Mudrick says to me, "We better sell these mirrors before the 911 comes."

"What are we gonna do if we don't sell them?"

"I'll have to walk them around to one of my buildings," he responds, referring to the buildings where he works taking out the trash and making minor repairs for cash.

Another black man in a suit comes over to the table and asks about the mirrors. "I'm trying to get twenty dollars apiece," Mudrick tells him.

"Twenty dollars apiece?" he asks.

"Yeah. That's a good price. But I can break it down a little bit for you."

"Oh yeah. Let me look at them," says the man.

"Hey, listen, when you pick 'em up, don't let it hit the wall, man."

"If he let 'em hit the wall, he bought 'em," says Butteroll, laughing.

"He bought 'em if they hit the wall and break!" says Mudrick. "Then they belong to him! Only thing he can do is look." He turns to the prospective customer and speaks in a louder voice. "Listen, I want twenty dollars each. The cheapest I can go is fifteen dollars. And you can't buy these nowhere in New York City for fifteen dollars. Nowhere. You can go to that price. You can pick it up and look behind it. All you gotta do is take that off. This come right off. You can take it, stick it right back on the wall. Or you can take the hangers and put the hangers in the wall and set it up in the rack."

A young Asian woman walks up to the mirrors with her white boyfriend.

They hear Mudrick explaining the mirrors to the black man. The Asian woman interrupts and says that she wants the mirrors but doesn't know how she's going to get them home.

"Where you live at?" Mudrick asks.

"Queens."

"How you going home?"

"Subway."

"That's easy," Mudrick responds with a straight face. "You take two and put 'em right under your arm and put 'em right on down in the subway. I brought all three of them by myself from Brooklyn."

The woman and her boyfriend confer a few moments. Then they walk away. "If you change your mind, come back," says Mudrick.

Two middle-aged black men stop at the table and look at the computer.

"What kind is this?" one man asks, looking at me.

"IBM," I answer. "It's not like the next generation of computer."

"I know. It's outdated. Well, how much is it?"

"Well, we were talking about fifty dollars," I respond. "For everything, including the keyboard, the wires, and everything."

"But you don't know how much K it is? How powerful the memory is?"

"I don't know."

"Was it your computer?"

"No."

I call after Mudrick, who is down the block. He doesn't hear me, and the men discuss it between themselves. By the time they decide to buy it, he is back. I walk to the other end of the table. Mudrick handles the transaction. They take fifty dollars out of their pockets and hand the bills to him, and Mudrick helps them put the computer into a taxicab.

"Who's he supposed to be?" one man asks Mudrick, pointing to me.

"That's my lawyer."

•

At seven that evening, the Asian woman and her boyfriend returned to Sixth and Waverly. The mirrors were still there. So were we.

Reaching into her pocketbook, the woman handed Mudrick two twenties. The boyfriend tried to pick up the mirrors, but he could hardly do it. Slowly, the two of them moved two of the three mirrors to the curb and hailed a cab. As a Prince song blared from a boom box that one of the scavengers had found in a nearby garbage can, Butteroll lay on the ground and announced to Mudrick, "I'm going to my office."

"I'm *in* my office," Mudrick responded.

"Give me my money," Butteroll said.

"Your money? You better sell the last mirror. There's one left right there."

Butteroll sat back down. Moments later, a cab stopped at the curb and the Asian woman got out with another twenty-dollar bill in her hand. "I'll take the last mirror," she said, and Mudrick helped her carry it to the waiting taxi, which had merely circled the block.

Butteroll stayed where he was. He knew he'd get paid soon. And it wasn't long before the man who had consigned the mirrors to Mudrick in the morning came back for the money they had agreed upon. "You have my ten dollars?" he said to Mudrick.

Mudrick said, again with a straight face, "No. But I have eight. I have to go and get the money."

He walked away from the table, pretending to get some money, but really getting change from the newsstand. He came back with seven dollars in his hand. "This is all I got," he said.

"I'll take the seven," said the man.

The man walked away, apparently pleased to have a few dollars in his pocket. I asked Mudrick why he hadn't given the man the full ten dollars, especially considering that he had sold the set of mirrors for sixty dollars.

"There's no way I'm gonna give him ten. It costs him for talking to me. He didn't understand that part of the game."

"Explain to me that part of the game."

"The game is that you gotta pay me for talking to me. And I took three dollars of his money for talking to me."

"How is he talking to you?"

"He asked me do I want to buy the mirrors. That's a dollar. I said, 'Yes, I want to buy the mirrors.' That's another dollar. Then he asked me for the money. That was another dollar. Talk is not cheap. I was just fucking around with him. But he went for it. So I didn't have a choice but to take it."

There seemed to be no question in Mudrick's mind that he would offer less than the full amount he had agreed to earlier. What is this? Is he a cheat? Perhaps he regarded the man who had sold him the mirrors as a stranger, someone he had never seen before and didn't expect to depend upon for merchandise in the future. Not long afterward, the man who had brought the computer in the morning, who regularly brings items to the block, came for his money and received twenty-five dollars—a full 50 percent of the sale price.

Next, Mudrick paid ten dollars to Butteroll in an act of generosity, though he had promised him only four. Again, Butteroll and Mudrick are friends and have known each other for twenty years; they might work together tomorrow.

After all the payouts, Mudrick still had seventy-five dollars in his pocket. Not bad for a man who came out to the street with nothing.

•

There was a time in his life when Mudrick robbed deliverymen and sold drugs to support his needs. It is not hard to understand why he and men like him believe there is a significant positive aspect to the choices they make, how they earn their own money, and how they give one another support on the street. This sphere of sidewalk life, largely unknown to most passersby,

reinforces conventional social norms. Not only do men serve as mentors for one another; they also fulfill economic roles that make it possible for them to support their habits and meet their everyday needs without robbing or hurting anyone.

As the street grew dark and music roared out of the boom box, Mudrick and I sat quietly for ten minutes, taking in the scene around us. Then he asked me if I was tired.

"A little," I said. "Are you?"

"The only thing I'm thinking is I gotta take my money to go see Dyneisha. I promised her. I gotta go."

I had always wondered whether Mudrick was as close with his three-year-old granddaughter as he claimed to be. Did the pictures he constantly pulled out of his back pocket really mean as much to him as he indicated? Did he really save his money for her? Or was this simply a "front," a respectable thing to say? Months later, when Ovie Carter and I were on the block, Mudrick's daughter's thirty-year-old live-in boyfriend, Anthony Merchant (who worked as a token clerk for the Metropolitan Transit Authority), came by. When he was alone, I asked him what he could tell me about Mudrick's relationship with Dyneisha.

"He comes to the house and he basically moves in," Anthony said, laughing. "It's not a like a visit! He comes and stays for a couple of weeks. It's like they are best friends, buddies. She's crazy about her grandfather. I have to fight to pull her away from him. Every dime he gets he gives to her. He takes her shopping. He just bought her a pair of sneakers. She's gonna get regardless, but he makes sure he puts his dollar in. He do the best he can to make sure she gets. I think that's all he lives for, basically. He don't care about nothing else."

Anthony had brought Dyneisha with him, and the girl was standing with Mudrick by the window of the lighting store, her hair in braids.

"Okay, Dyneisha," I said. "I want to interview you about your grandfather."

"What's your name?" she asked.

"My name's Mitch. Say your name into the tape recorder."

"Machine."

"Yeah. Say your name into the machine."

"You machine."

"No. I'm Mitch. Are you Dyneisha?"

"I'm not Dyneisha. You're Dyneisha," she said, smiling.

"No, I'm Mitch. I want to know what the name of your grandfather is."

She beamed.

"Granddaddy!"

PART TWO

NEW USES OF SIDEWALKS

How Sixth Avenue Became
a Sustaining Habitat

Although Greenwich Village has changed markedly since Jane Jacobs made the observations in her book, no subsequent work has had such a lasting impact on how sidewalk life is understood. Jacobs's influence might be attributed in part to her evocation of a way of urban life that minimized what she called "barbarism" or violence, which has come to concern many of her readers since the early 1960s. She begins with the assumption that "cities are, by definition, full of strangers,"[1] some of whom are "predatory."[2] She asks what makes it possible for sidewalks to meet the challenge of "assimilating strangers" in such a way that strangers can feel comfortable together. She argues that cities are most habitable when they feature a diversity of uses, thereby ensuring that many people will be coming and going on the streets at any time. When enough people are out and about, respectable eyes dominate the street and are fixed on the strangers, who will not get out of hand. Underneath the seeming disorder of a busy street is the very basis of order in "the intricacy of sidewalk use, bringing with it a constant succession of eyes."[3] The more people are out, or are looking from their windows at the people who are out, the more their gazes will safeguard the street. Jacobs drew most of her examples and observations from the streets of the part of Greenwich Village known as the West Village, but her ideas have become a fixture of the syllabi in urban-studies and urban-planning courses generally; for vast numbers, her book has become the bible of the field. Her ideas remain influential even though the systematic evidence for them is mixed.[4]

If you walk through the streets of the West Village today, you will find that the kind of street life Jacobs described is in some measure still evident.

On Hudson Street, where she lived, middle-class whites and blacks, gays, lesbians, artists and young professionals can be observed having a quiet walk on a summer's evening with the sense that others like them are paying attention.

But a few blocks away, at Sheridan Square (still in the West Village), or on Sixth Avenue near Washington Square Park, the people watching are no longer those whose eyes make it possible to assimilate strangers. In many cases, from the point of view of the residents, these people *are* the strangers. And it is not only the presence of poor black panhandlers, scavengers, and vendors that makes the problem of assimilating strangers here a different one; many of the pedestrians who must be assimilated into the sidewalk life are also members of racial minorities.

Though American society has very high levels of racial residential segregation, poor minorities from segregated neighborhoods do circulate through Greenwich Village, and the unhoused among them even sleep on the sidewalks. The intersection of Sixth Avenue and Eighth Street is historically the business center of this part of the Village. Once the home of shops catering to white middle-class residents, as well as a tourist destination for white youths from other parts of the city, the street has undergone a major transformation over the past two decades. Today, it is a destination for blacks and Hispanics as well as whites. Like the white youths of the 1960s, say, these visitors come from neighborhoods with less exciting stores, movie theaters, restaurants, bars, and the like, than can be found in the Village. They move about on the street among white youths from Long Island and New Jersey; older whites living locally in rent-controlled apartments; students, professors, and staff from New York University, the New School for Social Research, and Cooper Union; younger professionals of many races who have bought apartments in the Village; and gays of all classes and races.

These blocks of the Village are densely built up with retail stores, bars, and restaurants, primarily in mid-rise buildings. The residents in the three adjoining blocks have a median income of $66,869.[5] Traffic is heavy, on both the streets and the sidewalks. Adjoining side streets provide residences and additional commercial activity at varying levels of density, from large apartment buildings to single-family townhouses. Property values are some of the highest in the United States; narrow row houses can cost upward of a million

dollars, and condominiums sell easily for a quarter- to a half-million dollars. Partly because of New York's rent-control laws, many units rent at rates within the range of the lower middle class, as long as people are willing to make do with old and usually small units.

Like the Village as a whole, the neighborhood is known around the world for its cultural tradition, for an arty, bohemian, live-and-let-live way of life. For generations, it has been home for many of the country's important artists, intellectuals, and freethinkers. It has become the home of the city's highest concentration of gay men and women.

These blocks are dominated in the daytime (especially during the week) by the upper-middle-class white residents and students who live in the neighborhood. At night and on weekends it becomes a playground for black, white, Latino, and Asian youth participating in the hip-hop subculture, with its aspiration to defining the cutting edge in music, drugs, sex, and clothing. But at all times the neighborhood lends itself to the affluent and to the unhoused, to the Ph.D. and to the unschooled, on the same sidewalk at the same time.

Another element of the Village scene that doesn't appear in Jane Jacobs's description are the "head shops" selling drug accessories and paraphernalia and the drug dealers, who offer illegal substances as pedestrians pass by. For many years, Washington Square Park was the center of such activity, but in the late nineties the New York City Police Department installed cameras throughout the park. Now the drug dealing has spilled out onto side streets near the park and, most visibly, in front of the West Fourth Street basketball courts and up and down Sixth Avenue.

Every society has its places that give a clear indication of what it will and will not accept. Eighth Street encompasses much that is considered underground or off-limits in our society, and it draws many youths of various races and ethnicities who want to be in contact with these outer limits. An African-American barber named Hotis who works in the Village told me that Eighth Street is a downtown version of Harlem on a down low (DL). To him, a "DL" means a "low-key" place where people cannot be too "boisterous" but can be "hip" and "funky." "They can be the individual who they truly are, but they have to govern themselves to a certain extent," he says. "They have a good time doing it. And they realize the world is not just black or white when they are here."

Today, the sidewalks around Sixth Avenue and Eighth Street are bustling with many minorities from other parts of the city and the suburbs who must be assimilated into the neighborhood's sidewalk life. These include the vendors (housed and unhoused), and the pedestrians who live elsewhere. For Jacobs, their "assimilation" would mean that their behavior as strangers was contained in such a way that the working (and middle) classes did not feel threatened.

In Jacobs's description, the sidewalks could assimilate the presence of "strangers" because even most of those so called were alike in terms of race, class, and social standards. Today, the people sharing public space in Greenwich Village are separated by much greater economic inequalities and cultural differences. Some of the ways they interact bespeak cohesion and social solidarity; others—and these loom much larger in the minds of some pedestrians—suggest that things are tense out there. In any case, sidewalk life in Greenwich Village has changed gradually but significantly since Jane Jacobs wrote about it. My aim here is to bring about a better understanding of how those changes took place.

From Pennsylvania Station to Greenwich Village

Although there are two white men who work as table watchers on rare occasions, and a few others who occasionally visit the blocks, almost every one of the panhandlers, scavengers, and magazine vendors living and/or working on Sixth Avenue is African American—a number that only slightly overrepresents the large number of unhoused African-American men on the streets of New York City.[6] These proportions reflect the "dangerous, violent, and aggressive" image of African-American men, at times reinforced by racism, which makes it much more difficult for them than for men of other races or even black women to navigate through the social support system.[7] They also reflect a number of political, historical, and economic forces that sociologists have only begun to understand.

Without exception, they have grown up in Northern neighborhoods with high levels of racial residential segregation,[8] poor schools,[9] and spatially concentrated poverty,[10] or, in the case of older men like Mudrick, in the South under Jim Crow.[11] Three of them are Vietnam veterans (a population disproportionately prone to drug addiction). Almost all of them entered the economy in the years when the urban labor market began to deteriorate.[12] Though we cannot go back with these men and observe the effects of the political and economic forces in their lives—moreover, the men usually affirm that they are the authors of their own lives—vast social-science and historical evidence suggests that the lives of such men have been shaped by their interaction with broad structural conditions, including the lack of economic opportunity and the nature of American drug policies.

Furthermore, though it is now well documented and almost universally agreed that race is central to the makeup of high-poverty neighborhoods in urban America, it is less well understood how racial segregation and the sharp reduction in gainful employment in places like Harlem, the Bronx, and Brooklyn have had effects far beyond the areas of concentrated poverty. The results of these structural forces can be seen on the sidewalks of neighborhoods like Greenwich Village.

More than a third of the unhoused men on the sidewalk have told me that they spent time in state or federal prisons for possession or distribution of quantities of crack cocaine or for other crimes associated with drug use.[13] In some cases, if these men had been using drugs in private, as many middle-class people do, rather than on the streets, it is less likely that they would have been caught and become subject to the harsh drug penalties that are in effect in New York State. In a few cases of men who were sentenced under federal guidelines, they received penalties much more severe than they would have if they had been using powder cocaine instead of crack.[14] During the most recent year for which data are available, of those sentenced for crack cocaine, 88.3 percent were black and 95.4 percent were nonwhite.[15] Under the federal-sentencing guidelines, it has taken a hundred times the quantity of powder cocaine to trigger a penalty equivalent to that for crack cocaine. (In 1996, Congress reduced the ratio to five-to-one after ignoring the recommendation of the U.S. Sentencing Commission that it be reduced to one-to-one.) Crack is favored by poor people (most of whom, in New York City, are minorities) because it is cheaper. After the federal government has spent an average of a hundred thousand dollars of its resources for each incarceration of such persons for crack-related offenses,[16] they are released and come directly to the streets. In most cases, family ties have been shattered by their past behavior. Neither state nor federal prisons are organized to help ex-convicts make smooth transitions into homes and jobs. If these men had been given drug treatment, job training, help in finding employment, housing assistance, and follow-up counseling, rather than time in prison and an abrupt release back to the streets, many of them might be healthier.[17]

At the same time, as we implicate these large-scale structural forces, we must also acknowledge some uncertainty as to the extent to which these forces are determinative in the outcome of any life. More than half of the men who have lived on the street come from homes that conventional readers would call respectable. Butteroll, who lives in the "dungeon" and the "Bat Cave" of the subway, had a mother (recently deceased) who retired from a successful career in the U.S. Postal Service. In my meetings with Ron's aunts—Naomi, Esmay, and Macie—I witnessed the kind of propriety in manners and hypercorrectness in speech that one associates with the parents of many upwardly mobile Jamaican children. Each of these women worked as a domestic servant, and I saw statements indicating that Naomi had more than $180,000 in six bank accounts, saved from her years of hard work. When Marvin's mother passed away, his parents had been married for fifty-two years. She was a salad chef at Parkview Hospital in Toledo, Ohio. His father recently retired after thirty-five years as a precision grinder at the Dana Corporation. Many of these men on the sidewalk have brothers and sisters who are living successful, conventional lives. One of the open questions is the power of the above-mentioned structural conditions to devastate lives that should be poised for upward mobility. Structural conditions do lead a disproportionate number of black men to the sidewalks of our cities, but we must admit deep uncertainty as to why particular men give in to the power of drugs. In many cases, they are not the people who might be expected to end up on the sidewalks. Individual factors also have an influence.

Once these men succumb, though, the labor market which becomes most relevant to their lives is that for unskilled workers, especially day laborers. In the period when Jane Jacobs was researching her book, many alcoholics living on skid row earned their keep at jobs for which they could be picked from a day-labor pool on their good days. Today, there is consensus that demand for day laborers has declined substantially,[18] and that "African American recruitment networks into low-skilled industries . . . have dried up; the advent of immigrants means the newcomers have a lock on these jobs."[19]

Whereas the typical skid-row alcoholic supported his way of life through day labor, the men on Sixth Avenue today have moved in and out of prison for drug-related offenses and then from one unhoused domain to another during the past two decades. To understand how Sixth Avenue became a habitat for poor black men in a predominantly white upper-middle-class neighborhood—what I will call a sustaining habitat—it is useful to understand that not only broad social, economic, and political forces but also local social, political, and economic conditions have deeply influenced the lives of such men. How did the spatial distribution and redistribution of some members of this population occur? To answer this question, we must look closely at the neighborhood as the unplanned result of particular forces that, operating together, have made it a place where such persons could organize themselves for survival.[20]

Despite the common tendency to assume that a number of apparently unhoused people on the street are milling about, involved in a "great deal of random, restless, physical movement,"[21] the men on Sixth Avenue are not, as we have seen, engaged in random behavior, but in concerted action governed by norms and goals. Yet their social cohesion is based on a good deal more than the concerted actions depicted earlier. We can see on these blocks a collective self-consciousness that derives from a long, common history predating their time on Sixth Avenue. Understanding this history helps us see that these men are on these blocks as a result of forces far less random than they might appear.

Fifteen years ago, Mudrick, Randy, Ishmael, Joe Garbage, Grady, and Ron (along with as many as four hundred other people) slept two miles uptown from Sixth Avenue and Eighth Street—in and around Madison Square Garden and the Pennsylvania Railroad Station. They were part of a swiftly growing population of unhoused people, which doubled in size in the United States during the early eighties.[22] Train lines from Amtrak, the Long Island Rail Road, New Jersey Transit, and the New York City subway system converge in Penn Station. Each day at that time, two hundred thousand commuters made intensive use of a single space.

The area around the station has an abundance of social services available, as well as access to the Hudson River, parks, and other transportation, including Grand Central Terminal. Neighborhood services are so varied and extensive that it is very unusual to see a group of unhoused people from the station in another neighborhood, such as Greenwich Village.

Then as now, Penn Station served as a shopping mall of sorts, with bars, electronics stores, inexpensive restaurants, newsstands, restrooms, and public telephones. In a sense, the public areas of the station are passageways that link these establishments. Persons who do not hold tickets and are not planning to travel can legitimately be on the concourses as they walk from one facility to another.

To an unhoused person, the station offers all of the amenities for day-to-day survival. It is heated in the winter and air-conditioned in the summer. The snow and freezing temperatures of winter and the rain and heat of summer can be avoided here.

In the early 1980s, Mudrick, Ishmael, Randy, and Joe Garbage slept on the three hundred seats in the Amtrak waiting area; on the cracked terrazzo-floored concourses between the Long Island Rail Road and the New York City subway; and on several benches outside the station, in front of the adjoining Madison Square Garden, next to grates from which heat would rise in the winter.

Mudrick, Randy, Joe, and Ishmael cleaned themselves each morning in the lower-level men's lavatory between Nedick's hot-dog restaurant and McAnn's Bar.[23] As they tell it, the restroom was the special province of permanent unhoused residents of the station. The men would often strip naked in front of the sinks to wash themselves. In the corners of the restroom would be set giant plastic bags filled with aluminum cans, the men's belongings, or objects stolen from the suitcases of Amtrak passengers. From some of the stalls, the sounds of sexual activity (ranging from masturbation to intercourse) would periodically dominate the room. It was not uncommon for a few men to be lathering up their genitals while half a dozen others were stripped to their underwear waiting for a sink to open up—all this while train travelers who didn't know better were entering and then departing abruptly with shocked and disgusted looks on their faces.

In the mornings, men would sit inside Nedick's and Howard Johnson's, waiting for breakfast diners to leave half-full trays. Many of the fast-food restaurants in the station donated their leftovers to the unhoused at the end of the day. "We would wait for the food to come in," Joe Garbage explained to me. "Guys from the restaurants, like Kentucky Fried [Chicken], they had a Chinese restaurant that would give the food, and a pizza place that would give us the pizzas." Randy recalled, "We used to eat pizza from Reise Brothers and leftovers from a Chinese place. They used to put the bags outside and everybody would be scuffling for the food."

Many of the train travelers who passed through the station—most of them on their way to jobs in the city or homes in the suburbs—dropped money in the paper cups of unhoused men. Mudrick says he would often wake up with his cup full of dollar bills and change, more than enough money to buy drugs and food.

Each of the men I talked to found additional means of support in the station. Mudrick performed "services" for Amtrak passengers who came off trains with loads of luggage but were unable to find a "red cap"—an Amtrak employee charged with carrying bags. He would approach the new arrivals, gain their permission, and take their bags to waiting taxis. Some men would engage in taxi hustling—standing in front of commuters as they hailed cabs and opening the doors for them with the expectation of a tip. Though Mudrick acknowledges that some of these persons gave out of fear, he claims that most appreciated his "service," and their tips could be enough to sustain him for days without leaving the station. On occasion, the "service" provider refused to hand over a bag if the tip was not big enough, or simply disappeared with the suitcase.

Though they say they were often approached by Amtrak police and asked to leave, the officers in those days had no systematic tactics to eject people—to prevent them from merely moving, temporarily, to another part of the vast complex. At times, Amtrak police seemed to accept that the unhoused were legitimate users of the space, no less so than the traveling public.

When the unhoused *were* asked to move along, Amtrak police would usually watch them go up the escalator. Those who left would often linger outside for a few minutes and then return to the station through another entrance. Rather than go back to the same spot, they might move for a few hours to one of the subterranean areas or platform levels.

In the mid-1980s (from 1984 to 1987), the number of unhoused people in big cities outside of shelters had doubled again, even by conservative estimates. More and more middle-class commuters had come to see the unhoused men in the station as a nuisance, and they were beginning to make their voices heard. The relationship between commuters and such persons became one of social conflict, in which the groups had different ideas about the purposes of the physical space. The station was no classic ecosystem based on mutuality and balance. The unhoused needed the commuters who made donations, the restaurant owners who put good food outside, etc., but the commuters and merchants had no use for the unhoused, considering them obstacles to the proper use of the station. Pennsylvania Station had become an eyesore and an embarrassment to those who ran it, and there was a movement to clear it of men like Mudrick, Randy, Ishmael, and Joe, who were looked upon as worse than useless—detrimental—to the Port Authority's desire for cleanliness and order.

"They wouldn't let us sleep anymore," Joe Garbage recalls. "They would let us sit around, but we weren't supposed to go to sleep."

At first, Mudrick, Ishmael, Randy, and Joe say they took to sleeping on the grates in front of Madison Square Garden; then they joined a group of thirty men who would take over an entire subway car on the A train every evening to sleep. They picked the A train because it runs directly through Pennsylvania Station. The entrance is only a few feet from the area in which the men had previously slept. After leaving the station, it stays underground for fifty minutes to an hour, until it reaches the end of the line in upper Manhattan, shielding the men from extreme temperatures and natural light.

Between ten-thirty and eleven o'clock every night, they would meet on the platform. The men say that there was an informal agreement between them and the transit-police officers assigned to the station that they would be left alone when they were in a single car, a claim that transit officials confirm is highly plausible. According to one official, the MTA operates certain trains with ten or twelve cars but uses only a few of them. The unhoused would take over one of the closed-off cars.

"Sometimes I have rode the train at night for the whole week or two weeks straight," Joe Garbage recalls. "We'd go back and forth starting at 10:30 p.m. or 11:00 p.m. and wake up the next morning, come out, go back to the station."

This particular adaptation illustrates that what makes a particular attribute of a habitat like Pennsylvania Station (such as a space to sleep) valuable is not its utility alone, but its utility in relationship to other attributes of the setting. Because the men were able to find trains to sleep in that had entrances in the station, the subway became an important means for the men to adapt to the efforts to move them, especially at night.

Around this time, Randy went to prison for selling a small quantity of crack to support his own drug habit, something he had done earlier in his life. "I would wait outside the station for white boys from Long Island and places like that who would come up to me and say they wanted weed or crack. Sometimes they would be looking for prostitutes. The last one I remember was this white kid who bought cracks from me. I saw he had a hundred-dollar bill, helped him find a prostitute, and while she sucked his cock, I robbed his ass."

Ishmael and Mudrick have separately told me that they began working together, robbing for food and money for drugs. Mudrick says he began dealing drugs. "We used to [leave the station] and mess with the guys delivering food on the bicycles," Mudrick explained. "We used to take the bags from the Chinese guys and the pizza guys. Every time we'd take the food, we'd take the money, too. Sometimes they got a hundred dollars on them. If you take the food, you might as well take the money!" They say that Mexicans were choice targets, because they always had money from their deliveries and (as illegal aliens) they were usually afraid to report the crime to the police for fear of being reported to Immigration.

After six months, Ishmael says, he was caught robbing a delivery man. "While I was waiting for my trial on bail, I threw a guy down the escalator at the station. He disrespected me. He called me a motherfucker. He said my mom ain't shit. Then he pushed me in my back. When he said about my mom, I was gonna let it go. But when he put his hand on me, I pushed him down and his leg and arm was broken. I stood around. I felt that I had no reason to run, because he had started the fight. But when the police came it seemed like the shoe was on the other foot." Mudrick, Randy, Joe, and Ishmael say they were in and out of jail over the next couple of years, usually on charges of robbery or possession and distribution of small quantities of drugs. Joe Garbage was sent away for possession of heroin.

When they came out of prison, these men might have returned to the station and subway that had sustained them—but in the meantime, that habitat had become inhospitable.

Coping with the Environment

Amtrak's strategy of pressuring unhoused people to leave Penn Station continued for at least ten years after this particular group of men dispersed from the station, and remaining users devised new routines to evade them. In response to Amtrak's most arbitrary policies, including picking on people without evidence that they were not commuters, a lawsuit was filed in 1995 by Streetwatch, an association that monitored police treatment of unhoused people, with the *pro bono* legal assistance of lawyers at the Center for Constitutional Rights and the Jerome N. Frank Legal Services Organization at Yale Law School.[24] The case, *Streetwatch* v. *National Railroad Passenger Corporation*, received widespread attention when U.S. District Court Judge Constance Baker Motley enjoined the Amtrak police from arresting or ejecting persons from public areas of Penn Station without evidence that they had committed crimes, were loitering inside places of business, were sleeping in the station, or were sitting in areas reserved for ticketed passengers.[25]

Although Judge Motley ruled in favor of the unhoused people, the *Streetwatch* suit was ultimately the beginning of the end for mass numbers of unhoused persons living there. One little-noted aspect of successful litigation like *Streetwatch* is that the short-term benefits may be great for the plaintiff—authorities become more careful about the way they treat the plaintiff, and press coverage heightens public awareness of the arbitrary behavior—but that a decision that rules against arbitrary acts usually specifies neutral, systematic criteria that must be observed in the future. In *Streetwatch*, Judge Motley's instruction as to what was and was not permissible became a road map.

Shortly after Judge Motley's ruling, Amtrak undertook a campaign to transform the atmosphere of Penn Station and, in a systematic and rationalized way, to police unhoused people there. It hired Richard Rubel as director of a new "homeless outreach" program, which would provide services for the Amtrak-owned areas of the station and the Amtrak-owned properties outside. I visited Rubel at his office in the back of the station in 1997, and asked him what Amtrak had learned from *Streetwatch*. "The decision basically established that this is a public facility and you cannot target people by the basis of their appearance," he said. "You have to work with people based on their behavior. In other words, the station must have a prescribed set of rules of conduct. People who are in violation of those rules of conduct can be taken to task for that. But they cannot be taken to task based on their appearance or the color of their skin. So you are basically focusing on behavior, not individuals. And those apply to business folk—your customers—as well as noncustomers."

"In response to the lawsuit, what are some of the behaviors Amtrak specified as violations of new rules of conduct?"

"In the Amtrak-operated areas of the station, people are not allowed to smoke. You are not allowed to drink alcoholic beverages, sleep on the floor or lie in a way that blocks access, go through the garbage cans and take out recyclable materials, panhandle, or beg. There is a special code of behaviors for the restrooms, etc. And so we police the facility by enforcing those rules.

"The press that came out when the decision was reached suggested that Amtrak must endure homeless individuals and is not allowed to boot them out. That was not the case. I think quite the opposite came out of the case— that we do have the capacity to enforce the station rules, and that's exactly what we now do."

.

In addition to focusing on such behaviors—which are all activities of unhoused people—Rubel's program made other efforts to ensure that the station would not provide the means of subsistence. "One of the toughest battles I had was with the restaurants in the station. They know that they are not to be giving food to people in here, and they know it's a matter of self-preservation for their own businesses. Because if they gain a reputation for giving out food like that, they are going to be besieged on a continuous basis. And again, we know that, with our suburban customer base and people from far and wide in the nation, they do not want to take out money in a place where homeless people are congregating. So, for their self-survival, the businesses needed to clean up their acts."

Although it was possible for Rubel to speak to the managers of all the restaurants in the station, it was more difficult for him to gain the coopera-

When You Give
Money to the
Homeless, You
Help to Keep Them Homeless.

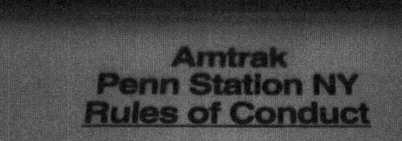

...trak is asking its customers to help us in our efforts to break the cycle of ...melessness in Penn Station by not giving money to homeless people in the Station.

...ANY ... PERSONS ... WHO VIO ATE
THIS LAW WILL BE PROSECUTED TO
THE FULLEST EXTENT OF THE LAW

Amtrak
Penn Station NY
Rules of Conduct

...ct shall govern all portions of Penn Station except the areas leased to ...re those areas of the facility which are intended for use by the public ... restaurants, shops, offices and other businesses in the facility, in t... ...o another, in waiting for transportation, and in utilizing public lavato... ...ervices as may be permitted pursuant to these Rules. Entry into a...

tion of the church groups and social-service groups who distribute food there. "One of my biggest problems is with volunteers who say, 'We know there's homeless people here and we have food for them.' What I try to tell them is, 'You are saying, "We will enable you, we will facilitate your living on the street by bringing a blanket and giving you a meal on a regular basis." ' My philosophy is that it is not an acceptable living alternative. You have to embrace people and take them indoors, not facilitate them living in transportation facilities or in the street."

Amtrak's idea in hiring Rubel, who had held a similar post at Grand Central Terminal, was to make a business decision to provide social services for the unhoused people of the station who had a legal right to be there. These social services would be on-site, prominent, and able to engage people and encourage them to receive help. I asked Rubel how he does that.

"To some degree, you have to treat them [the unhoused in the station] like a consumer and give them the services that they want and that they will accept. It's not against the law to be homeless, to smell bad, or to look bad. So you have to convince people to accept services, and you do that by providing quality services."

On a walk through the station with Rubel and the photographer Ovie Carter one summer day in 1997, two years after *Streetwatch*, I found it essentially bare of unhoused people. I told Rubel of my interest in the station as a place that had once sustained the lives of unhoused people, and asked if he could point out changes that had been made so that it would be less inviting as a habitat where subsistence elements could be found in one place. He pointed out a variety of design elements of the station which had been transformed,[26] helping to illustrate aspects of the physical structure that had formerly enabled it to serve as a habitat.

He took us to a closet near the Seventh Avenue entrance. "We routinely had panhandlers gathering here, and you could see this closet area where that heavy bracket is, that was a niche."

"What do you mean by 'a niche'?"

"This spot right over here was where a panhandler would stand. So my philosophy is, you don't create nooks and corners. You draw people out into the open, so that your police officers and your cameras have a clean line of sight, so people can't hide either to sleep or to panhandle."

Next he brought us to a retail operation with a square corner. "Someone here can sleep and be protected by this line of sight. A space like this serves nobody's purpose. So, if their gate closes, and somebody sleeps on the floor over here, they are lying undetected. So what you try to do is have people construct their building lines straight out, so you have a straight line of sight with no areas that people can hide behind."

Next he brought us to what he called a "dead area." "I find this staircase provides limited use to the station. Amtrak does not physically own this lobby area. We own the staircase and the ledge here. One of the problems that we have in the station is a multi-agency situation where people know what the fringe areas are, the gray areas, that are less than policed. So they serve as focal points for the homeless population. We used to see people sleeping on this brick ledge every night. I told them I wanted a barrier that would prevent people from sleeping on both sides of this ledge. This is an example of turning something around to get the desired effect.

"Another situation we had was around the fringes of the taxi roadway. We had these niches that were open. The Madison Square Garden customers that come down from the games would look down and see a community of people living there, as well as refuse that they leave behind." He installed a fencing project to keep the homeless from going behind corners, drawing them out into the open. "And again," said Rubel, "the problem has gone away."

IN THE NAME OF THE FIRST AMENDMENT

Some of the men who are currently on Sixth Avenue say they left Penn Station long before the *Streetwatch* ruling, because they could not endure the pressure that was being placed upon them by Amtrak authorities. In order to understand how each of these men and others came to Sixth Avenue in Greenwich Village, it is helpful to look at some political factors that helped give rise to these spatial patterns.

Above Grand Central Terminal in the MetLife building is the office of attorney Edward C. Wallace, a partner in the law firm of Greenberg, Traurig. In his office, as nowhere else in the city, we can begin to understand some of the political and legal forces that would operate in an unplanned way to make Sixth Avenue a new habitat with all of the elements necessary to sustain the vendors, scavengers, and panhandlers who live and work there today.

Wallace knows a great deal about the book vendors working in New York City. When we met in June 1996, he knew little about the magazine scavengers, the table holders, the movers, or other economic roles that poor people have assumed on Sixth Avenue. But he forthrightly took responsibility for them, so to speak, when I described my research.

In 1981, at age thirty-two, Wallace ran successfully for an at-large seat on the City Council, becoming the youngest council member. Wallace was a liberal Democrat and a civil libertarian, and soon after his election, he says, he was approached by Arthur Eisenberg, president of the New York Civil Liberties Union, who told him the story of David Ferguson. For more than a decade, Ferguson had been arrested and harassed in Greenwich Village for selling his own poems and a homemade literary magazine he edits, *Box 749*, without a vendor's license. Eisenberg suggested that Wallace meet Ferguson to discuss the problem.

"He told me firsthand the story of having the poetry magazine seized on a Sunday. That was quite outrageous. It seemed to be happening so thoughtlessly. They weren't sensitive in any way to the idea that you can't just go and grab somebody's poetry magazine. It's ironic that Greenwich Village is a venue for beatniks and the guy gets arrested for selling poetry without a license. Ferguson was repeatedly taken to the precinct house and repeatedly had his poetry seized."

Wallace believes that Eisenberg and the New York Civil Liberties Union were trying to bypass the courts because the police were not abiding by court rulings. "Though clearly there was a good lawsuit: poet gets arrested for selling poetry on street. That's Tom Paine. That's right up their alley."

On July 21, 1981, Wallace introduced a simple amendment to the General Vending Statute that stated: "The provisions of this article shall not apply to any person who vends or distributes newspapers, periodicals, or other written matter without the use of a pushcart, stand, booth or vehicle." He introduced his proposed amendment in the City Council and it was referred for consideration and a recommendation to the Committee on Consumer Affairs, which deals with issues of general vending.

Under ordinary circumstances it is not clear how easily an idealistic freshman member of the City Council with a civil-libertarian agenda could pass a piece of legislation to help one local poet. But before long, as Wallace tells the story, a broad and powerful constituency came out of the woodwork. "It was the circulation managers of the *New York Times*, the *Daily News*, and the *New York Post*. They wanted their newsboys and -girls to be able to sell papers without being harassed, and they became the reason why this exception got passed—not Ferguson and his politics. They came in and sat in the room."

Wallace explains that every elected official lives by three things—votes, contributions, and newspaper support. He says that, though the case can be made that the circulation managers have nothing to do with the editorial position of the newspaper, every now and then they would hint that they could affect it.

Arthur Eisenberg of the Civil Liberties Union also attended the meeting. He testified that, though Wallace's proposed bill was appropriately seeking to rectify a defect in the city's administrative code, it did not go far enough, because the proposed law did not explicitly state that people could sell written matter from pushcarts, stands, booths, or vehicles. It "fail[ed] to protect First Amendment rights to the full limits of the constitutional norm." In a statement that would become very important to the street life of the city, Eisenberg went on:

Under the First Amendment, an individual maintains the right to leaflet, petition or otherwise disseminate literature on city sidewalks so long as such dissemination does not substantially impede the convenient and safe passage of pedestrian traffic. . . . If one uses a card table or booth in connection with such dissemination the possibility of impeding pedestrian traffic is increased. Nevertheless, a blanket prohibition against the use of a card table or a booth cannot be imposed. Rather, an inquiry must be undertaken, on a case by case basis, to determine whether in the particular circumstances, the use of a card table or booth in the exercise of First Amendment activity causes a substantial impediment to pedestrian traffic.

When the council revised the bill, specific provisions for "table based written matter vending" were incorporated.

"I had put in my brief amendment, but the truth of the matter is that they generally mangled it by creating three pages out of three lines," Wallace now recalls. "Those three pages were written to satisfy the newspaper circulation desks, the merchants' associations who wanted certain things and not others, the newsstand vendors, the Civil Liberties Union, etc." According to Wallace, each section of those three pages was lobbied for.

The new draft of the bill began with the following legislative declaration:

The Council hereby finds and declares that it is consistent with the principles of free speech and freedom of the press to eliminate as many restrictions on the vending of written matter as is consistent with the public health, safety, and welfare. The Council further finds and declares that general vendors who exclusively vend written matter should be free from licensing requirements. It is further found and declared that general vendors who exclusively vend written matter with the aid of small portable stands should be exempted from restrictions on the time, place, and manner of their vending activity insofar as such exemption does not constitute a threat to the public health, safety, or welfare.

The bill went on to specify dozens of vending regulations from which sellers of written matter would be exempt, as well as issues such as the size of tables that written-matter vendors could sell from.

"I read the new draft," Wallace continues, "and I made a few changes, but the truth was that they were saying to me, 'We'll pass this and even make you the lead sponsor, but we're passing this the way the majority leader wants it passed.' "

On July 22, 1982, Mayor Edward I. Koch signed the Wallace amendment to the General Vending Statute into the Municipal Code as Local Law 33 of that year. Upon signing the bill, he declared, "We have all found that sometimes what seems to be a very simple issue is extraordinarily difficult to reduce to a draft bill which is both legal and addresses the specific need. In this case, it is believed that we have accomplished both goals."

What neither Koch nor Wallace knew was that Local Law 33 would help make the streets of a neighborhood like Greenwich Village a habitat where vendors, scavengers, and panhandlers could organize themselves for survival.

The Law as Technology

How did some of these men who had lived in Pennsylvania Station (along with others who did not) reconstitute themselves as written-matter vendors on the streets of Greenwich Village? How did they, and others, find out about the law? How did they learn to sell books and recycled magazines? How much of the law did they know in order to create such a life for themselves? And why did Greenwich Village in particular become a habitat?

After a municipal law has passed the City Council and the mayor has signed it, under the city charter it must be published in the *City Record,* the city's official daily paper. (It costs three dollars per issue.) Other than a few gadflies who make daily trips to the Municipal Reference Library to look at the *Record,* and a few law firms that have standing orders to be supplied with copies of all new laws (sending messengers or supplying the city with self-addressed stamped envelopes), very few citizens actually learn about new laws unless the media publicize them.[27] (This practice may change with the development of the World Wide Web.) A search through the *New York Times* index suggests that, like many laws passed in 1982, Local Law 33 was not referred to in that newspaper.

At the time that the law was passed, only three of the men currently working the blocks were present there. From their testimony, it is clear how they and others learned about the passage of the new written-matter excep-tion. After a law has been signed by the mayor, the executive branch of gov-ernment is responsible for enforcing it. In the case of Local Law 33, the agency of the executive branch responsible for enforcing it was the New York City Police Department, whose commissioner is appointed by the mayor. And indeed it was police officers who brought the new law to the attention of people on the street.

In the early 1980s, Greenwich Village was already a space in which un-housed alcoholics worked as vendors, often selling items they had produced themselves as craftsmen. The Village was known as a place where people would buy leather belts, jewelry, and incense, so many vendors—housed and unhoused—brought such wares there. Alfred Robinson was an unhoused al-coholic who sold his own handmade jewelry on Sixth Avenue. "By us know-ing some of the police, they would tell us, 'Listen, they getting ready to have a crackdown on you guys. The only thing that's gonna be legal out here to sell is gonna be books. So I suggest you get yourself some books.'

"And we had more than one cop tell us that. Marvin and myself and oth-ers who were out here selling jewelry and leather belts thought it would blow over. For at least three years, from 1982 to 1985, we thought that any day now this was gonna change. We thought, 'The Village will always be the Village.' So we said, 'Okay, I'm flexible enough to throw these books and magazines down on the sidewalk to make it look like I'm selling written matters.' You'd set your books out, but you're there making jewelry. Marvin was making belts. As long as you didn't have anything displayed except the books when the police passed by, they wouldn't bother you. But we were still making money off the jewelry and the belts.

"I was surprised when people started to buy the printed materials. When I realized there was a market for this, I filled a mail cart with hardcovers and another with magazines. Money was really good in printed materials. Because of the stuff that you would get, if you were just aware of what was selling, you could easily make a hundred dollars a day."

Marvin and Al's response was an adaptation governed by its efficiency and rationality. By the time most of the men currently selling written matter on Sixth Avenue arrived there, Marvin and Al's adaptation had been transformed into a norm of behavior that would gradually serve as a model for the other men. I asked each of them how they got into it, and in response every man emphasized some combination of imitating existing behavior, learning from others on the street, and learning from the police. We have seen in the chapter on the magazine vendors how Ron Harris, one of the first of the men currently on the block, learned how to sell magazines when he was given a stack by a panhandler who wanted him to stop working in his spot. Later, Ishmael, Mudrick, Randy, and Joe Garbage, who had known one another in Pennsylvania Station, came to these blocks from prison.

After Marvin and Al moved into written-matter vending from general vending, the next wave of men came to it from panhandling or without attempting any intermediate activity to support themselves. At the time I spoke to him about this, Ishmael had been working on the blocks for over four years. "I heard of Sixth Avenue from before. I heard it was the Village and a lot of things was going on. As the Village, it was a site to see and be. So, after I did my time, I came down [here]. I had a friend from Penn Station who had migrated down here and I knew he was down here. So I came to see him. This individual [pointing to Mudrick] is right here on the block. I knew him before prison, from the station.

"The first day I got out of jail was the first day I went looking for him. I got word when I was in prison that he was down here, so it only took me about two or three days to find him. I looked for him to find out what he's into, how we can take on life as it is. He was here as a vendor and he was selling his magazines. And I started to ask how to go about doing that and he told me what to do, so I took upon myself to take that chance of doing that."

"How specifically did you get into it?"

"I just came on the scene and brought myself a table and start selling magazines, too, and supported myself physically by buying myself clothes, treating myself out, and starting to respect myself as a human being by trying to live right and trying not to do what's wrong. It was four years ago that I came out of prison with a different type of attitude.

"I began working for that individual right there [pointing to Ron, set up on the next block from Marvin]. He used to leave me at the table while he go out there and get some magazines. The magazines on the table would sell, and I would collect the money, and I learned a lot from him. Marvin enlightened me to certain magazines, too, and he told me certain things to do and how to go about the situation.

"I worked first in front of the Blockbuster Video store, for two years. Then I moved to my current position on the corner of Sixth Avenue and Eighth Street. Anybody would try to get the corner, because that is where you catch all the traffic. There was somebody working there, but when that individual wasn't there I took it upon myself to go there. Since then, I verbally had to argue for the spot more than two or three times."

A third wave of men became written-matter vendors when their livelihood as panhandlers was taken away from them by severe restrictions on panhandling on the subways and at the doors of automated-teller machines.[28] Grady, for example, sells magazines next to the bus stop on Sixth Avenue near Waverly Place and sleeps on the lowest level of the subway platform. "I used to be seeing Mudrick and Ishmael over there [at Penn Station], but I didn't know them," he told me. "I started out here around 1988. I was panhandling. I used to see these guys here with their magazines. But it didn't interest me at that time. What started me to doing this was that this guy named Cowboy wanted to go somewhere and he didn't have nobody to watch his stuff. So he asked me to watch it. He went somewhere and I seen . . . I'm not gonna say I seen how *easy* they made money, but I seen *how* they made money. So, after that, me and this guy Cowboy start being together and doing little things, getting stuff and selling stuff. Then, as time went by, Ron asked me to watch his stuff. I was messing around with crack, and in order for me to come up with the drug money, that's what I did.

"Ron taught me how to get what I wanted to get for certain things. . . . He said you always try to find things marked 'Number One Best-Sellers.' In most cases someone will buy them. If it's an up-to-date bestseller, you ain't gonna have no problem selling it, and in most cases it says 'Number One Best-Seller' on the cover.

"He taught me that sometimes you might have older things. For example, if you have Plato or Aristotle or any of those Greek philosophers, it might only say thirty-five or forty cent on the cover. But during the time that this was printed or wrote or whenever this happened, maybe twenty-five or thirty cent was a lot of money. So by it being now, you know everybody be willing to give you twenty-five or thirty cent, but they ain't gonna be willing to give you four or six dollars. But then you know if it's in mint condition you can ask them for more money, because you know they can't hardly find it nowhere else. So that's what Ron means by getting your dollar for what you have, because you know it hard to find and you know they can't find it."

At the time of my interviews, Grady's partner in the sale of magazines was a man known as Heavy. "Ten years ago I met a guy who said he was going to make some money," Heavy explained. "I asked him what he was gonna do and he said he sold books and magazines in the Village. I says, 'Well, where do you get this stuff?' He told me, 'I get it for free.' I didn't believe him at first. I says, 'You get this for free and you make money?' He says, 'Yeah.' I said, 'How you get it?' And that started me off. He took me with him, showed me how to walk up and down the block, and we started collecting the magazines that people would set out, that they didn't want anymore—back issues, new issues—and we would take the magazines and put them on Sixth Avenue and sell them for a dollar each. And that's how I got to the Village, and I didn't leave since." (Two months after this interview, Heavy checked into a drug-treatment program, and he has not been seen again on the block.)

It is difficult to know how to think about the fact that men taught one another "tricks of the trade" so that those very people could compete with them. Perhaps such acts are a reflection of the kind of support we have already seen, whereby men on the street try to mentor one another and encourage one another to lead better lives. Regardless of how we explain it, this testimony makes clear that, by the time these men arrived on the scene, there were conditions conducive to magazine scavenging and vending. First, the sheer number of people engaging in the activity posited it as a workable alternative to stealing. Second, stable social norms governing the behavior made imitation easy, because expectations were clear.

It seems altogether plausible that, as Al and others have told me, the original written-matter vendors learned directly from the police that they could protect their livelihood as craftsmen by selling books and magazines as well. This means that whatever they knew about getting around the law they learned from the very persons responsible for enforcing it. I wondered what the men selling written matter on the streets today knew about why they were permitted to be there. I have found that most have a vague understanding of the law, which they learned about from one another.

"The police said the literature and books was all right to sell," Joe Garbage recalls. "At the time we weren't supposed to sell contraband. [The vendors refer to anything they try to sell other than written matter as "contraband."] But we set it up anyway and sold it. When I ran into TVs, watches, shoes, some clothes, I would set that up and sell it to make extra money."

"Did you know why specifically you could sell the magazines and not the contraband?"

"Because the magazines and the books was [pause]—how would you say it?—uh, educational! That's the reason why they let us sell that."

"Why was it okay if it was 'educational'?"

"Because the constitutional rights that they said. That we had the right to sell the reading literature. The reading material."

"Did you learn that from the man who taught you how to pick up the magazines?"

"No. I learned it from the police."

Although he had trouble articulating the legal basis for his work, he had some sense that the U.S. Constitution stood behind him. To be precise, it is a local law—not the U.S. Constitution—that makes his actions legal. In all of my interviews, the men working on the blocks believed that they had a constitutional right to be there. For example, when I asked Ron why he was permitted to sell recycled magazines, he explained:

When George Washington was running for president, this is one of the first principles of the First Amendment. There was no television or newspaper as we know it today. There was no telephones or computers for them to get their message across. They got their message across with written materials.

As a matter of fact, when the Revolution was starting to go against England, they needed written materials to get their message across. The only way they could do that was to write pamphlets. They needed money for the ink, for the presses, for the manpower, for all that stuff, you understand? So, a lot of the times, they had to sell this stuff. That's how you get about *selling* written materials. People need money to pay for the press to print this stuff. They can't stop us from *selling* written materials, the same way they can't stop the newspaper. Or that newsstand over there. They might say, "Oh, I don't like this newsstand, let me close his ass down."

Marvin, overhearing Ron, interjected, "It's like they couldn't stop freedom of expression and stuff like that."

"It's the foundation of this whole country," Ron went on.

"That sounds very feasible," said Marvin.

Ron continued: "A lot of people take freedom of speech to say whatever it is that you feel like. But it goes further than that. It's the ability to sell written materials. You understand? That's what freedom of the press means. Not just freedom for you to go out and slander somebody. But freedom of the press to print certain stuff and get your message across. The only way to get your message across is to write it up, like you are writing up yours now, Mitch."

.

Even Hakim, who was familiar with most of the municipal laws regarding written matter, initially believed he was exercising a constitutional right. As yet, however, the U.S. Supreme Court has not ruled on the issue of whether table-based written-matter vending is constitutionally protected under the First Amendment, and, indeed, many other American cities still have strict laws making it difficult to engage in such activities. In the absence of clear guidance from the Supreme Court on this issue, federal appellate courts have reached a variety of contradictory conclusions about the right to erect newsstands, news racks, and tables.[29]

In any case, the men working on Sixth Avenue were protected by a municipal ordinance which could be changed by the City Council at any time. What this demonstrates is that an understanding of the laws need not be very deep or accurate in order for people to develop a whole way of life based on them. All people need is a minimum of legal information. Even more important than an understanding of the law is the presence of many persons providing models of appropriate behavior guided by clear norms that can be imitated or taught.

This point is particularly striking in light of the long-standing theory of delinquency called "differential association," which argues that deviant subcultures come into being through a process by which people associate with those who are deviant, just as lawful behavior is fostered through a process of association with those who are law-abiding.[30] On Sixth Avenue, it is possible to see something more complex than this theory would predict: that the subcultural or, in the eyes of some, deviant behavior of these men takes shape through their association with police officers and other people working the street; it does not merely develop and occur through associations between so-called deviants.

It is likewise possible to see that the relationship between "disorder" and crime is more complex than social scientists have posited. It has been said that " 'untended' behavior leads to the breakdown of community controls," and this is no doubt often true.[31] But the actual relationship between "disorder" and crime is more subtle on Sixth Avenue. Here we can see that the existence of scavenging and vending led to the emergence of norms and models of behavior that could be followed and imitated by persons interested in supporting their drug habits by making "an honest living." The precise relationship between "disorder" and crime is, today, taken for granted, but it surely deserves further investigation.

How Sixth Avenue Became a Sustaining Habitat

How did Sixth Avenue in Greenwich Village become a habitat able to sustain the daily lives of unhoused men? What makes an attribute like food or shelter or trash valuable is not its utility in itself, but its utility in relationship to other attributes of the setting. Rather than assuming the complementarity of the habitat's elements, I wanted to know *how* the various elements came together in this particular neighborhood.

On Sixth Avenue, there were the same basic characteristics of a sustaining habitat that had been found at Pennsylvania Station: density of people, convergence of transportation lines carrying many persons from various parts of the city, people willing to make donations, cheap or free food, places to sleep, and what Richard Rubel of Amtrak calls "niches." These were supplemented by two elements vital to an economy in used written matter: an abundance of high-quality recycled trash in the neighborhood, and sympathetic local residents willing to donate used books and magazines.

BASIC CHARACTERISTICS

Perhaps the most obvious of the basic elements of this habitat is a density of pedestrians. The block between Eighth Street and Waverly Place, near a major entrance to the West 4th Street subway station, is especially busy. A variety of businesses draw a diverse range of passersby: B. Dalton's bookstore, Village Lighting, Sam Goody's records, Payless Shoe Source, Supercuts, Starbucks Coffee, and Duane Reade Drugs. Across the street, McDonald's, a newsstand, Coconuts Records, Lechters Housewares, Emigrant Savings Bank, Pizzeria Uno, Petland Discounts, Mignon's sandwich shop, and the Waverly Restaurant.

The businesses on the block between Waverly and Washington are Urban Outfitters, Pacific Sunwear (formerly a Blockbuster Video), Gothic Cabinet Craft, Saga Shoes, and Radio Shack. Across the street is The Vitamin Shoppe, Village Cadeau (a head shop), Taj Jewelry, and St. Joseph's Roman Catholic Church. The businesses serve, among others, residents of a twenty-four-unit condominium complex called Washington Court, above Pacific Sunwear and Urban Outfitters. This condominium is only one of several dozen buildings in the area, their many occupants constantly coming and going.

Another characteristic of the habitat is the availability of cheap or free food, as was evident one winter day when Mudrick walked over to Marvin's table with a full plate.

"I got a plate of that food they got from the church," he said. "That shit is smokkkeenning!"

"Yeah," said Marvin. "What is it? Chicken?"

"Chikkkkkeeeeennnnn!" Mudrick responded.

"Dressing, carrots?" Marvin asked. "Pie?"

"Pie!" said Mudrick.

"Every Christmas they have pie," said Mudrick. "Every Christmas is good."

"I went into the kitchen at twelve o'clock and was fixing my own plate," said Mudrick. "Me and Butteroll got one. I'm gonna get me another one, too."

The presence of St. Joseph's Church (which runs a soup kitchen) and other shelters and charities makes it possible for many unhoused persons to eat for free. This has the effect of drawing persons to these blocks who might not otherwise venture there, as well as making it easier for those working on the blocks to remain there.

A third characteristic of the habitat is an abundance of public places to sleep with little impunity. As at Pennsylvania Station, we find on these blocks "niches" where men can lie down out of plain sight. For a long time, Ron slept inside the Chemical Bank's automated-teller-machine vestibule (now a Duane Reade drugstore). Others who sell written matter on Sixth Avenue sleep in chairs on the sidewalk, on the steps of the church, or in the subway dungeon and Bat Cave.

"Where do you live?" I asked Grady, who sells magazines down the block from Ishmael.

"On the steps of the church in the summer and winter, and in the train station, in the tunnels, during the fall and spring. You gotta fix it yourself.

It's a place where you put maybe two mattresses, a bunch of sheets, a bunch of blankets, clothes. At one time there were six or seven people down there. It's too hot in the summer and too cold in the winter."

"Are you scared down there?"

". . . I used to think about rats and stuff like that, but it's not that bad. The main thing you think about is a derailing, but that would be the end anyway. So you wouldn't have to think too long about that! The trains come about two feet from you. You hear the train come by constantly. But you put your body in a position like listening to music. You tune yourself to the roar of the tracks and the making of the noise and you go right to sleep. You sleep right through it. You wake up during rush hour, because you hear so many trains coming so close together. That gives you an idea of what time it is. Otherwise you wouldn't know if it was day or night."

"Do you ever feel that someone might hurt you down there?"

"That thought don't even cross my mind. It's like, whoever be down there, they try to be together, and it's like a little family. You know you're sleeping near this guy, or this person is around you, so you look out for each other."

"Do you ever take your girlfriend down there?"

"Sure, you ask guys to leave, or whatever. I take girls down there. Some was afraid and some is not. Some go for it and some didn't go for it. They say, 'Oh, man, I can't go down here.' So you can't make 'em go. One of my girlfriends . . . always says she's gonna write a book about dungeons and dragons! But she got used to it."

In Pennsylvania Station, unhoused people used the public restrooms to perform toilet functions and to have sex as well. On Sixth Avenue, Grady is able to find in the subway dungeon a place to have a physical relationship with his girlfriend, Phyllis. Many unhoused people urinate and defecate at the bottom levels of the subway tracks, too. Others urinate in the crevices of the walls of the Washington Court Condominium, which provide just enough space for them to turn against the wall and urinate without being seen. (This is a topic I will take up in some detail in a later chapter.) What these facts reveal is that the absence of one element in a working system (such as bathrooms) does not break the "lifeline" of the habitat. People are more than capable of adapting, as long as the habitat provides other, complementary elements that make it worth their while to be there.

SUPPLEMENTAL ELEMENTS

Several other elements serve to make Greenwich Village a sustaining habitat that is ideal for magazine scavenging and vending. The neighborhood is the home of many people who are sympathetic to unhoused people and are willing to give money and food to them. Further, it is not uncommon for residents to come up to the tables and offer to donate stacks of books or magazines. When Ellen, a fifty-year-old white woman, came up to Marvin's table on a hot June day, she told him she wanted to donate a number of magazines, but in exchange she wanted him to reduce the price of a graphics magazine on his table.

"You know I gotta charge full price," Marvin told her in a defiant but joking manner.

"But I'm going to give you a lot of magazines!" she told him, smiling.

"So you want me to take out your garbage *and* give you a discount?" Marvin retorted. "It gotta be good magazines. I gotta have an eye for them. I can't just take a whole bunch of average stuff and put it on my table."

"No!" she responded. "They're all good ones. They're all ones I got from you!"

They both laughed.

"Well, they dies out after some time," said Marvin.

"Well, I need to get rid of them," she responded.

"Okay."

"So you'll let me have this magazine for free?" she asked.

"I don't know," said Marvin.

"Come on. I'm gonna give back a *lot*."

"I'll tell you what," said Marvin. "Give me a dollar for this magazine and then send me out the batch."

"What?" said Ellen, laughing.

"I'm taking your garbage out *and* I'm giving you a deal!" said Marvin.

They both laughed. She gave him a dollar and then pointed at me. "Why don't you send your assistant with me to pick them up."

As I rose from the milk crate I'd been sitting on, I asked Marvin to introduce us. "Ellen, he's a sociology professor and he's writing a book about us," explains Marvin.

"Uh-huh. Okay," she said, and we walked toward her apartment. "I've lived in the area since 1962," she told me. "I have an antique store and I live

up above it. We used to be publishers. We published magazines and books—political. We published a magazine called *Lies of Our Times* about the *New York Times,* and we had a book-publishing company called Sheridan Square Press. And we still publish a magazine in Washington called *Covert Action.*"

"How long have you been patronizing these magazine sellers?"

"All the time. Since they've been out there. Some of my neighbors say they want to get rid of these guys. I think they are wonderful. I go to Marvin, mainly."

We entered her apartment and went directly to a cabinet in the back, which was filled with back issues of *Architectural Digest, Elle Decor,* and *Art and Antiques.* Above us were framed photographs of Fidel Castro and Ernest Hemingway.

"These are all things you bought from Marvin?" I asked her.

She knelt and shuffled through the piles.

"Yeah. And I'm giving them back. Because I've read them and someone else can read them now and he can make some more money. My husband is a First Amendment lawyer and Marvin is doing First Amendment work. And I think it's *great* that he is out there."

A Hunt Through Recycled Trash

In Greenwich Village, high-quality magazines can be found in the trash cans, too, and in fact most of the magazines sold on the street are gotten there. When a scavenger goes looking for new material, he is said to be out on a "hunt." Very early most mornings, one can hear the rattle of stolen shopping carts and discarded baby carriages as these hunters make the rounds of a neighborhood's Dumpsters and cans. Marvin carries with him a standard map of New York City, printed in the Yellow Pages, which indicates when recyclable trash will be picked up in every neighborhood. The goal of a scavenger is to sort through the trash sometime in the period between when the material is put out, after sundown, and when the collection truck comes, early the next morning.

In Greenwich Village, Marvin's hunt begins at 6:00 a.m. on garbage-collection days. Marvin tells me to meet him then in his regular place on Sixth Avenue. We both arrive on time and walk to the first building, at 64 West Ninth Street, across the street from Balducci's market. "See these boxes right here? I have a brilliant way of going into the boxes without messing it all up."

He takes his box cutter and neatly opens the side of a bundle to see the inside. Holding a flashlight up to the cut, he quickly scans the magazines without unsettling them. "That's the reason why they don't like us. Because we mess up what is left neat and organized, and these buildings will get tickets if the garbage is not tied up."

The magazine scavengers of Sixth Avenue tend to take great pride in leaving the trash they sort through neat and orderly. Marvin has relationships with many of the building superintendents. They make accommodations for the scavengers by putting cans and bottles in one place and magazines in another, so that the men don't rip into every single bag and make a huge mess. At the townhouses and brownstones, which generally do not have supers or porters, many residents lock their trash in wooden cabinets to avoid waking up to a mess on their front stoop and receiving an Environmental Control Board summons from a sanitation-enforcement agent.

In New York City, the theft of items from garbage is a Class E misdemeanor, punishable by up to a year in jail and a fine of one thousand dollars. It is also considered "interfering with sanitation operations," and "removing material put out for collections," two other violations. The Department of Sanitation has its own police force of about one hundred persons,[32] but scavengers like Marvin are among the least of their worries. Their focus is on environmental issues such as illegal dumping, medical-waste disposal, and enforcement of recycling laws. So Marvin does not seem very concerned as police cars pass us by.

Without opening a bundle of newspapers, he discovers some books stuffed inside.

"How did you figure out those were in there?"

"Well, you feel it. When you need more you go for more! You go through more avenues to get it."

He picks up a box and puts it down without opening it.

"How do you know nothing is in there?"

"You can tell by the feel. You can feel the edges of books or magazines through a box, or you can see the impressions on the side of a box."

He gets nothing at that stop and pushes the baby carriage he uses to carry

the magazines on to the next stop, passing a building with a number of boxes outside.

"Why are you skipping this one?"

"I know what to hit. On the first part of this street right here, you never find anything good. But here, at this next building, I always find a lot of good stuff."

The first box he opens has three old issues of *Artforum* magazine. "This one is September," he explains. (It is now December.) "If it was current, I would take it. But I probably won't be able to sell a copy that is two months old."

Next he moves across the street. "This place right here, I don't stop here all the time. They usually throw out a lot of research magazines. Like medicine and science magazines that I can't sell."

It is ten to seven, and the sun has come up. Now and then people pass on the street, and a truck moves slowly down the block. At the time of this hunt, Marvin had grown concerned about high-tech scavengers who rent trucks and remove newspapers and magazines without being contracted to do so. "I am in competition with the paper haulers, legitimate and illegitimate. You see, when paper went from one cent to two cent a pound, that doubled it, so it became much more valuable to them. The guys in these trucks think they own it. They don't like to see little scavengers like me out here." At the time, the price per ton of recycled newsprint was high; when the bottom fell out of the newsprint market a year later, the high-tech scavengers disappeared.

A man with a cart full of soda cans passes by.

"Who is that guy?"

"Who? Him? He cans. He just does cans."

The can scavengers are an unintended consequence of aluminum-can redemption, which New York State has had in effect under its Bottle Bill since 1980. There are hundreds of them in the city, so that one rarely finds an aluminum can or a bottle in New York City street litter.[33]

Marvin finds a box full of *New Yorkers*, *Times*, and *Newsweeks*, but he passes on most of them. He explains that he isn't going to pick up anything that's heavy and won't sell. He is looking for monthly magazines, because weeklies become outdated too quickly. Other scavengers, with different approaches, will pick them up. But for Marvin, it is the monthly magazines that are lucrative. He is proud of his focus. "I saw other people selling weeklies, but I don't do it the way they do it."

As we continue up Sixth Avenue, Marvin says that the next building will be important to the success of the hunt. "Now we're going to this one shot up here, this one building that I depend on for some very good things. At the later part of the month, the magazine pickings really die out. People are looking for the next month. I always go out early. You see, if you go early, when nobody else is here, you can always find a couple of magazines."

He finds a copy of the December issue of *Architectural Digest.* The subscriber apparently threw it out after only a few days. Marvin puts it in his carriage, though he says he isn't as excited about this magazine as he once would have been. "When I first started, this was one of the magazines I could really sell. But because of Candy Nast [sic] . . . or whatever . . . a company that bought *Architectural Digest,* it fell down. And the reason why it fell is because they started throwing a whole bunch of nonsense advertisements and articles to sell the ads, and people don't want it anymore. In the old days, every month people used to come every day and ask, 'You have the latest one?' I would have five or six customers that would stop by looking for it every day. I would go to the Upper West Side and Upper East Side, where the professional people live, and I would get the latest issues as soon as they came out, even sometimes thrown away before they were taken out of the plastic bags [they were mailed in]."

Marvin moves on toward the next building. He passes another man like himself with a wagon filled with magazines.

"Hey, boy," Marvin shouts.

"What you doing?" the man asks, pointing to the white man with a tape recorder.

"I'm giving an interview."

A Working System

The men who live and work on Sixth Avenue share a common history and a collective self-consciousness; having come to the avenue, they have remained there because it is a habitat that can sustain a person's minimal existence.

How Sixth Avenue became a sustaining habitat, of course, is no simple matter. My ethnographic method, which gives us access to the social worlds of individuals in small groups at one point in their lives, is hardly adequate for precisely calculating the political and social forces that operate to make these streets the way they are. Nor is it adequate for fully comprehending other forces which shape these blocks: the segregation, concentrated poverty, flawed or inequitable drug policies, and the failure of the state to help the newly deinstitutionalized (including ex-convicts and the mentally ill) make smooth transitions to jobs and homes. No concise look at the circumstances of these men's lives can explain how they came to live this way. In the case of the written-matter vendors, the political actions of Councilman Edward Wallace on behalf of a lone poet, and the legal interests of circulation managers of major newspapers, worked directly in an unplanned way to bring this particular habitat into being.

These forces would have been nothing, of course, without the activities of many other people working together in an indirect, unplanned way: police officers offhandedly teaching people working the streets as much of the law as they needed to know; new scavengers imitating the behavior of more experienced ones as a means of self-preservation, and developing differing amounts of specialized knowledge about subjects ranging from the law to the print industry; ecological movements that led to local residents bundling their magazines for recycling; great numbers of persons making an intensive use of local space and providing a market for used written matter.

A habitat came into being where these complementary sustaining elements were brought together in a working system. Mudrick, Ron, Marvin, Grady, and Ishmael could have a legal right to sell, but it would have meant nothing without a source of merchandise in local trash cans, a way to get food, and sleep. By virtue of its contextual connections, Local Law 33 became a resource—and a valuable one.

PART THREE

THE LIMITS OF INFORMAL
SOCIAL CONTROL

Sidewalk Sleeping

In the early 1980s, residents of many American cities came to see their sidewalk life as a new kind of struggle. They perceived that conventional standards did not apply on streets like Sixth Avenue. Politicians responded by advancing programs for restoring order and reducing crime that seemed to be the exact opposite of Jacobs's "eyes upon the street." Jacobs wrote: "The first thing to understand is that the public peace—the sidewalk and street peace—of cities is not kept primarily by the police, necessary as police are. It is kept primarily by an intricate, almost unconscious, network of voluntary control and standards among the people themselves, and enforced by the people themselves."[1] For many city dwellers, informal social control was no longer enough, because the eyes upon the street were no longer conventional. The police were essential to the maintenance of order and could no longer be the "or else" of social control.

The most prominent argument for using formal methods of social control was advanced by the social scientists James Q. Wilson and George Kelling in an article entitled "Broken Windows," which appeared in *The Atlantic Monthly* in March 1982. They grounded their argument in the 1969 report by social psychologist Philip Zimbardo, who had arranged to have automobiles without license plates parked with their hoods up in the Bronx and Palo Alto, California. In both places, according to Wilson and Kelling's summary of Zimbardo's study, vandalism occurred once passersby sensed that the cars were abandoned and "no one cared." In Palo Alto, it was middle-class white passersby who did the damage; in the South Bronx, it was poor minority ones. Using Zimbardo's experiment as an analogy, Wilson and Kelling went on to argue that the appearance of a single broken window in a neighborhood (not merely in an abandoned car) gives a sense that "no one cares." Once the "no one cares" threshold is met, they claimed, "serious crime will flourish." And even before crime increases, citizens will begin to feel the anxiety that comes from "a sense that the street is disorderly, a source of distasteful, worrisome encounters. . . . One unrepaired broken window is a signal that no one cares, . . . so breaking more windows costs nothing."[2]

Although for Jacobs disorder serves many positive functions and for Wilson and Kelling it does not, their approaches are only superficially different in other ways. Both ask what sorts of unintended consequences flow from particular sorts of publicly visible practices. Jacobs's argument, in part, is that public characters (who in her analysis are respectable figures) generate a sense of predictability by acting as eyes, and this generates social order, by creating a set of cultural meanings and expectations that "someone cares." Wilson and Kelling and those who advocate stronger police control believe that visible forms of disorder and disrepute have the unintended consequence of producing crime, by creating a set of cultural meanings or expectations that "no one cares."

Through what came to be called the "broken windows" theory, Wilson and Kelling laid the scholarly groundwork for a political combat plan that responded to the concerns of vast numbers of city dwellers who wanted to feel safer on their streets. In the 1980s and 1990s, these issues became the substance of two successive New York City mayoral elections. In 1989, Democratic Mayor David Dinkins initially tried to show tolerance for sidewalk vendors, scavengers, and panhandlers even as he hired William Bratton, a transit-police chief who vigorously applied Wilson and Kelling's ideas. In 1993, Dinkins went down to defeat to the Republican Rudolph Giuliani, who intensified the same policies (as he would later promote Bratton to the post of Police Commissioner) as he ran an unrelenting campaign against the forces that were said to be diminishing the "quality of life" for conventional members of the electorate. Since 1993, crime rates have dropped dramatically in New York City. Because crime rates have also dropped in cities where the "broken windows" theory has not been applied, the extent to which the dramatic drop in New York can be attributed to "broken windows"–style social control is a matter of fierce debate.

Having examined the way that the informal ties of the sidewalk help men as they struggle to live in accordance with standards of moral worth, I want to look now at the very acts that lead policymakers to classify these same persons as "broken windows." These are acts which seem not to be regulated by informal social controls among the vendors themselves, and which have made sidewalk life seem like a new kind of battleground for many conventional citizens. In what follows, I will focus on four apparently indecent behaviors: when some men working the sidewalks urinate in public, detain local residents in conversation, sell stolen goods, and sleep on the sidewalk. (I might have focused, say, on the sale of marijuana or crack, but during the time of my fieldwork such petty dealing was uncommon—only once did I see a man working with the vendors sell marijuana to a passerby—and also has been addressed in detail by other scholars.)[3]

Thus far, I have tried to show that what makes sidewalk life viable is an informal system of social control, maintained in part by people like Hakim, Marvin, and Jamaane. The question is this: If the informal system is so powerful, how and why do some men persist in these acts? And aren't the people who do these things the very people I claim are trying not to give up on basic standards? How is it that the same person who makes a conscious decision to "respect" society by scavenging trash or panhandling (instead of breaking into parked cars or selling drugs) turns around and urinates against the side of a building? How much respect does he really have for society if he engages in such behavior? In examining some of the hardest cases and the most contradictory evidence, I hope to address the limitations of informal modes of social control.

A Puzzle

On a late night in August, Ron came up to me and asked if I would hold sixty of the ninety dollars he had earned that day. Even if he asked for it later on that night, he told me, I shouldn't give it to him.

Marvin, Hakim, Jamaane, and Alice were also often asked to hold other people's money (mainly because they did not use drugs). By the end of my first summer working full-time on the block, I sometimes found myself holding someone's money as well.

What is the significance of a person's giving me fifty or sixty dollars to hold and insisting that I not give it back to him later on that night, even if he asks? It means he is about to buy some five- or ten-dollar vials of crack co-caine ("nickel" or "dime" vials) and does not want to spend all of his money on drugs. A nickel in a crack stem is often referred to as a "good hit," a dime as two "good hits." The high from a nickel lasts for about five minutes, but can be made to last as long as fifteen minutes if the person has no more of the drug. Then a depression tends to set in, leading him to smoke more. A person with a hundred dollars can do a nickel every two or three minutes, going through a pocketful of money in less than an hour. Some smoke up to a hundred dollars in a night, usually extending their supply over a few hours. It is no wonder that a man might give someone else money to hold so as to have enough left over the next day to buy food, purchase merchandise to sell, or settle debts.

Sometimes when Ron asked me to hold his money, he returned at one or two in the morning and insisted on getting it back. Once, when I refused and reminded Ron what he had told me earlier, he said, My money is my money! Give it to me!

Okay, Ron, I'll give you twenty dollars, I responded, and did so.

An hour later, Ron laid his body down and went to sleep.

When I arrived on the block the next day, I noticed Ron sitting on a milk crate, evidently drunk. Rather than give him the rest of his money, I walked away before he saw me. A few days later, now sober, he expressed appreciation that I hadn't returned the money to him earlier. He then used it to buy some extra books from Joe Garbage, who had struck gold on a hunt. He also bought some food, and paid back a debt of ten dollars to Marvin.

Instead of having me hold his money, he might have used it to stay at the White House Hotel on the Bowery, which now charges ten dollars for a cubicle room, or at one of a number of other hotels. He could have gone and checked into the hotel *before* he smoked, a common practice of men who know they don't want to sleep outside after they get high. Or, like Conrad, another vendor of scavenged magazines on the block that night, who was (at that time) addicted to crack, he could have reserved three nights at the White House with a lump-sum payment.

When I told Hakim that I found this behavior puzzling, he said he could offer no explanation to help me out. But he offered to take the tape recorder and do an interview with Ron.

"Do the other guys that [are] out here know about the White House?"

"Yeah! But they [don't] want to spend that money. Ain't nobody gonna save up no eight dollars!"

"But, Ron!" exclaimed Hakim. "Eight dollars! Save up? You can make eight dollars out here in five minutes!"

"In one sale!" Ron laughed.

"You just made a sale for . . ."

"Fifteen dollars!" said Ron.

"That's two nights right there!" said Hakim.

"Yeah, that's two nights."

"It's warm?" asked Hakim. "It's clean?"

"Yeah, it's clean."

"It beats sleeping out here on the sidewalk?"

"Yeah, definitely."

"But you are saying these guys don't want to spend eight dollars a day, which out here is peanuts, to stay somewhere rather than the sidewalk?"

"Yeah. And you get a bed, towels for a shower, and soap. They have a big shower down in the basement."

The Logic of the Habitat

Approximately a third of the men working on Sixth Avenue sleep on these sidewalks, in the subway, or on nearby blocks. In his influential 1994 book, *The Homeless*, sociologist Christopher Jencks argues: "A bed in a New York or Chicago cubicle hotel currently costs about $8 a night. Most people who have enough money to buy substantial amounts of crack could therefore afford to rent a cubicle instead. A large fraction of the single adults in New York shelters who test positive for cocaine presumably think that a crack high, however brief, is worth more than a scuzzy cubicle." He goes on: "We badly need more reliable information on where the homeless get their money and how they spend it. But the only way to collect better information is to spend endless hours with the homeless, observing what they do instead of just asking them about such matters on surveys."[4]

In responding to Jencks's plea for more and better evidence, I did *not* find that these men spend every bit of additional money they have on drugs. Why, then, do they continue to sleep on the street?

As we have seen, the blocks are a place in which various survival elements can be networked together, making it a particularly good subsistence habitat for the street entrepreneur. A defining feature of unhoused persons on Sixth Avenue is that a complex social organization has arisen from the work they do to sustain themselves.[5] There are two basic reasons, rather than a lack of available housing or a lack of money, why embeddedness in a habitat leads a person to remain on the street. First, a man will sleep on the blocks as a function of the complementarity of the various habitat elements (such as food, basic shelter, and an opportunity to make a little money) coming together in one place. Second, he may sleep there because his friends are out there watching tables, which makes the habitat a place where he feels safe and even comfortable. He is there for the same reason that Jane Jacobs says a busy sidewalk life makes pedestrians feel safe: because those who are out know that eyes are upon the street.

Because resources are valuable in the setting by virtue of their contextual connections, people working the street use the sidewalks in accordance with a logic that derives from the complementarity of different elements. To understand the act of sleeping on the sidewalks, rather than assuming a person is making a trade-off between drugs and a room, it is always useful to consider a person's overall logic and how it is encouraged or structured by the existence of the habitat.

Why might a man choose to sleep on the sidewalk? Some common answers:

To save a vending space. "If you see the spot that Ishmael got, he want to be there all the time, twenty-four hours," Ron told me. "He don't want to leave the spot and have it be taken by somebody else when they get here in the morning. So he figure he just stay there."

Ishmael confirmed that he stays there because doing so maintains another resource, a space on the sidewalk from which to sell his magazines. We have, of course, already seen a variation on this theme: a person who earns his money as a table watcher may stay on the block all night to earn his pay.

To save money. Grady, a longtime drug user, now clean, who recently discovered that he is HIV-positive, sleeps on the sidewalk or in the dungeon of the subway because of the complex of other activities that exist within the

habitat. He told me that someone is always getting on or off the train in the middle of the night, so that he usually feels safe and comfortable on the sidewalk or in the dungeon. His plan is to to sleep on the streets in the summer and fall, so that he can have enough money saved up for the winter, when it gets cold. Such a plan would not be possible unless the habitat provided a space for sleeping that Grady considered a safe and comfortable alternative to a hotel.

For a time, he went to a hotel on days that he spent with his girlfriend, Phyllis. But when she was locked up in the Riker's Island prison, a hotel hardly seemed worth it to him anymore. In one month he saved a thousand dollars for the winter and for a trip to see his mother in Florida. (I counted the money.)

Hakim interviewed Grady about his finances and sleeping. Grady explained that he was saving his money for the winter. He knows that, like other men, he could earn enough money in the winter to afford housing then, but this would force him to be working outside during the coldest months of the year as he tries to combat HIV. His choice is not between drugs and an apartment, but between an apartment in the warm weather and an apartment

in the cold, or between an apartment when his girlfriend is with him and one when she is not.

To use crack. Even though there are many police officers around Sixth Avenue, a person who is using crack often prefers to be on the sidewalk, near those police, rather than in a hotel (presumably away from the police). Why? Because he knows that in a hotel the manager can call the precinct and say that something suspicious is going on in a particular room. "The police can get a key from the front desk and walk right on in," Ron told me. "You might be engaged in some kind of activity and you are busted. That's one of the reasons they say hotels is not safe."

Also, Ron, like other crack users, is paranoid about being in small, enclosed spaces when he is high. This might also help explain how crack use became associated with the rise in the number of unhoused persons. And, of course, the continuous stream of money that comes from the entrepreneurial activity of the sidewalk makes it possible for Ron to keep bingeing all night long—smoking or drinking until he passes out, or sitting in his chair at the table until he falls asleep.[6]

"Once You're Homeless, You're Always Homeless"

The person who sleeps on the blocks to save a space, to save money, or to use drugs is making use of the complementarity of the various subsistence elements available in one place.

In each case, the person who regularly makes the decision to remain on the sidewalk overnight has a vocabulary for expressing its acceptability to him. Hakim used my tape recorder to conduct an interview in which Mudrick made a number of statements that illustrate this point. Mudrick often sleeps on the steps of the church, on subway trains, or on the floor of a storage room in the building where he makes extra money taking out the trash. Here he keeps his clothes neatly folded.

"Once any man is homeless, he's always homeless," Mudrick told Hakim.

"In what respect?" asked Hakim.

"You got a bed, Hakim? You sleep in your bed, right?"

"I prefer to sleep in my bed," responded Hakim.

"I sleep on the floor," Mudrick continued. "Ask my daughter where I sleep when I go see Dyneisha. Me and my granddaughter go get a blanket and sleep on the floor. My daughter asked me why I can't sleep in the bed. I said, 'Listen. It's a long story. One day you might hear it . . .' She don't know what streets I live on. You see, I sleep on the sidewalk."

"Would you spend ten dollars a night to stay in the White House Hotel?"

"I can't afford it!"

"But, Mudrick, you making money!"

"What I'm gonna stay in the hotel for when the same thing as the hotel is sleeping in the street? What's the difference?"

"So, if tomorrow you won the lottery or you inherited an apartment on Tenth Street with a bed and furniture and everything, you gonna sleep on the floor?"

"That's right! I choose to be homeless."

"You choose to be homeless?"

"I choose to be! Where else I had to go when I come here? I didn't have no money. I came here to find a job and work. But that didn't work and my money ran out."

"If a man who sells magazines or books makes fifty to sixty dollars a day, what would stop him from taking ten dollars and going to the White House?"

"People who sleep in the street that make that kind of money want to do this."

"So you saying it's not a question of money?"

"Listen, a bed is made to sleep in. I don't sleep in it. I'm not used to it. I don't want to get used to it. I got a choice. I gonna stay in the street. I ain't going to go nowhere."

"No matter how much money you make?"

"No matter how much. Once you're homeless, you're always homeless."

•

In speaking of their own deep acceptance of their condition, men sometimes refer to their initial unhoused condition as a choice, sometimes blatantly contradicting biographical facts from the same interview or an earlier conversation. (In this case, Mudrick claims to be "homeless" by choice in the same sentence in which he recalls his inability to find a job that would put a roof over his head.) Once again we are reminded that interviewing does not

necessarily produce a clear understanding of the men's personal choices, even if we do get to hear the vocabulary through which they explain their condition.

Two of the most common explanations for remaining on the street are "I can't afford a room" and "The hotel is not safe." Yet, when challenged on these claims, many men will state that sleeping in certain hotels (like the White House) *is* as safe as sleeping on the sidewalk, and few men will stick to their claim that they really can't find in their earnings the money for a hotel. "Safety" sometimes seems to refer to being free from police searches.

Mudrick's "Once you're homeless, you're always homeless," seems to be linked to his body's response to the social and physical experience of sleeping on a hard surface. His body seems to have grown to prefer a particular physical experience, which makes the social experience of homelessness acceptable in ways it would not be for the average person. For some of these men, sleeping in a bed no longer feels natural. Although most Americans take sleeping in a bed as basic to decency, the conventional bed is not a physical necessity but a cultural artifact; many people of the world regard a bed as less healthy for sleeping than a hard surface.[7]

Ishmael hardly ever leaves the corner of Sixth Avenue and Eighth Street. Yet, when Hakim asked him if he considers himself homeless, he said, "No! I don't consider myself homeless. No. See, I don't sleep on the street. I don't lay out on the street. I don't act like I can't work."

"You say you don't sleep on the street. But I've seen you for quite some time in a chair on the sidewalk, asleep."

"On the sidewalk, sitting down, asleep. Okay? At a job, asleep. Okay? I'm at my job, asleep. It's not like I'm not at a job! I'm not stretched out on the ground."

So some men deny being homeless even as they demonstrate an acceptance of that condition in other terms. The "homeless" condition itself does not constitute the basic role through which these men define themselves. *The entrepreneurial activity*—more than the person's unhoused state—is central to personal identity. If you ask a person to tell you about himself, he'll likely say, "I'm a vendor," not, "I'm homeless." (Here recall Ron and Marvin's bargaining techniques, the way they sell their wares and "get over," producing self-respect and a sense that they are independent businessmen.)

Although passersby regard him as a "homeless" man, Ishmael's answers suggest that he sees his work as basic to who he is. Indeed, most aspects of Ishmael's day on Sixth Avenue are tightly scheduled in accordance with the demands of work and the principle of complementarity within a habitat. He knows that the police will walk the beat at certain times, and he *must* be present at his table during those periods if his belongings are not to be taken. He knows that trash is put out at certain times, so that he must be out "hunting" then. He knows that customers will purchase the most magazines at certain other times, so he must be present on the block then. He knows it is good to be present on the block if he is to be there when a random person appears with a donation of magazines.

He may tell a researcher that he would choose to have a place to live, but not if that means he must give up the things that otherwise sustain him: yes, a place to sleep; but also free or cheap food, social networks, abundant trash, and, most important, a place to earn a living by selling what he takes from the trash. Into his presence on these blocks must be read more than the existence of "homelessness." We must see in the uses to which he puts the sidewalk an embeddedness in habitat, a series of complementary elements tied together in an encompassing manner that ultimately sustains. In networking together complementary sustaining elements, Ishmael chooses to sleep on the block—not because this is the best sleeping alternative he has, and not because he has spent all of his money on drugs, but because he is on the block first and foremost to work and, through that work, to live his life.

•

To speak about the little choices people make on a day-to-day basis is not to comprehend the circumstances that led them to the street. Nor does a close look at this population solve the problem of understanding other types of unhoused people whose sustenance activities have not led to complex forms of social organization.[8] We must not begin with the assumption that the unhoused on Sixth Avenue are the same as single mothers with their children walking the streets, unhoused families living in cars, individuals sleeping by themselves underneath bridges, or persons who cannot find a place to stay.[9] Research suggests, for example, that the destruction of New York City's Single Residence Occupancy (S.R.O.) housing stock was a primary contributing factor to the rise in visible big-city homelessness in the 1980s.[10]

Nevertheless, when people sleeping *on these blocks* decide to stay there, it becomes questionable to many passersby whether they are really struggling to live "decent" lives. The answer, I think, is that such acts pose no challenge to what we saw in the first three chapters of this book: each of these men is engaged in such a struggle. This is most evident in the way they choose to support themselves: through honest entrepreneurial activity. If they were using drugs, could not work for other people in a tolerable manner, had no marketable skills, and then robbed to support their habit, we might reasonably conclude that they had given up on the struggle to live in accordance with society's standards. In this case, the men have made clever use of a local ordinance to appropriate public space and avoid engaging in criminal activity that hurts others. As Ishmael sees his life, others can do the same thing with the space that he did, appropriating it from him. So he has to protect it by staying there, or at least he thinks he must.

Some argue that no matter how "degraded" or "victimized" a man is, he must be held up to the same standards as everyone else. Actually, a sociological analysis gains power when it takes up such a challenge, comparing the acts these men engage in with those of other members of society who are not viewed as "victims." Ishmael brings to mind people whom society considers respectable who, like him, choose to sleep where their jobs are. Owners of small retail businesses may have spent the first ten years of ownership sleeping in the attic. They are afraid that, if they are not present, things may get fouled up. Even once their store runs like clockwork, they seem to believe they mustn't be away from it.

It is tempting to believe that the difference between Ishmael and "decent" people is that the latter have solved problems of where to sleep in ways that fit in better with standard ways of doing things. To some extent, this is true. But when "decent" people have not done so, few people accuse them of being indecent. This is because they don't fit the delinquent stereotype and aren't as public in their behavior. Few people actually see what they do.

There are, of course, many people in America and throughout the world who appropriate public space and sleep outside. In Santa Barbara, California, some people sleep in beat-up Volkswagen buses by the Amtrak station, sometimes for months at a time. There are many other people who appropriate the public lands with sleeping bags and camp out as they make their way up and down the coast. These people are white, and often come from middle-class families. That they use drugs while they do their camping seems of little concern to anyone. Fewer people question their decency.

If Ron is too paranoid to rent a room when he is high on crack, and if Grady is afraid of being outside in cold weather and wants to save his money, it is hard to argue in consequence that they have given up on the struggle to live a "decent" life.

It is important to note that of the sixteen men who have at one time regularly slept on these blocks, only five currently spend their nights out there. Like Ron, of the eleven men who left the blocks for a housed existence, *all* still work out on these or other sidewalks as vendors. At any given time on the blocks, someone is looking to take the money he has saved and get himself a place to live. As I write this, Grady has now secured an apartment and his partner Keith White has saved $1,000 to be able to afford a security deposit for an apartment in Brooklyn. The opportunities to vend ultimately do help many men to stabilize their lives.

But there are always some people who take sleeping on the blocks to an extreme. When I asked Hakim to account for the failure of people like himself, Marvin, and Jaamane to stop sidewalk sleeping altogether (in cases where it does not seem necessary), he said: "It's not as if, in the case of Ishmael, that we have not tried to talk to him and say, 'This is what we would like for you to do to move your life beyond sleeping on the sidewalk.' In the early days I was optimistic about it, but I came to the conclusion that he was not interested in creating a balance in his life beyond work, work, work. Once a guy gets used to living a certain way, it takes a long time to adjust to doing anything better."

The practical test of whether the informal controls have been a failure is whether a system of control brought in from the outside could do better. If the kind of mentoring depicted in the first part of the book does not discourage sidewalk sleeping on its own, could the government implement formal regulations that would work? For example, if the city were to assign spaces to vendors, it would be unnecessary for men to sleep on the sidewalk to maintain their rights. In theory, this would encourage some people who are living on the streets to go elsewhere at night. If a person had a property right to a particular sidewalk space, he or she would not feel a need to sleep there to maintain it.

Such a regulation might well lead to greater order on our sidewalks and among the people dwelling on them. But the evidence suggests that many of these particular unhoused people would not go to hotels anyway. Even if the right to vend at night were taken away, men who are out on the sidewalk because they are accustomed to hard surfaces would likely remain outside. And those who are there to make money for drug bingeing would also likely remain outside, panhandling or stealing the money, instead of vending. From what we know about these men and their lives, it is fair to speculate that the effort to reduce disorder through more formal regulation might even result in greater disorder; that eliminating vending and scavenging might result in more theft.

Informal mentoring and controls simply cannot contain all acts that go against common notions of decency, nor could we expect government to establish a policy that would do any better. The best alternative, of course, would be better drug treatment and men who are willing to avail themselves of it. But even with the best programs in place, some people will choose to binge. Some of those will choose to earn their money honestly. And some of those will sleep on the sidewalk. The contribution of the informal system of social control inherent in sidewalk life is to encourage men to live "better" lives within the framework of their own and society's weaknesses.

When You Gotta Go

If you walk down Sixth Avenue between Waverly Place and Washington Place, you will sometimes see men urinating against the side of the Washington Court Condominum. Although Sixth Avenue is a habitat that can sustain a fairly well-rounded life, it lacks one of the best amenities of Pennsylvania Station: bathrooms open to the public. So men must find their own places to urinate and defecate.

When I asked Phillis Gross, a resident of the condominium, how people in Washington Court felt about this, she replied: "Clearly, one of the design flaws the architect of this condominium made was placing indentations in the side of the building, which makes it very convenient for people to use it as a bathroom. The fact that a *human* would have to use the street [is disturbing to me] . . . but they really don't [have to], because there is a bathroom in Washington Square Park [a few blocks away]."

Mudrick: "This Is My Bathroom"

"I gotta get me a paper cup and I'm gonna be all right," Mudrick tells me as we walk down Sixth Avenue at 10:00 p.m. After he finds one in a trash can, he pauses, unzips his pants, and begins urinating into it. I ask him why.

"This is for the street, Mitch. This is for Guiliano," he laughs, referring to the mayor, who is more commonly known as Rudolph Giuliani. "Guiliano say you can't go to the bathroom. I invented this thing. Now everybody out here gets a cup. You can't go to the bathroom in the stores and restaurants, because they don't want you in there if you ain't got no money to spend. So how you gonna piss? You gotta get a cup."

"And then you just throw it in the street?" I ask.

"Throw it in the street!" said Mudrick.

"And that's for Giuliani?" I ask, surprised that urination is being described as a political act.

"Yeah. I went to Riker's Island jail for pissing in the street. Now I get a cup. I'm gonna give the city a hundred dollars for pissing in the street? Shit! Now I get a cup. When the cop says, 'What you doing, pissing?' I say, 'Yeah, I'm pissing in a cup! Not in the street! The street is over there! I'm in the cup!' "

"You can't go to the bathroom around here," Mudrick continues when I ask him more about this on another day. "Like McDonald's [across the street]. Yesterday, I went in the morning time. I had to take a dump real bad. They said, 'You have to buy something.' I'm a regular customer. Ten minutes later, another guy walks in and he ain't buying nothing and she gives the key to the man and lets him go in."

A few days earlier, I had noticed Mudrick flagging down a cab. None stopped for him. A few seconds later, he turned away with a cup in hand and dumped it in the sewer. While Mudrick pretends to be hailing a cab, he holds the cup and urinates under an untucked shirt. Passing pedestrians and motorists don't seem to know what he is doing. "I'm gonna show you how I do it. I put my thing here like this. My shirt over here. And I hold it like this here. And I say [yelling], 'Taxi.' They have no idea, 'cause I look like I'm catching a cab."

On another occasion, after dumping his urine in the sewer, Mudrick placed the Starbucks cup he had just used on the branch of a tree on Sixth Avenue. (The tree had been planted by the local Business Improvement District to cut down on space for vendors.) I had occasionally noticed paper cups hanging from tree branches but had never thought twice about them.

"[I] hang the cup on the tree. That means that's [my] cup. You gonna put your private thing in somebody else's cup? So you put your cup up and that's your bathroom. Like this here. Here's my cup. When I finish my cup, I don't want nobody to use it. This is my bathroom. I got to put my bathroom right here. [Puts the cup on a branch of the tree.] Then I walk back over to the bookstore [his table], and every five minutes I keep watching my bathroom, because I know I gotta take a leak sooner or later."

"Everybody do's it," he continues. "Marvin do's it. You know why? Because they can't get into the bathroom."

Mudrick says that New York City could afford to put more public bathrooms on street corners so that he wouldn't have to walk seven blocks "to take a piss" or, if he has to move his bowels, be gone so long that the police will confiscate his books. "Giuliano making all this money and a homeless man like me got nowhere to go. I respect the public and I respect everybody but I cannot use the bathroom."

"That's where I took a dump at yesterday morning," he continues later in the day, pointing to the Dumpster on the corner. He shows me how he unlocks the Dumpster, sits down in it, and defecates. To guard against hepatitis, he says, he keeps paper in his pocket all the time. I ask to see it and he pulls out a large wad of toilet paper. "Both pockets I got some. Because, when I get ready to use it, if I got to go somewhere, I'm going right behind the truck over there. I'm not ashamed of my game, 'cause I ain't got no game."

"This is all going to be in the book," I remind him.

"I don't care what have to be in the book. You got to let people understand!"

Ron: "There Are Times When I <u>Had</u> to Pee in the Street"

Are people who work the streets routinely forbidden to use public washrooms? On a Friday in June, I was passing by Pizzeria Uno when I noticed Ron enter and dart toward the men's room in the back of the restaurant. I then went into the washroom myself, noting that Ron was in the only stall. I left and waited for him to come out. Two minutes later, when I hadn't seen him, I walked back inside and found him washing his hands with soap.

"Mudrick told me they won't let people working the street use this bathroom," I said to Ron.

"The other day the manager came out and said he don't want us over here no more because the bathroom was messed up and he believed it was one of us," Ron responded. "But I told him, 'We've always been able to use this bathroom. I've been here for ten years and I've always been welcome. As a matter of fact, the previous managers before used to give us food.' And he said, 'All right, forget about what I said.' So right now anyone can use it."

"But Mudrick says he's not allowed in any of these restaurants, including Uno's."

"He's probably never tried! I've never seen him trying to go in there. I don't think he could go in there with a beer. I never see Mudrick trying to go in there. He always use his cup." Ron then explained that he hasn't always used the Uno's bathroom, welcome or not.

. "I used to pee by the [Washington Court Condominium] building. Then I would have people come out of the building and say, 'Oh, that's disgusting.' So now I don't even like doing that. If I *have* to pee in public, I pee in the street."

"I can't believe that you would ever go against the building. You must have been drunk."

"No."

"Was it because you were angry with the people in there?"

"No. It was just some place to go and pee. [Laughs.] That's all. Not that I was drunk. I don't see anything wrong with peeing on the building."

"How come you don't see anything wrong with it?"

"It's just a *building*. It's not like it's the inside of an apartment or something. It's just a structure. It's only natural for someone to want to pee against *something* rather than pee in the open. When you use the toilet, you pee against the wall of the toilet. And even dogs, they go up and pee against the side of the building. If they have so much against humans' peeing against the building, they shouldn't let the dogs pee against the building. Dogs' pee are stronger than humans' pee. You understand? If they worried about the smell going up inside their apartment, they shouldn't let the dogs pee against there. . . . But anyway, I don't do it anymore. I try not to."

"Why?"

"People might be looking through the window and see you. Some people get pretty upset. They say, 'Hey, that's my building!' "

"Do you think they are justified to get upset?"

"If they want to. You can't tell people how to feel. So what I do is just try not to do it. I go between the cars now. And I try not to pee *on* people's car, either. If someone sees you pee on their car, they get pretty upset."

"Do you ever do it into a cup like Mudrick does?"

"I don't like that. Because the pee gets all over your hands."

"What are the circumstances under which you would *have* to pee in the street?"

"I am out here at three o'clock and most of the places are closed. The ones that are open are too far away. I'm not gonna walk four blocks and lose my table, so I might just go down to the street between the cars. [While you are gone from your table], anything can happen. Someone may steal your stuff, or you may lose a sale. You've been waiting all day to make a sale, and the second you are gone, someone walks up to buy the stuff.

"Sometimes you can't help but pee in the street. Because when a person is dirty or stinkin' he don't want to go to a bathroom with decent people in there. You just don't feel good about yourself. There are times when I *had* to pee in the street. My body and clothes was dirty and stinking and smelling of liquor from the night before. And my pores are sweating and dirty. I don't want to be going in no bathroom."

"So peeing in the street is a way of showing respect?"

"Right! Especially in the morning, people dress up in decent clothes getting ready to go to work. So I don't go into places like that. So I *have* to go in the street."

Even if both Mudrick and Ron say they are pressured to engage in nonconformist conduct, there is a difference in the means they have adopted to pee: Mudrick does it in a cup, whereas Ron used to go against the side of a condominium. Yet, even if Ron doesn't understand why people look down on such behavior ("You can't tell people how to feel"), he still adjusts his behavior in response to their views by going in between the cars. He seems to be quite concerned about the feelings of his fellow citizens; so concerned, in fact, that he refuses to enter restaurants when he believes his body odor will be offensive to paying customers who are well groomed and dressed for work.

The Newsstand Worker: "I Don't Feel No Good"

While Ron and I were talking, Raj, the Indian worker in the corner newsstand shack at Sixth and Waverly Place walked up and greeted us. He was dressed in his Italian silk slacks, ironed cotton shirt, and tennis shoes; he was well groomed and had the appearance of a man who had showered earlier in the day. Since he also worked on Sixth Avenue and had no bathroom inside his newsstand, I asked if he engages in similar behavior.

"Let me ask you a question: when you are in your newsstand and you have to urinate, where do you go?"

"I go over there," Raj said, pointing to Baluchi's, the Indian restaurant across the street, at Sixth and Washington Place. He says that, when he is in the newsstand by himself and can't get away, he "makes it" in a cup and puts it in a garbage can.

Unlike Ron, Raj spoke with embarrassment in his voice.

"How often do you do this?" I asked.

"Very few. Because I ashamed. I don't feel no good."

Addressing Raj, Ron said, "But you do it inside the booth. Nobody can see you. He's private. You understand?"

It seemed that for Ron the only reason to be embarrassed was at the thought of others' seeing him in the act of urinating. For Raj, however, the sense of shame seemed to be derived from his own belief that he was violating a societal standard, whether others saw him or not. The contrast may be meaningful. It is very likely that the need to look for sidewalk opportunities to urinate has eliminated any sense of shame that Ron might feel at having to "go" somewhere other than a bathroom: he is simply too accustomed to doing it this way. But he still feels embarrassed at having others see him. Since embarrassment is based on our own sense of the way others view us, it is a thoroughly social emotion, demonstrating embeddedness in society.

"Do you also use the bathroom over there?" I asked Raj, pointing to the Waverly Restaurant, directly across the street.

"Yes."

"Is that because you buy something?"

"No. I just say, 'I'm the newsstand,' and they say, 'No problem.' Over there and over there. [He points to the Waverly Restaurant and Baluchi's.] No problem. Over here and over there? Any time! They have a nice bathroom downstairs."

For Customers Only?

Mudrick and Ron have different claims with regard to whether it is necessary for them to do their bodily functions in public. Mudrick claims that he does so because he is unable to gain admission to local washrooms. Ron says that he sometimes urinates in the street because it is more respectful to do so in the street than to try to enter a restaurant when he is dirty or drunk.

It is certainly possible that Mudrick could be admitted to a restaurant but has had certain experiences that make him believe he cannot. It is possible that he has completely rejected the importance of using a toilet and is exaggerating when he says he cannot be admitted. It is also possible that the weight of his experiences makes it painful for him to try to use the washroom and risk rejection. The risk of rejection may be a higher cost than he wants to pay.

During my years on the block, I was sometimes presented with independent evidence that people working the street have trouble gaining access to public restrooms. We have already seen that Ron was told by the manager of Pizzeria Uno that men on the street could not use the washroom. He gained access only after pleading his case; other men might have been intimidated and walked away in similar circumstances. There were other examples as well. On one August day, for example, John Stewart walked over to Hakim's table and said: "These people in McDonald's have a bad attitude. I came in to use the bathroom and they locked the door. I've been going to McDonald's for twenty-five years. All the money I spent there!"

Hakim recently had a similar experience, and the two men decided to go into the McDonald's to protest, bringing the tape recorder with them.

"I would like to speak to the manager," said Hakim to an African-American man behind the counter.

"The manager will be back in an hour. What's it about?"

"A number of African-American men in this neighborhood who buy stuff in this restaurant have been systematically denied use of the bathroom. We work around here and we would like to speak to the manager to see if we can resolve it at this level."

"If anyone just walks in to use the bathroom, they've got to be a customer."

"What's happening is, people who are spending money in here are being denied the right to use the bathroom," said Hakim.

"As long as you are a paying customer, you can use the bathroom," interjected a black female worker.

"You talking about paying customer!" said John. "I've been coming to McDonald's twenty-five years."

ED.	8 AM	10:00 P
HUR.	8 AM	10:00 P
FRI.	8 AM	11:00 P
SAT.	8 AM	11:00 P
SUN.	8 AM	10:00 P

BATHROOMS
ARE FOR USE
OF TODAYS
CUSTOMERS
ONLY

THANK YOU FOR
NOT
SMOKING

"Not here," said the worker. " 'Cause this branch has only been here for less than a year."

"You see," said John, "you still got that mentality. How old are you?"

"Twenty-one."

"I was coming to McDonald's before you was born," he said.

With that, Hakim and John left the restaurant and went back out to Hakim's table.

"If this doesn't stop, we're gonna take a picket sign, stand in front of the restaurant, and start boycotting," said Hakim. "Until everybody else around here understands what's going on."

"I came in there yesterday and when I walked toward the back the manager said, 'Can I help you?' " said John. " 'Can you help me? Help me with what?' So I bought a cinnamon roll. Then I still couldn't use the bathroom!"

A black man of about fifty walked up to the table and joined the discussion: "Sometimes we have a tendency to go and shop and beg. But we shouldn't shop where we not respected. And a message should be sent to these plantation Negroes that McDonald's has in there."

"Yeah," said Hakim. "At McDonald's, once you get past frying and stuff, you ain't gonna see too many black folks."

The episode illustrated a few issues that I have seen come up again and again.

First, it appears that, even though John ultimately purchased a cinnamon roll, he was told that the bathroom was closed. This is not uncommon. I personally witnessed Ishmael being told that the bathroom was being cleaned and could not be used, even after he had made a purchase. Though I had not bought anything, I got the key and entered the bathroom myself without receiving any warning, only to discover that it was empty. Many people who work outside on Sixth Avenue seem to be hassled in similar ways, even when they have made a purchase. The stories are repeated constantly.

Second, the person on Sixth Avenue who needs a bathroom needs it now. He often has little or no money in his pocket at the time he needs it. He may be faced with the dilemma of trying to get by a manager without making a purchase, or urinating in the street.

Who Is a "Customer"?

Third, and crucially, it appears that John initially tried to use the bathroom without making a purchase. Indeed, many people who work and live out on the street believe that they are entitled to use the washroom of any establishment in which they normally spend money. Whether they have spent their money at the moment they need the washroom is irrelevant to them. When John said he has been coming to McDonald's for twenty-five years, he was actually giving voice to the common view on the street that this long-term relationship with McDonald's defines his rights as a customer.

Mudrick also has this view. "You go in and buy one thing—say, French fries—this week. Two weeks from then, you go back to use the bathroom and they tell you no. But you *still* a customer! If you buy something, you be a customer."

"Do you think you are a customer for life?"

"Once you go *in* there, you supposed to be a customer for regular. You spend that money there. You supposed to be a customer. They seen you there and you spent your money there and they know ya. They gotta know you. You gotta take a leak, but you can't use the bathroom."

"What do you have to do in order to be a customer?"

"That's what I'm trying to find out," Mudrick continues. "If you go to the restaurant, they ain't gonna let you use it, because they think you ain't a customer."

"If you tried to use the bathroom at the exact moment when you bought the coffee, would they let you use it?"

"I never tried it that way."

"How come?"

"If I buy an order of French fries now, and I go out to eat the French fries and my stomach turns like I want to go take a dump, they say you gotta be a regular customer. Hey, hey: I just bought an order of fries. What's the difference?"

A year after my conversation with Mudrick about these issues, we entered a restaurant on Sixth Avenue to have some Cokes. He walked to the back and asked to be buzzed into the bathroom. The waitress refused, saying something like, You never buy anything here. Reaching into his pocket, he pulled out a wad of dollar bills, and tried to stuff a few into her hand. Here's a nice tip for you, he said. But the bills fell to the ground and the waitress refused to pick them up. Don't disgrace me, Mudrick told her. The cook and I made eye contact as he buzzed open the door. Mudrick bent over, picked up the money, and then went in.

Where Else Can a Man Go?

If Ron believes he is too dirty or drunk to enter a restaurant without offending his fellow citizens, or if Mudrick believes he will not gain admission, what alternatives do they have?

Why don't these men go to the brick public men's room located in Washington Square Park, a few blocks away, as Mrs. Gross of Washington Court Condominium says they could? I have repeatedly asked Mudrick why he does not go there.

"It is too nasty," he tells me about the bathroom in Washington Square Park. "The toilet bowl has no seat on it. You have to sit on the little rim. And there's shit all round the rim. Now, who going to sit their ass where there is shit all round the fucking rim?"

Mudrick and I walk over to the park to take a look. It is 4:00 p.m. on a weekday in June. The floor is covered with brown water. The room has six toilets, with no partitions between them. There are no toilet seats, either. The stench of feces and urine is strong.

On the way out, we visit the manager of the park, K. C. Sahl. As we walk into his office, Mudrick says, "Turn on the fucking speaker," referring to my tape recorder. I turn it on.

We introduce ourselves and exchange handshakes with the manager. Then I ask him, "How come there's no seats on the toilets in there?"

" 'Cause they'd get ripped off the minute we put them down."

" 'Cause they *would* be ripped off, or because they *have* been ripped off?" I ask.

"They *have* been," Sahl says.

"So, basically, there's not gonna be any more toilet seats in there in the future?"

"No," the manager continues. "I think that's the kind of gravy, that's the kind of minutiae you'd be shooting for—is to be able to leave toilet seats on there, and then maybe even have walls for privacy."

Mudrick and I leave the manager's office. He is visibly enraged. "Washington fucking Square Park and they can't put toilet seats right here? They could fix it, but they don't want to fix it. They want to keep our ass out of there. I can't go in there and take a dump in there. I can hardly hold my breath to go in that motherfucker. If I had to take a dump right now, I'd go right behind that tree right there. It's air out here. You go in there, you ain't got no privacy. That thing suppose to have a partition."

Mudrick continues: "Everybody in there, when you pull your dick out, everybody be looking at your dick. Trying to see what you got. You take a shit in there and the motherfucker is looking at your ass. This is a fucking crazy city!"

A Solution: Provide Public Bathrooms

I have spoken to managers of McDonald's and the Waverly Restaurant. Both said that, if they welcome one person working the streets into the restaurant, they will soon be welcoming them all. If each person working the streets uses the bathroom a few times a day, there will be a steady parade of men walking through the restaurant, creating an atmosphere that will be unpleasant for customers. At McDonald's, the assistant manager explained that, every time the toilet gets dirty or floods, someone must be taken off the counter to clean it, leading to longer lines in what is, after all, supposed to be a fast-food joint. The very existence of the bathrooms is a source of great frustration for people working at both restaurants.

Whether a man comes to see the bathroom as *the* natural or best way to do his bodily functions is conditioned by access to the bathroom resource itself and the fear of having his table and belongings seized by the police when he leaves it. These conditions lead to a resocialization of the individual. Mudrick seems to see his behavior as a natural response to constraints that he seems to believe exist. The information he has is not universal in its application to others, as Ron suggests, but it likely accords with his experience.

The men working the street have been accustomed to living in this manner for a long time as they have gradually been differently socialized. Those who once lived in Pennsylvania Station, for example, became used to stripping in public in the washrooms and cleaning themselves at the public sinks. It seems that acceptance of one's place on the street entails a certain resignation, which makes such behavior more acceptable. Consider the difference in reactions between Ron and Raj, the newsstand worker.

The behavior these men engage in is indecent from the standpoint of mainstream society. But their actions can, of course, be compared with the behavior of wealthier, white men. I have witnessed apparently middle-class white men urinating on buildings in Greenwich Village on a busy Saturday night. I have also heard from Adam Winkler, a friend who plays golf at the Hillcrest Country Club in Beverly Hills, that it is not uncommon to see men urinate on the golf course, despite the restrooms scattered throughout the tract. In all socioeconomic classes, the male act of urinating in public seems to be common, though those who work the streets seem to have fewer options as to where to go.

As we have seen, Ron, possessed of a sense of embarrassment, stopped urinating on the condominium building and did not enter restaurants when he thought his body odor would be offensive. In this context, he may actually see the act of urinating in public as a way of respecting his fellow citizens when he is too drunk or dirty to be in the same bathroom with them.

The problem of public urination is not one that could easily be solved by better informal social control or "mentoring." It is in the nature of the kind of stigmatization we have here observed that some people on the sidewalk will always be excluded or feel excluded, whereas some others, in a slightly different condition, will create a solution for themselves. Hakim has access to the bathrooms. So does Jamaane. These men have developed relationships with restaurant owners who are willing to let them in. It is unlikely that anything Hakim could say to Ron and Mudrick would make them feel more comfortable going into a restroom. The difference is that Hakim and Jamaane take daily showers and look presentable, and do not use drugs or sleep outside. They also frequently make purchases where they use the restrooms.

Likewise, over the years Alice has not had any problem using bathrooms in the local restaurants, or at the parking facility, where she and some other vendors store their goods at night. When Store 24 (a convenience store) was being converted to Go Sushi, Alice developed a rapport with the owners of the new store. She began keeping an eye on their two parked cars, putting money in the meters from 11:00 a.m. to 7:00 p.m. with the unspoken *quid pro quo* that she could use their bathroom. Her five-year-old granddaughter, Marcisa, uses the bathroom in Go Sushi as she pleases, and Alice changes the diapers of Monisia, her two-year-old granddaughter, in that same bathroom.

In some ways, this is an area where a better system of control—a formal system—actually might supplement the sidewalk's informal folkways and mentoring. There is evidence that these problems may be caused partly by severe police policies. By disposing of vendors' belongings when they leave the blocks, police encourage people working the streets to use cups, Dumpsters, and the sides of buildings. There is a strong similarity between the vendors' problems and those of workers in companies that do not respect excretory rights. Indeed, many employers have conflicts with employees who wish to go to the bathroom on company time.[1]

In the end, however, there is clearly a problem with access to the bathroom resource itself, and this is the leading cause of the men's problem. The city's approach to solving such problems has been to lock up a person like Mudrick when he is seen urinating in public. But this has not solved the problem, because the men working the streets believe they have no choice. An alternative would be to provide self-cleaning public bathrooms of the kind that are currently on the streets of Paris and San Francisco.

On even this point, I feel some uncertainty. On a recent trip to Paris, I walked the streets with a French sociologist, Henri Peretz, looking for one of the maintenance trucks that perform upkeep for the city's self-cleaning public toilets. When we tracked one down, and I told the driver (through Henri) of my hope that one day the people of New York would have such resources, he complained that in Paris some unhoused people had taken up nightly residence in the bathrooms, using them as shelters. This suggests that even public bathrooms will not always be available for people to do their bodily functions. Every policy has its unintended consequences.

Furthermore, to provide such a toilet would, of course, enhance the viability of the neighborhood as a habitat, something many policy makers would not want to do. Nevertheless, the lack of such resources does not break the lifeline of the people on the streets. It merely leads them to engage in behavior that is unsanitary and appears indecent to those who are not aware of its social genesis.

Talking to Women

On a late-August day, as I was selling written matter with Mudrick, he kept trying to gain the attention of women who passed by on the street.[1]

"Hi, pretty. You look so nice. I don't see no ring on your finger. When you want to get married?"

"You *know* you see a ring on my finger," says a white woman, perhaps forty years old.

"Oh, listen, let me marry you!"

"Sorry!" she says, looking straight ahead.

"Jesus Christ! You gonna come back?"

She walks on.

"Lord have mercy! You gonna give me a heart attack if you don't come back!"

A white woman of about twenty-five walks by.

"I love you, baby."

She crosses her arms and quickens her pace, ignoring him.

"Marry me."

She is gone.

I tell Mudrick that she looks like a nice person.

"Nice in a fucking dream," he responds. "No women nice. All of them full of shit."

"You don't think she's really nice?"

"No. It's hard to meet a nice woman. There are very a few womens that are nice. Very a few."

Next, it's two white women, in their mid-twenties:

"Hi, girls, you-all look very nice today. You have some money? Buy some books."

A black woman in her twenties passes, ignoring him.

"Hey, pretty. Hey, pretty."

She just keeps walking.

" 'Scuse me. 'Scuse me. I know you hear me."

Then he addresses a white woman in her thirties.

"I'm watching you. You look nice, you know."

She ignores him, too. But Mudrick doesn't think so.

"She was looking dead at me, Mitch. You could see it. They be watching you. Most ladies, they be waiting for you to say something to them."

•

For a few of the people working the sidewalk, a defining feature of Sixth Avenue is the opportunity it provides to look at and talk to pedestrians. To some of the pedestrians, especially the women, this behavior is unsettling, particularly when men like Mudrick sometimes deliberately work to entangle them, detaining them through conversation.

All of the more than fifty apartment dwellers I have spoken to over five years (regardless of race, class, gender, or sexuality) have reported some difficult encounters with someone on the sidewalk. But of the interactions I watched every day between pedestrians and men working the street, only a small fraction were "difficult" by the criteria I will soon describe.

Most of the interactions between pedestrians and people working and/or living on the street show social solidarity, as illustrated in the conversations between vendors and their customers depicted earlier in the book. I found that, on these blocks, only three of the twenty-one "regulars" make efforts to entangle passersby. However, it may only take a small number of men who insist on getting the attention of strangers, and a small proportion of the total number of encounters on the street, to create an occasional "quality of life" problem in the minds of local residents.

I pay special attention to interactions between poor black men and upper-middle-class white women, because only interactions between these groups struck me as troubled when I heard them on the tapes. I end by speculating why this seems so. I also ask whether these interactions constitute any real threat to the passing women, and why it is that informal mechanisms of social control seem unable to regulate such behavior.

While my analysis here centers on behaviors that some passersby find objectionable, it cannot be overemphasized that at other times on the sidewalk (and at other times in their lives) each of these men would be seen acting in "positive" and straightforward ways toward others, including the women in their lives—girlfriends, mothers, and granddaughters as well as general passersby.

My purpose in this chapter is to show the process by which a few of these men are upsetting some of the passing women. By looking carefully at how these effects are produced, we can see an important dimension of what is so unsettling about these interactions. Scholarly and lay wisdom is that the tension felt by women when they receive suggestive comments from men stems from the content of what gets said.[2] Other scholarly and lay wisdom is that the tensions felt by whites in the presence of poor blacks occurs because many whites are not sufficiently "streetwise"—able to differentiate between different kinds of blacks, or skilled in the art of avoidance.[3] The conventional wisdom surely is very helpful, but there is more to see. On Sixth Avenue, I found there was an added layer of reasons that explained why some of the people feel a tension well out of proportion to any material or physical harm the interactions might involve.

Entanglements

For Jane Jacobs, the sidewalks gave people the chance to interact regularly, and informally. Her stress on the importance of "eyes upon the street" implies that, on a successful sidewalk, if something happens to you, others will come to your aid. The simple exchange of hellos with the butcher or locksmith or candlestick maker is of great importance because it gives you the sense that they'll pick you up if you fall down, and that nobody will assault you while they are watching. She believed that the knowledge that others are watching added up to "an almost unconscious assumption of general street support when the chips are down."[4] Because of the presumed good intentions affirmed by the experience of even minor interchanges, people felt safe and thus spent more time on the streets, making them safe. Jacobs saw the

problem of managing one's social life when there are many different people in one's environment. The ideal of urban life is to have superficial contact with all of these people whose eyes and ears bode security without getting *too* involved with them:

Sidewalks bring together people who do not know each other in an intimate, private social fashion and in most cases do not care to know each other in that fashion. . . . Cities are full of people with whom, from your viewpoint, or mine, or [that of] any other individual, a certain degree of contact is useful or enjoyable; but you do not want them in your hair. And they do not want you in their hair either.

A good street life consists in part of the freedom to walk along without getting entangled, and to feel safe while doing so.

Sidewalk life today is different from how it was when Jacobs was writing. In Jacobs's time, sidewalk life brought people into limited contact with other strangers substantially like themselves.[5] Because the strangers appear so different now, so do the problems—and specifically the problem of entanglements.

It is, of course, possible that sidewalk life is not so different now as Jacobs's account would suggest. For critics of her generation, including William H. Whyte—the author of *City*, a great study of urban public space—the sidewalk is equally unproblematic for everybody: men and women, blacks and whites. As long as eyes are on the streets, there is reason for everyone to be happy.[6] In recent years, however, a number of feminist geographers and sociologists have emphasized that public spaces are not neutral; rather, such spaces put women at a disadvantage, forcing them to endure threats of violence as well as verbal assaults from men.[7] One reason Jacobs's account did not refer to white men catcalling women may be that her times were not as sensitive to this issue as ours are; her account of sidewalk life is different not simply because the sidewalk was different but because the lens for viewing the sidewalk was different.

Nevertheless, at the time Jacobs was researching her great study of city life, a scene such as exists today on Sixth Avenue would not have been possible, mainly because of the differences in race and class that are represented here.

Unreciprocated Openings

Out on Sixth Avenue one day, I ask Mudrick to tell me a little about his relationship to women on the street. Since most women ignore him, he says, he talks to all of them. That way he might get to have conversations with some of them.

Three white women in their twenties approach, and I am given a demonstration of his method. "Hi, ladies. How you-all feeling, ladies? You-all look very nice, you know. Have a nice day."

I have seen Mudrick engage in such behavior over and over again, but there is no doubt in my mind that this demonstration has been for me, a way of responding to the question I had just asked.

"Let me ask you a question, Mudrick. When you do that, explain to me the pleasure you get out of it."

"I get a good kick out of it."

"Explain to me the kick you get out of it."

"It make me feel good and I try to make them happy, the things I say to them, you understand? The things I say, they can't accept. They gotta deal with it."

"What do you mean, 'They gotta to deal with it'?"

"They *have* to deal with it. I say sweet things to a woman. Make her feel good. Like, You look nice. You look very nice. I'd like to be with you someday if I can. Try to make you happy. Some womens treated so wrong they scared to talk to the right man. Men treat women *so* wrong. Women don't give a fuck about men. Now they go to women. They gets a woman to be their man. They turn into be a lesbian. Because they scared to mess with a man."

A woman walks by without acknowledging him, and Mudrick tells me that she must be a lesbian. He claims that the women he addresses never feel harassed, because he gives them respect, and he can tell from their smiles that they *like* the attention.

A white woman wearing sunglasses approaches with her friend.

"Hey, you, with the shades on. You look very nice."

"Thank you," she says.

"Your friend look nice, too."

"Thank you."

He tells me that the women never respond by turning away or looking angry.

"What's the worst things that women will do when you say that to them?"

"They can't do anything. Because, the words I say, they don't have any choice."

He says he doesn't care if a boyfriend gets mad: it should "make him feel good to have something nice-looking," just as it makes Mudrick feel good when she smiles at him. "Anybody look back at me and smile, I say, 'I'll get you when I catch you by yourself. I'm taking you to bed!' "

I ask Mudrick if he's ever yelled out like that to a woman and actually gotten a date.

Mudrick replies that he has gotten many telephone numbers out there, and that he's indifferent to what the women look like.

"Oh, come on."

"I'm serious. Hey, pretty," says Mudrick to a white woman in her thirties with blond hair. "Look at her smiling!"

"She smiled back at you," I say.

Next he addresses a white woman with a Walkman on. "Hey, pretty. You got your earphones on. That's all right! Some you can't play with. What goes around comes around."

Mudrick begins talking to a woman as she walks past the first of four tables, which belong to Marvin. She responds, which happens rarely (probably less than 10 percent of the time).

"Hi. How you doing?"

"You all right?" asks Mudrick. "You look very nice, you know. I like how you have your hair."

"Oh."

"You married?"

"Yeah."

"Huh?"

"Yeah."

"Where's the ring at?"

"I have it home."

"Ya have it home."

"Yeah."

"Can I get your name? My name is Mudrick. What's yours?"
The woman waves goodbye and walks away.

•

Although the things that Mudrick said are likely disagreeable to the passing women, we can see further why the conversation itself might have been a source of tension by looking at aspects of it which are not evident from the words themselves. Studies of troubled public interaction have tended to rely on subjects' post-event reports or reconstructions based on a combination of interviews and observation. But during the past couple of decades sociologists have made some important findings about the technical properties of conversation, which make it possible to go beyond impressionistic accounts and data culled from interviews. The specialty is called Conversation Analysis, or CA.[8]

Conversation Analysis looks at conversations in micro-detail—how they are ordered sequentially, and how participants organize them moment to moment in responding to one another's moves. CA scholars have developed a systematic way of making discoveries about how people manage to converse at all.[9] I thought the CA method could show something the other methods cannot: *how* the entanglements are produced, and certain other unseen aspects of *how* they become a source of tension for some pedestrians.

In the encounter depicted just above, all but one of the things Mudrick says is a question (six times) or a compliment (three times)—in effect, a request for conversation. CA shows that compliments and questions normally get responses. In contrast, the woman asks only one question (in response to the first compliment) and offers no compliments of her own. From Mudrick's standpoint, he got some talk, but under circumstances that many people would find demeaning. From the woman's standpoint, she made clear to the man that she did not want to talk, but her signals were ignored. To most people these cues are obvious when one does not reciprocate, by asking questions, offering compliments, or using other techniques to show a desire to carry on. But faced with cues that the woman does not wish to do so, Mudrick ignores them.

It is important to emphasize that these cues are based on elements of normal conversation that almost all people take for granted. For example, a formal indicator from within the talk itself that something is indeed "going wrong" is that the women so often do not respond to questions or compliments. Nor do they, as people do in ordinary talk, ask for a repeat of the question or for a clarification. They are not interested in responding. This is all striking from the viewpoint of CA, which shows that questions ordinarily induce some kind of answer, requests produce a declination or are granted, compliments are an engine for acknowledgments. These expected couplets are examples of what CA calls "adjacency pairs"; they recur again and again.[10] Generally, the withholding of the second part of such a pair is noticed, as evidenced in a participant's tendency to repeat his or her first part if the second does not follow. Not to respond at all is notably "disaffiliative." For men to keep asking, when knowing "perfectly well" they have been heard, is a kind of "disaffiliative escalation."[11]

We can use the techniques of CA to see further evidence of *how* disaffiliation occurs. In this case, not only the woman's responses but the timing of her responses show that she is reluctant to talk. Conversation Analysts have shown that, in ordinary conversation, not only do questions and compliments usually elicit responses, but those responses come *immediately*; even three-tenths of a second's delay is enough to signal a conversational problem to the interactant, as well as to the analyst (e.g., the compliment or question was not heard or was misunderstood).

By presenting the same conversation using the transcription form of Conversation Analysis, we can see the timing (as well as other features of interest to specialists).[12] Let us look at it again, this way (numbers in parentheses indicate the length of silences, in seconds; brackets indicate "turns" that overlap).

1 Mudrick: Hey pretty.

2   (0.8)

3 Woman: Hi how you doi [n.

4 Mudrick: [You all right?

5   (2.2)

6 Mudrick: You look very nice you know. I like how you

7   have your hair (pinned)

8   (0.8)

```
 9   ( )   (O(h()   (                    )   ((said   in   high-pitched
     voice))     ((tape recorder shakes))
10   Mudrick:   You married?
11   Woman:    Yeah.
12            (0.1 )
13   Mudrick:   Huh?
14            ( . )
15   Woman:    Yea[:h
16   Mudrick:        [(              ) where the rings at.
17            ( 0.5 )
18   Woman:    I have it ho: (me(
19   Mudrick:   (Y') have it home?
20   Woman:    Yeah.
21   Mudrick:   Can I get your name?
22            ( . )
23   Mudrick:   My name is Mudrick what's yours.
```

Notice that the woman delays her responses (when she responds at all) but Mudrick speaks immediately following her—evidence, as derived from textbook Conversation Analysis findings, of his desire to keep the conversation open and her desire to close it. Even asking a question in line 4 ("You all right?") gets Mudrick not an answer but a 2.2-second silence that he must end by taking still another turn.

After noting the woman's efforts to get away, including her answer to the question of whether she is married, Mudrick asks for her name. At this point, we can see that he has been given three different kinds of signal that the woman would like the discussion to go no further. First, she has answered yes to the question whether she is married. For the average person, this would be enough, but Mudrick asks where the ring is. It is notable that she owes him no answer to this question, but politely answers anyway: "I have it home." This shows her going the extra step of trying to close the conversation without "rudeness." But Mudrick won't accept this cue, either, and persists in asking for her name until she walks away. From the standpoint of normal etiquette, there is nothing rude in the woman's behavior as she leaves at this point. But Mudrick has forced the woman to be "technically rude":[13] walking away from a person while he was talking to her.

A second level of cues Mudrick received were embodied in the turn-taking itself. Beyond the woman's specific words and the asymmetry in the turns they took, Mudrick was also informed of her lack of interest by gaps and silences in inappropriate places, after questions and compliments. Ulti-mately, *he* comes across as rude, because he ignored a string of cues, layered on top of one another, that were supposed to serve him notice that the woman did not want to give him something as personal as her name. By ask-ing for the name after receiving so many prior notices, Mudrick paid no alle-giance to the background expectations with which conversation is normally organized.

In my interviews I consistently discovered that the sort of rudeness Mu-drick showed this woman—more discernible through CA than through anything "rude" that was said—makes some residents of the Village feel annoyance and even anguish. This was confirmed in my interview with Monica, a college professor who walked through the neighborhood with her baby in her arms.

"That's what cities are about," she says. "You want to be able to trust in the kindness of everyone around you. You want to be able to talk to them. . . . There is something that one does in New York as a woman: you can't ever look anyone in the eyes, you have to be really guarded, and it actually ends up being sort of rude. . . . I don't have the vocabulary to not be rude. And what ends up happening is that one has to be rude. And that's actually what's really upsetting about it."

With the experiences of an entire adult life in urban, mixed-race neigh-borhoods, Monica has a lot of it right, but she shares with her neighbors a ba-sic misunderstanding of the situation. She is wrong to think that her "vocabulary" is amiss. Neither the women nor the men lack anything in terms of word knowledge; they also know how to use verbal cues and time their responses. And many of them, like Monica, must be given credit for be-ing "streetwise," in the sense of knowing how to distinguish "between differ-ent kinds of blacks" and being skilled in "the art of avoidance." The problem manifests itself through tactical sabotage, as a few men use their tacit knowl-edge of conversational technology against those of higher status—a kind of interactional vandalism. But unlike assaults against property, interactional vandalism leaves victims unable to articulate easily what has happened. Having a benign encounter requires more than a vocabulary for saying no. It requires conversational partners who are willing to accept one another's cues, including gaps and silences, so they can avoid being "rude." This is what we depend upon in everyday life.

"How did you feel about her?" I asked Mudrick of the woman who had waved him away as he finally asked for her name. "Did you feel she rejected you just now?"

"Nah. Mitch, if I wanted to get a real woman, I could find her. When I'm getting ready to have sex, I know where to go. There's a lot of women I know I could talk to, you know? But I got my mind on my granddaughter, Dyneisha."

I believe that Mudrick was quite sincere about being more concerned with his granddaughter than with any of the women on the street. But that doesn't mean he is more concerned at any one moment with his granddaughter than he is with how some woman receives his performance.

Though Mudrick is in a lower social-class position, he uses his status as a man to create entanglements with women on a public sidewalk whereby he can achieve a limited measure of power. This is not the power one sees in the police's ability to confiscate a vendor's merchandise when he sets up outside the lines, or even the mayor's ability to win an election by making the "quality of life" part of his policy agenda. Mudrick's power is nevertheless palpable, because it enables him to influence a social encounter. In effect, he can use the privileged position men enjoy in the public sphere to influence what will happen on the street.

With every interaction, Mudrick reasserts his right to set the terms for an encounter that he initiates and maintains. He talks as if he has no doubt that this way of behaving is a good thing. If he treats women as objects of desire, they love it. He is bringing them pleasure with his words. The women who pass him by do not feel harassed. Look at their lips: all except the lesbians smile. If they don't like his repartee, they are not normal, because a normal person would like it.

The power he feels is indicated by his insistence that "they gotta deal with it." That much he knows for sure. Even their boyfriends can't do anything about it. It may not merely be a control over women in public space that enables him to feel his own masculine prowess. He also feels a sense of power and control in relation to other men, by his influence over their women. When these women look at him and smile, he knows what time it is! He'll get them when he gets ready.

This is mostly fantasy, and deep down he knows it is mostly fantasy.[14] Surely he's been working a game to impress me. But even the efforts to entangle, which occur independently of my presence (according to Hakim and women I have interviewed), are enough to give him a feeling of power as he sits at his table; he gets a response, if only a tense looking-away.

•

Though many women clearly are entangled, there is evidence that when Mudrick wants to he knows how to treat other women the way they want. In the following example it is a woman of his own race and class. Two years after my initial conversation with him, I was sitting on Sixth Avenue when I got a glimpse of him putting a black woman into a taxi.

"Who was that?" I asked him.

"She's about the most beautiful thing I ever see," he said.

"I didn't even see her," I said.

"She's short, weighs about 190 pounds, long hair, black, light-skinned. Some womens you gotta give a lot of respect. We've been dating for six months."

"Where did you meet her?"

"I met her on Sixth Avenue by the subway station. She was waiting for a friend. She takes care of an old man in Long Island. On Friday and Saturday night I take her up to Sixth Avenue and 41st Street, to the big park. And we relax there."

A few weeks later, I again saw Mudrick put his friend into a cab. I asked if she knew where he lived.

"She didn't know I was homeless. Now she found out, because I keep telling her, little bit by little bit. And she understand. At first she didn't understand. Now she understand what people have to go through."

"Do you curse in front of her?"

"No! No cussing! No drinking beer! No smoking cigarettes! I cannot do that with her. She's a beautiful person. That's the respect she want from me. Not in front of her."

"How do you treat her differently than you do women passing in the street?"

"When I'm talking to women in the street, I treat them beautiful, too. When I'm talking to a woman, some wants to talk to you and some say get the hell out of here. You just never could understand a woman. Never. But this one I think I know."

He explained that sometimes his friend stays with him in the storage room of the building where he gets paid to take out the trash. "She always comes there. Now I'm having a set of keys made."

"You've told me you sleep on the ground. When she comes over, what do you do?"

"I have a mattress for her. I sleep next to the mattress on the floor."

"What does she think of that?"

"She don't think too much of that! She said, 'Why don't you sleep on the mattress?' I said, 'Listen, if you sleep on the ground for fifteen years, on a piece of cardboard, it's hard to get back on the mattress. She look at me like I'm crazy. 'Get on the mattress, Mudrick.' I said, 'No. You sleep on the mattress. I'll sleep on the floor.' "

"What's her name?"

"Yvette."

Unreciprocated Closings: Keith and the Dog Walker

Keith Johnson, forty-two years old, is an unhoused alcoholic who panhandles next to a Korean deli and outside the ATM vestibule. Carrie, a thirty-four-year-old white woman, lives in a small apartment nearby and regularly walks her pug dog, Daisy, down Sixth Avenue.[15] A graduate of Smith College, she has lived in the Village seven years and works as a secretary to a venture capitalist. At the sight of Keith and me one Wednesday evening, she straightens her back and looks dead ahead. As she passes, Keith stops talking to me and calls the dog by name. Men working the street often know the names of neighborhood dogs (and toddlers) and routinely call out to them.

"Hold on, I gotta talk to my baby," says Keith. "Come here, Daisy."

"Hi, Daisy," I say. "This is Daisy, right?"

"Yes," says the woman.

"Miss," says Keith.

Pulling on the leash, the dog tugs her owner over to Keith, who begins playing with Daisy.

"Sit down," says Keith.

The dog sits as the woman stands by, looking distracted and pulling on the leash. As Keith pets the dog he says to me: "One o' my babies. No, no . . . pushy woman [in jest, looking down toward the dog], kiss me. Okay. Get off me, get off me. Oh, that's better. Look at 'er. She's a-laughin' or somethin'."

"How old is Daisy?" I ask the woman.

"Eight months," she responds.

Referring to another dog nearby, Keith asks her, "She see her boyfriend? She likes younger men."

"They ran into each other tonight for the first time."

"An' he's big as a ox," says Keith.

"She looks very happy," responds the woman.

"He's about five months old," says Keith.

"Six," corrects the woman.

"Six," says Keith. "He's like this much bigger than her owner. She's like, 'Ohh, what a man.' "

"She's a pioneer," says the woman. "She's out there."

"Always," says Keith.

"Yes," says the woman.

"Well, she can't make me no grandpa," says Keith. "That's my baby here."

"Come on, Daisy Dog. [Claps.] Hey! Come," the woman says.

"Drop the leash for a minute," Keith responds. "Walk away, I wanna see what happens."

"No, you know I can't. I'm not gonna drop my leash."

As is characteristic, Keith, not the woman, initiates the interaction. Also characteristic, he does so in the form of coming on to a female ("my baby . . . I love Daisy . . . pushy woman . . . where you goin?"). But in this case the female is a dog. Because Keith has a dog to talk to, he is spared the need to open with a compliment or a question. Rather, he can give an order: "Come here." Indeed, this gains Keith the dog's attention—her movement toward him—and hence a strengthened capacity to hold on to the woman. Because the dog—unlike its human owner—does not recognize class, race, or gender and is not in a rush to get to work, she comes to Keith in a way an even slightly streetwise or busy woman might not. As events unfold, Keith uses the dog to bring the woman into interaction as she follows the dog's lead. The woman has the dog by the leash; in gaining a kind of control over the dog, Keith, so to speak, has the woman by the leash.[16]

We have seen how women resist invitations to open conversations. Because the women generally succeed in avoiding being entangled in such talk, it is rare that any kind of "real" conversation takes place. But this stretch of talk involving Keith and Carrie is such an instance. As such, it allows us to focus on how the men may not respond to women's cues for closure of conversations once they are under way.

Something about my presence helps elicit "easy talk" from the woman. It might be my own race and class, or it might be the differences in the ways Keith and I talk to her. I ask a simple question, whereas he uses the language of a sexual come-on in addressing her dog. Here it is again, in CA transcription:

1   Keith: . . . . Hold on, I gotta talk to my baby
2   Come here, Daisy
                (1.0)
3   Mitch: Hi, Daisy. This is Daisy, right, =
     Woman: = Yes

Whereas there is a pause after Keith's turn (after line 2), the woman responds to me immediately (the "=" indicates there is no detectable silence between my question and her answer; it comes so fast that it is a virtual continuation of my "turn"). This immediacy, by Conversation Analysis findings, shows the woman's acceptance of my behavior and standing (or both) in contrast with Keith's.

Nevertheless, Keith's control over the dog introduces a level of parity into his interaction with the woman. In what follows, Keith talks to the dog, which is alternately in his arms, on his lap, or otherwise in his control. Keith does all the talking, either speaking to the dog or referring to the dog. In the 14.2 seconds that pass from line 1 to line 18, the woman offers not so much as an "umm" or any other kind of "speech particle" or "monitoring device" (in Conversation Analysis parlance) that people ordinarily use to indicate they are interested and paying attention.[17]

But Keith's control over the dog allows him as well to tolerate silences

(4, 11, 15, 18 in the following excerpt), relaxing his need to fill in with compliments and questions that otherwise might appear necessary to delay the woman's departure. Here is the Conversation Analysis version:

4		(0.8)
5	Keith:	Miss
6		(0.2)
7		((car alarm goes off))
8	Keith:	One o' my BABIES = NO (.) no.
9		(1.0)
10	Keith:	(pushy woman/ kiss me)
11		(0.5)
12	Keith:	Okay. Get off me (.) GET OFF me::
13		(2.2)
14	Keith:	Oh, that's better?
15		(3.0)
16		(Look at 'er)
17		(She's a-laughin') in 'er ( ) or somethin'
18		(3.0)

For my part, the woman's silences and the imposed constraints on her movement made me tense: I felt conversational conventions being ignored. Her last silence, at line 18, is especially long—long enough to signal a lack of interest in continuing the conversation[18] and leading to goodbyes. Such silences, in CA findings, make unmistakably clear that there is nothing more to say and hence prepare for the upcoming closing. The awkwardness of the moment (Keith is not saying goodbye and the woman is not able to) is the interpretation that I give, in retrospect, for coming to Keith's aid (line 19) by asking the woman a question of my own. Predictably, the woman again responds readily to me:

19	Mitch:	How old is Daisy?
20	Woman:	= Eight months.

The smoothness of this couplet (no silence between turns) again shows that the woman's unease has to do with Keith, not strangers in general. In terms

of the meanings established at the scene, my ability to again "help" Keith reinforces the contrast between me and Keith, to all concerned.

Much of the conversation that follows (lines 21 to 35) is a result of my interchange with the dog owner, which, along with Keith's hold over the dog, has given new life to the conversation. It is worth noting that, when the woman does finally volunteer a comment to Keith and so appears to "affiliate" with him, she does so to disagree with him: she contradicts his opinion that a second, nearby dog is Daisy's "boyfriend," asserting that the two dogs were only just then meeting (lines 22–24). Further, her disagreement comes even faster than immediately, actually overlapping Keith's turn.[19] Whereas people frequently overlap when agreeing with one another, Conversation Analysis teaches, they delay their response when it is going to be negative (by leaving silence or prefacing it with a softener like "well," "umm," or "gee"). The swiftness of the woman's reply tactically underscores her difference with him (in technical terms, a strongly "disaffiliative" move). Her only other comment to Keith (lines 29, 30), correcting his estimate of the dog's age, is again a kind of contradiction, and again it contains no cushioning delay. Here it is again in CA:

```
21      (1.0)
22   Keith:            Sh' see her boyfriend (0.1) She likes youn[ger men.
23   Woman:                                                     [They ran
24        into each other tonight for the first time
25   Keith:            An' he's big as a ox=
26   Woman:      =(She looks) very happy.
27   Keith:            He's big as a ox=
29   Keith:            He's about five months old
30   Woman:      Six
31   Keith:            ( . ) He's like this much bigger than her
                       (own/owner).
32   She's like, "Ohh, what a ma::n."
33   Woman:      She's ( . ) a pioneer. She's out there.
34   Keith:            Always
35   Woman:            Yes.
36   (3.0)
```

This last three-second silence (line 36) is reinforced by other cues the woman provided to show that she wanted to end the conversation: distracted facial gestures, continual jerks on the leash, and, although it is a subtle cue, her use of "yes" (line 35), which in this context is a "summary statement" that ordinarily prefaces a conversational end rather than, say, "yes, how interesting" or as the answer to a question that might invite further comment. Keith does not take the hint of the woman's silences, or of the gestures that accompany them. He does not let go of the dog or the conversation.

Rather, Keith introduces a new topic:

37	Keith:	Well, she can't make me no gran::pa.
38		(0.5)
39		That's my baby here.
40		(2.5)
41	[Daisy:]	yelping, whining sound.

Standing in silence, pulling on the leash, the dog owner fails to respond to any of Keith's statements; seconds pass and the dog begins to whine (line 41), which leads the woman to make still stronger moves for closure. She looks only at Daisy and yells at the dog (lines 42, 44, 46, 48) to come, while Keith continues, now silently, to maintain his hold:

42	Woman:	Come o::n.
43		(0.5)
44		Du::na Dog.
45		(0.2)
46		((clapping)) Hey!
47		(0.5)
48		Come
49		(0.5)

The woman's agitation, coupled with the dog's movement toward her, seems to encourage Keith to act boldly: he makes a substantive demand. The woman shows, in an uncharacteristically direct way, that she will not abide:

50 Keith: Drop the leash for a minute walk away I wanna see what
51   happ[ens
52 Woman: [No, you know I can't. I'm not gonna drop my leash.

Again, the woman's denial comes as an overlap, with none of the prefatory buffers that allow a person to withdraw or reformulate his request before it is turned down (for example, by saying, "Maybe some other time, where its safer"). Her "no" (line 52) is harsh and, because of its timing, likely to be considered rude. She does soften her technical rudeness by following up with the substantive "you know I can't."

The woman desists from telling Keith to let go of the dog, it seems, because this would risk prolonging the conversation by initiating a set of turns. Keith tries to hold on, asking a stream of questions that "should" result in answers. But the woman, once she gains control of her dog, need no longer bother:

53   Keith: Where you goin'.
54   (1.0)
55   Where you goin.
56   (2.5)
57   Now wait 'till I get (.) you can't wiggle down like a
58   snake. You gotta wait 'till I get ready. See ya later
59   baby.

The woman walks off without so much as a simple "goodbye" or "see ya."

.

Having summarized the research finding about entanglements that I feel the most confident in reporting, I would like to end by speculating about the puzzle to which I referred at the beginning. Why is it that I only have examples of upper-middle-class white women getting waylaid in these encounters that are deeply problematic from the standpoint of Conversation Analysis.

Consider the ways in which both gender and race might be decisive on these blocks, possibly leading troubled encounters to occur with more regularity between certain categories of people.

It is well known that streets and sidewalks are places where women are disadvantaged by public harassment. While the things we are witnessing are a case of the larger public harassments that occur between some people working the street and pedestrians of both genders, perhaps for women it is a problem in distinct ways. Keith is attempting to control the woman *as a woman*, knowing that even privileged women occupy vulnerable positions in public space. Like most males (black and white), he has been taught that to be a male is to possess this power, and he feels entitled to control her. I asked after his awareness of the dog's owner as a woman.

"So, you know the dog's name," I said after they left.

"Yeah."

"Do you know the woman's name?"

"No. I'd rather have the dog than her. You know why? Dog don't want nothing but a little attention. Give him some food. Take the fucker out for a walk. Let him watch TV with you, and it's cool. But she wants room and board, clothing, makeup, hairdos, fabulous dinners, and rent, plus they want a salary for giving you some pussy once in a while."

Keith's comments are a recognition of the limits of his own control. Yes, he is a man and as such he can try to control a woman, any woman. But he also thinks that since some of the domination is based on money, he could never take the control he exercises on the street into a relationship. His resentment is couched in terms of his inability to do things for her that are expected of a man.

It is true that men, too, are often waylaid on the street, and the same lack of respect for the practical ethics of conversational closings exists in male-male encounters. But the nature of those violations is different. The sense of an entitlement to control another man is notably absent. Although I have seen many breaches of conversational ethics, in five years on the block I have never seen Keith or any other panhandler try to control a man with a comment akin to telling a dog walker to drop the animal's leash.

Although I did not do a comparative study, let me cite one single stretch of interactions, to give a comparative example which I think illustrates the difference:

A blond woman of about thirty-five walks past the table.

Hello, gorgeous, Keith says loudly.

Hello, she says as she crosses her arms and ignores him.

A white man in a suit walks by in the opposite direction.

Help the homeless help themselves, he calls out.

The man looks in his direction.

What's up? Keith asks.

The man hesitates but keeps walking.

Help! he calls out as he shakes his cup.

The man walks on.

The words are broken only by the rhythmic shaking of his cup. Help!

A forty-something black woman passes.

Help! Help! Throw something in my cup.

She ignores him.

A phone number or something!

Two black men in their thirties pass by.

Help the homeless, Keith calls out.

You got a habit? one of them calls back.

Yeah, I got a habit, Keith yells. It's called eating.

None of these situations produced an entanglement, but there is a difference in the way Keith tried to waylay men and women. Only in the case of the women did he offer compliments or say things which they might interpret as intimate or coming-on. In the case of interactions with the men, his requests were far more simple. When a white man looked in his direction after the initial pleas for help, Keith said to him, "What's up." We have seen in the case of both Mudrick and Keith that a large number of the things they say to women are either compliments or statements that try to achieve intimacy. How, then, might gender work to systematically create more entanglements for women than for men? First, through the sense of entitlement that these men feel in entangling women—an entitlement one does not observe in their interaction with men. And, second, gender works through the form that conversation takes. With both men and women, they refuse to take no for an answer, engaging in basic conversational breaches. But with the women there is an added layer—a series of compliments and assertions of intimacy which are particularly difficult to ignore without feeling rude.

But why *white* women, and particularly the upper-middle-class white women of this neighborhood? Here, again, we remain on speculative territory. My discussions with over twenty women of different races in the Village, as well as my own personal experience, lead me to think about the nature of the anguish these residents feel in being forced into rudeness. At times, *I* have felt a special anguish in erecting boundaries between myself and men that I am aware of as poor blacks. I would not be surprised if for many of these residents their anguish is also exacerbated by their sense of themselves as people who have chosen to live in the city so that they can have contact with a heterogeneous population. My interview with the dog walker supports this interpretation of her experience. I gave her a stenographic transcript of the materials quoted above as well as my own interpretation of them (largely intact in this version):

"I think what you said about our white liberal guilt is true . . . I was thinking about the fear in my voice and I think you are right about people having a hard time saying no, that you're not supposed to say no."

The detailed analysis of the cues, using the transcription conventions of Conversation Analysis, provides evidence of how this particular woman was forced into "rudeness." The transcript may put into perspective her concession about what she called "white liberal guilt." Perhaps the residents of the Village are erecting boundaries not only *because* the men are poor and black (which is often the case) but also *despite this.* Maybe that is why they must literally be forced into "rudeness." In general, people don't want to deprive others of common courtesies. And it is possible that many of the whites of Greenwich Village—most of whom would classify themselves as liberals— have a double dose of angst. Few human beings like to say flat-out no, and Conversation Analysts show how we avoid doing so. (Mudrick won't even take no for an answer, much less 2.5 seconds of silence as a cue.) My interviews suggest that the liberal white residents of the Village may feel especially uncomfortable being rude to people who are poor or black. The desire to avoid rudeness may be compounded by the surface morality of wanting to be nice to those at the bottom of the racial and class structure.

This leads me to wonder: Could it be that black women passing by tend not to feel this double dose of angst? That in sharing a common history with these men, they feel no guilt for the circumstance in which the black men now find themselves?

•

Here on Sixth Avenue we have two groups of victims confronting each other. Whether they like it or not, many of the white women are very much implicated in the history and politics that have engineered this poverty, and even in the politics that would chase it away. Whether he admits it or not, Mudrick is using the system of gender inequality to harass passing women who do not like what he does.

Sixth Avenue sometimes takes on a character more like the edge of the proverbial construction site than anything approaching Jane Jacobs's idealized sidewalk. A few poor and unhoused men behave like some workingmen—black and white—who engage in sexually suggestive banter.[20] Sometimes, the men exploit gender inequality to achieve a sort of power, making unreciprocated conversational openings and refusing to accept signals to close.

Much more is going on than the breaking of conventional rules of etiquette or even the expression of outright vulgarity. Through the pacing and timing of their utterances, the men offer evidence that they do not respond to cues that orderly interaction requires. The men deprive the women of something crucial, not just to them but to anyone—the ability to assume in others the practices behind the social bond.

For the residents of the Village, "eyes upon the street" do not necessarily make the street welcoming and comfortable. Sometimes, eyes have the opposite effect. For Jacobs, "eyes upon the street" implied an "almost unconscious sense of street support when the chips are down." But it is hard for the residents of the Village to assume that people will provide support when the chips are down when those people will not cooperate in something as basic as acknowledging basic social cues to end a conversation. The lack of such cooperation gives notice that every other encounter, especially when the chips are down and more is needed, may well be difficult. So-called small talk is a kind of proving ground for benign intention.

Jacobs celebrated the restraints that play out in urban life and enable people to function without others "in their hair." These restraints ultimately depend on the mutual observance of the routine grounds of interaction discovered by the Conversation Analysts. The balance between privacy and interaction is no longer as casual in the West Village as Jacobs suggests it was. Between some poor black men and upper-middle-class white women, at least, the norms of interaction that are the basis of Jacobs's restraints cannot be taken for granted.

When people separated by such a gulf can assume in others the practices behind the social bond, less tension is bound to be felt, even where there are irrational patterns of prejudice or stereotyping. Likewise, when strangers who are not separated by large social gaps find one party betraying the system of "practical ethics" that underlies conversation, they are more likely to experience the stranger as weird than as threatening. We might speculate that the layering of race-class-gender differences on top of micro-level conversational trouble leads to a tension well out of proportion to any material or physical harm the interactions themselves might involve.

In the year after the exchange described above took place, a medical condition made it very difficult for Keith to walk, and he began doing his panhandling from a wheelchair. According to his medical records (which I obtained after he signed a release), the condition began when Keith drank a half-pint of vodka and did not perceive that he was getting frostbite. Over time, he got gangrene, leg ulcers, and cellulitis. The condition was treated with antibiotics, but he was released back to the street, where it worsened in the bitter cold. In the end he lost most feeling in his ankles and toes and was soon unable to move about on his own. When the police arrest Keith for being too close to the automated-teller-machine vestibule, he often stands up from the wheelchair to prepare for being taken away in the squad car; I've seen some passersby sneer, in the apparent belief that the wheelchair is nothing more than a prop.

Perhaps because Keith is now in a wheelchair, in the year after the exchange I transcribed, Carrie, the dog walker, became more at ease in his presence, choosing sometimes to talk with him and sometimes to ignore him: "I have been rude to him and I'll be rude to him in the future," she told me, in a tone resigned to the awfulness of the situation. My interviews with local residents suggest that many others become similarly resigned. This helps to explain the body language when they pass certain panhandlers and magazine vendors, noted so often in random photographs from the street.

·

The informal social control vendors exert among themselves is usually unable to regulate the kind of behavior detailed in this chapter. The existence of self-regulation is somewhat apparent in the fact that most of the men on Sixth Avenue do not engage in such behavior. And those who do behave in this way are challenged by vendors like Jamaane and Marvin, who shout out requests to desist. In these instances, they tell the entangler that he is stopping them from making money, that he is giving everyone a bad name with his bad behavior. Sometimes the men listen. If Marvin or Jamaane yells loud enough, sometimes the entangler will go away. But often the behavior persists despite the entreaties to stop. Jamaane, in response, left the area to find a vending space on the corner of Houston and Broadway, where he can be alone.

And behavior of this kind occurs away from the others who would be on the lookout and would point out how "dumb" it is. Hakim and Marvin and Ishmael have told me that this behavior is very bad for those who must live with it every day. It comes as no news to them that the attack on conventions of talk is a form of interactional vandalism (vandalism against propriety), perhaps as unsettling to some passersby as vandalism against property.

Once again, we are confronted with behavior that is indecent from the standpoint of mainstream society but which has its counterparts within the conventions of middle- and working-class white America. Not only the workers on construction sites in towns and cities across America are similar to these men, but also the telemarketers who call and ask us to change our long-distance carrier, practiced as they are at mobilizing people's dependence on conventional cues to keep them on the phone. What makes the breaches on the street especially unsettling is that they are layered on top of race-class-gender differences, which have their own accompanying tensions. Furthermore, it is more difficult to walk away from a face-to-face encounter (which feels more threatening anyway) than to hang up a telephone.

We know that social problems outside the talk permeate problems of the talk. We have seen in previous chapters that many of these men are on the street in the first place because of an interaction between their lives and broader structural conditions. But here we can see that the street encounters are themselves not irrelevant in shaping attitudes and politics that then—in the form of laws on welfare, policing, drugs, and public health—come back to influence, in turn, the life of the street. "I'm getting more conservative as I get older," Carrie told me. "And it's not taxes. I don't mind paying taxes. I guess I don't mind some of the street cleaning-up around here. . . . [And I] *hate* my reaction."

The situation in the Village can be clearly seen. For the men who sell written matter and panhandle, almost all of the women are so beyond the reach of friendship, romance, or even common sociability that the men treat them as objects upon whom interaction tricks can casually be put into play. In turn, this behavior and the predicaments to which it leads increase the men's exoticism, reinforcing their identities as dangerous objects to be avoided. For the women, the men's "eyes upon the street" do not bring about a sense of security among strangers but a feeling of deep distrust. So some Villagers avoid sincere relations with the men, for fear that sincerity will be exploited. In avoiding the street men's gaze, walking past them as though they were not there, they further reinforce the men's view of them as beyond human empathy and, in their coldness and lack of respect, appropriate as interactional toys. For the women, the men's behavior and the predicaments to which it leads further reinforce their view of these men—and others who appear to be like them—as dangerous. Anxiety transfers to innocent panhandlers, book vendors, and, to some degree, perhaps, black men in general. Stereotypes are given their life.

Accusations: Caveat Vendor?

One afternoon the owner of a local bookstore, Jill Dunbar, her face flushed with anger, marched up to Hakim's business partner, Alice. Accompanied by a younger woman, Jill grabbed several copies of *Push,* a novel by the performance artist Sapphire.

"Hold on!" Alice yelled. "What are you doing?"

"These come from my store," Jill said. "The author signed them, and the signatures in the books all have the date she was in my store. They were stolen from me today—just now—and now they're on your table."

"They're my books," Alice said. "You can't just pick them up off my table."

The argument grew louder as Alice, accusing Jill of trying to harass her, insisted that Jill call the police. Hakim left his customer at an adjacent table and joined the two women.

"I'm not accusing you of coming in and stealing my books," Jill said to her. "I'm just saying that someone stole from me. They fenced to you."

When a police officer arrived, he appeared unconvinced by Hakim's explanation that authors sometimes came to their table to sign books. He told them they had to give the books back or they'd get locked up for possessing stolen property.

"You let them take the books," Alice said to Hakim as Jill walked away.

"What do you want me to do, Alice?" Hakim said. "I'm not about to get arrested over four books. When a white woman comes here and says something is hers, it's hers. It's as simple as that. There's nothing I can do here. I'm not going to get locked up over four books."

I'd known Hakim and Alice for nearly four years when I saw this incident, and I was disturbed by Jill Dunbar's accusations. I went to see her at her little store on West Tenth Street called Three Lives & Co. "I've lost a lot of colleagues lately among small bookstores, and it troubles me," she told me. She had founded Three Lives in 1978 with two friends and was concerned about its future. "The vendors who are set up with new books definitely affect our business. Some of them are stealing books, so I get hit by losing merchandise. And they sell books for less than I can buy them for wholesale, so that hurts a second way."

At Coliseum Books, in midtown, and the St. Marks Bookshop, in the East Village, the owners say they feel threatened by the sidewalk booksellers. Terry McCoy and Robert Contant, at St. Marks, told me that they stamped all their display copies. "When something is missing," Contant said, "we have to go out and look at what's on the tables. We sometimes find the book with our stamp on it. Some of the vendors give the book back to us, because they don't want to have trouble with the police. Some of the vendors won't. We can have guys arrested, but nothing ever comes of the court cases, because the vendors never show up for their appearances. Their goods are confiscated. Our merchandise winds up in some police lockup for six months. By that time, it is shopworn and devalued."

The store owners don't believe that sidewalk vendors are always directly responsible for the thefts from their stores. Yet, Jill told me, if there is a thriving population of thieves, there must also be someone who will buy and sell the stolen goods. In other words, there must be a fence. "If there weren't a fence, then it wouldn't happen. It adds an extra dimension of vigilance—something that I did not go into bookselling for. I'm a seller of ideas. Not a policeman."

During the following months, I took more careful notice of where Hakim's and Alice's books came from. I saw that around twenty percent of them came from people in the neighborhood who would drop off their used books, often bought and read during that publishing season. Another twenty percent (especially the "black books") came from a distributor in Brooklyn called A & B Books. And another main twenty percent—mostly used—came from scavengers.

The remainder of their books—up to forty percent—came from people who approached them at their tables with one, two, or a few copies of new

books. Anyone who brings a box of assorted books from the same publisher, Hakim said, is generally an employee of that house. Many publishers give their employees free books, and the sale of these is one of the gray areas of American publishing, rarely discussed in employee manuals. (There are also many cases in which publishing employees gain access to books they were not given.) One regular supplier often sells books from Penguin, for example, and once I watched as a woman sold Alice twenty books published by St. Martin's Press for two dollars a copy. There are also editors and editorial assistants at magazines and literary journals, both large and small, and freelance book reviewers who sell review copies sent to them by publishers.

"There's large numbers of people in the publishing industry who are grotesquely underpaid," Hakim once said. "And this is not just the underlings. It's the editorial people, too. A lot of these people see these books as a way of supplementing their income. Sometimes it means lunch for a day, or carfare."

As I watched Hakim buy books and listened to his conversations with the sellers, it became apparent to me that most of his sources were both easily identifiable and relatively legitimate. While brand-new books, perhaps stolen, were sometimes dropped off by scavengers, this was rare. But there are many professional fences on the sidewalk, consisting in large part of those who specialize in current best-sellers. These vendors, who set up in certain prominent sites throughout the city, sell brand-new books at prices that are well below those of the chains. Once a man whom I'll call Steve asked Hakim whether he'd thought about his earlier offer—that he would supply Hakim with best-sellers to sell from his table, and they would split the profits. Hakim asked how many titles the man would want him to sell.

"What we do is we play it by ear," Steve said. "We'll go a little bit at a time. I'm getting a shipment tomorrow. So, hopefully, there's some really good, brand-new stuff. I'd give you ten, twelve, fifteen titles. Twos of each. And we keep in touch on a daily basis. If you sell them out—bingo." He added, "The last Tom Clancy, I got five hundred copies before Barnes & Noble got it."

"Now this Tom Clancy thing," Hakim said. "The fact that you had them even before?"

"Actually," Steve said, "it was a guy in Brooklyn who gave them to me. Two days after I put them out, he called and said, 'Listen, don't put those

Clancys out yet, because they're not due to be released for another two weeks.' I had already sold all of them. I haven't had any problems. I do things aboveboard."

Over the next few weeks I waited to see whether any of Steve's books would turn up on Hakim's table. And Hakim, meanwhile, continued to complain about the bookstore owners who, he said, were trying to demonize him. He felt that Jill Dunbar was making him a scapegoat for an economic atmosphere that had been created by the chains, and not by the street vendors. He also repeated his claims that both bookstores and newsstands sold stolen goods.

"You and everyone else hold me up for special inspection because I'm a little guy working on the street," he once said. "In some cases, because I am a black male working in public view. What you need to understand is that the sale of written matter is always a corrupt enterprise. Yes, sometimes the books I receive are stolen. Most of the books I sell are not. But the biggest bookstores and newsstands in this neighborhood, including the chains, are receiving stolen material. And then when a little guy like me tries to enter the marketplace everyone points the finger at him. But this is how all the big fellas got started."

Hakim's attitude reminded me of the techniques delinquents often use to justify their behavior to themselves and others: denying their own responsibility, denying that they are injuring others, claiming that the injuries they caused are justified under the circumstances, or condemning the condemners. These ways of justifying deviant behavior are known to sociologists as "techniques of neutralization."[1] They are ways that society's behavior is turned back or "neutralized." The effect is to allow the deviant to engage in his acts while remaining committed to the dominant value system of the society.

Yet there was something more to the conflict between Hakim's remarks and my interpretations of them—a sense that Hakim never saw his behavior as deviant in the first place. This is what the sociologist Dianne Vaughan, in *The Challenger Launch Decision,* calls "the normalization of deviance." In studying the culture and structure of the dynamics of decisions that led to the space shuttle's explosion, Vaughan shows the importance of looking at the culture and processes that "allow organization members honestly to view their actions as normal, rather than as deviant."[2]

I noted that Hakim's tendency to "normalize" his own actions by turning the accusations back on the bookstores had a sympathetic audience at his table. In this sense, some of his customers were insiders in ways I wasn't, especially in their belief that the only difference between a store and a peddler selling stolen books is that the store has the cloak of official or corporate legitimacy (which, in the words of one man, "everyone knows is corrupt anyway"). I noted that, when Hakim tells this to his customers, generally a substantial number of them nod their heads in agreement.

.

I ignored Hakim's accusatory questions initially, but as I started to look into them I was surprised by how many people involved in the publishing industry acknowledged that theft was part of the business. A major newspaper distributor in New York, who, like most of the people I spoke to, wished to remain anonymous, told me that it was hard to ignore swag, meaning stolen goods. "Drivers pull up and say, 'I have two extra bundles. Do you want to buy them?' " A newsstand owner will buy the papers from the driver for half the cover price, when he would pay the wholesaler eighty percent. "Back in the early days," the distributor said, "I probably bought them."

The _Daily News_ has been hard hit by such practices. In 1992, the District Attorney tried unsuccessfully to indict a number of leading newspaper executives and distributors. As part of the investigation underlying the case, a brief had been filed in the Supreme Court of the State of New York. It consisted of testimony submitted by a sergeant assigned as a senior investigator in the Special Investigations Unit (SIU) of the Bureau of Criminal Investigations of the New York State Police.

Among the claims made in the investigator's report was that "over 20,000 papers are printed each night at the _Daily News_ plant in Brooklyn that cannot be accounted for. The papers simply disappear. In fact . . . the theft is so large and so regular that the _News_ has been forced to create an accounting line for the missing papers so that their statements balance."

The investigator reported that the missing papers "disappear" after they reach the drivers. "Specifically, there is a gap each night between the number of papers counted at the bundler . . . and the number of papers on the computerized manifest."

In a later section of the report, the investigator explains that this scheme involves making deliveries to certain places by "hiding deliveries to them on the *News* manifest." The investigator had spoken to "an employee of the *Daily News* about the falsification of business records. The employee ha(d) seen the falsified manifests. Both from his own knowledge of where retail shops do and do not exist, and from conversations with other drivers and employees of the *Daily News*," the employee knew those manifests contained false entries.

I asked a retired newspaper-circulation director why a paper like the *News* didn't just cut off the newsstands that it suspected were buying stolen copies. "That's the stupidist thing in the world to do," he said. If you cut the guy off, then he takes all stolen papers. Then you're not his partner anymore. So I used to tell my guys, "Don't cut 'em off. Keep them supplied."

I also spoke to a woman who had been working for the same book distributor for several decades. Distributors, who stock books from various booksellers in central warehouses and act as middlemen between publishers and bookstores, are thought to be particularly vulnerable to theft. She told me that there is a multitude of sources for the books that someone like Steve is selling on the street: they come from wholesalers' warehouses, from leaks at binderies where workers secretly bind up extra copies of books, from delivery drivers, and from returns from bookshops which are sent back to warehouses but are then often left there by large publishers, who don't put them back into the inventory. "There are always people who are feeding these out," she said. Then I asked her whether street vendors were the only people selling stolen books.

"No," she said. "Everybody has an angle, because the margins in the book business are not that great. And there are bookstore owners who will protest, and say, 'Oh, this is so terrible,' while they are buying these stolen books, too."

Even the most famous bookstore in the city, the Strand, has been accused of buying and selling stolen books. A family-run business, now in its third generation, the Strand is a book lover's paradise—especially for people looking for books they can't find elsewhere at low prices.

In May 1983, a month after Farrar, Straus and Giroux, a New York publisher (and, as it happens, the publisher of this book), discovered that the Strand was selling copies of their books at half the cover price, the publishers filed an action against the Strand for $3,019.14, to cover the value of two hundred and forty-five copies of thirteen different titles which they claimed had been stolen from their Brooklyn warehouse and sold to the Strand. One possibility was that the Strand, well known for buying and selling review copies, was doing just that. "The clearest case," Roger Straus said, answering this scenario in his deposition, involved *Aunt Julia and the Scriptwriter,* by Mario Vargas Llosa. "All the copies that were sent to reviewers," he continued, "came from the first printing of the work. But the book (which was highly praised by critics) went through four later printings. The books found at the Strand came from the fifth printing, which had not been sent out for review."

At his deposition, Fred Bass, the Strand's owner, testified that he obtained his copies from George Foss, the owner of another bookstore, the Abbey, situated around the corner. Foss, in turn, testified that a man named Danny, who visited his store several times over a two- or three-month period, had sold him many of the books. Foss paid Danny about ten percent of the cover price (generally between two and three dollars), and then sold them to the Strand for "five or six dollars apiece." The trail stops at Danny: neither Foss nor Bass explains who he is or how he obtained the books.

The case did not go to trial. Bass claims that Roger Straus never had a case. "He probably accomplished what he wanted to," Bass told me. "He got negative publicity for the Strand." Jill Dunbar, however, also seemed vexed by the Strand, believing that they acted as a fence, buying books that they knew were stolen. "I've alerted them when my books are missing," she told me. "And they've said, 'Hey, your stack is here.' And I had to buy them back." Bass, for his part, claimed that he was simply extending a courtesy to the trade. "I will buy the book and offer to return it," he said. "The bookstore generally compensates us for what we pay for it."

Bass was the only store owner I spoke to who seemed to accept the theft of books from his own store with some degree of equanimity. He also offered an alternative view of the vendors. "They don't affect us one way or another," he said. "They're scavengers. They're recycling stuff. The amount and effect that they have on our business is minor. Some of them are selling fairly low-end stuff. Then, there are the street vendors that are selling new books and discounted books. That doesn't seem to affect us one way or another. My customers don't come in and say, 'Hey, I saw that book cheaper on the street.' And it's not mainly street vendors we catch stealing. It's good customers we catch stealing—people who come in here and spend a lot of money and steal books at the same time."

The investigation I had undertaken in response to Hakim's questions had been more educational for me than for him, though even he seemed quite interested in the details about the *Daily News*. Although none of the evidence I had come across is conclusive in any particular case, it all adds up to a suggestive picture of crookedness in the sale of written matter in New York City.

This has been going on for a long time, possibly longer than any of the people interviewed in this chapter have been in the business. Even the owner of one of the largest news delivery companies in the country claims to have received swag in the 1950s, when his family controlled only one paper route. It appears that many people involved in the business know about it, and many people are benefiting. This does not mean that everyone benefits. Jill, for instance, might get hurt the most, and the *Daily News* may put up with it so that they won't have trouble with their drivers and so that, as the newspaper distributor I spoke to pointed out, on some level they will remain partners with the newsstands who are cheating them.

How does all this bear on the question of whether Hakim is selling stolen books and in so doing engaging in deviant behavior? It tells us that this is how parts of the economy in written matter work. People in various aspects of the business generally understand this, and they also make accusations periodically to keep one another in line. But the people in the business are not using rationalizations or "techniques of neutralization" —because the culture to which they belong shapes a perspective from which they don't see such behavior as deviant in the first place. In Vaughan's phrase in the *Challenger* study, the sale of stolen written matter has occurred through "the normalization of deviance."

When deviance has been "normalized," members of the culture must still find ways of setting limits on *how much* of such behavior will be considered normal. The incidents reported here suggest that one way participants in a business or subculture enforce limits is by making accusations. One condition in which accusations get made is when someone has become too greedy: when the Strand suddenly has so many of FSG's books for sale that someone notices and tells Roger Straus; when the *Daily News* begins losing so many papers that an accounting line must be created for them; or when Jill loses a stack of books of particular value because they were signed by the author. The norm of the industry is that theft is okay but it can go only so far. The norm gets highlighted by making noise every once in a while.

It is noteworthy that none of these cases about books or newspapers moved forward to any conclusion. Although Jill told Hakim and Alice, "I can't take it anymore," she did not try to have Alice arrested for possessing stolen property, which she could have done. She merely served notice.

If such behavior is a "normal" way of doing business, who is vulnerable to being accused? On the face of it, Hakim and others who sell written matter on the street seem to be more vulnerable to accusation, with people of color being the most vulnerable to fitting the delinquent stereotype.[3] But people at other levels of the system are vulnerable as well. Hakim is probably correct in saying that, when whites make an accusation to a police officer against a black male on the street, it has the force of truth because blacks fit society's delinquent stereotype.

But ultimately, the accusations are made at every level—by FSG against the Strand, by the district attorney against the *Daily News,* by Jill against Hakim and Alice. Where theft is the norm, the accusations serve notice that someone is getting greedy, thereby enforcing the limits.

When I asked Alice, she told me that the copies of Sapphire's novel must have come from Jill Dunbar's store. Hakim later said that at the time Jill had marched up to the table he was not even aware that Alice had purchased the books in question a short time before. "If Jill had talked to me instead of just grabbing the books," Alice added, "we would have cooperated with her." (By comparison, Jill does not grab her books from the owner of the Strand, accompanied by a police escort. She expects to pay the store for the books.)

The best-sellers that Hakim had been promised by Steve never appeared on his table. I asked him what had happened. He said he'd quickly realized that Steve wasn't aboveboard. "It was also," he added, "a nefarious attempt to use me as a front to establish another table right here in the neighborhood." Hakim had decided, in any case, that he didn't want to be "operating under circumstances" where he would "one day be dealing with law enforcement."

In an extraordinary study published in 1974, entitled *The Professional Fence,* the criminologist Carl Klockars documents the life of a fence known as Vincent Swaggi. Klockars shows that a fence must be "public," explaining that the fence "must acquire a reputation as a successful dealer in stolen property and he must arrive at a way of managing the full significance of that reputation." The vendors on Sixth Avenue sell books and magazines at prices that are often well below those of a bookstore. Perhaps some of their economic success derives from their fitting the very stereotype of delinquency that makes them more vulnerable to accusation. Even if only an incidental percentage of Hakim's business derives from fencing stolen goods, some of his customers may wish to believe that the percentage is far higher.

Hakim is correct that his own periodic sales of stolen written matter do not make him an economic deviant in the business he is in. Ultimately, the business he works in, and perhaps American business as a whole, allows him to view his actions honestly as normal, rather than as deviant—an example of "the normalization of deviance." Though there may be a tendency for stores' practices to be considered legitimate, and the practices of people on the street to be seen as illegitimate, there seems to be a good deal of consistency from the bottom to the top in how the sale of written matter works. The activities are normal at every level, but their apparent deviance on the street derives from the following: first, the patterns at other levels are usually well hidden from those who do not know, whereas Hakim's must be public; and second, the informal economic activity of the street fits the delinquent stereotype, whereas the activity of the formal economy does not.

Initially, I assumed that the stolen books gain a market on the street because street vendors provide a unique outlet for them. This would be an example of the street economy's providing an atmosphere in which criminal activity flourishes, and informal social control's failing to contain these acts. But a comparative investigation of the economy in written matter shows that the most "organized" outlets are engaging in the sale of stolen materials.

This suggests that we must not assume that the criminal behavior we observe on the street is caused by a "disorderly" atmosphere, or by a unique failure on the part of these men to regulate themselves. A better analytical strategy is to compare the acts these men engage in to those of more conventional city dwellers, asking if their logic is as distinctive as it might appear, and whether these men are, anyway, altogether different from conventional persons in the quantity of their indecency. Indeed, in the case of stolen books, we have no better reason to believe that the instances of deviant social behavior (real or imagined) on the street are caused by an atmosphere of disorder, than to believe that these instances in the lives of the "normal" have such roots.

PART FOUR

REGULATING THE PEOPLE

WHO WORK THE STREETS

The Space Wars: Competing Legalities

It is not difficult to understand why the 1990s saw a movement for formal social control in response to minor civic infractions. The politics of Mayor Giuliani and the scholarly arguments of Wilson and Kelling echoed the opinions one could easily hear from many local merchants and business leaders, who complained about the people that were panhandling, scavenging, and "laying shit out." Take José Torres, who managed the Store 24 (a convenience store) on Greenwich Avenue near Sixth Avenue for seven years before it closed in 1996. "Aside from the nuisance they create," he explained to me, "they sometimes don't look presentable. They sometimes smell bad. They sometimes smoke drugs or urinate. Right in front! Without any regards for law or anything! As customers even try to walk into the store, sometimes they have to be met by these people, and it's very uncomfortable, especially when you have someone who doesn't look presentable, smells bad, and is begging for money."[1]

The formal social control of small infractions also reflects the concerns of local business groups. When I met with Andrew Manshel, the attorney for the Grand Central Partnership and the 34th Street Partnership, he frankly declared that the group's policies were influenced by Wilson and Kelling's "broken windows" theory. He argued not merely against the panhandlers and scavengers, but even against book vendors like Hakim Hasan. "Why is it that these people choose to be in the street?" he asked. "Is it a legitimate lifestyle choice to operate your business in the public way? My own view—and I'm not speaking for the Grand Central Partnership—is that it's an antisocial act. They have chosen to defy certain social norms, such as working in the formal economy. It seems to me we could agree as a society that occupying public space to sell things is antisocial. Why do we have to make it illegal in order not to have it? We've gotten to a place as a society where people say, 'Anything that's not illegal on the streets, I can do!' "

The Grand Central Partnership and other Business Improvement Districts have sought to limit the number of vendors by reducing the total space that vendors can legally occupy. In this chapter, I will attempt to show how the policy operates: how a law cutting down space got passed thanks to the input of politically influential business associations, and the impact the new law had on the street life.

The Business Improvement Districts

Business Improvement Districts (BIDs) are "geographic areas within a city in which property owners agree to pay for enhanced services and capital improvements to benefit an area."[2] These districts are created to improve the quality of the commercial and physical environment in a part of the city by providing services to complement those provided by the city, including enhanced security, sanitation, and social services. In addition, the BIDs organize visitor services, sponsor public events such as concerts, and coordinate the quality and variety of retail stores and their façades. The importance of BIDs cannot be overemphasized in understanding the distribution of power in New York City and the daily life of the streets in neighborhoods like Greenwich Village.

BIDs emerged as a significant political force within New York City during the 1980s, motivated by the business community's sense of helplessness over its inability to control the public spaces, which affected the value of its real estate and the success of its commercial activities.[3] By employing their own security forces and sanitation workers, the BIDs have brought about the degree of civic order called for by the "broken windows" theory. Some BIDs are politically powerful, working to achieve their ends through close associations with the mayor and/or members of the City Council.

In New York City, the most significant such associations are the midtown BIDs, which include the Grand Central Partnership, the 34th Street Partnership, the Fifth Avenue Association, and the Times Square Business

Improvement District. BIDs approach the problems of their neighborhoods differently, but they have a good deal in common. Many of the Manhattan BIDs, for example, employ uniformed safety officers who patrol their areas on foot from 7:00 a.m. to 11:00 p.m., with the objective of providing a deterrent to crime and a radio link to the local New York Police Department precinct. In addition, uniformed sanitation workers patrol surrounding streets seven days a week, picking up litter, reporting clogged storm drains, painting over and removing grafitti and illegal posters, and emptying trash receptacles.

A visit to the Fifth Avenue Association's Field Bureau in the basement of Rockefeller Center shows how a BID supplements the police. A uniformed officer sits at a desk with a radio and telephone wired directly to dispatchers of local New York City police precincts. "Ten four, let me know the disposition of that shoe-shine guy, okay?" says the radio operator to one of his own safety officers.

"Your message is coming in broken up," responds the officer.

"Please let me know if that shoe-shine guy has been removed," repeats the operator.

"Ten four."

A few moments later, a safety officer calls in. "Food vendor still in the same spot." (Under the municipal law, neither food vendors nor shoe-shine men are permitted on this street.)

"Stand by," says the radioman, as he presses a button connecting him to the police precinct. "Hello. I'm calling from Fifth Avenue Business Improvement. This is Mr. White and I'm calling about a food vendor that we have on the northwest corner of 50th and Fifth Avenue."

He hangs up, and I ask what they said to him.

"The usual story. Someone will take a walk by, or drive by, and check it out. It's not really a major emergency for them, but my bosses want them out of there. [Or else] everybody else will set up, and they'll start getting away with murder."

Another call comes in. "Post Six to Base. We have two guitar players in front of FAO Schwarz."

"Ten four, I got it."

A Law Is Passed Restricting Space

During my years of research, only one legislative initiative to deal with written-matter vendors passed the City Council, and this was chiefly due to the influence of two BIDs, the Grand Central Partnership and the 34th Street Partnership. To find out more about how this happened, I paid a visit to their counsel, Andrew Manshel, and asked him to describe the "philosophy" behind his legal efforts on behalf of midtown property owners.

"We have a general program here to deal with quality of street life," he explained to me. "Building on the work George Kelling of Northeastern University, James Q. Wilson at UCLA, and William H. Whyte, who wrote *City* . . . everything that gets done in this office is very self-conscious and very studied, and draws principally on these intellectual sources.

"A lot of what we do flies in the face of what a lot of academics, especially sociologists, have to say," he added. "There are professors who do work on public spaces and we drive them crazy. I mean, we're right across the street from them and we're everything they're against. They are these people who distort Jane Jacobs. I've taken to calling them believers in grit. They believe that anomic stuff that happens on the street is good and healthy and organic. They believe drug dealing is a small-scale business, and that to believe otherwise is kind of racist. They're people who believe that grafitti is a valuable cultural expression. That's not what we're about.

"People say we are trying to Disneyfy downtown and exert fascistic control over public spaces. That is a gross overstatement." He goes on to explain why the BIDs oppose unlicensed street vendors. "It's mostly about how they look as much as what they're doing. It's not just that they're selling things in public space, but they don't look like they've made a capital investment in what they are doing. They are not selling high-quality goods. When they are selling high-quality goods, there is an implication that the goods are stolen. It's not clear that they are part of the social fabric. The problem—besides that it looks disordered because of the lack of capital investment and the lack of social control imposed upon it—is that there is an element of unfairness with people who are renting stores and are selling similar merchandise and are paying taxes and minimum wage and rent."

BIDs are often accused by their political opponents of being completely closed and unaccountable to the public, but Manshel let me look at his voluminous files on his efforts to pass the law.[4] I asked what he and Daniel Biederman, then president of these two midtown BIDs, had done to deal with the written-matter vendors. Ultimately, they hired as a paid lobbyist the very man who had fought for passage of Local Law 33 of 1982, the original written-matter exemption, Edward C. Wallace.[5] After leaving the City Council when his seat was abolished, he had gone into private practice as an attorney.

Meanwhile, Wallace says, before Manshel contacted him he had already concluded for himself that Local Law 33 had gotten out of hand. "We gave a roadmap for how to do business on the sidewalks," he says. "On speech issues I am a total civil libertarian, which does not mean uncontrolled speech in all cases. It means 'subject to reasonable time, place, and manner restrictions.' Clearly, [civil liberties] was driving my enthusiasm for the orginal written-matter exemption. But the turnaround came when my enthusiasm for *that* had resulted in something completely unintended and not in my mind connected with *any* civil liberty: the proprietary taking of the sidewalk by private enterprises.

"I guess what I learned is that my youthful absolutist view has to be tempered by a practicality. In the end, that doesn't mean giving up the free-speech principle. It means recognizing how it can be distorted and twisted or abused for no First Amendment benefit."

•

On June 9, 1992, Wallace represented the Grand Central Partnership and 34th Street Partnership BIDs at a public meeting convened by the Consumer Affairs Committee of the City Council. In his presentation, Wallace summarized the views of representatives of many of the real-estate holdings who had been organized by the partnerships to attend the June 9 meeting. These included the Real Estate Board, the Fifth Avenue Association, the Shubert Organization, the Rockefeller Group Inc., and 665 Sixth Avenue.

"Ten years ago, I introduced a minor amendment intended to protect pamphleteers from arrest for unlicensed vending on the general vending law," he told those present. "Unfortunately, that well-intentioned minor exemption grew during the legislative process into a loophole big enough to spawn a table-based sidewalk industry which has clogged the sidewalks to the point where pedestrians cannot pass, and police officers cannot chase the

chain snatchers and muggers who prey on tourists in congested places. These table vendors form a virtual blockade, which prevents firefighters, ambulance crews, and police officers from moving quickly from curbside to building. The need is urgent for the council to take back the sidewalks for pedestrians and emergency services."

After the public meeting, Peter L. Malkin, a local property owner who had founded the Grand Central Partnership, wrote a letter to Mayor David Dinkins claiming that the exemption of book vending from general vending regulations had led to serious abuse. In response, Mayor Dinkins wrote that the sale of books on public streets raised constitutional issues: "In deciding upon restrictions on book vendors, we must be sensitive to First Amendment values," he emphasized.

It is likely that the mayor regarded the American Civil Liberties Union as an important political actor. Though not influential on their own, written-matter vendors like Hakim, Alice, Marvin, Ron, Ishmael, and Mudrick would have an influential interest group on their side.

According to Manshel, Wallace brought to the table a technical knowledge of how to recast the law so that it would be constitutional and the kind

of "political moxie" to get the bill through the City Council. He also had contacts with civil-liberties groups to persuade them that this law would not raise constitutional concerns. Wallace carefully crafted his draft law in an effort to address the concerns of the ACLU.

In particular, he proposed legislation to ban written-matter vendors from setting up tables on streets where food vendors and general vendors were already banned. Thus, the new law would not be said to target speech specifically, but would be seen as balancing First Amendment rights with the health and safety of the public.

Twelve months later, as the 1993 mayoral election approached, there was a bitter campaign between Democratic Mayor David Dinkins and the Republican challenger, Rudolph Giuliani, focusing on the "quality of life." Both candidates ran against the deviance symbolized by panhandlers, squeegee men, vendors, and the like. Two councilmen introduced Local Law 45, which had been meandering its way through the legislative process since the previous year. The measure was overwhelmingly approved by the City Council, and on June 1, 1993, Mayor Dinkins signed it into effect, with the following legislative finding:

"The Council hereby finds and declares that a threat to public health, safety, and welfare exists due to the practice of permitting general vendors who exclusively vend written matter to vend on sidewalks without subjecting them to certain placement and location restrictions which have been found to protect the health, safety and welfare of the public." The Council further found that this threat to the public health was worsened by the placement of vending tables along major commercial thoroughfares. It claimed that "these tables blocked the access of emergency services, including fire and police personnel, to the entrances to buildings and to fire hydrants; caused pedestrian congestion at major tourist points and transportation facilities; and impeded the movement of police foot patrols along the sidewalks."

These legislative findings were adopted by the City Council even though there was no evidence presented to support them. The new law included prohibitions on the mandatory number of feet between a vendor's table and a street corner, the entrance to a building, or a subway entrance.[6]

Local Law 45 had immediate implications for all of the avenues under the jurisdiction of the Grand Central Partnership and the 34th Street Partnership. There, because food vendors and general vendors were already prohibited, written matter could no longer be sold once the new law went into effect. Those vendors would have to move to side streets in midtown, and perhaps to other parts of New York City.

Like all general vendors, written-matter vendors throughout the city now had to set up their tables in such a way as to allow at least a twelve-foot-wide pedestrian path. They could not lean themselves or an "item" against a building or window; they were prohibited from being within twenty feet of an entranceway to any building; and they were not allowed to set up within ten feet from bus stops, taxi stands, subway entrances and exits, or street corners.[7] Many vendors realized that the spots they had worked in had suddenly been eliminated.

A Public Reckoning

In Greenwich Village, the amount of space for written-matter vendors was cut in half. For quite a while, instead of bringing about greater order on the streets, Local Law 45 led to a further deterioration of sidewalk life on Sixth Avenue. Those vendors who did remain would routinely fight with the police and one another for the remaining legal sidewalk space.

Because vendors want to be able to set up in the same place each day, so that their customers will know where to find them, and because the municipal law does not recognize any person's claim to a particular piece of public sidewalk, the vendors had devised their own system to order their relations with one another regarding the distribution of space. Under the municipal law, any vendor who arrives first at a space is entitled to set up there; but under the unofficial system each vendor has his or her own space, which is usually honored by the others.[8]

Before the passage of Local Law 45, my discussions with vendors indicated that they looked with great disdain on the idea of calling on the police to settle disputes. Often I heard a vendor who threatened to call 911 (the police) referred to as a "plantation boy" or a "snitch" by other black vendors.

The unofficial system for settling disputes was orderly. It had long worked without overt conflict. It seemed to me to be part of a larger set of unquestionable truths on the block, based on notions of black collective consciousness. When the amount of space was cut in half, however, I observed that the unofficial system was not based on unquestionable values at all; it existed because it maximized the interests of vendors, whose method of allocating space had depended on minimizing contact with the official law. The professions of brotherhood had kept the official legal system from interfering with an unofficial system that regulated vendors' affairs, but it could not withstand the strain of decreased space; those values now competed with more practical concerns such as "who got here first."

This is illustrated by one dramatic episode involving Hakim and Muhammad, a vendor supporting a family of eighteen who had worked on the corner at the busy intersection for many years (it is not clear how many). Like Hakim, he is an African American who changed his name when he became a Muslim; unlike Hakim, he is still a practicing Muslim and a member of the Nation of Islam. When I arrived at 9:00 a.m. one Monday, I noticed that Hakim was set up in the spot where Muhammad usually puts his table. Around 9:30, as I talked with Ishmael, Muhammad arrived and put his table directly in front of Hakim's. The two men began to argue.

You're not listening to what I'm saying. I was here since seven o'clock in the morning, Hakim said.

My brother, if you charge me with doing something to you and that's why you're doing it to me, that's not right. I've never hurt anyone. I've never hurt you, Hakim!

This is not about what's right or wrong, answered Hakim.

Yes, it is about what's right or wrong, said Muhammad.

It's about what you're doing, responded Hakim.

It's about right or wrong, said Muhammad. You accused me. And I wanna defend that.

A crowd of ten or a dozen men working the block quickly surrounded Hakim and Muhammad. Many of them had been upset that Muhammad was arriving on the block late in the morning and yet claiming a spot that they could have been using. Hakim's assertion of his right to challenge the longstanding custom might have been interpreted as a threat to the collective solidarity of these men, who were united by their customs, or simply as a technical argument about a specific rule. It was a public reckoning about how life on the street should be ordered.

During my years of observing the blocks, I had never seen such a dispute occur. It was established that particular spots "belonged" to particular vendors if they occupied them every day. If Hakim were to establish his legitimate right to the location, the entire unofficial system that governed property rights on the street would be transformed.

As Muhammad and Hakim and their supporters yelled, passersby steered around them, apparently disconcerted by the sight of ten black men circling around one another and raising their voices. I walked over to the assembling men as I turned on my tape recorder.

"You can't prove it, brother, because I've never done anything like that," said Muhammad.

"Nobody can prove anything with you!" responded Hakim.

"Oh yes, brother . . . you . . . hey . . . if you get witnesses you can prove it to them," said Muhammad.

Hakim turned to the crowd of vendors and looked for his witness. "Was I out here at seven o'clock this morning?"

"Brother? . . . Brother?" called Muhammad.

"Did you see me come out here seven o'clock this morning?" repeated Hakim. "Right or wrong? What time did *you* get here?"

"Granted," said Muhammad.

"What time *did* you get there?" asked Hakim.

"Everybody was here when I came. No problem on that. I haven't concerned that as a problem. It's just that you made an accusation against me," said Muhammad.

"What time did you get here?" demanded Hakim. "What time did you get here?"

"I got here later than . . ."

"What time did you get here?"

"I got here later than all of you-all," Muhammad admitted.

"*About* what time did you get here?" continued Hakim.

"I just got here not too long ago."

"How long ago was not too long ago?"

"You want to play the legal game, Hakim? You got here first!"

"Right! Then you put that table there for what reason?" asked Hakim.

"I have never hurt you, brother," responded Muhammad. "You accuse me of trying to hurt you."

"You are playing games here. You not smart enough to be playing games with me."

"No, brother! Truth is truth. Truth is light."

"I'll guarantee you one thing," said Hakim. "You put that table up right there today and I'll have the police confiscate it. I'm telling you now. Watch. I'm gonna play the same game they play with me."

Hakim's comment was a bombshell, violating the stigma against bringing in the police as a way to settle disputes. Since Hakim was a seller of black books who was looked upon as a good "race man"—one who feels "an intense responsibility to 'the race,' to the point of viewing most events, especially public ones involving white society, as having definite implications for the well-being of other blacks"[9]—it was unlikely that anyone could successfully frame Hakim's motives as anti-black. In order to undermine the unofficial system previously supposedly based on black collective consciousness, Hakim was defining the issues in narrow, practical terms ("What time did you get here?"), whereas Muhammad wanted to keep the discussion at an abstract level ("No, brother! Truth is truth"), which would enable him to avoid confronting the issue of whether the rules needed to be changed. He wanted to keep the issues on a level that would indicate a potential crisis for group solidarity.[10]

"I came down here to fight with truth against all falsehoods," said Muhammad. "And that's what I'm doing."

"You know what they call that?" yelled Hakim. "They call that rhetoric."

"They call it a brother talking to another brother," said Muhammad.

"You know what? Let me say the following: from now on, whoever gets here first in that or any other spot, they can set up."

"If you wanna do that, that's up to you," responded Muhammad.

"I'm *gonna* do that," said Hakim.

"Right! That's up to you."

"I don't need your permission to do that," said Hakim.

"No. You know what? You know what? You going with that because you want the white man's permission to do that!"

Hakim was ready with a rejoinder. "If you don't care about the white man, why are you fighting with me over a space? Why don't you set up outside his lines?" asked Hakim.[11]

"We brothers," said Muhammad. "You know I got eighteen mouths [to feed] . . . eighteen mouths, brother, and you know another one is on the way. Hey, brother, I've been here for eleven years on this corner. And you don't want to respect that?"

"I'm not afraid of you. I'm letting you know, from now on, I'm setting up anywhere on this block."

"Allah-u-Akbar," said Muhammad, meaning, "God is Great."

With that, two squad cars from the Sixth Precinct rolled up on the curb, evidently prompted by a passerby.

"What's up?" said an officer, a white male, as he got out of one of the cars.

"How are you? I'm trying to hold a discussion with *this* man," said Hakim, turning away from the officer.

"We're having a discussion," said Muhammad, turning his back on the officer as well. The body positions of the two men signaled to all of the surrounding vendors that neither of them was going to defer to the white officer in solving an internal dispute.

"No, but you out of order," said Hakim.

"I'm not out of order," said Muhammad.

"You out of order! You've been out of order for a long time!" said Hakim.

"Islam is order. I came to you Islamically," said Muhammad.

The officer tried to move between the men.

"Sergeant, everything is all right and we at peace," said Muhammad. "We just here having a discussion."

"What I'm trying to explain to him is that he doesn't own this corner at the top of the block," said Hakim.

"We already know that," said Muhammad.

"He's just determined he owns the corner," said Hakim.

"That's not true," responded Muhammad. "You made a falsehood and that's not true. Now, you can act plantation boy if you want to . . . in front of the slave master."

"All right, come on," said the officer, as he dispersed the crowd.

Muhammad's claim to a particular space had long been acknowledged, as were the claims of other vendors to "their own" spots. Now Hakim had made an open declaration in front of all the other vendors that "First come, first served," would be the new norm on Sixth Avenue. But it was not a norm that could be adopted quickly or easily. As it turned out, there would be even more fighting.

The Unhoused Rule

The first to benefit from the new norm were those who slept on the block. They had first claim on spaces not eliminated by Local Law 45, whereas vendors who went home or elsewhere at night found themselves at a disadvantage in obtaining any legal space at all.

This led to a major transformation in the informal system that governed property rights on the street. For some time, as we know, a number of men had earned money by serving as "place holders"—guarding a spot of public sidewalk overnight and selling it to a vendor in the morning. Whereas once this had been done at the vendor's request, however, now the unhoused men insisted on "holding" spaces overnight, regardless of whether vendors had asked them to do so. The men who had been "place holders" became extortionists of a sort.

"The only way you could come into that block, you had to go through me," a scavenger and place holder named Leo Porter once explained. "There were so many vendors coming to the neighborhood, and there was no room for no one to set up. So we had a special little crew, and everyone had their own specific spot. They would pay me twenty dollars per spot. One day a guy who sells comic books said, 'Yo, I'm not giving you nothing no more.' I said, 'But, brother, you got your spot, now give me my money.' He told me to go fuck myself, so I grabbed him by the neck and put a blade to him. Before he knew it, I had him pinned up against the wall of B. Dalton. The men on the block were yelling, 'Leo, don't kill him,' 'cause they seen death in my eyes, because I *am* capable of killing. I backed up and let him go, and he ran to the precinct. By the time I finished with him, I was incarcerated for three months while I waited for a trial. Then I got it thrown out." I had heard a similar version of this story from others on the block.

Whereas vendors were once the source of their own system of apparently workable, mutually advantageous norms and rules, it seemed as if the lack of space resulting from Local Law 45 had led to conflicts that were being solved with weapons and by the police. Needless to say, such conflicts contributed to a mood of disorder on the street. More and more vendors turned to the official law and the New York Police Department to establish their rights. That Hakim and Muhammad had turned their bodies away from the police officers had been powerful symbolically, but the meaning seemed to apply less and less in their daily lives.

Howard Refuses to Pay for Space

One hot evening in August, Howard, a vendor who had long been setting up his table of comic books on Sixth Avenue, threatened to call the police when Mudrick and other vendors and place holders refused to make room for him upon his arrival.

The next morning, Howard (who is white) was standing on the sidewalk when Mudrick approached him. "I don't like what you said yesterday. I gotta tell ya. I don't think you mean what you said. You can't tell the police what we do in the street. That's not right."

"Let me explain," said Howard.

"Listen to *me*," said Mudrick.

"No, let me talk," said Howard.

"I'm the one who called *you*," said Mudrick. "To straighten this shit out. You listen to *me!* Don't tell the police anything! We have to straighten it out with the people in the *street*. Don't call the police down on the people."

"I don't want to," said Howard. "But if people want to keep on . . ."

"Then why you say that [yesterday]?" demanded Mudrick. "I want to hear this shit. Because I couldn't sleep last night behind this bullshit. Make sure you say it right, 'cause it's gonna cost money to talk to me anyway."

"Let me finish," said Howard.

"First, let me tell you what you getting into," said Mudrick, trying to intimidate him. "You gotta pay me to talk to me!"

Howard was speechless for a moment or two. Mudrick said, "Now you can go ahead and talk."

"If someone is taking up everything and putting you out of business," began Howard, "you gonna tell me that you're not gonna do anything about it?"

"You gonna get a spot anyway," Mudrick responded. "All you gotta say to these guys is, 'I need a little space.' "

"I can't even get . . . like yesterday . . ."

"You can get it! All you gotta do is say, 'I want a little space.' You know how to settle about space in New York. You put your shit over there and they make room for you and you make room for them. You don't have to go to the police. . . . You understand that? Do you understand English? I know that you do!"

"Yeah, I understand English."

"Well, they gotta make a space for you!"

"They say it's too bad," said Howard. "I myself, personally, do not have any love for the police."

"Ain't no love in this game," said Mudrick. "There's enough money for everybody."

"The bottom line is, I have to make money," said Howard.

"You gonna make money," said Mudrick. "But you don't have to go to the police and let the police know what we're doing over here."

"I haven't gone to anybody yet. But, I mean, if somebody does it to me enough times, I'm gonna . . ."

"What you're trying to say is, if they don't do what you want them to do, you're going to have to go to the police?"

"If they take up seven tables for two people . . ."

Mudrick laughed.

"What do you think? That I'm going to be a nice guy? You wouldn't be a nice guy, either," Howard said. "Listen, I'm not looking for any hassles, my friend. All I [have to do] is make money. If I don't make money, I'm in trouble."

"Do me a favor," said Mudrick. "Listen, don't call the police."

"I'm not calling nobody."

"The police is the wrong thing to call. Don't put the police in. We trying to get organization here and try to straighten out things. Then, when you call the police, it don't make no sense."

"Then let's work together," said Howard.

"That's what I'm trying to tell you. Let's work together with this shit."

"That's the bottom line," said Howard as he walked away.

"Don't call no police," called out Mudrick after him in a voice loud enough for everyone on the block to hear. "That's wrong. Don't be a snitch."

Turning to Butteroll, Mudrick continued loudly, "Motherfucker snitch on me because he can't get a spot. If you want a spot, wake up in the morning and get a fucking spot. I'm here all night, you gonna come here twelve o'clock [p.m.] and look for a spot? Get the fuck outa here. Everything is took over."

As a black man talking to a white man, Mudrick could not appeal to black collective consciousness to establish that it was taboo to call on the police to resolve problems among vendors. Instead, he tried to intimidate Howard, and then, when Howard wouldn't back down, to stigmatize him in the eyes of other vendors. But Howard made it clear that he was not intimidated. As a middle-class white man, he would likely have power with the police that the poor black men lacked. When he came to the blocks in the weeks to come, Mudrick and the other magazine vendors made space for him.

Over the next five years, a new informal system would emerge, with intricate relations to the official legality. Nobody tried to stand in Howard's way. Other vendors, such as an elderly white man who never threatened to call the police, paid B.A., a place holder, fifty dollars to hold his spot. This sometimes led to fights over who had the right to collect "rent" for holding particular spots.

A System Prevails

As the months after the passage of the new law turned into years, a combined version of the older and newer systems for determining property rights prevailed. Muhammad continued to occupy his place on the corner, but he was challenged for the space whenever he showed up late.

On one day at Christmastime four years later, a dispute showed that the public "scenes" had never come to an end. I came to the block around 11:00 a.m. and noted that Ron and Marvin were set up in Muhammad's usual space. A few minutes later, Muhammad's wife drove up in their van and dropped their fifteen-year-old daughter off on the corner with two tables and a load of merchandise on a large pushcart.

"No, no, no!" yelled Ron. "How she gonna come in here? Marvin, don't let nobody in. What you gonna cut down on our money for? Don't move none of our stuff. Then you'll have to move for others."

"Right," said Marvin. "Let her put her stuff outside the line. Why should we move our stuff outside the line for her?"

Muhammad's daughter stood silently with her pushcart to the side at the corner of Sixth Avenue and Eighth Street.

She likely heard the two men talking, but never approached or asked for a space.

Turning to me, Ron said, "You see, Mitch, I feel for these people. I've been out here since six o'clock this morning. I didn't set up until just now. I waited until ten o'clock."

"What was going through your mind as you waited?"

"I figured, 'I don't want no argument,' you understand? I figured I'd set up outside the line down there [in an illegal space], because I know this is where Muhammad wants to set up at. But then it looked like Shorty and Conrad were getting ready to come over here. I was thinking to myself, 'Muhammad didn't come yesterday. The space was here empty all day. Why should I lose out?' "

Before Local Law 45 was passed, there was plenty of space for those who wanted to engage in entrepreneurial activity on the sidewalk. It would have been inconceivable that Shorty, Conrad, and Ron would "eye" a space that had gone unclaimed for a few hours.

"Did you feel while you were waiting that if you did set up here you were being some kind of bad person?"

"Yeah. Like I was trying to move in on their territory or something like that. It was some kind of informal understanding that this is where these guys set up all the time."

Four years after Local Law 45 was passed, vendors were still respecting a person's right to set up in a specific place, but only if he arrived "on time." Yet, as Ishmael joined the conversation and Ron continued talking, it became clear that even on this point there was still disagreement. My presence became an occasion for the men to discuss what constituted suitable behavior.

"Let me show you another example," Ron said. "Ishmael can confirm this. When Ishmael don't set up here, I set up [in his spot]. But if I knew he was coming, I wouldn't have set up here in the first place. Not because I think it is his spot, but because I know he like to set up there. So I figure, Let me give him the first crack at it. But if I see him not coming, I'm not gonna wait around all day and don't make no money. I'm gonna try to make some."

"I believe like this," said Ishmael. "If you've been there and you consistently there, he can come two or three hours late, but I'm being considerate.

Let's work this outside of arguing. Because, if you're gonna argue, it's gonna go further than that. So, if you take it on a considerate basis, something is gonna be worked out."

"No," said Ron. "Sometimes you gotta look out for *you*. You can bend over backwards only so much. . . ."

"When it's coming down to a kid who is coming out here by herself," interrupted Ishmael, pointing to Muhammad's daughter standing on the corner.

"That's her father sending her out here," responded Ron.

"That's her personal money," said Ishmael.

"*They* sending her out here in the cold," responded Ron. "I need money to pay bills. . . . I gotta pay rent. . . . I lived on the street for years. I'm not getting ready to go back to it."

"I have feelings for a kid," said Ishmael, pointing.

"If all the cops was here right now, they would say I have a perfect right to be here," said Ron. "Because I was here first."

"This is greed," responded Ishmael, as Marvin joined the discussion. "You should sacrifice one of your tables for her. You and Marvin have two tables."

"We need money to pay bills," responded Marvin.

"I don't care," said Ishmael. "That's not being considerate."

Shorty joined Marvin, Ron, and Ishmael, taking the side of Muhammad's daughter. "Hey, give her a little space," he yelled.

"Shorty, what bills she has to pay?" yelled Ron.

"I don't know what bills she has," yelled Shorty.

"She gotta pay rent?" asked Ron.

Shorty put his body up against Ron's. "Next time I'll get this space," he said.

"Get out of my face," yelled Ron. "Don't be shoving up on me and swinging your hand."

Shorty backed off.

"Yo, I didn't plan on setting up here," said Ron. "Nobody was here and I set up here. And that was it. If you want to give up the end table, it's up to you, Marvin."

"Okay, we'll move the end table over," responded Marvin. "But we ain't moving no other tables."

"If we move our little table, how she gonna get her big table in there?" asked Ron. Turning to her, he said, "Young lady, if you got a smaller table, I'll move that one over for you and you can set up here."

"Even if I set up there, though, I'm outside the line," she said.

"I don't think you're going to get any problem," said Ron.

With that, she went across the street to the public telephone, perhaps to call her father.

"I will fight for this space," Marvin yelled.

"We don't have to fight, Marv," responded Ron. "It's first come, first served."

The yelling of all of the gathered vendors rose to a high volume. Passersby were crossing to the other side of the street rather than pass the angry, fighting men.

•

Mrs. Gross of the Washington Court Condominium was well aware of this situation on the block. "They fight with each other—hitting each other with objects, picking up chairs and smacking them into each other," she explained. "Which does bother me, because I have a twelve-year-old, and the issue, as he walks to and from school, is, they are out of control and it's not as if they can control themselves and let a kid walk by. The homeless guys feel that they have their spot. The other vendors, who are not homeless, like the guy who sells comic books, come and they fight with them. So they *do* all fight with each other over the space."

To make matters worse for the neighborhood, once space became scarce, more and more vendors with quality goods had their merchandise seized by the police for setting up outside the lines. These vendors could not afford to replace their seized merchandise, whereas the vendors who sold scavenged items could make one trip around the block and find a new stock of magazines in the next round of recycled trash. This drove away the vendors of quality goods:

"The people that *buy* their merchandise, they can't afford to have the police taking their stuff," said Ron. "Only people that can afford to have the police take his stuff are the guy who go get it from recycling."

"Yeah," agreed Marvin.

The police well understood that seizing a vendor's new books could be

an effective method for driving him out of business. "They'll say, 'I don't mind taking a summons, but I'm not going to lose my valuable merchandise for a month while I wait to see a judge. I'm gonna get out of the business,' " one officer told me. "A lot of them feel the pressure is too much. Only your real die-hards stay. To them, it is just the cost of doing business. But most of them will get out or go to flea markets or places like that."

This, then, was yet another way in which Local Law 45 would have an effect that was as unintended to its proponents in midtown as was the impact of the original written-matter exception to general vending. Rather than encouraging vendors who sold new merchandise to set it out on the sidewalks, the local law ended up causing most of those vendors to disappear.

After the passage of Local Law 45, a Business Improvement District called the Village Alliance was formed in Greenwich Village in an effort to make the neighborhood more attractive, cleaner, and safer. Although this BID would never have the resources, influence, or talent of the Grand Central Partnership, it would work in small ways to make life difficult for the vendors. Most notably, it would get permission from the Department of Transportation to plant trees where vendors had once worked, further cutting down on the amount of space on the sidewalk, and causing more wars over space. The "philosophy" toward people on the street that stood behind these efforts was possibly epitomized in BID President Honi Klein's words to me: "Where I think that there should be a change in the law is that I don't think that the First Amendment should protect people who are street people. They are not homeless. These people never had homes."

A Christmas on Sixth Avenue

In 1996, for the second consecutive winter, the holiday season came to New York City without snow. In the towers above Rockefeller Center, men and women who were engaged in international transactions and the coordination of global production could look down on sidewalks packed with tourists glimpsing the ice skaters and the famous Christmas tree. The sidewalks throughout midtown were so congested that it took five minutes to make one's way the length of a city block. There on the streets of the influential Fifth Avenue Association and Grand Central Partnership Business Improvement District, no vendors, panhandlers, or unhoused people could be seen.

A few subway stops south, on Sixth Avenue in the Village, the Volunteers of America had their Sidewalk Santas ringing bells near Eighth Street, asking people to "help our neediest neighbors." Halfway down the block, a Santa from the Salvation Army rang his bell. A few steps away, Keith Johnson cried out from his wheelchair, "Help the homeless," and then complained about the institutional panhandlers, who were cutting in on his proceeds this holiday season.

On Greenwich Avenue, next to Hakim's table, the florist had taken over the sidewalk space where Conrad usually puts his magazines, setting up a dozen Christmas trees for sale.

And across the avenue, Balducci's market had taken over the sidewalk in front of its store with straw baskets filled with gourmet items. The lines flowed outside and around the block as local residents waited for their chance to buy fancy cakes, imported cheeses, and other delicacies.

Meanwhile, Ishmael was raising hell on the sidewalk.

You heard they took my table, Mitch? he says when I arrive on the blocks around eleven on the morning of December 23. He continues telling Hakim and Alice that all of his belongings had been seized by officers of the New York City Police Department between two and two-thirty that morning.

He says, They took my magazines and they took my personal belongings, too. I went shopping, bought some new clothes, had a receipt and everything. They took all that. And they didn't give me no summons for my stuff, nothing. They just took it.

Ishmael says that he is being punished because two other men on the street, Joe Garbage and Al, had placed their goods for sale on the ground, in violation of local laws; in response, the police had punished them by removing everything that was out on Sixth Avenue, not merely Joe's and Al's belongings. If the problem's down there, he says, don't take *my* stuff.

Ishmael does not have anywhere else to keep his belongings, so the bags underneath his table can contain anything ranging from a family photograph to clothing. Often men will say that everything they own is under their table, that a certain bag is their survival bag: "That bag is my life," Warren once said. "That bag can do nobody any good than me. It had my clothes, my ID, my toiletries, just things that I need to survive on the street. Some people out here stay in the same clothes, don't care about their hygiene. But that's not me. I wasn't brought up like that."

A few weeks earlier, Ishmael had met a young Japanese woman named Tina, a graduate student in music who was trying to support herself as a singer, and she had begun to visit him regularly on the block. After many conversations, they developed an amorous relationship, and they had planned to go out on a date that very evening. Ishmael had used his earnings the day before to purchase new trousers and a shirt on 14th Street so that he could look neat and clean on the date. "He [the officer] took my new clothes that I went shopping for," Ishmael explained. "I have nothing to wear on my date tonight."

•

If we look closely at this incident and others like it, we can better understand how unhoused vendors are regulated in New York City. After his election victory, as we have seen, Mayor Rudolph Giuliani advanced a change in the strategy of the police department that was already taking place, from responding to 911 calls to maintaining order and eliminating public disorderly behavior.[1] The new model of policing, again, began with the assumption that felony crimes spring from environments in which forms of nonviolent deviance are tolerated—aggressive panhandling, scavenging, and "services" such as opening car doors, flagging taxis, locating parking spaces, and washing motorists' automobile windows at intersections without their permission.[2] The laws and their enforcement have been made part of a quality-of-life campaign that is widely described as intended to "clean up" the city.[3] It is accompanied by offical disparagement of "street people." In this climate, as we will see, individual police speak as if the vendors occupy places on the street at the discretion of the police; their presence is a privilege bestowed by the community and regulated by the beat-patrol officers. The police engage in a kind of micromanagement—making sure vendors set up within precise lines, stay close to their tables, and keep merchandise off the sidewalk.

On Sixth Avenue, fixing broken windows entails constant face-to-face relations between police and vendors. The police must rely on the cooperation of the vendors, and the vendors must rely on the police not to abuse the

law. As we shall see, this is hardly an optimal set of expectations for either side to rely upon.

The system of sanctions police have at their disposal to regulate the vendors consists mainly of civil penalties. Whereas under a penalty of criminal law someone might be put in jail for an infraction, in controlling minor offenses (like putting merchandise on the ground) police rely on summonses and tickets, which bring fines. The difficulty people working the sidewalks have in not committing minor infractions, and the failure of these tickets and summonses to have any lasting effect on their behavior, lead to crises of personal respect between police and those who do not comply. These crises lead to abuses of law on the part of both vendors and police.

Advocates of "broken windows"–style policing acknowledge that such regulation puts more power in the hands of the patrol officer on the beat, and that in their discretion the police will occasionally harass the poor. They also contend that, through effective education,[4] such abuse of discretion and harassment can be minimized. But the problem is not merely one of discretion or education. Rather, it inheres in the very structure of such a policing process.

Let us look more closely at the way this all works.

A Visit to the Sixth Precinct

Ishmael asks me if I will accompany him to the precinct that evening, as he tries to get his belongings back. He says that he wants me to see the way he is treated there. He had gone to the precinct a half hour after his belongings were seized, but now he wants to go again. Marvin and Mudrick had told him that it would do no good, that he would have to get a Legal Aid attorney and sue. But Ishmael says he wants to let the police know that if they pick on him he will be on their backs; that, unlike some other vendors, he will not take such treatment lying down. I say that I'll come along.

When we arrive at the station at 5:00 p.m., I stand to the side and listen. After a short while, I move to a seat in the waiting area, outside the view of the desk sergeant, in a place where I can take rough notes on the conversation.

What's up, man? says Ishmael to the officer. It is clear to me that they have met before.

I came here last night about a table that was tooken from me and was not unattended. Right? The incident that was taking place that happened down the block was that somebody threw some stuff on the floor. The cop took his attitude and came all the way up on the block, where I am, and took my table.

What's the cop's name? asks the sergeant.

I can't recall. But I know what he looked like. He was driving a scooter. A little slim guy with a short mustache. And I was in the right at the moment. Plus he took some personal belongings that I just bought from the shopping center.

Did he give you a summons?

He didn't give me none of that. He just seized it.

Where were you when this happened?

I was approaching the table when the other guy was working the table. And before I went away, the officer told me he would not touch my table. And when I left to go and get something to eat, I see he called in a car, and the next minute they was throwing my stuff inside the car, and they did not give me back my personal belongings and whatnot that they took. I mean, they took the table, they took my clothes. And when I got to the precinct, they told me I could sit down. So I sat for a while, and finally the officer called in who took the stuff and, knowing that I was here, said that he threw it in a sanitation truck somewhere on 14th Street.

Listen, you know me, right? asks the desk sergeant.

I know you very long.

Have I ever treated you with any disrespect?

No, you didn't.

Never, right?

No, you didn't.

I've always treated you with the utmost respect and, to tell you the truth, I don't know why anybody would have a hard time with you, because you've always treated me with respect. But to be perfectly honest with you, I don't have the officer's name, and I can't tell you what happened to your property until I find out who that officer was. And I'm gonna ask around to see if anyone knows what happened to your property, and if it got thrown in the Dumpster, I apologize for that, but there's not much I can do. Now, you know me. You know how I deal with you. And if I did know, I would be straight up with you.

I know that, says Ishmael.

But I don't know. So all I can say is, I'm sorry. If I had more information to go on, I'd help you. I don't have a summons number.

No, there was no summons written up.

You understand that I'm not stroking you here, right?

No, you're not stroking me here, responds Ishmael. I respect what you're saying. I know, if you knew who did what, there would be something coming out of that. But I'm just asking him to leave me alone. Because, the way I conduct myself where I work at, this officer, he told me sometime I may get in the way, but as long as one person is at a table, keep the area clean, don't have nothing on the ground, and be by your table. So I've been respecting that with this officer. I'm at the point where I'm tired. You understand? Him coming and taking on me like I'm somebody's poodle. Like you can come bang up on me for somebody else's actions. Okay? I don't give nobody no problem. I don't give no officer no problem.

I agree with you one hundred percent, says the officer. But I don't even have nobody I can talk to, because I don't know who it is. You understand what I'm saying?

Yeah, says Ishmael.

All I can say is, keep your eyes out for him. Once you see him, take down his shield number.

All right. Nice talking to you, my friend, says Ishmael.

Take it easy. Better luck next time, says the officer.

All right. I'll talk to you.

I left the station behind Ishmael and met him on the sidewalk. Though I could not tell whether my presence had influenced what was said, the conversation reflected two things that I have witnessed over and again in my observations on the sidewalk: the general conversational ballet over the issue of respect, and the suggestion by the vendor that he was being punished for the actions of other vendors.

The radio has long been full of rap songs by young black males who sing of being "dissed" or warning others not to "dis" them. These, of course, are references to being "disrespected"—to being treated in a way that is inconsistent with the way the individual wishes to present himself to others. When the officer said to Ishmael, "You know me, right? Have I ever treated you with any disrespect?" he was asking, "Have I ever treated you in a way that is inconsistent with the way you sense you have a right to be treated?" To do otherwise would be, in the parlance of the street, to dis Ishmael.[5]

It is taken for granted among social psychologists that all human beings seek to avoid being treated in ways that are inconsistent with the way they believe they have a right to be treated.[6] It seems that on Sixth Avenue the concept of respect sometimes is invoked in response to embarrassment, but sometimes it is a verbal formula that is not necessarily grounded in actual feelings. In fact, the idea that a person should not be subjected to embarrassment is so well understood on the street that even the prospect of a perceived slight will often lead a person to use the verbal formula. Social psychologist Thomas J. Scheff proposes that one sign that a person has been humiliated but does not acknowledge it is that he becomes obsessive, and his thoughts, talk, and actions become very rapid.[7] But as in the case of the desk sergeant and Ishmael, it is common to see the verbal formula used when there is no apparent sign of humiliation. The use of strategies to avoid shaming the other seems to be a structural aspect of relations between police and street vendors.

The content of the conversation between Ishmael and the desk sergeant was carefully framed by the two men in reference to the long-term history of the street. As much as 50 percent of the dialogue was focused on issues of respect, and it did not seem at all strange in this context for the officer to respond to Ishmael's statement that his belongings had been thrown in the back of a garbage truck by saying, "You know me, right? Have I ever treated you with any disrespect?"

By emphasizing that he has always treated Ishmael with respect, the sergeant showed that he had assimilated the verbal formula into his approach. The greatest measure of "respect" derived from his treatment of Ishmael as a worthy individual, rather than an anonymous black male. In a study of the relations between black men and the police, Elijah Anderson notes, "The anonymous black male is usually an ambiguous figure who arouses the utmost caution and is generally considered dangerous until he proves that he is not."[8] Many black men are accustomed to this sort of treatment in public. By treating Ishmael as a respectable person, rather than making him prove his worth, the officer, it seemed to me, defused some of Ishmael's anger and frustration.[9]

It is understandable that Ishmael showed great deference to the officer.

His purpose was to establish a rapport—to be recognized as an individual worthy of respect who had been mistreated—as much as to recover his belongings. He wanted to let the police know that if they take his belongings he will be there to complain. Unlike some other vendors, who might not pursue the matter, he will be on their backs. In fact, Ishmael did more than show respect; he was also deferential, a behavioral norm I have witnessed over and over again in interactions between police officers and black men on the streets.[10] On the streets of New York, I have observed police officers demand this respect to different degrees. Officers abuse discretion and the laws regularly enough so that many men working on the sidewalks realistically fear police power. Ishmael assumes that if he does not defer to the police they may be vindictive in response. As we shall see, this assumption suits the facts of his life.

Taking the Law into Their Own Hands

"Broken windows" policing places great faith in the discretion of individual police officers in the field—on their ability to regain control of the street, and to establish orderly, conventional standards of conduct.[11] Although police always have enormous discretion, the attention paid to minor infractions broadens the scope of situations over which they have authority. It also increases the number of situations in which police and people working the streets have direct interaction, times when issues of respect must be faced. And when other methods seem to fail, it encourages police to take the law into their own hands.

Every day, some vendors, scavengers, and panhandlers violate the Municipal Code by setting up in illegal spots, laying miscellaneous scavenged items for sale out on the ground ("laying shit out"), or leaving their tables unattended. With the mayor directing the police department to focus on "quality of life" issues, every day the police issue summonses for these code violations. The summons requires a vendor to appear before the Environmental Control Board, a civil tribunal. If found guilty, he will be fined.

According to the Environmental Control Board's statement of purpose, fines and other civil penalties are incentives meant to encourage violators to change their behavior. The vast majority of civil fines are leveled against property owners for building- and fire-code violations, excesses of air and noise pollution, and sanitation and asbestos violations. If the owner of a building does not answer such a summons, the city can put a lien on his or her property.

Civil penalties like fines are not likely to be effective against the people working on Sixth Avenue, however. Many don't carry identification. (When asked by the police for some form of ID, a scavenger or vendor will, not uncommonly, pull out a wad of other summonses he has received.) Some give the police false names, and often a police officer has known the same vendor by the wrong name for years. Moreover, only 10 percent of those summoned appear before the Environmental Control Board. The other 90 percent of summonses go unanswered, and fines against vendors mount.

All this is frustrating to individual police officers, who are pressured by their commanders to do something about the "quality of life." When the police officer must repeatedly tell vendors on the block to pick up their stock-in-trade from the sidewalk, when every time the policeman turns his back the vendor puts his materials where they do not belong, the officer feels he is not being treated in a way that is consistent with how he is entitled to be treated. Inevitably, from time to time an officer seeks to avenge this—for example, by throwing a person's table, crates, and goods into the back of a garbage truck.[12] As we shall see, the officer's sense that he has been disrespected may be the variable most likely to lead him to go beyond the official limits of his discretion and take the law into his own hands.

A lieutenant in charge of policing the vendors has told me that, rather than write a ticket, officers sometimes prefer to wait for a person to leave his table unattended, and then confiscate his goods. In such an instance, the officer can claim that the goods were abandoned and take the vendor's belongings to the nearest dump truck or Dumpster in the trunk of the squad car. Such punishment serves to achieve a measure of social control by getting vendors to stay close to their belongings; more important, such measures are moralistic, bringing personal satisfaction and a sense of justice to police officers who have been embarrassed or shamed by vendors' attitudes or behavior.[13]

In ordinary life, when we speak of people taking the law into their own hands we are referring to situations in which citizens settle their own grievances without resorting to law enforcement.[14] But just as many citizens who take the law into their own hands do not want to depend upon the police to

settle their disputes, many police officers do not want to be entirely dependent on the law. The law can be frustrating. For example, the local law states that when an officer seizes a vendor's merchandise he or she is supposed to issue a summons, label the goods, and bring them back to the precinct house; this can take an hour or more. Many officers see it as wasted effort, since the vendor can recover his goods from the property clerk by paying a small storage fee, without appearing before the Environmental Control Board. And it makes the property clerk a kind of warehouse for recycled trash. Besides, most scavengers never come to collect their goods at all—it is easier for them to replenish their stock by picking through a new round of trash.

These incidents are repeated over and over again, so that the relationship between the vendor and the police officer is ritualized. The individual police officer who methodically labels trash that has become merchandise, takes it to the precinct house, and then returns to the street only to see more trash for sale as merchandise feels that he has not been treated with the level of respect to which he is entitled. Though the street person is inconvenienced by the enforcement of civil penalties, they have little or no effect on his behavior. It is much easier for an officer to throw a man's belongings away than to place them in storage at the precinct. And since the officer knows that so much of the merchandise comes from the trash anyway, he sees the Dumpster as the proper place for it. From the officer's point of view, throwing away Ishmael's stock of magazines while he is away from the table—taking the law into his own hands—is a way of moving beyond penalties that have no effect and toward penalties that do.

The "Legitimacy" of Retaliation

After Ishmael and I arrive back on the block from the police station, Marvin asks, "So what happened? Was I right? Did you learn that you should get a lawyer?"

"Get a *what*?" Ron asks.

"Get a *lawyer*," Marvin repeats. "They took Ishmael's stuff. They fucked with him."

"He wasn't there, though," says Ron. "How you going to do it? By fucking lying?"

Even though vendors will complain about the police's behavior, there are times when they will recognize in talk among themselves that their own misdeeds may have brought on the results they are frustrated about. In so doing, they show awareness that taking a man's belongings is a prescribed method of punishment. In this case, Ishmael was unwilling to admit that he was away from his table, a denial that didn't make sense to Ron:

"I *was* there, man."

"You was there, Ishmael?" asks Ron.

"Yeah," says Ishmael.

"You wasn't there."

"You gonna tell me yesterday they took my stuff and I wasn't there?" says Ishmael.

"How you gonna have a case if you wasn't there?" says Ron. "What if the man at the newsstand left his stuff and someone took all his shit? You think he could say anything?"

Turning to Marvin, Ishmael defends himself. "Marvin, what Ron's saying is irrelevant right now. He don't know nothing, because he just got here today. He's just going by earsay."

"That's what everybody says, Ishmael," responds Ron. "That you wasn't there. So you need a witness to say you was there. Nobody said you were there."

"You know what your problem is, Ron? You want to be so right. At the moment you are wrong. I got a witness there."

"You was there?" asks Ron. "So why did you let them take it?"

"Why I let them take it? They took it because they wanted to take it. Because the motherfuckers throwing shit on the ground like you doing right now. They say every time they see shit like that they taking everybody's table."

"That's not why they took yours!" says Ron.

"They came from down here and took my fucking table because Joe laid shit all over the fucking ground."

"How come they didn't take Grady and them's table?" asks Ron. "How come they only took your table?"

"Look, Ron, right now I don't need you to get me upset. You got your shit. You here. Be happy with that. I got my shit tooken and I'm not too fucking happy. Leave it alone, okay? The whole issue is based on you laying your stuff on the ground and the officer specifically saying, If I see anything on the ground, I'm going to look for anybody's table and take it."

"That's what the issue is," says Marvin.

"You right, Marvin," continued Ishmael. "But the issue remains that the same officer took the table spoke to me and said, 'I'm not gonna mess with your stuff at all.' I said to him, 'I'm gonna walk off, I'm gonna go to the bathroom, get some food and stuff.' He said, 'You don't have nothing to worry about.' See, that's a form of entrapment."

An Asian woman, about twenty-five years old, has been standing a few feet away, waiting for us to finish talking. When Ishmael sees her, he says to me, "Look at this. That's my wife," using the word loosely to describe in a possessive way the woman with whom he has begun to have a romantic relationship. "What's up, Tina?"

"Hey!" she says.

"They took my stuff, Tina!"

"I heard it," she says. "You have to tell me! Because I was waiting, waiting, waiting, waiting. And I went outside and I was standing outside. . . ."

"That's the one I was supposed to take to the movies," Ishmael says to me in a low voice.

"The reason they took my stuff, Tina, is just because another guy put his stuff down on the ground," Ishmael continues. "They took every last thing that I had."

"So you ain't working today?"

"I don't know. I've just been taking care of business all day, dealing with the law all day. . . . I went to the precinct to get my stuff."

"They want to keep it? They don't want to give you back?" asks Tina.

"They didn't even give me a summons for it, hon!"

"What's that?" asks Tina.

"A paper where they write up the stuff that they take from you. It's like a receipt. Tina, I've been busy all day."

After another minute of conversation, Tina leans over and kisses him on the lips. "Well, I'll come back and see you tomorrow, Ishmael."

"I be thinking about you." They embrace. Then she goes away.

Marvin and Ron turn to their customers. Ishmael goes for a slice of pizza, and then on a hunt to find a new supply of magazines.

•

Whatever the facts may be (recall that Ishmael told the desk sergeant that he was approaching the table when the officer removed his belongings), the argument illustrates that Ishmael and Ron understand the rule of the street: that police can seek vengeance under certain circumstances. By refusing to admit that he was away from his table, Ishmael shows his assumption that a table left unattended can be taken *legitimately*, even though there is no municipal ordinance to this effect. Police are free to control the "quality of life" through routine discretionary acts that they establish in the minds of vendors as legitimate.

When the Law "Means Nothing" to the Police

Two days later, on Christmas afternoon, I saw Ishmael again. When I arrived, Hakim was standing on the corner. Ishmael had set up his table in his usual spot on the corner of Sixth Avenue and Eighth Street. Ten minutes later, Of-

ficer X (as I'll call him) approached and said something to the effect of: Ishmael, you have to break down, guy.[15]

I'm not breaking down, man, he responded.

Ishmael clearly was not showing the kind of deference the men on the block normally observe. I took out my tape recorder and turned it on, though neither Ishmael nor the officer saw me do so.

"You have to break down," the officer insisted.

"But I'm not. Because there's no such thing as a law telling me that. I'm not gonna break down, man. If I can't work, what the hell you working for?"

"Step over here for a second. Ishmael . . ."

"I'm not, man. Come on, that's my food. . . ."

"Listen to me," said the officer.

"I'm the only one out here."

"Listen!"

"I'm not doing nothing wrong!"

"Listen. Listen, Ishmael. The captain says he don't want anybody out here. Now, by all means I should be out here closing the table down, putting your stuff in the car, but I'm not gonna do that to you. I want you to voluntarily do it yourself. 'Cause, listen, if he comes out here and you out here, he's just gonna take your shit away, probably collar you or something like that. And you know, it's not a good day for it."

"Collar me?"

"Listen. Of all days, I don't want to break you down today, because it's Christmas, but I've got to do what I'm told. All right. So, please, don't give me a hard time."

"I'm not giving you a hard time. You giving me a hard time."

"I know. It's just something he said I have to do out here. That's all."

"But do you think it's right?"

"No, I don't think it's right. But I have to follow his orders, man. You know. 'Cause he is my boss. And if I don't follow his orders, the guy could fucking do anything to me. Do you follow me?"

"You saying he could write you up?"

"Yeah, for not following orders. Listen, you know what, why don't you go set up across the street? But not on Sixth Avenue. That way he's not gonna say shit to you. Thank you."

With that, the officer walked away. Ishmael called after him.

"What is the thing about Sixth Avenue?"

"Ishmael, it's a lot better to be over there. Maybe you'll sell a few books. It's better than having your shit broken down and being locked up."

"I'll be locked up for that, too?"

"Listen! For not complying with orders, right? Take your stuff across the street. Take your chances over there. It's better than over here right now. All right?"

"All right."

The officer walked away. Ishmael walked over to Hakim and me. We were standing on the corner.

"You heard that, Mitch."

"What happened?" asked Hakim.

"He said I could be locked up for not complying with the orders."

"With what orders? What law?" asked Hakim.

"The captain's law," said Ishmael.

"The captain said you can't be here today? There's something in the Municipal Code that says you can't work on Christmas Day?"

"He didn't tell me that," said Ishmael.

"Is there exigent circumstances, an emergency circumstance that does not allow you to be here?" asked Hakim. "Is that what he said to you?"

"It's just his captain telling him this. And I asked him, What do you think? And he said he know it isn't right, that he gotta go along with what his captain says. . . . Right now he's saying that, if I don't comply with what he's saying, then I can be collared."

"You can be arrested?"

"For not complying."

"In other words, they gonna take you *and* the table?"

"Yeah."

"That's deep," said Hakim, and went on: "What is the legal basis for him telling you to leave? You in a legal vending space. Unless he say there's an exigent circumstance going on that has millions of people walking down the street. But what did he say?"

"He said that I can't be on Sixth Avenue today because there's no vendoring on Sixth Avenue today. If you choose to stay on the block, the captain will take you and your stuff. There's no law to find out. But I don't want to go through this procedure with these people. I'm gonna have to break down. I don't feel like getting locked up for nobody today."

"Well, if you feel that way, then break down. But I'm just saying to you, they make up the law today, they make up the law tomorrow. So you gotta put him in check. You see, he don't have nothing to say to me. Because, the last time, I let his ass have it down here. If you don't know the law, they abuse you."

"Well, this is what I don't know," said Ishmael.

•

Ishmael began packing up his magazines. After a few minutes passed and about half the material was packed up, the officer returned.

"You know, it really affects me," Ishmael told him as he continued packing. "Because this is first year out of seven years out of all the Christmases that I've worked out here and this is the first time that I've heard something like that. And I don't know where that captain comes off at saying that statement that I know for sure is not documented in no kinds of papers. They've got vendoring up there on 14th Street. And it's a holiday weekend. So what's the difference? If I'm being shut down, what about the newspaper stand [pointing]? Why isn't he being shut down? He's on Sixth Avenue."[16]

The officer stood silently as Ishmael continued. "That's like taking the bread out of my mouth, man. And that's something that I have to go and confirm with this captain. It's not right, man. And if it's allowed to be done this time, it will keep being done. It's not right. Lawfully, it's not right." Ishmael continued: "That's like superseding over everything, man. That's like violating my rights for trying to make my livelihood of money. Come on, man. I'm not saying it's you. It's that individual who's sending that law down that you have to do that. Out of seven years, this is the first time that I've ever heard of some crap like that, man!"

"You the only one out here, Ishmael," said the officer.

"They see me is the only one out here. Other people choose not to be out here and work. If they had a table, I guarantee the tables would have been set up today. But since their tables got tooken from them . . ."

"Those guys got their tables taken from them?" asked the officer.

"Yeah, they had their tables tooken from them!"

"When was that?"

"The other morning."

"Did they have their shit all over the floor?"

"No. It was unattended. And legally it can be tooken when it's unattended."

"You know how many times I've warned them about that, too?" the officer asked rhetorically as he walked away.

As Ishmael packs up his belongings, I read and reread my own crumpled copies of the municipal ordinances that govern the sale of written matter. I am certain that Hakim is correct. Barring some special circumstance that makes it dangerous to remain on the street at a particular time—a parade, say, or a demonstration—the officer has no legal reason to insist that a vendor move from a legal space.

I have spent years studying these laws and spoken to experts on the codes. It seems to me that I may be witnessing an example of the discretion taken by police officers as they engage in policing against "quality of life" infractions. The officer had justified his actions in a variety of ways (my captain says to close you down, you are the only one out here today) without making reference to the law—because, indeed, the law would not have stood behind him. But since Ishmael does not know the law, and so has no confidence that he is correct ("That's what I don't know," he told Hakim), he was afraid to stand up to the officer and risk arrest or a summons. Perhaps, he thought that as an unhoused black male, even if he was in the right, the officer would not necessarily acknowledge it.

I wanted to see what else I could learn by setting up in the very spot Ishmael had just vacated. As he was hauling tables away, I asked him to loan me a small table and a set of *National Geographics*.[17]

Five minutes later, I stood behind a table just as Ishmael had earlier in the day. I was wearing a leather winter jacket, with the microphone from my tape recorder sticking out the front pocket. I wondered what I might discover about the police's use of their own discretion to improve the "quality of life."

Alice walked up to the table. "You see, Mitch, that's the thing. These cops is full of shit. Because they don't have nobody else to bully around."

The vendors moved away from the table against the front of the B. Dalton bookstore about twenty feet away. "If they take you in, we're going with you," Ishmael called out to me.

At two minutes after five (I checked), a Sixth Precinct police car drove by and a white officer stared at me from the passenger seat. When the car had passed, one of the vendors yelled, "As long as it's a white guy out here it's okay."

If this was a test designed to find out whether an upper-middle-class white person would be treated differently from an unhoused, poor black vendor, I thought to myself, then it was not a good one. To begin with, the officer had just closed Ishmael down. The odds were very small that a black police officer who had to enforce the law against black vendors every day would let himself be seen as one who would allow a white man to stay in the same spot. Furthermore, he might notice the microphone sticking out of my pocket, and this would probably affect what he'd say to me.

I had been standing at the table for about ten minutes when I saw the officer and his beat partner walking toward me.

As I waited, approximately ten black vendors, including Hakim and Ishmael, stood by, offering their support.

"It's showtime!" yelled Ishmael.

"Yo, if they take you in, Mitch, we're coming down there," offered Al.

Then the police were at my table—or, as the vendors would say, "on my ass."

"My man. There's no selling here today. Break it down."

"Excuse me," I said.

"No selling here today. Break it down."

I took a copy of the municipal law out of my pocket. "I'm exercising my right under Local Law 33 of 1982, and Local Law 45 of 1993, to sell written matter."

"Break it down," said the officer. "There's no selling here today."

"Am I within the spaces?" I asked.

"I'll tell you one more time."

"Am I within the spaces?"

"I'll tell you one more time. Break it down."

"Under what law?" I asked.

"No vending here today. Break it down."

"For what reason?"

"Listen. There was somebody here who broke it down, all right? Break it down or I'm gonna take your table away."

"Just tell me the reason I'm being broken down. I have the law right here. I just want to know what reason I'm being broken down."

The officer grabbed the copy of the municipal law out of my hands. "*This*, listen to me, *this* means nothing to me right now."

"But *this* is the local law!"

"I don't care. Break it down."

"Can I please have my copy of the local law back?"

"After you break it down."

"No. I'm not breaking down. How can you say the law means nothing to you?"

"Because *he* broke it down," he said loudly, pointing to Ishmael, who was out of earshot on the corner.

"I'm set up within the lines. Correct or not?"

"Listen," the officer responded, "vending on Sixth Avenue is a privilege that is bestowed on you guys by this community over here."

"A privilege?"

"Yes."

"I'm set up under the law. Can I have my copy of the law back?"

"Listen."

"You just confiscated my property."

"Listen. Break it down."

"Officer, give me back my property."

"You can have it back when I give it to you."

With that, he walked away from the table and conferred with his beat partner on the corner. Then they put in a call on their radio.

"What are they telling you?" Al cried out. "That they're gonna give you a ticket?"

"No. He confiscated my copy of the law and he won't give it back to me."

A few seconds later, the same patrol car that had passed by earlier pulled up to the curb behind the table.

"Listen, man. We gonna be with you, man," one of the vendors called out.

Officer X walked over to the car and conferred with the officer in the passenger seat for a full minute. Then that officer, a white man of about fifty, got out of the car and slammed the door behind him. He walked around my table and inspected its contents.

Another patrolman appeared on the block, walked up to the table, inspected the magazines closely, and said to Officer X, "This guy looks good."

At the same time, Officer X pulled me aside and said, "What's your name?"

"Mitchell Duneier."

"Mitchell Duneier. Can I talk with you over here, please. Mitchell. This is what happened earlier. Okay. There was a gentleman over here. I had asked him to move and go across the street, because—"

"Can I have my law back, please?"

"You'll get your law back."

"I have to stand at my table. Please talk to me at my table. I'm distributing written matter in accordance with the local law. I must stand with my materials."

"Mitchell, 'cause you and I are talking, you can leave the table. Nothing is going to happen to you. All right? Now, like I was saying previously, there was a gentleman here. I asked him to go across the street, because apparently they don't want anybody on Sixth Avenue today."

"Who?"

"Mitchell. Listen. All you have to do is listen."

"Okay, I'm listening. But you have to understand that I'm frustrated with you, because you said to me before that the law means nothing to you."

"Listen."

"Can I have my copy of the law back?"

"Are you gonna listen? Or are you just gonna ramble on?"

"I'll listen if you respect me. I want my copy of the law back."

At this moment, the officer who had been in the passenger seat of the car, whom I'll call Captain Y, approached us at the table.

"Here's your copy of the law back," said Officer X.

"Listen," said Captain Y. "Regardless of what that says [pointing to my copy of the law], *we* decide where you're allowed to vend and where you're not. So don't cop an attitude with the officer."

"I'm not."

"Listen to me carefully! Don't cop an attitude with them, because they know the law better than you know the law. And you can take this [pointing to the law] and bring it to Central Booking. You don't want to do that on Christmas. So just cooperate with the officers and don't cop an attitude. You understand? 'Cause the last thing they want to do is get tied up in court."

"Okay, Officer."

"And we don't want to put you in jail tonight."

"Okay, Officer."

"So I told him you can stay for now. Put your magazines and do what you got to do. But *we* decide, not you, where you stay. Do you understand that?"

"Can I ask you a question?"

"Surely."

"Do you have any idea why he came here and told me I had to move? I mean, I'm set up within the legal lines."

"Well, actually, it's so many feet from a doorway."

"It's measured out exactly," I said.

"How many feet is it?"

"It's supposed to be more than twenty, and this is more than twenty."

"No, it's not. From that door to here is not twenty feet," said the captain.

"You see these painted lines here? These are the vending lines that are set up by the police."

"Listen to me carefully! They've been changed!"

A number of vendors had crowded behind the captain to hear what he was saying. One man yelled, "Its twenty-one feet. The reason I'm listening is I'm a vendor, too."

"Listen to me," said the captain. "That door to this table is how many feet?"

"Twenty-one feet."

"Wanna bet? All right, the fact is, you can stay for now. All right? So the point is moot."

"Okay," I said.

"I don't want to argue with you on Christmas."

"Okay," I said.

"As long as you understand that!" said the captain.

With that, the police left.

"I see he gave you back your paper," Al called out. "I think that was a point well made. Now Ishmael can put his stuff back there."

"Where is Ishmael?" I asked, looking to the corner. "Is he gonna put his tables back here?"

"He said he's waiting until you leave," said Hakim.

"Okay."

I left the table and approached Ishmael. "Here's my tape recorder if you want it." It had occurred to me that this scene with Officer X might not be Ishmael's last encounter with the police.

"Yeah, let me just keep it on." He took the machine and put it in the milk crate under his table, and I went inside an open coffee shop, the Bagel Buffet, to warm up.

•

As I sat by myself at a small table, I reflected on the events that had occurred on the block. Although I hadn't given careful thought to what might be gained by setting up in Ishmael's spot, I had long sought to understand the ways of the police as they used their discretion to enforce the municipal laws against written-matter vendors and unhoused people on Sixth Avenue. I had tried to interview police officers, but had always been told that to conduct an interview I would have to get permission from the New York City Police Department's Bureau of Public Information. When I finally did get such permission once, after months of waiting, the sergeant in charge of policing vendors sat with me in the back of the Sixth Precinct and answered all my questions, but somehow said nothing of any significance. This reminded me of what I had read of others' experiences, including that of Paul Chevigny, a leading American scholar of police. "It must be admitted that the NYPD is difficult to study," he writes. "Bureaucratized as it is, it turns a bland face to the public as well as to scholars. Everything has to be done through channels; hardly anyone in the department will talk to an outsider without approval from above, and once the approval is obtained, hardly anything of substance is revealed."[18]

As a sociologist, I would have liked to use as my example taped conversations between police and vendors when neither party knew they were being recorded. Likewise, I would have preferred to see Hakim and the vendors win or lose this battle without any interference or intervention on my part. Nevertheless, it seemed that my encounter with the police might have analytic value.

Because I possessed a copy of the local law and understood it, I had witnessed a striking example of the extent to which officers of the Sixth Precinct will use their discretion to circumvent the law, even when someone waves that very law before their eyes. But how did I *know* that this abuse of discretion was characteristic? It was possible, for instance, that the officer had tried especially hard to get me off the block because he wanted to prove to Ishmael and the other vendors that he wouldn't show favoritism toward a white vendor. Possibly, if one of the regular black vendors had waved the law in the officer's face, he would have been allowed to stay.

In the end, of course, I *was* allowed to stay, by the captain, even though this embarrassed the officer. There is no way for me to know if this was because I knew the law and had a copy handy, or because I was an educated white male. In everyday life, of course, race, class, and education are correlated: white middle-class people are more able to mobilize the law than poor people of color. An altogether thorough experiment would have required one more trial, with Hakim at the table, in order to test what happens when a person with education and a knowledge of the law, but a low social status, challenges the police. Lacking this, the closest that I can come to such an experiment is some observations of the way Hakim was treated under similar circumstances.

In a letter he wrote to me after the passage of Local Law 45 in 1993, Hakim tells of setting up his table in front of Balducci's gourmet market. I quote from the letter with his permission:

Yesterday I came into New York and set up twenty feet from the entrance to Balducci's Supermarket and ten feet from the intersection.

There is nowhere else to work right now.

I knew that, if necessary, I was going to set up on the block where Balducci's is located a long time ago. I never told anyone that I studied the location and placement logistics for every block in the Village. I do not wait for other vendors to do anything. I act alone. No one is going to help me anyway. No one. I was holding on to my trump card for a long time. I knew there was a legal space in front of Balducci's Supermarket.

Within ten minutes a Puerto Rican Balducci's security guard with a cheap "March of the Wooden Soldiers" uniform says to me, "I am just trying to be nice. You can't stay here. You gotta leave."

"This is public space," I told him. "This is a *legal* location for vending. I do not want to be here, but I can't work down the street. So, you are gonna have to call the police."

Anyway the police come in an unmarked wine red car. Two patrol officers and the Sergeant in the back seat.

The measure tape comes out.

Are you ten feet from the intersection?

I'm more than ten feet and I'm twenty feet from the entrance to their store.

They measure. I got her ass! She has that "I'm tired of this smart-ass Nigger" look on her face.

One of the patrol officers says to me, "You know the law pretty well, huh?"

"Yeah, I read it like some people read *T.V. Guide*. But, I don't want to be here, Officer."

The sergeant had to get back in her car and leave. They *cannot* move me. They have no *legal basis* to move me without running the risk of being *sued*. She knows this.

The manager of Balducci's does not like this and I overhear him say "That's ridiculous."

If the Sergeant thought she could "make it up" as she imagined it, she would have lied to force me to move. But she *recognizes* I have done my homework.

No *sane* African-American should ever trust what any police officer says. Get the law and look it up. Know your basic rights.

What have I found? That people down here do not know how to look up basic laws, and they cannot afford experts.

Because I am generally regarded as a Nigger, many white folks, even well meaning white folks, think I am stupid. Stupid means: The inability to achieve the tactical intelligence of a white person.

Hakim's letter strongly suggests that the crucial difference between Ishmael and me may not have been race alone, but level of education and confidence about the law. What seems more important is that if the officers will speak so cavalierly about the law with an educated middle-class white vendor—"this means nothing to me"—it seems reasonable to infer that their treatment of poor and uneducated black men who cannot cite the law chapter and verse is potentially far more arbitrary.

It is helpful to see this incident in the larger historical context of how skid rows used to be policed. In a classic sociological study of the mid-1960s, Egon Bittner shows that in skid-row districts the law was invoked somewhat arbitrarily, but mainly "as a resource to solve certain pressing practical problems in keeping the peace."[19] Patrolmen saw it as their goal to help people on skid row and to engage in service activities. Those officers whose "roughness is determined *by personal feelings* rather than situational exigencies, are judged to be poor craftsmen."[20] Officers did not expect or demand deference.[21] They used the law "to keep skid-row inhabitants from sinking deeper into the misery they already experience."[22] Officers kept the peace on skid row not merely by knowing names, but by having a detailed personal knowledge of the people on the street. Supervisory personnel understood that such knowledge was crucial, so they exhibited "a strong reluctance to direct their subordinates in the particulars of their work experience."[23]

Some of the officers who regulate vendors on Sixth Avenue today know their names; others don't. Regardless, the police on Sixth Avenue today have less detailed knowledge than the patrolling officers on skid row did. They do not view it as their job to help salvage souls or to develop a detailed knowledge of the men on the beat, which they can draw upon in difficult situations. And their supervisors, having less respect for such detailed knowledge, give commands from far away.

A Cop's Honor

While I thought about these issues in the coffee shop, Ishmael was setting up his table with the tape recorder in his crate. A few minutes later, Officer X returned.

"Why did you fuck with me last week?" called out one vendor from against the brick wall of the B. Dalton bookstore.

"You're unprofessional!" yelled another.

"Stop picking on brothers," called out another.

"I've known Ishmael for three years now," the officer responded. "I've never had any problems with him whatsoever. These other guys give me problems, except for him. He's never given me any trouble. Today, I asked him respectfully. I said, Look, the man says he don't want anything out here. You was upset. I can understand that. All right? You was upset, but you respect me and I respect you. I never give you any beef out here, do I?"

"No, you don't," said Ishmael.

"And he'll tell you. If anything, I'm the most tolerant cop out here. You guys bust my balls. Every time I take your stuff, you guys do it again. If it were another officer, and you know who I'm talking about, your shit would have been kicked on the floor, kicked in the street. I don't want to do that to you guys. Granted, let me get upset. But I'm not gonna take your shit away. Just do what I ask you."

"You say the problem is us?" asked Al.

"Yes."

"Well, let me say something," said Al. "We also have a problem with the police, too. Just because you have a problem with some knuckleheads out here doesn't mean that Ishmael is a knucklehead or that I'm a knucklehead."

"Did I ever say you was a knucklehead? I'm just saying I don't want your stuff on the floor."

"I understand what you're saying. But we have problems with individual police officers."

"Fine."

"Because you walk by and you're on duty today and we do what you tell us, we know how you feel, and everything works out fine. Tomorrow or the next day, somebody else is on duty, and he says, 'Get your shit outa here. . . .' So on a day-to-day basis we don't know which way is up and which way is down. We want the relationship to be balanced. You know what we're saying? It has to happen. This is America."

"Hold on," said the officer. "Ishmael, if you're the cop and you say, 'Don't put your stuff on the floor,' I say, 'Yeah, Ishmael, no problem.' I take it and I pick it back up when you're there. When you walk away, I put it back on the floor. This happens several times. How are you going to react?"

"I have to act like you didn't respect me. I have to take your stuff. But I'm asking you now, is it permissionable for me to put back my table?"

"Yeah. Listen, Ishmael, I don't know if you know the guy that set up over there. Do you know him?"

"Do I know him?"

"The guy who set up. Do you know the white bread that set up over there?"

"No, I don't know him."

"So I asked you to move because the captain said he didn't want anyone on Sixth Avenue. All right? Meanwhile, after you leave, I see that guy. I asked him to leave. He said, Why? I said, Because you can't be here. He says, Well, my right's to be here. So I said, 'I don't care about that right now.' You have to leave. It's not right to you if I ask you to leave and then he comes and sets up. I was like, bullshit, you have to leave. I told my partner, 'If anything, I want Ishmael back here, not him. Fuck him. I don't know fucking Joey White Bread from Adam.' "

"Yeah."

"I've known you for three fucking years, man."

"Yeah," said Ishmael.

"You've done nothing but show me the utmost fucking respect. Why should I let him stay?"

"Right. That's what I'm saying," said Ishmael.

"We had a big argument. You were over there. The captain came out here."

"Your captain?"

"Right. The captain was like, If my patrol officer doesn't want you out here, we don't have to let you stay out here. I was just about to kick that boy's table into the fucking street. But then the captain came here. And then I told him, You know what, take my name and take my fucking shield number down. I don't give a shit. You know? You not supposed to be out here. Period. He said, Oh, this is my right under the law. And I was like, I don't care about your rights now. And he got offended because I said that. Then he's being like fucking defiant to me. I don't like that. Because, honestly, if the captain didn't pull up, I would have knocked his fucking block off. All right?"

Ishmael laughed. "You crazy, man."

"Fuck that. I don't know him from Adam."

"That's why I didn't understand that," said Ishmael.

"You see, now I feel badly. 'Cause he let this fucking guy stay out here. So, now, fuck it. You put all of your shit back. Fuck him. I feel bad now because you had to leave."

"Well, that's part of the game, man. I'm just glad that I did not get collared behind the situation," said Ishmael.

There was silence. A few seconds later, the officer continued.

"Then, after that, these guys said to me, 'Why did you come yelling at me last week?' I said, 'Four times I told you not to put your shit on the floor. Every time I turn my back on you, it's on the floor.' They said, 'It's not right. You're not a pro.' What do you mean, I'm not a pro? I'm asking you. I'm not fucking telling you. You know how I am out here."

Ishmael changed the topic.

"Yeah, but the thing is, I've seen him set up before as a vendor, working."

"That's the first time I've seen him out here," said the officer.

"But I guess he sees what going on down here and he probably figured he could set up, too," said Ishmael. "But since that blew over right now, it's over, and I just want to do what I have to do. And that's why I have to come back to you to ask you again, is it permissionable for me to set up so I won't have to worry about my stuff getting tooken again?"

"Set up, set up," said the officer. "You know what, though?"

"What's that?" asked Ishmael.

"That guy [pointing to Hakim]—he tried to fucking defy me once, he made me look like an idiot. When I see him fucking up, my man's getting a summons. I'm gonna tell every cop out here. Every chance they get. Nobody does that to me out here, man."

"But don't worry about that, man," said Ishmael.

"But, Ishmael, it ain't right, man."

"There's a lot of things that ain't right. But it happens. But what can we do? The best thing we can do to solve the situation is to bring out the rightness. All right?"

"All right, man."

"Anyway, let's just make this day a better day." said Ishmael. "Still, it's Christmas, right?"

"Let's look at it that way."

"All right."

The two men were quiet a few moments. The police officer broke the silence.

"Ishmael?"

"Yes."

"Here. Buy a beer on me, man," the officer said, his voice quavering.

"A beer? I don't want no beer. I want just two franks."

"Here you go. Two franks on me, bro."

"This is five dollars, though!"

"Come on, man. Listen. So I'll probably be out here Friday. So we'll talk."

"We have to talk," said Ishmael. "Because I respect you a whole lot, man."

"You know," said the officer, "these guys, they say, Why am I this way? That I'm not a pro. They don't fucking know me."

"That's right," said Ishmael. "They have to get to know you. They don't know you how I know you. They haven't been around you. They don't know how you *really* is."

"You know what, though? If I was the sergeant? You know that shit would have been kicked out of here a long time ago." (He was referring to the sergeant who had backed off when Hakim had shown her he knew the law.)

"That's what I'm saying," responded Ishmael. "The sergeant would have went off already."

"And you know what it is," said the officer. "I don't like to pick on brothers. You know what I'm saying? Because it's hard enough for all of us out here? But these guys, they push me too far, man. How could they get respect if they don't respect their own kind?"

"But you have to understand their mentality at the moment. These are people that was out here for so long and so much was taken from them, they'll just explode. They like walking bombs now. And it's not really toward you, officer."

"I know."

"It's not really you. And at the moment, they walk around because so much been done to them."

"All right, man," said the officer. "I'll be on Sixth Avenue somewhere. All right?"

"Relax," said Ishmael.

"All right, I'll talk to you later. Enjoy your franks."

A few moments later, Ishmael spoke into the microphone. "I hope you got that on tape, Mitch. That was a good conversation. That justified for a lot of things."

The discussion between Ishmael and the officer seemed to be charged with emotion: the officer's anguish over the prospect that the vendors see him as unprofessional, and possibly Ishmael's own embarrassment at the officer's humiliation, as well as anger over the way he thinks he has been mistreated by the police. The officer is part of an occupational subculture that rewards conformity, and it is through conforming to the commands of his superiors that he is rewarded with the positive evaluations that lead to pride and fellow feeling, leading to further conformity.[24] It is well established that a police officer will support his fellow officers at almost all times, but here the lack of support from his fellow officers (namely, the captain) led the officer actually to speak ill of fellow officers, including the sergeant who had let Hakim stay in front of Balducci's when he demonstrated that he knew the law. The officer contended that if he had been the sergeant, he would have long ago kicked everybody's items into the street.

When he is challenged as unprofessional by the vendors, the officer's immediate response is to defend himself vigorously (even at the cost of attacking his fellow officers). He seems to have reacted to the shock of having the members of his occupational world fail to stand behind him (a usual source of pride and fellow feeling), while also sensing that he has been made to look like a fool in front of the very men he must discipline every day. This leads to a highly unusual exchange between a police officer and an unhoused vendor in which the vendor becomes confidant and even therapist.

This exchange suggests the predicament of black officers who engage in the "quality of life" policing of black vendors. In defending himself, the officer points to the vendors' actions as the basis for what he does to them. We see here extreme frustration at having to enforce the law with what seems like so little effect.

The officer defended himself with great self-confidence, possibly in order to stop the vendors from further shaming him by referring to his unprofessionalism. He may perceive that, if he does not do so, his shame will be remembered on the street in the future. But when he is outside the earshot of other vendors, the shame he feels becomes apparent. Why does Ishmael respond with seeming sympathy? When he says that the vendors don't really *know* the officer the way he does, is he supporting the officer out of some calculation regarding his future dealings with police on the street? (The officer had made it clear that he seeks revenge against Hakim.) Or is he genuinely embarrassed for the officer, able to see the world through the eyes of the man who earlier made him break his table down? There is no reason why both motives cannot enter into Ishmael's response, and there is no reason to dismiss either of them. Ishmael seems intent on giving the officer more than a sympathetic ear: he actively works to prop the officer up, deferring to him until the very end, asking over and again whether it is okay to set up now. Asking this question again and again may be Ishmael's attempt to make the officer feel that he is still respected.

When the officer hands Ishmael five dollars and tells him to buy a beer, he seems to be acknowledging the shame he feels for the way Ishmael was treated. He wronged Ishmael, and he "owes" him for it. But once he has given over the five dollars, he seems to need to save face for that act, too. As a way of doing this gracefully, he distinguishes between Ishmael and indecent men like Hakim, who defy their own kind. The charge against Hakim reveals the special logic that a black officer employs to deal with the dilemma of policing black people: how could these black vendors get respect when they don't even respect their own kind? As the officer suggests, it is not only the black vendors who feel betrayed by black officers. The vendors' logic is turned right back on them. When a black vendor defies a black officer, that is a betrayal with special effect. We see here how self-respect for all concerned is tied to being a good "race man."[25] And this distinction becomes the officer's way of making it clear to Ishmael that he is apologizing for no other reason than that Ishmael ultimately showed respect—the lens through which much is seen on Sixth Avenue. As the officer said to Ishmael in defending himself vis-à-vis all of the vendors, "You respect me and I respect you."

•

Soon afterward, Ishmael walked to over to Hakim, a couple of frankfurters in his hand. "Listen, you gotta tell Mitch that me and him can't talk for a few days. 'Cause this cop is upset. He flipped out. Everything he said is on this tape. You gonna bug the fuck out."

"Yeah, I know he's flipped out," said Hakim. "But he gotta calm down. Because he took instructions that were completely unenforceable and then was forced to be made a fool out of himself because a white supervisor came here again and told him, 'No, we can't do this.' That's his fault. Because he could have easily called up and gotten clarification on this. But he didn't do that."

"Yeah, he didn't do that."

"And then what happens? The white guys in the car roll in. He's made to look like a fool again in front of some other black people. That's his problem."

"And then the guy gives me five dollars. Ain't that something?" exclaimed Ishmael.

"The cop? Damn! That's deep!"

"Where do you think I got the two frankfurters?"

"Let me ask you this question," said Hakim. "Are you gonna work?"

"Yeah, I gonna get my stuff."

"Well, you gotta do what you gotta do."

"Where's Mitch at?"

"Inside the coffee shop," said Hakim.

"Yeah, I got to send him this tape machine," said Ishmael. "Yo, I'm gonna set up. Take this out and give this to him. The officer asked do I know Mitch. I told him no."

"I'm going in the coffee shop with this."

"Merry Christmas, Hakim."

"Merry Christmas, Ish."

•

A certain arrogance has accompanied the success of replacing voluntary social control on the sidewalks with "broken windows" social control. The proponents of this idea (including many business associations, police chiefs, and other policy makers with great influence) have moved into a new phase of advocacy heralded by George Kelling and Catherine Coles's book, *Fixing Broken Windows*, and perhaps unanticipated by the original *Atlantic Monthly* article by Wilson and Kelling. The authors of the new book state that the future of social control depends not merely on taking violent people or criminals off the sidewalks, but "disreputable or obstreperous or unpredictable people: panhandlers, drunks, addicts . . . loiterers, and the mentally disturbed." Elsewhere they target "unlicensed vending and peddling."[26]

As we have seen, many of the men on Sixth Avenue who are succeeding at living a "better" life through their entrepreneurial activity are panhandlers, drunks, addicts, loiterers, and possibly the mentally disturbed, as well as unlicensed vendors. This new phase of "broken windows" regulation is proceeding on the premise that such persons must be removed from our sidewalk life because all these types of behavior can be designated as "disorder." Such claims should no longer be accepted without solid evidence. Indeed, if we take the time to know the people who fit the labels, there is evidence to the contrary. In justifying the argument that a broken window in a neighborhood leads to a series of larger harms, Wilson and Kelling had no hard evidence, nor did they claim to. But they reasoned from Zimbardo's demonstration of what happened when cars were abandoned in Palo Alto and the Bronx. Now that crime rates have declined by 50 percent in cities that have adopted their ideas, Wilson and Kelling's claims about "broken windows" seem self-evident.

My purpose has not been to debunk the "broken windows" theory. In fact, the anti-crime programs that Wilson and Kelling originally advocated, which enable many cities to "catch some problems early and nip them in the bud,"[27] as well as other programs that involve citizens in problem solving,[28] have probably contributed to lowering crime rates. But the "broken windows" programs that target people trying to make "an honest living" on the sidewalks are intellectually the weakest parts of these prescriptions. On Sixth Avenue, we can see the unanticipated consequences of such policies.

According to Wilson and Kelling, once passersby got a sense that "no one cares" about the car in Zimbardo's demonstration, they were willing to break windows and steal random parts. Wilson and Kelling use this demonstration to argue that unrepaired minor disorder leads to a spiral of crime and decay in a neighborhood.

When Zimbardo did the broken-windows demonstration on abandoned cars in Palo Alto and the Bronx, he was interested in only one form of disorder—vandalism. Defined as the apparently senseless destruction of property, vandalism is a form of disorder that is physical in nature. Proceeding from Zimbardo's demonstration, Wilson and Kelling begin with the quite plausible inference that some potential criminals who see physical disorder get a sense that "no one cares" in a neighborhood. Then these people think they can get away with committing crimes.

But Wilson and Kelling made a significant untenable assumption that went unrecognized in the widespread adoption of their ideas. They used Zimbardo's demonstration with the abandoned cars, which was merely about *physical* disorder, to justify a set of ideas about *social* disorders, such as loitering, unhoused status, vending, drug use, and begging. This assumes that physical and social disorder are the same in their effects. But we should pause before accepting this assumption without good evidence.

Wilson and Kelling appeal to our willingness to believe that the mechanism for serious crime is the sense that "no one cares" and that social disorder, like physical disorder, means to people who would commit crimes that "no one cares."[29] They write, "The unchecked panhandler is, in effect, the first broken window. . . . If the neighborhood cannot keep a bothersome panhandler from annoying passersby, the thief may reason, it is even less likely to call the police to identify a potential mugger or to interfere if the mugging takes place."

My research leads me to be skeptical about the assumption that, in the signal given a potential criminal, there is a useful comparison to be made between a broken windowpane or graffiti on a wall and a panhandler or unhoused vendor on the street. Unlike a broken window, social disorder consists of human beings such as the vendors, scavengers, and panhandlers on Sixth Avenue, who are capable of thinking and creating meanings that range from "everyone cares" to "someone cares" to "no one cares."

It seems that an intellectual weakness of the "broken windows" theory as it is applied to people on Sixth Avenue is that it is formulated as a claim about the behavior of people who *look at* the broken window, rather than also being a theory about the behavior of the person *who is* the broken window. In a theory that moves by analogy from physical to social disorder, this is not tenable. The reaction of the potential criminal (the person who looks at the social broken window) cannot be divorced from the reaction of the social broken window who on Sixth Avenue sets up behavioral expectations quite different from those that Wilson and Kelling would propose. Even the panhandlers who refuse to respect propriety when they refuse to accept a signal to close a conversation know that this is just about as far as they can go when

Hakim, Marvin, and Jamaane aren't around. They, too, are being watched by the vendors and scavengers.

It is more reasonable to assume that physical disorder expresses the "no one cares" attitude than that apparent *social* disorder does so. I think that Wilson and Kelling may make a valid point when they argue that property damage is a symbol that tells potential lawbreakers that it is open season for such activity in the neighborhood.[30] But how do Wilson and Kelling know when they see instances of *social* broken windows that tell potential criminals that they can break the law? "Social disorder" is not the same as a public telephone that has been vandalized. The men working on Sixth Avenue may be viewed as broken windows, but this research shows that most of them have actually become public characters who create a set of expectations, for one another and strangers (including those of the criminal element—as, indeed, many of them once were), that "someone cares" and that they should strive to live better lives.

The "broken windows" theory as applied to street life seems to have worked so well because it has been used so broadly that it can hardly fail. In effect, with an unsystematic definition of disorder, it has been applied unscientifically, with a large margin of error that is usually unobserved: events such as occurred on Christmas between Ishmael and the officer usually go unseen and unheard. A better approach would be to define disorder with greater accuracy. In particular, I would like to see "broken windows"–style regulation work without "disrespecting" people who are engaging in innocent entrepreneurial activity.

PART FIVE

THE CONSTRUCTION

OF DECENCY

A Scene from Jane Street

Not all has changed on the sidewalks of Greenwich Village since Jane Jacobs wrote *The Death and Life of Great American Cities*. Although economic inequalities, cultural differences, and extremes of behavior can make sidewalk life difficult and unpredictable, there are places in the neighborhood where sidewalk life still provides strangers with a source of solidarity and mutual assurance.

A year after Ishmael's incident with the police, he was still set up on Sixth Avenue in the usual spot. I wanted to see how sidewalk life can work where there are no salient inequalities in race and class, where the public characters on the sidewalk are seen as decent and as posing no threat to passersby. Accompanied by Ovie Carter, I went to Jane Street, only five blocks from Sixth Avenue and in the heart of Jane Jacobs's old West Village neighborhood. We visited with the Romps, a family from Shoreham, Vermont, living in a camper on the streets of the West Village. The Romps were there to sell their Christmas trees to New Yorkers, and had lived on Jane Street, by the intersection with Eighth Avenue, ever since Thanksgiving.

Billy and Patti Romp have been coming to this block for ten years. They bring their three children—Ellie, seven; Henry, three; and Timmy, two—who are schooled at home and can be away from Vermont between Thanksgiving and Christmas.

The Romps have spread balsams and Douglas firs the length of two city blocks, in two-by-four wooden racks that Billy has built to keep the trees out of the way of pedestrians. On the curb are a saw and clippers, and an assortment of stands that New Yorkers will buy and use to mount trees in their apartments.

The Romps have set up in accordance with Local Law 17 of 1984, which states, "Peddlers may sell and display coniferous trees during the month of December . . . but in any such case the permission of the owner of the premises fronting on such sidewalk shall first be obtained."[1] The family has received the necessary permission from the West Village Committee, which administers the Jane Street Community Garden that fronts this sidewalk.

The sidewalk may not have been designed for such an enterprise, but somehow everything is neat and orderly. There is always a clear, if narrow, pedestrian path.

When we first catch up with the family on December 23, Billy is leaning against the side of his camper.

"How did you come here originally?" I asked.

"It was a bit of luck," he explains. "People we know in Vermont had been selling trees in Manhattan, and we had been asking about it for a couple of years. It was just an idea we had. Something to be adventurous. We really lucked into this corner here. We didn't know that we had the nicest corner in Greenwich Village, and we didn't know it would be profitable enough to come back for ten years."

Billy is interrupted by a woman who wants to talk to him. He greets her warmly.

"Hi, how you doing?"

"Do you know where 299 West 12th Street is?" she asks.

"Yeah, it's that giant building right there. You just go down there and take a right."

"So you know all the buildings in the neighborhood?" I ask.

"Yeah! I give directions all the time."

"But you're from Vermont!"

"I think these people must assume that, if I'm in the neighborhood, I must know my way around. And that's right. I do deliveries. I know all the restaurants and some of the addresses of most of the main buildings. I've been in a lot of them from doing deliveries. I deliver for free. Which shocks a lot of people."

He has customers. A white woman in her forties with a little girl.

"Hi. How you doing?"

"We want a tree. How much is this one?"

"This one is fifty. This is a big, plump, grade-A, premium balsam. Want me to move it out here so you can get a better look?"

The little girl thinks the tree is too small.

"Of course she wants the big one," says Billy, pointing to another tree. "Look at all the room for presents under there, will ya?"

The girl laughs.

"And will you put a fresh cut in?" asks the woman, wanting him to cut the last inch off the bigger tree.

"I will. Would you like me to bag it up?"

These local people seem to feel comfortable with the tree sellers. Billy does his part to make them feel that way.

His brother-in-law, Joe Gilmartin, is helping out. Joe brings a family from around the corner, where more trees are being displayed. "These folks are from Germany. They just moved here in October," he says.

"This is the *Tannenbaum*, right?" asks Billy, using the German word for "Christmas tree."

"You know a lot!" says the customer.

"We'll charge them in deutsche marks," he tells his brother-in-law. "We'll make them feel at home!"

I ask, "What is it like, coming from Vermont and living here with your family, in a camper without a bathroom?"

"First year we showed up, some of the first people that walked by say, 'Oh, you got a little baby in there. Have you got a friend in the neighborhood?' I said, 'No, we don't know anybody.' 'Oh, well, listen. My mom's got a place down here that's empty. I'll drop the keys off.' "

"Did you ever expect that in New York City?"

"No. Personally, I thought this would be one tough thing. I thought we'd have to pee in a bottle and use the restaurant when it was open. But as it turns out, that was the first of three people who offered us the keys to their apartments. You know, I'm a stranger here! And I had the typical cliché attitude toward New York City: that it's tough, and I was gonna have to tough out three weeks down here. It turned out that it's a nicer Village than the one I live in in Vermont. Here's an example: Garber's hardware is right around the corner. If I go there and buy some stuff and I'm three or four dollars short, 'Drop it off tomorrow! You'll be here.' Garber is Jewish. They don't buy a tree. But they come by and stand here every year and they let me give them a wreath or something. Great people."

A middle-aged white woman approaches the table.

"What kind of tree is that?"

"This is a Douglas fir from Pennsylvania."

"How much would it cost?"

"This one here is sixty-five dollars."

"It's beautiful."

"I know. They are beautiful trees. Now, how much did you have in mind to spend for a nice towering giant Christmas tree?"

"Forty bucks."

"Forty bucks? I bet I could fix you up with a forty-dollar balsam. Wanna look at one of these?"

Billy and the middle-aged woman are forced by a series of passing pedestrians to take a step backward, close to the trees.

"People like to walk by and smell," Billy explains.

The woman says she will come by later with her husband, and Billy begins telling me about his sales technique, how he works to make the customers feel comfortable.

"I find that a little patter is what people are used to. I don't mind silent spaces myself. But if I sense that someone does, I just go with the patter: 'How big is your ceiling? Look down there: plenty of room for presents.' Keep the patter up, which is partly good retail and partly it's my friendly nature. You know how, if you're in a conversation and there's a lull, especially with a new person, it's a little uncomfortable? If there's a big, long silence? Many people, their instinct is to say something, just to break the silence. I'm one that has never minded that. You know, if you and I are standing here for a while and"—he stops talking for two seconds to make the point—"and nothing happens, I'm fine with that. But I've noticed that many people get uncomfortable when there is a long silence."

"Is that more so in New York than in Vermont?"

"I think so. So, being here, you sort of find yourself developing a different technique with regard to those silences."

A woman from the neighborhood walks up with her little girl.

"Hi. How ya doin'?" asks Billy.

"Good. Mary wants to say hi to your kids. Okay?"

"Sure, they're in [the camper]. I think Ellie is getting her hair braided. Henry's being naughty and getting chewed out. So go right ahead in there."

"Is this a bad time?" asks the woman.

"No, no, no. Wanna step in the little camper? [Opens the door.] Climb right in there."

When the little girl sees Santos, the Romps' dog, she hesitates.

"Is this big doggie scary?" asks Billy. "Or are you just shy?"

She is quiet.

"I'm shy, too," Billy tells her. "Ellie, say hi to this young lady."

A woman named Barbara stops by and says, "We're making gingerbread cookies around 3:00 p.m., if your daughter wants to come."

"You still in the same apartment?" Billy asks.

"Yeah, you know the address—"

"Thank you, Barbara."

•

Billy catches a glimpse of his son Henry and tells him to grab a broom and clean up the needles from the Douglas firs all along the sidewalk.

I ask Billy where he gets his trees.

"Well, a bunch of the Christmas-tree stands have a single buyer. Actu-

ally, I should stop talking. Just say a friend who has a Christmas-tree business . . . I shouldn't even use his name. He hates publicity."

Another neighbor, named Terry, comes by with her dog. "Hello, Santos,
my gorgeous dog," she says. "Can I pet him?"

"Sure," says Billy. "Here, give me Star."

The two dogs bark uncontrollably at one another.

"You like that, Henry?" asks his father.

Henry points to the skateboard hanging on the side of the camper.

"You got shoes on?" his father asks, placing the board on the ground.
"There you go, buddy." Before he can finish saying "Be careful," Henry is
down the block.

Billy introduces me to Star's owner. "Mitch, this is Terry. She is one of
the very first people, late at night, walking her dog, to know us."

"Well, I've been on the block for quite a while," Terry responds. "When
Billy's working here, I have the luxury of coming out at one-thirty in the
morning to walk the dog. 'Cause he's on the corner. 'Cause there's someone
standing there."

"Whereas, if there was nobody there . . . ?" I ask.

"Well, would you come out at two in the morning to walk your dog casually around?" she responds, turning to Billy. "Find something else to sell
and be here year-round!"

"A lot of people wish I was here year-round selling stuff," said Billy.

"Well, start selling perennials!" responded Terry.

"I've thought of it all, Terry. There's nothing that will pay like Christmas
trees. Christmas trees are like magic. I can't sell enough flowers here."

Patti, Billy's wife, joins us, and Joe, her brother, carries a tree past the
ladies. He is single. When he isn't selling trees, Joe talks to some of the
women as they go by. They respond without hesitation.

1 Joe: Hi you doi [n.
2 Woman: [Good. How are you?
3 Joe: Breathe deep. Smell the pine.
4 Woman: Smells nice.

After he gets positive responses from a few different women, Joe
explains, "You can definitely tell the women that have lived here longer,

because they're into fashion. Especially the ones that got those black shoes on with those big heels, and it can be freezing cold out and they're in a little leather jacket and tights. You can tell." He points to a tree and calls out:

1 Joe: How does it look?
2 Woman: Nice. Very nice.

Two elegant old ladies approach Joe and tell him, in thick New York accents, that they are looking for branches. As he refers them around the corner, they walk in single file to avoid the trees. "Sorry about our crowded showroom," he says.

The women ask specifically for little Henry.

"He did it last year and he did very well," says one of them.

Billy explains that Henry runs the branch branch of the business. Billy used to give branches away as part of public relations, and then Henry took it over. Soon he has gathered some branches together, and the women are ready to pay.

"We'll give you a couple of extra, just in case, and you can put them in a vase," says Billy, adding to the impression the Romps give of never "getting over" on their customers.

"Now, how much do I owe you?" one of the women asks Henry.

"That's a dollar," he says.

"Talk it over with your father first."

"It's Henry's business," says Billy.

"No, no, no. Give him a hint."

"He charges what he wants."

"Do you think two would be better?" asks the lady.

"That's a dollar," says Henry.

"You could pay him a dollar and give him a little extra for his kindness," says Billy.

"Does he have a bank?" asks the other lady.

"Absolutely!" says Billy. "He's saving for a motorcycle. Maybe I shouldn't tell you that."

"On second thought . . . !" responds the lady.

"I have more than a hundred dollars," says Henry.

"This is for Dad for the branches. And this is for your motorcycle. Okay?"

Henry is quiet.

"What do you say?" asks Billy.

"Thank you," says Henry.

"Thank you very much!" says Billy. "Merry Christmas! Have the best, okay? If you need more, come back."

A few seconds later, Henry approaches his father.

"Dad? Why did the ladies give some of the money for the branches to you?"

" 'Cause I do all the chopping and clipping," Billy retorts as he hands over the money to his son.

When Billy and I are otherwise alone on the corner, I ask him to tell me more about how his family uses the local bathrooms.

"If it's daytime, I usually go to Bonsignour [the gourmet deli at 35 Jane Street], right in the back, the employees' bathroom. Or the Tavern on Jane."

"And they let you in?"

"Oh yeah. They love us. They welcome us with open arms. They give us

free food at both places. Late at night, when they're closed or too busy, the
Corner Bistro has one. They like us there. Now, that's if I don't want to
bother dealing with keys. But in that building is an apartment that belongs to
a lady named Angela. From the very first year, she's one of the people who
gave us the keys to her place. She's nice. She's been up to visit us. Stayed a
week with us in Vermont and everything. Wonderful woman. And then, in a
second building, I have the keys to an apartment up there where the person
. . . nobody lives there. It's a small studio with a nice white couch. And it's
funny: I use the one up there. My wife never goes up there. My wife goes to
Angela's. I never go to Angela's. And my kids have friends around the corner. They often go there for baths and stuff. So it's funny. We all go to different places."

"How do you get electricity in your camper?"

"See that wire?" Billy responds. "The one going across the street. It goes
down into the basement of Philippe's [Philippe Bonsignour, the owner of the
gourmet deli across the street]. See them under his bench over there? I've got
my own circuit there with my own circuit breaker. So I don't interfere with
his electrical stuff."

"Does he make you pay for that?"

"He won't accept any money."

"How long have you known him?"

"Well, this is the seventh year. The first three years, there was a lady named Priscilla who treated us the exact same way. And she sold the business to Philippe. So she treated us just as nice. And the next year we came here—this is a cool story—I showed up here and I knew from talking to her that she had sold it. And so I walked over and said, 'Hi. I'm Billy. We're the Christmas-tree people.' Philippe said, 'Great. Welcome.' Shook my hand. 'What do you need? You need anything? You need bathroom, electricity, anything like that?' I figured Priscilla had talked to him. I just found out last year that he had no idea who we were and no idea that we were coming. He just saw us, we shook hands, had instant rapport, and he opened his heart to us."

The Construction of Public Characters

On the sidewalk, certain similarities among people seem to be most crucial for bringing about helping behavior, for they lead strangers to a sense that the others involved in the interaction are decent, unthreatening people.[2]

One obvious difference between the Romps and the new public characters on Sixth Avenue is their race. Some might speculate that the different reaction to these two groups is partly or completely based on this factor—that the West Village residents (most of whom are white) feel an immediate bond with the Romps because they, too, are white, whereas they are unlikely to feel such a rapport with blacks, even if those persons were similar to them in class and behavior. If racial similarity as such predicts rapport, though, we would expect that if the Romps went to an affluent black neighborhood they would not be able to establish immediate rapport. I have myself been treated very warmly in many middle- and working-class black neighborhoods, where I look very different from the people on the street, so I am unwilling to make an assumption that middle-class blacks would not help the Romps.

It could be argued that the different reaction to these two groups is based *mainly* on class. The Romps are relatively similar in class to the people of Jane Street, whereas the men of Sixth Avenue are not. But Hakim, who is surely as educated, articulate, and well mannered as Billy Romp, tells me that he has never once been offered keys to an apartment, even though he has many long-standing friendly relationships with whites on the street.

Another possibility is that something else about the Romps brings them closer to the people of Jane Street. Perhaps two sets of circumstances—they are selling Christmas trees and they are a family—make the people of Jane Street feel a rapport with them and consider them decent, law-abiding people like themselves. Or perhaps Hakim simply does not possess Billy Romp's almost scholarly conception of the significance of speech and silence in making local residents feel comfortable. Perhaps without such an understanding it is unlikely that people will have the instantaneous rapport that is necessary for them to trust him with their keys.

Another real possibility is that it is not race or class or behavior *per se*, but the way that all people (including blacks) react to blacks in the context of the street. There is good social-science evidence that on the street whites are more afraid of blacks than blacks are afraid of whites.[3] It has also been found that blacks are more wary of blacks in some public places than they are of whites, including in black neighborhoods.[4] On a more anecdotal level, even Jesse Jackson has stated that, when he hears footsteps behind him on a dark street, if he turns around and sees white people he feels relieved. It is worth remembering that, when I first met Hakim, I assumed he was unhoused, largely—I think—because I viewed him in the context of the street.

The Struggle of the New Public Characters

Let us imagine a hypothetical conventional black family from Vermont (the "black Romps") selling Christmas trees on Jane Street. The actual white Romps developed an *instantaneous* rapport with the owner of the local deli, Philippe Bonsignour, who immediately offered them use of his bathroom, electricity, and telephone line. If the reader accepts the above reasoning, the "black Romps" would develop an instantaneous rapport with the local residents only if they were regarded as decent and nonthreatening. Despite common family values and other class similarities, in a culture where a fear of blacks in public places is layered on top of a history of racial tensions, there are barriers to the development of rapport. In the present circumstances, I think it unlikely that any residents of the West Village would offer their keys to the hypothetical "black Romps" upon first meeting them.[5]

It is possible that the "black Romps" would have received keys to apartments after the residents got to know them. But by then the "black Romps" might have been seen urinating in cups, or become known to have no way to bathe their children, making it less likely that local residents would regard them as decent people. Tension between economic classes and racial groups does not emerge all at once. It comes about through a series of steps, a process, which we often don't notice as we go about our lives. Part of this process occurs through a history that is shared by all involved but is seen very differently by blacks and whites.[6] And part of the process occurs right here on these streets, though not always visibly.

Other local residents might have asked where this black family got its Christmas trees in the first place. Once the community saw the black family engaging in "pathological" behavior and risking their children's welfare, they might have questioned why the police allowed them to take over two city blocks with their balsams and Douglas firs. They might have discovered that the local law stipulates that the sidewalk can be used to sell Christmas trees only during the month of December. They might have asked why the police allow this black family to use the sidewalk for this purpose beginning in the month of November. Some concerned neighbors might have called the city's Department of Child and Family Services, suggesting that the "home-schooled" black children living in a camper on Jane Street be put into foster care. The Sixth Precinct would likely have warned the black family that they must leave. Before too much time passed, the police—in response to their own frustration—might have thrown the black Romps' tools and skateboards and trees into the back of a garbage truck.

All of these elements of their situation would have stigmatized the black Romps, and social psychologists have found that stigmatized people receive less help than those who have not suffered stigma.[7] In other words, the black Romps would likely never have received keys to local apartments, because obtaining such keys would involve achieving a high level of decency in people's eyes—which, as we can see, would be very difficult.

Furthermore, those who live in public space engage in acts that are constantly seen and viewed by passersby. And as we have seen in a previous chapter, those whose acts are public are ultimately more vulnerable to being accused of indecency, if not illegality. On the other hand, those whose most basic functions as well as deviant behaviors take place in the privacy of apartments are much less vulnerable to appearing indecent or being stigmatized by accusations of breaking the law.[8]

In Jane Jacobs's account, the built-in eyes that kept sidewalks safe were a group of local shopkeepers, including the butcher and the locksmith. What we will never know is how many of those people, while furnishing the built-in eyes that kept the street safe, helped themselves in the privacy of their stores by dealing in "swag" off the backs of trucks. Nor do we know how many of the housed men and women of the city are in positions of power that allow them to "be distanced from criminal events and that can obscure their involvement in them,"[9] or who commit acts of deviance the men on Sixth Avenue can't commit, such as domestic violence, tax fraud, or insider trading. As we fix the "broken windows" of their homes and places of business, we naturally contribute to the impression that the quantity of "deviance" in street spaces is necessarily greater. But is it? Or is it simply more public, perpetuated by persons who are labeled "deviant" in the name of making the housed people feel safe on their streets?

These are not merely rhetorical or polemical questions, but ones that illustrate how difficult it is for the new public characters to establish their decency. Most housed residents of Greenwich Village have both time and space to protect them from assumptions of indecency. The Romps have time on their side and, in the privacy afforded by their camper, some private space as well. Many of the vendors on Sixth Avenue have neither. Without time or space to achieve decency, they are likely to engage in behavior that will be seen as indecent.

Ultimately, their indecency feeds back into the community structure of action toward them and belief about them. As more and more local pedestrians refuse to help, their stigmatized behavior spirals to new extremes. For example, the conviction based on experience that he is not permitted to use a bathroom leads a person to urinate in the public places where he makes his life. In so doing, he confirms local residents in their view that men like him are indecent. As residents become colder and more implacable in their reactions, the men on the street come to believe the residents are beyond their reach socially; since the men can't change the minds of the people in the neighborhood, they take the opportunity to subvert the social conventions that make normal interaction possible. And a few of them engage in "interactional vandalism," further reinforcing the sense that they cannot be trusted.

By contrast, as more and more people in the community come to look forward to seeing the tree sellers every day, and openly encourage them in their work, the Romps find it easier and easier to be decent. Billy and his family have a place to earn a living, and the community has exactly the kind of public characters it wants.

Because decency, like social cohesion and conflict, is achieved in a temporal *and* spatial process, the way the Romps and the vendors on Sixth Avenue are treated is more likely due to some interaction between their race and the constellation of other factors summarized by the terms "class" and "public behavior." Being white is not enough to get a person the keys to strangers' apartments. But being black in public space probably is enough to ensure that one will not get the keys right away, thus making likely some level of "deviant" behavior (urinating in public, say, or changing diapers on the sidewalk), which further ensures that no keys or electricity or free food or restaurant bathrooms or leeway from the police will be offered.

Alice and Her Black Grandchildren

The closest we can come to a family of "black Romps" is the case of Alice and her grandchildren. Alice, a Filipina, has a daughter, Jeannie, by a black man. Jeannie, who is twenty-one years old, completed her GED degree (with Hakim's encouragement) after dropping out of high school. She had been receiving public assistance, but after some months she took a job at a clothing store down the block on Eighth Street.

Jeannie has two children—Marcisa, five; and Monisia, two—by a black man. She says that on her salary of $5.50 per hour, she cannot afford child care. Alice does not make enough money for child care, either, and the father of the children apparently makes no contribution. So Alice ends up babysitting her grandchildren on the street in very hot and cold weather while she works.

Since the children are black, many passersby assume that Hakim is the father and that Alice is the stepmother. Some think she is a nanny or babysitter because she is Filapina, not black. Some regulars in the neighborhood refer to her as the Chinese lady.

Now that Marcisa is in school, Alice must leave the block (sometimes with Monisia in tow) to pick up the older granddaughter. She leaves the block around 1:15 p.m. and travels at least an hour to pick her up at school at 2:30 p.m. in Jersey City. This means that Alice must pay double carfare: instead of spending $4.30 per day, she has to spend $8.60. And on those rare days when Hakim is not there to watch her table in her absence, Alice must close it down and put her goods back in storage before she goes away.

Despite the fatigue that sets in from taking care of two grandchildren and working to help support them (and their mother), Alice works seven days a week. When I ask her how she does it, Alice shrugs her shoulders and says, "I just work."

There are times when Alice is too tired to carry Monisia, and at the end of a long day the child can be irritable. Monisia cannot take regular naps and must adjust, almost like Mudrick and Ishmael, to the noise of the street and to sleeping outside. When she needs to be changed, she says, "Wet, wet." If Alice is too busy, Conrad will change her.

Having one's grandchildren on the sidewalk all day can be expensive. In the warm weather, Alice has to be careful about bringing cooked food or milk from home, because such items spoil quickly. She spends about twenty dollars a day on food for herself and the grandchildren.

The most generosity Alice has received from the community comes from Richard, a white man in his fifties, who every few weeks gives her bags of dimes, nickels, and quarters (usually adding up to about thirty dollars) for the children; and another well-dressed retired white man, who buys candy and ice cream for the kids. One white woman, Jill, brought Alice a sweatsuit that her sister had discarded. Sometimes the managers of the local Ferrara pastry shop (who are black and Puerto Rican) and the Go Sushi (who are Chinese) give strawberries, watermelon, soda, or sushi. Most of the generosity toward her children, though, comes from vendors like Conrad and Mudrick, who sometimes buy the children ice cream, cookies, candy, and food from McDonald's. Sometimes Mudrick gives the children dollar bills.

Unlike the Romps, Alice receives little other support from community residents. Never once have local residents invited her grandchildren home to play with their own children. Never do they offer keys to apartments so that the children can nap or use the bathrooms, or so that Alice can store food in

the refrigerator. Never has Alice been offered keys to local apartments during blizzards or storms.

Whereas the Romps depend largely on local residents and businesses, who don't question their child-rearing practices, Alice sometimes elicits threatening remarks. "These children should not be in the street," said one woman, holding the hand of her own little boy.

"What is *your* child doing in the street with you?" asked Alice.

"I'm the mother!" said the woman.

"So am I," said Alice. "This is my grandchildren."

The woman walked away.

"They think these kids from the street," Alice told me. "Or that we are addict parents. That is their opinion, because they don't *know* my children."

An elderly white man walks by and tells Alice he feels sorry for her. He says he doesn't think the children belong on the street and doesn't understand why Alice has no choice.

Recently, a white man in his thirties saw Alice disciplining Monisia on the sidewalk (something white residents do all the time as they pass by), and yelled, "Somebody should hit *you*. The next time, I am going to hit you and call the police." Alice lives with the fear that someone will complain that her grandchildren are being neglected or mistreated, which they are not.

Whereas the Romps were assimilated immediately by local residents on the basis of race, class, and public behavior (including having a family on the sidewalk selling Christmas trees), Alice, perhaps because her grandchildren are black, cannot depend on their presence to win a place in the hearts of local residents, including at Christmastime. Perhaps it is because she is there all the time, because she is not selling Christmas trees, or because she is not black and therefore is not obviously their grandmother. These things we cannot say with certainty. What we can say is that nothing has come for Alice and her children without the *very* hard work of establishing herself as a public character who can be trusted. Nothing has come immediately, and what helping behavior has been directed toward her has come from local storeowners as a result of her hard work in their behalf as a public character. Once, when Alice was busy and Conrad was not helping her put quarters in the parking meter for the owners of Go Sushi, Alice said, "Conrad, because we are using the store, you have to cooperate with them. We have to work hard just to let them know we can be trusted. We *have* to return *something*, and then we can use their facilities."

It is notable that the two businesses that do cooperate with her are owned or run by members of ethnic minorities. Whether this is a coincidence is hard to know. For example, as noted previously, it is only through helping out the Chinese owners of Go Sushi that she was able to gain regular unrestricted use of their bathroom for herself and her grandchildren. She might get this help from white people if she were putting coins in the meters for them. In any case, Hakim and the owners of Go Sushi rarely speak to one another, and it seems to be through Alice's standing that he is permitted to use the bathroom regularly without making purchases.

In the case of the Romps, good manners and family values and Christmas trees and middle-class status layered on top of whiteness seems to have been enough to create an *instantaneous* sense of them as decent and non-threatening. And this has led to a rapport that has reinforced the Romps' own ability to live as decent human beings, leading to goodwill and mutual support on Jane Street.

Conclusion

"They gotta deal with it." These words of Mudrick's, a crude justification for his remarks toward some women, are nonetheless a useful metaphor for framing a basic question about the practical attitude of pedestrians toward people working the sidewalks: Do conventional citizens *have* to deal with it?

The recent history of efforts to use criminal laws to control minor disorder demonstrates that, at one level, pedestrians don't have to deal with it. In New York City, it is now illegal to wash a car's windshield without the driver's permission or panhandle by the doors of automated-teller machines. And cities around the world see New York City's "zero tolerance" strategy as a model for how to control their public spaces. In Las Vegas, barkers and criers may no longer give out handbills on the Strip; in Santa Barbara and Seattle, it is against the law to sit on the sidewalks of many downtown blocks; in Santa Monica, would-be panhandlers must stay at least three feet away from those they solicit. Laws like these, in combination with a demand that people move from welfare to work, show that greater conformity can and will be exacted from the most marginal members of urban society.

Many politicians incorrectly think that, if only they were to pass more laws to make life difficult for disreputable people working the sidewalks, these people would go away. But I think we can see that the subsistence uses to which the city is put are difficult to cancel out in the first place. City councils have a tendency to try to eliminate different elements of the habitat—cutting back on the right to panhandle, putting up signs telling citizens not to give food or money to unhoused men and women, legislating against the Dumpster-diving of scavengers, or cutting back on sidewalk space for vendors—in an effort to find the weakest link, which, if broken, they believe, will destroy the group life.

Surely, the people working and/or living on the sidewalk cannot be done away with so easily, even if it were desirable. Those determined to make "an honest living" will keep deploying their creativity, competence, and cultural knowledge, as the men and women on Sixth Avenue do, to survive. And where the symbiotic system is so small and self-contained (as in Pennsylvania Station) that those who run it can find the weakest link—sleeping space— to destroy the group life, such "solutions" will merely lead people to find other habitats, like Sixth Avenue, and other means of survival, like vending written matter. The interlocking net is capable of reconfiguration.

What to do, then? A new social-control strategy is needed. At its core can be unrelenting demands for responsible behavior, but there could also be new kinds of enlightened understanding from the citizenry, leading to greater tolerance and respect for people working the sidewalk.

Citizens can begin by trying to understand the motives of the people who seem to upset their sensibilities, why they do the things others find so offensive. Often, these acts are not unlike those the wealthier classes engage in, such as when an upper-middle-class man urinates on a golf course or the shoulder of a highway. At times, they are simply more notable because people working on the street lack the resources of time and space that middle- and upper-class people take for granted. Many people working the sidewalks rarely develop a strong rapport with their neighbors, who live in houses and apartments. They have less supportive behavior directed toward them. As people living in public, they appear deviant because most of what they do occurs in plain sight. Whether it be selling swag, using drugs, or arguing out loud, almost every act they engage in makes them appear more indecent than the owners of local stores or the housed people passing by. Sometimes they behave the way they do because they have been stigmatized and so lack access to basic resources, whether bathrooms or common sociability with the upper-middle-class white people who populate the neighborhood they, too, call home.

While we grant that the "broken windows" theory has viability, and that it has been used to lower crime rates, we need not learn the wrong lessons from that success. In particular, we ought not begin with the assumption that the deviant behavior we observe on the street is caused by a disorderly atmosphere which gives rise to crime. Sometimes this may turn out to be true, but comparisons of the vendors on the street with more conventional city dwellers often demonstrate that the supposed indecency of the street is not unique and is no more caused by an atmosphere of disorder than is indecent behavior in the lives of more conventional people.

Learning to "deal with it" entails recognizing that the forces that bring about the entrepreneurial activities of the sidewalk help us to define what America has become for many poor people. The people who work on Sixth Avenue, like many of their ancestors, have lived their lives in interaction with a variety of political, economic, and historical conditions, including housing segregation, spatially concentrated poverty, deindustrialization, and Jim Crow. The failed politics of drug reform, best seen in disparate penalties meted out for possession of two different forms of the same drug—crack and powder cocaine—is especially obvious on these particular sidewalks. As we have seen, a combination of the effects of drug use on a person's life, repeated encounters with the criminal-justice system on the part of those who use crack, and the loss of day-labor and low-wage jobs that addicts and alcoholics could once depend upon—all have likely influenced these lives. Aggressive and intolerant reactions to the people on the sidewalk will have no effect on these larger conditions, which will continue to lead people to work on streets like Sixth Avenue.

In the end, some of them will not be agreeable to conventional city dwellers. At the same time, it is useful to understand why the interactions are unsettling—not always so much because any real threat is present and not because anything offensive is being said, as because practical conversational ethics are being betrayed in a search for power and dignity. The few men who commit "interactional vandalism" give a bad name to others on the street. Given the racial and class differences in play, it is in the nature of such conversations to create tension, but rarely to harm. Intolerant reactions to breaches of practical ethics might change some behavior. Nobody *has* to deal with that. Technical rudeness is often a way out for those who understand how it works.

On these sidewalks, the vendors, scavengers, and panhandlers have developed economic roles, complex work, and mentors who have given them encouragement to try to live "better" lives. This is the story of the largely invisible social structure of the sidewalk. For many of my readers, and certainly for myself, these redeeming aspects of the sidewalk have come as a surprise. At first glance, it strikes us that the visible practices of the street create an atmosphere for crime. Accordingly, much public policy today begins with the assumption that it is possible to know without systematic study which kinds of people make life safer and which kinds by their mere presence lead to serious crime. But it cannot correctly be assumed that certain kinds of human beings constitute "broken windows," especially without an understanding of how these people live their lives. Nor can it be assumed that the role of the public character need be filled by conventional people like the Romps, as valuable as they are to the neighborhood they visit each fall.

To be sure, there are some "broken windows" on these blocks. But mainly there are windows that look broken to people who are just passing by. Because Americans ruthlessly use race and class categories as they navigate through life, many citizens generalize from the actual broken windows to all the windows that look like them—and assume that a person who looks broken must be shattered, when in fact he is trying to fix himself as best he can. Only by understanding the rich social organization of the sidewalk, in all its complexity, might citizens and politicians appreciate how much is lost when we accept the idea that the presence of a few broken windows justifies tearing down the whole informal structure.

As a complement to the "broken windows" theory (and not in necessary contradiction to it), I would propose a "fixed windows" theory, which explicitly follows the "broken windows" logic in reverse. When the government abdicates its responsibility to help persons who come out of prison to find homes and jobs, such persons are left to their own devices if they are to transform themselves into persons that make a contribution to society. Some behavior that appears disorderly to the casual observer is actually bringing about community controls, rather than leading to their breakdown.

Thus, we can observe the following process. A man comes out of prison and goes to Sixth Avenue to panhandle. He watches another man's vending table and in time learns how to scavenge and find magazines that citizens will buy. Through his positive relations with customers and the self-direction that comes from being his own boss, he begins to feel the self-respect that also comes from knowing that he is earning "an honest living." After a time, as Marvin, Ron, and Grady have done, he makes his way off the streets to an apartment.

At this point, it is still not inevitable that he will maintain his positive connection to society, especially if the forces of formal social control constantly try to eliminate his entrepreneurial opportunities. But if he gets some encouragement, that can matter. If residents come to see his behavior as a positive contribution, they treat him with a respect that he isn't used to. At the same time, other men who come out of jail or who know no other way of self-support than robbery will see models of positive behavior and begin to imitate them. "Fixed windows" and "broken windows" can work together. A city that is serious about fixing its disorder must do more than take a surface approach to determining what disorder is.

The informal structure actually leads some people to mentor or help other people to turn their lives around. One of the most surprising things I learned in hearing the life histories from Sixth Avenue was how many of these men had actually taught one another how to hunt for magazines, how to set up their tables, and how to make "an honest living." There was likely imitation in the production of law-abiding modes of self-support, just as there might be imitation in the production of "broken windows." Tearing down the informal structure carries with it the cost of eradicating positive and inspiring models that are misunderstood for their opposite. This implies the need to rethink the relationship between disorder and crime. It may not be that the "broken windows" theory linking these two variables is incorrect, but rather the tendency to define disorder by incorrectly using race and class categories is.

We will improve our well-being by making provision for more persons, not fewer, to engage in informal entrepreneurial activity. City governments can do much better in regulating those trying to make an "honest living" on the sidewalks if they accept such activity as inevitable and, in its way, admirable as well. Certainly, the New York City Council never intended to increase public disorder by cutting down space for vendors. Proponents of fixing "broken windows" surely did not mean for police officers to be reduced to committing vandalism against unhoused vendors.

What does this mean, practically? It means that order must not be prized as an end in itself; rather, order is a by-product of a system of social regulation that is grounded in an understanding of city life in its uneasy complexity. Cities should not establish too rigorous standards for pedestrian congestion, and judges should be careful of efforts to use pedestrian congestion as an excuse to eliminate vendors from high-rent districts. In my interviews with the assistant to the director of a small BID, he admitted that his boss tries to protect her neighborhood from vendors by arguing that they interfere with the free flow of pedestrian traffic, even though she has no evidence to support her point. The standards set up by local departments of transportation or street-vendor-review panels make it far too easy for a business association to advance claims about congestion that are often highly subjective and speculative (while said to be objective and rigorous). I have also observed business associations arrange to have planters, trees, bike racks, and news racks installed on the sidewalks to make it impossible for vendors to work. New standards should be set up to make it more difficult to place plants where human beings need to earn a living.

Business Improvement Districts can even go so far as to encourage the presence of new public characters like Hakim, Marvin, and Ron. Rather than installing planters and news racks to stop vendors from setting up, they might build simple permanent vending tables, with benches under which peddlers could store their merchandise. And even while recognizing that every good intention might have some unanticipated consequences, they might consider building more public toilets of the kind that have been placed on the streets of Paris. Business Improvement Districts must understand that the informal economic and social life has great value and need not be aesthetically displeasing.

Any society with high levels of economic inequality, racism, illiteracy, and drug dependency, and with inadequate transitions from mental hospitals and prisons to work and home, will have vast numbers of people who cannot conform to the requirements of its formal institutions. Given this, the correct response is not for the society to attempt to rid public space of the outcasts it has had a hand in producing. It is vital to the well-being of cities with extreme poverty that there be opportunities for those on the edge to engage in self-directed entrepreneurial activity.

There will always be people who, faced with dispiriting social conditions, give up. The people we see working on Sixth Avenue are persevering. They are trying not to give up hope. We should honor that in them.

Afterword
by Hakim Hasan

The streets that are the focus of these pages are places of metropolitan refuge, where the identities of the men and women who work and live are hidden in public space. In the pedestrian's eye these men and women are reduced to a horrific *National Geographic* photograph come to life. It is as if they were born on these streets and have no past, or other life experiences.

My decision to leave the corporate world and sell books on Sixth Avenue was incomprehensible to my family and friends. One of my black former co-workers saw me selling books one evening, walked over to me and asked with comic disbelief, "So this is what you are doing now?" I did not want to answer this embarrassing question, so I replied, "No. I'm just watching the stuff for a friend of mine. He went to the bathroom."

In effect, I went into exile on the street. I began the process of exile long before I arrived on Sixth Avenue. In an attempt to avoid the everyday formalities of corporate life, in 1988 I began working as a legal proofreader on the night shift in the word-processing department of the law firm Robinson, Silverman. Nothing made the futility of my efforts more evident to me than an incident that occurred one evening when I had no work to do because of an upcoming holiday. I sat at a secretary's work station and read a copy of *Business Week*. A white attorney walked over to me. He leaned over my shoulder, saying not a word, and began to read. The crumbs from the popcorn he was eating fell on my head. I thought to myself, "Man, I should stand up and slap this guy senseless." In the moments that it took for me to weigh this option, I imagined paramedics working on his limp body and a phalanx of television reporters and police officers interviewing my co-workers in the corridor. I did not say a word to him. My silence was simply another in a series of concessions I made to those who provided me with my daily bread.

I was abruptly fired during an employee-review meeting in 1991 by the director of administrative services, a middle-aged white woman. Why? I had been accused of being incompetent, she said, by an attorney she refused to identify. I still remember the cadence of her words: "I'm so sorry, but we're going to have to let you go," as if it were a refrain to a song; and I recall the way I sat in a chair opposite her desk, statue-still, paralyzed by their unforeseen and immediate implications. I recall the way she stared at my face and the way my silence prompted her to say, "You seem to be taking this so calmly."

The director of administrative services was not my supervisor. How did she conclude that I was incompetent? What were her criteria? I worked on the night shift and saw her rarely—only when she was working late. The night-shift proofreaders and word processors had very little contact with her or the members of the legal staff, as it was my supervisor's responsibility to deal with them.

Prior to this meeting, my supervisor and I traded the normal office banter. She never gave me any verbal or written notification, during the time she was my supervisor, that my work was not satisfactory, nor was she present at the meeting.

Incompetent? What about those three years, working under deadlines and enormous pressure, proofreading legal documents inside a room the size of a prison cell with three other proofreaders? The director of administrative services believed the expression on my face was one of calm. It was an expression of shock. That night I left this insular world in order to salvage whatever was left of myself and forge a new identity.

•

Mitchell Duneier recalls that he was thoroughly surprised when, during our first conversation at my book-vending table, I told him that I had a Rolodex. His surprise was a matter of social context. But what if I had not mentioned the word Rolodex to Mitch? Because the word Rolodex is associated with people who work in offices, and because I was perceived as a "street person," my use of it stood out. It caused a shift in Mitch's perceptions of me. I am now inclined to suggest that this book would not have been written if it had not been for this conversation, which challenged his assumptions about me and my social status.

In the first chapter Mitch recalls his difficulty in convincing me to become a subject—at that time the sole subject—of the book. Indeed, I found myself hearing the decree of my mother, whenever she had to leave my siblings and me at home alone: *Do not open the door for anyone while I'm gone.*

If I defied the maternal decree and opened *this* door, on what basis would I weigh Mitch's intentions? How could I prevent him from appropriating me as mere data, from not giving me a voice in how the material in his book would be selected and depicted? How does a subject take part in an ethnographic study in which he has very little faith and survive as something more than a subject and less than an author?

Because I believe my disastrous experience in the corporate world was the effect of racism (a claim many whites these days liken to that of the proverbial boy who cried "Wolf!"), I asked myself, "Can I expect Mitch, as a white sociologist, to understand why that experience led me to work as a book vendor on Sixth Avenue in the first place?" The idea of race as a lived experience could not be avoided; at the same time, if I made the mistake of denying Mitch *his* humanity on the basis of race, without giving him a fair chance, there would have been no way for me to know whether he could write about my life accurately.

I did not know how Mitch would construct an account of my life on these blocks. Would he conduct his research as a descendant of a sociological tradition which historically has found it all but impossible to write and theorize about blacks, especially poor blacks, as complex human beings? I worried this way, oddly enough, even after reading Mitch's book *Slim's Table*, despite its insights into the lives of working-class black men, because my life, not the lives of the men depicted in that book, was at stake.

Over several weeks, I talked with Mitch informally at my book-vending table, and whenever possible at a restaurant where we could speak candidly without being interrupted. These exploratory conversations revolved around the basic facts of my life and, more to the point, the circumstances that prompted me to become a street bookseller, and they were emotionally charged. Mitch did not react to what I had to say with the cool, clinical detachment I had imagined to be the sociologist's stock-in-trade. He listened attentively. I came to respect his sensitivity, and soon I trusted him to write about my life.

After reading the original manuscript three years ago, I concluded that the events and conversations that took place at my book-vending table could not convey, by themselves, the complexity of the social structure that existed on these blocks. I sent Mitch a long, handwritten letter outlining my concerns. I expected him to think I had overstepped my bounds as "subject." True, I knew Mitch's research agenda had been shaped by my reference to Jane Jacobs's intriguing idea of the "public character." But, since I was a subject, how far did my right to theorize go?

Not long afterward we spoke on the telephone—I from a public telephone as I watched my table, he from his office. Mitch told me that he appreciated my sociological insights and that he was grateful for the letter. He wondered aloud if it might be productive for us to co-teach a seminar where we would discuss the issues raised by the book with students and each other. Shortly thereafter, Mitch received permission to invite me as a paid lecturer to co-teach a ten-week undergraduate seminar with him. This course marked the beginning of a process whereby the other men and women on Sixth Avenue would no longer be mere data.

I literally found myself selling books on Sixth Avenue one day and on the next seated opposite Mitch at a huge conference table at the University of California at Santa Barbara. This was new terrain, since I had no formal experience whatsoever teaching in a university environment. Up until that point, I had jokingly told Mitch that the sidewalk had been my classroom, so to speak, and that I was contemplating charging tuition.

The nineteen students whom Mitch and I had selected on an "instructor approval" basis to enroll in this seminar represented diverse ethnic backgrounds and demonstrated a keen interest in the way the seminar was structured, as well as a willingness to tackle an arduous series of reading assignments. Race, of course, was an unavoidable component of our meetings. This was due to the choice of reading materials and to the issues that emanated from the street.

We encouraged class participation based upon the assigned reading materials so that individual seminars would not be reduced to "rap sessions." The reading material we assigned was twofold: some books provided structural and conceptual understanding of issues of street life (*The Death and*

Life of Great American Cities, Streetwise, Urban Fortunes, and *The Home-less*), others were "black books" that working and middle-class blacks purchased at my book-vending table (*Pimp, Dopefiend, Volunteer Slavery, Africa: Mother of Civilization, Makes Me Wanna Holler, Breaking Bread, Race Matters,* and *Confronting Authority,* to name a few).

Co-teaching this seminar with Mitch was not easy. Not only was there a tremendous amount of preparation involved, but it gave me a firsthand understanding of the magnitude of his responsibilities as a college professor. Teaching undergraduates, where a professor must contend with the occasionally base intellectual instincts of some students, is a difficult enterprise. Standards and critical thinking are of the utmost importance.

I was given an office in which to work and conduct meetings with students during my office hours. Before each of the first four seminars, I would sit in my office stricken with such anxiety that I would find myself taking two Tylenols to help ease the onslaught of a headache, even though I had spent years at my book-vending table conversing with ordinary and famous people day after day.

And yet I adapted easily to this new social context. The seminar proceeded wonderfully, with Alice and Marvin visiting us in the middle of the academic quarter for two weeks. What became evident from the questions and responses of students was the shortcomings of the book. Why were the lives of the magazine vendors not included in the first draft? What about the panhandlers? What about homelessness? Why didn't these people simply find jobs? What did the whites have to say to these people? What were their interactions like with neighborhood residents? How did I get my books? Could a white professor really be trusted to write about black men without succumbing to stereotypes? These were difficult questions, and Mitch and I talked about them at length in between sessions. As a result of the seminar and our conversations, Mitch began writing this book all over again, returning to Sixth Avenue to document the lives of the other men.

My telephone communiqués back to New York proved to be meaningless as Alice recounted the general assessment of my trip to me. The men on Sixth Avenue could hardly believe that I was actually co-teaching a class with Mitch. They thought I was in Santa Barbara vacationing and enjoying the high life.

The social hierarchy of the book vendors and magazine vendors was characterized by long-standing antagonisms (as described in the chapter on the space wars), and I had a good but far from perfect relationship with the magazine vendors. In order for Mitch to gain access, he needed a sponsor among them—both to help him gain their trust and to ensure his safety. This is why Marvin was crucial. As a sponsor, he had greater credibility than I would have had, because he and Mitch had had no prior relationship.

Marvin and I briefed Mitch on what to expect and avoid as he initially moved about these blocks conducting fieldwork. Many of these men believed that Mitch was "rich" (that is the word I often heard) and they were prepared to take advantage of him. On these blocks, life is measured on a day-to-day basis, often in terms of the money one can obtain from people of goodwill. In those early days of fieldwork, the question of whether or not Mitch was really writing a book about the meaning of their lives was secondary. Their question was: How much money can I get out of him?

Some of them had earned as much as one hundred dollars apiece selling magazines the day before, but had spent that money on crack or alcohol before dawn. They invariably asked Mitch for money to buy breakfast, which had a variety of shaded meanings: a two-dollar ham, egg, and cheese sandwich from Gray's Papaya, a bottle of St. Ides malt liquor, or a hit or two of crack.

As far as money goes, none of these men were aware that Mitch had covered all of the costs associated with the research for this book out of his salary. He did not have a research grant, and would not wait to get one before conducting his research. Marvin was shocked when I told him this, but I knew that it would not have mattered if I told it to the other men.

Mitch eventually learned how to say no to requests for money from seemingly desperate people. He established goodwill through his seriousness of purpose and sincerity as a sociologist. I watched him gain access to the magazine vendors as I periodically peeked around the corner from my table and sometimes looked from the second-floor window of Userfriendly (a pay-by-the-hour computer center, now closed). I could see him working for Marvin and slowly but assuredly easing his way into the life that existed at that table. There was an "invisible" social world there unknown to most pedestrians and, as I would later learn, even to me. Through intensive fieldwork,

Mitch managed to document this subtle and complex social structure. It is fair to say, in retrospect, that his reception among these men was actually far easier than I anticipated it would be.

Alfred Robinson, who was among the "first generation" of men to make their lives on Sixth Avenue, told me that Mitch would have become a "victim" on these streets had there not been a consensus among the men and women that what he was trying to do was important. In the end, any sociologist who simply believes that time spent in the field qualifies him as "one of the boys" is not only sadly mistaken but in grave trouble. The street is the street. Make no mistake about it. Mitch understood this from the outset. He never pretended to be anything other than he was: a human being and sociologist attempting to understand the meaning of our lives.

Not one of these men or women (including myself) had any coordinates for this kind of undertaking, but in order for Ovie Carter to photograph these men and women, they had to put their faith in him too. People who work and live on the street, as a general rule, do not like, let alone permit, photographs to be taken of them. Some do not like the idea of their lives being reduced to a tourist attraction, while others see photographs as an aspect of police surveillance. Many think that unless they "get paid" the photographer is "getting over" on them.

Ovie is a black staff photographer for the *Chicago Tribune*. He is a soft-spoken man who has spent over twenty-five years photographing the inner city, with a particular focus on problems like drug abuse. This would be the third major project on which he and Mitch would collaborate. I can say with assurance that Ovie's status as a black man was not the sole criterion for his admission into the lives of these men and women. Jamaane, for example, initially expressed his reluctance to be photographed. I recall Ovie talking to Jamaane about his reluctance in front of Store 24 (now Go Sushi) on Greenwich Avenue, the very block I work on. It was an intense yet cordial conversation. Within fifteen minutes, Jamaane changed his mind. Jamaane, who is a man of great integrity, had come to respect Ovie and his intentions as they related to this project. The wealth of Ovie's Chicago experience photographing men and women very much like those on Sixth Avenue had never really occurred to me in my own assessment of how he would manage to be accepted on these blocks. Compared to Mitch's, his rapport with the men and women was almost instantaneous.

When Mitch had written another draft of this book and photographs had
been carefully selected, he came back to New York, rented a room at the
Washington Square Hotel, and brought each and every man and woman involved with this project there. He read chapters of the book to them and so-
licited their opinions. This was not easy, but it proved (particularly when
everyone involved had heard their own words) that the book was a work in
progress that portrayed their lives accurately. Mitch had made his own judg-
ments after listening to everyone first.

There was no way for me to know that my desire to survive as something
more than a subject and less than an author *would* influence the way this
book was conceived and written. Let me elaborate: my determination to participate in this project forced me to discover that a dialogue with Mitch, in
his capacity *as a social scientist*, was possible. This was no small achievement. This was a departure from the "scholar knows best" paradigm. The ro-
manticized idea of "the subject's voice" that I often hear about from graduate
students studying at New York University and the New School for Social Research who come to my table is one thing. The radical willingness of the social scientist to listen is quite another.

Mitch's research compelled me to realize that I knew less about the lives
of the men and women on these streets than I thought, although I had spent
years working right next to them. For instance, I was quite surprised to learn
that a sub-group of these men had actually known one another for over fifteen years and had "migrated" to Sixth Avenue after having lived in and
around Pennsylvania Station. Because of social distinctions that exist between the magazine and book vendors, I was not privy to this fascinating information. Had Mitch failed to talk to each and every man who inhabited
these blocks, there would have been no way to determine, let alone document, their shared history and their migration from Penn Station to Sixth Avenue. The story of their migration raised profound questions for me, since it
demonstrated their tremendous adaptability and ability to create a milieu in
public space in which they could survive. Perhaps, in the final analysis, migration of any kind is a story of survival and adaptability. But this seems
never to occur to people who encounter these persons, including policy makers, who think street vendors can be eliminated with laws that cut vending
space or ordinances that make the world less comfortable for them.

When I read the first draft of the chapter "A Scene from Jane Street," I found it unimaginable that Billy Romp and his family are allowed to live in a camper on Jane Street (an unusually narrow street, no less) and that residents think so much of the Romps that they give them keys to their apartments. I explained to Mitch, I have never been offered keys to any resident's apartment, and even if I were, I doubt that I would have accepted. The limitations that I place upon trust would not allow me to do so. Maybe this is not important. What is important is the keys, which symbolize that the Romps are accepted by the residents.

The juxtaposition of Ishmael being told by the police officers that he could not sell his magazines on Christmas Day and Billy Romp selling his Christmas trees made me angry. Let me say something about the comparison between Billy Romp and me as public characters: while it is admirable that he is widely accepted on Jane Street, and undeniable that his presence creates a sense of "eyes upon the street," the role I came to play on Sixth Avenue is markedly different from his. Without the signs of race, class, and family stability (I have no children) that might have allowed me to gain immediate acceptance on Sixth Avenue, I had to earn my place there through my wit, presence, and perseverance. There is no indication that I, or any of the other men and women, have ever been accepted altogether on Sixth Avenue.

Despite the fact that it was a labor of love, working on the Avenue for over seven years took a toll on me. Two days after Alice handed me a letter on the sidewalk notifying me that our relationship was over and that she was romantically involved with another vendor on *our* block, I decided to leave Sixth Avenue. While this news was a precipitating factor, I had endured poverty and the lack of health insurance long enough, and the prospect of entering middle age with no financial security was frightening. I had to leave.

My departure from Sixth Avenue was no easier than my arrival. One does not spend seven years working on the sidewalk and make a swift foray back into the formal economy. I thought that I could. My attempt now to move into publishing, public school education, or urban policy research is marred still by bitterness and my contempt for corporate whites who thwarted my ability to simply earn a living, which is what brought me to Sixth Avenue in the first place. This conflict between my aspirations and my bitterness is the essence of my story. It has not been resolved. It may never be.

I am still trying to understand how Mitch and the people whose lives he documented developed relationships on several New York City streets where race and class conflicts derail most efforts to transcend such barriers. Does this mean that people sometimes find ways—the will, actually—to work through their phobias and prejudices on these streets? Is it a matter of being willing to listen to one another with respect? Does it hinge on the sheer willpower of a subject, in this case myself, who was determined not to be reduced to a theoretical formulation or mere "data"? Given the vast inequalities, racial misunderstandings, and violence found on the street at every turn, I believe there was some measure of good luck involved here—the kind of luck that scholars and "subjects" of different races, classes, and genders will need when they encounter one another "in the field."

New York
August 1999

APPENDIX

NOTES

ACKNOWLEDGMENTS

Appendix

A Statement on Method

... I am convinced that the actual evolution of research ideas does not take place in accord with the formal statements we read on research methods. The ideas grow up in part out of our immersion in the data and out of the whole process of living ...

WILLIAM FOOTE WHYTE, *Street Corner Society* (1943, 1993)

I am only going to report on what I conclude from studies of this kind that I've done. And I can only begin by repeating ... that what you get in all of this [attempt to articulate techniques] is rationalizations, and we're in the precarious position of providing them.

ERVING GOFFMAN, "On Fieldwork" (March 1974)[1]

On the Evolution of Sidewalk

On my shelf is a manuscript about the everyday life of one street vendor and the people who come to his table to buy and talk about books. I wrote the manuscript after observing at Hakim Hasan's table for two years. In 1996, the manuscript was accepted for publication by Farrar, Straus and Giroux, which intended to bring it out the next year.

But I was uneasy, and ultimately I told the firm's editor in chief that I wanted to start the research all over again and write a new book. To explain why, I have to say more about how the research developed. In the process, I hope to give a sense of some of the most important methodological issues I faced.

Co-teaching a Seminar with Hakim

After completing the draft of the original bookselling manuscript, I gave it to Hakim and asked him for his comments. He read it and brought to my attention a major limitation. As he saw it, my study focused too closely on him and not enough on the vendors who occupied other spaces on Sixth Avenue. As I listened to what he had to say, I realized that we needed to have a sustained conversation about the material in the manuscript. I proposed that we teach a course together at the University of California–Santa Barbara, where I was that year. Hakim was clearly well read, and I had admired his pedagogical relationships with young men like Jerome. Surely my students in Santa Barbara could benefit from working closely with him. I told my idea to Bill Bielby, the chair of my department, who arranged for Hakim to receive a lecturer's salary for the ten-week quarter.

Hakim and I taught a seminar for undergraduates called "The Life of the Street and the Life of the Mind in Black America." In it, we discussed a number of books which Hakim had sold at his table and spoke in detail from the draft manuscript, showing the students how "black books" entered into the lives and discussions of people who came to Hakim's table. As a teacher, Hakim was organized, insightful, and patient with students on subjects of race, class, and gender, although the discussions were sometimes quite heated.

In the class, Hakim felt that the focus on him did not give a wide-angle view of the sidewalk that he knew. (Some colleagues, too, suggested that I study the vendors who sell scavenged magazines.) Hakim thought we should invite his partner, Alice Morin, and Marvin Martin to participate in the seminar. The next month they joined us in Santa Barbara, and they participated in two weeks of classes.

My research focus was evolving as I came to get a sense of what might be gained if the book included a more comprehensive view of the street. I asked Marvin if he thought it would be possible for me to do interviews with the men he knew on Sixth Avenue, and he said that would not be a problem.

On Marvin's last night in Santa Barbara, we walked down Cabrillo Boulevard, by the ocean, reflecting on how much ground we had covered in this setting so different from Sixth Avenue. As he thought about going back to New York, he lamented that his business partner, Ron, was going through a stage of being unreliable. Every time Marvin left the table to place bets at Off-Track Betting, he had to depend on Ron to remain by the table; if Ron was drunk or high, he might abandon the table, and it would be taken by the police.

A thought occurred to me. I could work for Marvin during the coming summer. I would learn a lot more about the sidewalk, if I worked as a vendor myself, than I would by merely observing or doing interviews, and he would have his table covered. So I proposed that I work at his table for three months and give him the money I made. "What will the fellas think when I have a white guy working for me all summer?" he asked. We decided he should just tell them the truth—I was there to do research on a book about the block—and he said he would think about it.

When I told Hakim, he had reservations. Would I be safe on the streets? Could Marvin look after me? Would the toughest and most violent men on Sixth Avenue accept what I was doing as worthy of respect? Meanwhile, Marvin called from a pay phone in New York to accept my offer. I would begin in June. My summer internship, so to speak, had been arranged.

Getting In

On June 8, 1996, I appeared on Sixth Avenue at about 6:00 a.m. Ron, whom I recognized from the time I had spent on the block (but whom I had never met), was already there. I had heard enough about his violent episodes to think that I had better wait until Marvin arrived before I approached.

Marvin appeared half an hour later. He greeted me and introduced me to Ron, who, it turned out, had been expecting me. As the two men began unpacking magazines from crates which a "mover" named Rock had transported from Marvin's storage locker, Marvin told me to watch how the magazines are displayed, with the foreign fashion titles placed at the top of the table where they will catch the eyes of passersby.

As I joined in the work, I removed a tape recorder from my bag. Ron looked down at

the machine and scowled. He hardly spoke that day. I put the tape recorder back in my bag, never having turned it on.

I was wearing the same clothes I had been wearing in the classroom a few days earlier: a blue button-down shirt, beige pants, and black shoes. Even if I had dressed differently, I would have stood out. My speech and diction alone would have made me seem different. Had I tried to downplay these differences, though, Ron would have seen through such a move immediately.

So right away on the block I was being a person not unlike the person I am with my friends in casual settings, my family at home, and my colleagues at work. Of course, in each of these settings, I adapt somewhat, accentuating some traits and downplaying others. In small ways I am not aware of, I doubtless did the same as I began my work.

Using myself as a participant observer, I was there to notice by taking part, trying to observe and retain information that others in the setting often thought unimportant or took for granted. I had research questions vaguely in mind, and I was already making mental comparisons between what I was seeing and what the sociology literature had to say. I had only approximate notions about what I would do with the data I collected and what I sought to learn. In some participant-observation studies, fieldworkers let the specific research questions emerge while they are in the field. For example, I couldn't have told Marvin and Ron that I was interested in studying the way a few men on the street talk to passing women, because I didn't know that could be an issue. Nor was I fully aware that I would be interested in comparing present-day sidewalk life to sidewalk life in the period when Jane Jacobs was writing about the Village. I was there simply to observe and record, and I was asking the people working the sidewalk to let me be there.

One of the most difficult situations I faced as I tried to make an entry into these blocks was avoiding the conflicts which already existed. Hakim, with whom I had become closely associated, got along well with everyone on Sixth Avenue except Muhammad. (See the chapter on the space wars.) But if I was to get to know all the men on the block, it was essential that I not be viewed as especially associated with Hakim.

The act of "getting in," then, sometimes led me to be less than sincere about my connection to Hakim. Fieldwork can be a morally ambiguous enterprise. I say this even though I have never lied to any of the persons I write about. The question for me is how to show respect for the people I write about, given the impossibility of complete sincerity at every moment (in research as in life).

The gulf between the other vendors and myself was much greater than it was with Hakim. How could I expect these men to trust me? The vendors were wondering the same thing. One conversation captured on my tape recorder illustrates this. I had been interviewing one of them, who had been holding my tape recorder, when I got called away. While listening to the tapes a few months later, I came across the conversation that ensued after I left. (The participants, who forgot the tape was running, have asked me to conceal their identities in this instance.)

"What you think he's doing to benefit you?" X asked.

"A regular black person who's got something on the ball should do this, I would think," said Y.

"He's not doing anything to benefit us, Y."

"I'm not saying it's to benefit us," said Y. "It's for focus."

"No. It's more for them, the white people."

"You think so?" said Y.

"Yeah. My conversations with him just now, I already figured it out. It's mostly for them. They want to know why there's so much homeless people into selling books . . . I told him because Giuliani came in and he said nobody could panhandle no more. Then the recycling law came in. People voted on it."

"Case in point," said Y. "You see, I knew he had to talk to you. I can't tell him a lot of things 'cause I'm not a talker."

"I told him in California there's people doing the same thing that we're doing. They doing it on a much more higher level. They are white people. You understand?"

"Yeah."

"They have yard sales."

"Yeah."

"They put the shit right out there in their yard. He knows. Some of them make a million dollars a year. But what they put in their yard, these are people that put sculptures. They put expensive vases. These are peoples that drives in their cars. All week long, all they do is shop."

"Looking for stuff," said Y. "Like we go hunting, they go shopping."

"Right. Very expensive stuff. They bring it and they put it in their yard and sell it. And they do it every weekend. Every Saturday. Every Sunday. So they making thousands. He's not questioning them: How come they can do it? He's questioning us! He want to know how did the homeless people get to do it. That's his whole main concern. Not really trying to help us. He's trying to figure out how did the homeless people get a lock on something that he consider *lucrative*."

"Good point," said Y.

"You gotta remember, he's a Jew, you know. They used to taking over. They used to taking over no matter where they go. When they went to Israel. When they went to Germany. Why do you think in World War II they got punished so much? Because they owned the whole of Germany. So when the regular white people took over, came to power, they said, 'We tired of these Jews running everything.' "

"But throughout time the Jewish people have always been business people."

"But they love to take over."

Y laughed.

"Of course," X said, laughing hysterically. "That's what he's doing his research on now. He's trying to figure out how did these guys got it. How come we didn't get it?"

Y laughed.

X continued laughing hysterically, unable to finish his next sentence.

"I don't think so," said Y.

"But he's not interested in trying to help us out."

"I'm not saying that, X. I'm saying he's trying to focus on the point."

"I told him that, too," said X. "Everyone he talk to, they're gonna talk to him on the level like he's gonna help them against the police or something like that. They're gonna look to him to advocate their rights."

"No. I don't think that, either. I think it's more or less to state the truth about what's going on. So people can understand that people like you and I are not criminals. We're not horrible people. Just like what you said, what happens if we couldn't do this? What would you do if you couldn't sell books right now?"

Hearing those stereotypes invoked against me made me realize that—conventional wisdom to the contrary—participant observers need not be fully trusted in order to have their presence at least accepted. I learned how to do fieldwork from Howard S. Becker, and one of the things he taught me—I call it the Becker principle—is that most social processes have a structure that comes close to insuring that a certain set of situations will arise over time. These situations practically require people to do or say certain things because there are other things going on that require them to do that, things that are more influential than the social condition of a fieldworker being present.[2] For example, most of the things in a vendor's day—from setting up his magazines to going on hunts for magazines to urinating—are structured. This is why investigators like myself sometimes can learn about a social world despite not having had the rapport we thought we had, and despite the fact that we occupy social positions quite distinct from the persons we write about. (More about social position later.)

It was hard for me to know what to make of that discussion between X and Y. Maybe they were "just" having fun, but I don't think so. Though I was not astonished by what I heard, I had no idea that X harbored those suspicions toward me as I had gone about my work on the blocks throughout the summer. In this sense, fieldwork is very much like life itself. We may *feel* fully trusted and accepted by colleagues and "friends," but full acceptance is difficult to measure by objective standards and a rarity in any case. If we cannot expect such acceptance in our everyday lives, it is probably unrealistic to make it the standard for successful fieldwork.

At the same time, participant observers like myself who do cross-race fieldwork must, I think, be aware that there are many things members of the different races will not say in one another's presence. For blacks in the United States, it has been necessary to "wear the mask," to quote the black poet Paul Laurence Dunbar, who wrote:

> We wear the mask that grins and lies,
> It hides our cheecks and shades our
>
> > eyes,—
> This debt we pay to human guile;
> With torn and bleeding hearts we smile,
> And mouth with myriad subtleties.[3]

Dunbar's words are no less relevant today, for, as a survival mechanism, many blacks still feel that they cannot afford to speak honestly to whites. Surely, it would have been a methodological error for me to believe that apparent rapport is real trust, or that the poor blacks I was writing about would feel comfortable taking off the mask in my presence.

I believe that some of the vendors may have let me work out on Sixth Avenue with them because they eventually saw what I was doing nearly the way I did; others merely wanted to have me around as a source of small change and loans (something I discuss later); and a few others may have decided to put up with me so that there would be a book about them and the blocks. But it would be naïve for me to say that I knew what they were thinking, or that they trusted or accepted me fully, whatever that might mean.

Using the Tape Recorder

To write my first draft, I had collected many quotations by jotting things down when I could—sometimes minutes after they were said, sometimes that night, sometimes a day later. Where I learned to do fieldwork—university sociology departments—this was the convention. I had never seen any discussion of the meaning of quotation marks in any research-methods textbook.

I decided that if I was interested in getting meanings right, I had to strive to my utmost to get exact words right, too. The meanings of a culture are embodied, in part, in its language, which cannot be grasped by an outsider without attention to the choice and order of the words and sentences. Reversing the order in which words are spoken, or getting the words wrong, allows the reader to come away with a meaning different from what was intended. I began to think that, for a discipline in search of meanings, it was well-nigh indefensible that so little attention was paid to exact quotes and quotation marks.[4]

For participant observers, it is perhaps especially crucial to be aware of this when people of one race and class rely on casual records of words to depict people of another race and class. If the observer is not careful, the different meanings found among people of divergent social positions can be easily misunderstood and misrepresented.

With this in mind, I brought a digital tape recorder to Sixth Avenue. One might think that to use such a device on the street, a researcher would need to have a great deal of trust from his or her subjects. As we know from the recorded conversation between X and Y, this is not altogether the case. But I believe it is overwhelmingly true. The fact that I was sponsored by Hakim, and that Marvin and Alice had been to see me in Santa Barbara, meant that these people knew a great deal about me. Although X states in the tape that what I was doing was for the "white people," it is notable that he did not go so far as to speculate that I might be a plainclothes detective or an informant for the police. They believed that I was a researcher and a professor and it appears that their trust in me on this point led them to let me run the tape recorder on the pavement.

Because I had a tape recorder running all the time, I didn't have to make a special effort to remember verbatim what people said or make written notes right away. The field notes I did write were based on what the tapes prompted me to remember, not on memory alone. This was a great advantage, since I find it difficult to take notes when I am actively involved in the daily routine of a group of people.

I wanted everyone I was planning to identify to develop an awareness of the machine. Sometimes one of the vendors, scavengers, or panhandlers would pick it up, beginning a performance for the microphone that might last a few minutes. The tape recorder was discussed at one time or another with every man out there, and after a few days such awareness of the machine ceased. With passing pedestrians (such as the dog walker) who could not be efficiently notified it was on at the time, such discussions occurred if and when I needed to identify them in the text. With the police officers whose voices were captured on tape, I decided not even to try to find out their names. Not only was I reasonably sure they would not consent, but I did not wish to demonize those police officers, and to create an inaccurate sense that the problems were personal rather than systemic.

It was my responsibility to know which behavior was not for the tape and which behavior was, and I was able to discern this before introducing the machine. A good example is the account of the interactions with customers in the section on magazine scavengers. In the moments leading up to the interaction, the men were bantering with one another for the benefit of the tape. When the customer came near the table, however, Ron turned to her, and the ensuing interaction was typical of hundreds of vendor-customer exchanges I had witnessed.

The tape recorder may have distorted certain things. But the machine did not hide the things I was interested in as a sociologist: the ongoing life of the sidewalk. Once again the Becker principle comes into play: most social processes are so organized that the presence of a tape recorder (or white male) is not as influential as all the other pressures, obligations, and possible sanctions in the setting.

It was through the tapes that I came to realize that the topic of talking to women who don't want to was important. On one occasion, with the machine running, I asked Mudrick a few questions about his drug use. While telling me that he never used drugs, he interrupted himself with loud calls to passing women, as I had seen him do many times. He didn't want to talk about drugs, but he felt no reserve in letting my microphone pick up his banter, which he seemed to engage in with little awareness that it might interest me. This was true about much of significance that I learned on Sixth Avenue. Here the researcher trades on the difference between what a subject thinks is significant to the sociologist and what turns out, in fact, from the dense stream of utterances and activity, to be of analytic use. These were things that showed up over and over again on my tape. They were typical and/or incidental to the people of the sidewalk. (Of course, it is possible that I have made a great deal out of things that people were not completely aware they were doing, or were not aware that I thought were noteworthy.)

My collaboration with a photojournalist has taught me the importance of getting an incident or conversation on tape when I can. To use the tape recorder effectively, the sociologist can mimic the photojournalist, who often has no choice but to make his or her picture in a given moment, because he or she has another assignment, or because the light is waning, or because the event is singular and may not be repeated. A good example of this is Ishamel's encounter with the police on Christmas Day. When I went to the block that morning, only Ishmael was set up and it was dark and cloudy. I had made plans to go to see a film with Hakim and Alice later in the day, and approached Ishmael's corner to meet them. I had expected to do no fieldwork that day, so I might have left my tape recorder at home. But to use a tape recorder effectively, it is good to get used to having it along all the time. I had it that day, and the tapes I made enabled me to study the episode far more carefully than I might have without it.

Diagnostic Ethnography

When I went back to Sixth Avenue to work as a magazine vendor, I hadn't yet formulated a precise research question. I had no theories that I wanted to test or reconstruct, and

I didn't have any particular scholarly literature to which I knew I wanted to contribute.

During my first summer working for Marvin and Ron, I began with a loose but useful sense to guide my data collection. I would take note of the collective activity between and among the vendors and others they worked with. I watched the relations between them and their customers; I went on hunts with the men to see how they acquired magazines; I watched them interact with police officers, trying to get a sense of *how* those encounters unfolded. I also talked to men in depth about their lives. At this stage of my research, I sought mainly to diagnose the processes at work in this setting and to explain the observed patterns of interactions of people. I also have a general theme that guides me in collecting data in all of my work; whether and how the persons I am with are or are not struggling to live in accordance with standards of "moral" worth.

The fact that I did not know my specific research question at the start may seem counter to the way sociologists are supposed to operate. I take a different view, however. In much of social science, especially much of quantitative research using large data sets, a research design often emerges *after* data has been collected. Of course, survey instruments themselves require design, which requires some sort of theoretical agenda or conceptual foundation to begin with. (My focus on "moral" struggles provides that framework for my data collection.) But a well-designed survey allows the researcher to raise a variety of questions and topics later on, some of them unanticipated. This is essentially what happened there to me. Like quantitative researchers who get an idea of what to look at from mulling over existing data, I began to get ideas from the things I was seeing and hearing on the street.

In Madison, Wisconsin, the following fall, at some distance from Sixth Avenue, I realized that I might make use of Jane Jacobs's study to do a loose comparison of today's sidewalks and those of a few decades ago. Something had changed in this neighborhood, and my recognition of this change was the beginning of a research design. At the same time, I began the process of listening to the many tapes I had made on the street, as well as looking at all my notes. And I began to write down various topics that seemed important.

While I was in Madison, Ovie Carter made his first trip from Chicago to New York to photograph the scene on Sixth Avenue. During my summer as a vendor, I had called Ovie weekly to tell him what I had been seeing. Now it was his turn to show me how things looked to him.

As Ovie showed me the first batch of his photographs, I began to get a better sense of how things worked on the blocks, for he is committed to capturing relations among people and their environments and not mere individual acts.[5] For example, Ovie's photograph of a man sleeping in the doorway of Urban Outfitters is not a picture of just the man; it shows the man in the context of a table where he does business. This photograph led me to think about the relation between sleeping outside and saving a space, which led me to focus on how "habitat" is formed and works through contextual connections.

Ovie's photos also helped me make a more complete description. I recovered details, such as where goods were kept and how space mattered. With some of his photographs tacked on my office walls, I continued to listen to tapes and to look at my notes to try to figure out what could be said about life on Sixth Avenue. Many of the topics I realized were important back in Madison had not stood out as important when I was in New York. For example (as discussed in more detail later), while I was listening to a tape in my office, I heard Marvin talk about being kept out of a restaurant's bathroom. I also heard on the tapes constant references to the "Fuck it!" mentality, which was far more pervasive on the tapes than I had realized.

After fall classes ended, I returned to New York to work with Marvin and Ron until New Year's Eve. On the blocks then and on subsequent occasions, I began researching some of the above issues, now with clearer research questions in mind. During this period, I witnessed the incident between Ishmael and Officer X that is discussed in the chapter called "A Christmas on Sixth Avenue." This incident (and my account of it) demonstrates the necessity of being there. Had I been in Madison or Santa Barbara that December, or had I tried to do a study based on interviews instead of participant observation, I could never have gotten such a perspective on police-vendor relations.[6]

In the end, I had many separate research questions, each of which might have served as the basis for a monograph or article but which were fitting together into a book. I spent more time thinking about how these chapters would fit together than I did about any other research topic.

The structure of the book ultimately resulted from considering alternative interpretations. I wanted to be open to new information and counter-evidence in regard to my theme, and this led me to follow three chapters on informal social control with four chapters on the limits of such control. The desire to look carefully at counter-evidence and explore alternative interpretations was certainly helpful as I organized the book. But as Karl Popper has argued, "there is no such thing as a logical method for having new ideas."[7]

A colleague of mine who teaches courses in the philosophy of science, Erik Olin Wright, calls my approach "diagnostic ethnography," and I agree with that characterization. I begin observation by gaining an appreciation of the "symptoms" that characterize my "patient." Once I have gained a knowledge of these symptoms, I return to the field, aided by new diagnostic tools—such as photographs—and try to "understand" these symptoms (which is some amalgam of "explain" and "interpret" and "render meaningful"). I also read in more general literature, seeking ideas that will illuminate my case.

It was much later in the process that I began to understand that some of the things I was observing had relevance to "broken windows"–style social control, and that the principles of urban life articulated by Jane Jacobs might actually be seen to require a certain kind of sidewalk life, which was not in evidence here. It was also much later that I began to use as a sort of tool kit the scholarly literature of, say, "work and personality," Conversation Analysis, feminist theory, urban poverty formation, the sociology of emotion, or the sociology of law, among others, to make sense of what was taking place on the sidewalk.

This approach might usefully be compared with the influential "extended case method" elaborated by Michael Burawoy in *Ethnography Unbound.*[8] The contrast is with research that begins with theory reconstruction as its pivotal agenda and seeks cases that cause trouble for received wisdom. Burawoy advocates an approach that begins by looking for theories that "highlight some aspect of the situation under study as being anomalous," and then proceeding to rebuild (rather than reject that theory) by reference to wider forces at work.

Burawoy is a scholar known for his theoretical agility, and such an approach understandably appeals to ethnographers of that ilk. I, by contrast, don't set out with theories that

I know I want to reconstruct. So I observe patterns of interactions that I wish to explain, and move from diagnostics to theory reconstruction, almost in spite of myself.

The Ethnographic Fallacy

In a paper given to mark the thirtieth anniversary of Herbert Gans's *The Urban Villagers*, Stephen Steinberg warned participant observers against what he calls "the ethnographic fallacy."[9] He argues that, unlike Gans, people who do firsthand studies often become too enmeshed in cultural details. Steinberg warns against "an epistemology that relies exclusively on observation—in other words, that defines reality by what you see." He explains: the ethnographic fallacy "begins when observation is taken at face value. Too often—not always—ethnography suffers from a myopia that sharply delineates the behavior at close range but obscures the less visible structures and processes that engender and sustain the behavior."

Steinberg's ethnographic fallacy emerges from his desire to avoid inappropriate concreteness. In researching this book, I was aware that the people I wrote about sometimes took complete responsibility for their own failures, unable to comprehend the obstacles and opportunities in their lives, the pressures and constraints they may have faced, and thus the probabilities of particular outcomes independent of their own actions. Sometimes the men inadvertently referred to such obstacles, as when Mudrick told me he was homeless by choice in the same sentence that he talked of being unable to find a job when he came to New York. But in general, if I had simply taken the men's accounts at face value, I would have concluded that their lives and problems were wholly of their own making.

A common way for a fieldworker to avoid the ethnographic fallacy is to suggest that economic or political forces all but guarantee that a particular person will act in a certain way. Such analysts avoid the ethnographic fallacy, but in doing so invoke determinism rather than tendencies, dispositions, and constraints. Another common way fieldworkers try to avoid the ethnographic fallacy is to discuss political and economic forces in distinct chapters, without providing evidence for the links between those conditions and the lives and behaviors they write about elsewhere in the book.

In short, the reader is asked to believe that the researcher who knows his or her subjects can also be trusted to be the guide to understanding which conditions are engendering and sustaining their behavior. But the details of everyday life on the sidewalk are much easier to account for with clear evidence than are the connections between those lives and the constraints and opportunities that shaped them. It is easy to learn that Ron dropped out of high school, but it is much more difficult to show that his choices in ninth grade were limited because of an interaction between his family's structure and its residence in a neighborhood with racial and class segregation, violence, and joblessness.

The scholar who wishes to avoid the ethnographic fallacy must sometimes ask the reader to make a leap of faith. On the one hand, the ethnographer makes a great effort to document and verify vast numbers of details, and in the process to tell how a social world works in everyday life. On the other hand, when it comes to the connection between these details and constraints and opportunities, his or her claims can seem quite skimpy by contrast.

My approach to this problem was to try not to get so caught up in the details of Sixth Avenue as to lose sight of their connections to constraints and opportunities. I read and reread the writings of contemporary analysts of such conditions as various as William Julius Wilson, Douglas Massey, Christopher Jencks, Andrew Hacker, Saskia Sassen, Reynolds Farley, Melvin Oliver, Orlando Patterson, and Roger Waldinger, as well as Stephen Steinberg, in an effort to be sensitive to these connections.

I certainly want the reader to know that the lives of the people on Sixth Avenue are engendered, sustained, and/or complicated by social forces. But I do not believe there is any easy way to avoid the ethnographic fallacy. If ethnographers shy away from analysis of constraints and opportunities because they cannot be substantiated with hard evidence, they will leave the inaccurate impression that the manifest behaviors are self-generating. But the ethnographer who allows theory to dominate data and who twists perception by invoking it to cover the "facts" makes a farce of otherwise careful work.

There is a middle ground: to try to grasp the connections between individual lives and the macroforces at every turn, while acknowledging one's uncertainty when one cannot be sure how those forces come to bear on individual lives. That, I think, is the best a committed scholar can do, and I hope my own uncertainty rings out loud and clear when appropriate in these pages.

Further Issues in Linking Micro and Macro: An Extended Place Method

Constraints on individual lives such as residential segregation were much more difficult for me to monitor than conditions of a more medium range. Much of my effort was spent doing more middle-range work: focusing on how institutions of various sorts, especially institutions that organize power, affect the microsettings I studied. This entailed looking for proximate linkages and visible traces of organizational structure on the sidewalk. I call my strategy an extended place method.

This approach, too, is usefully explicated through comparison with Burawoy's extended case method.[10] Burawoy, too, is interested in understanding the connection between the macro and the micro, and he collapses two distinct concerns—the importance of (1) reconstructing theory and (2) making the micro-macro link. My view is that theory reconstruction, while a fine objective on its own, was not the most efficient or rigorous way for me to make links between micro and macro.

What, then, *was* the most efficient way, and how was my approach an extended place method? For me to understand the sidewalk, that place could only be a starting point. Later, I needed to move my fieldwork on out, across spaces, to some of the other places where things had happened that had a role in making Sixth Avenue what it is. For example, having listened to unhoused men describe their day-to-day problems using public bathrooms, I paid visits to local restaurant owners, to learn more about the structural links between the sidewalk scene and the surrounding commercial reality. I also walked with Mudrick to Washington Square Park, to see an available public toilet and why it was unacceptable to him, which led to an interview with the park manager. In all these cases, the process of interviewing off the blocks grew out of participant observation on the blocks, out of seeing and hearing evidence of these problems in the day-to-day lives of people. It would have been difficult to understand the public urination I witnessed on the sidewalk without extending my fieldwork outward from the sidewalk itself.

Sometimes my effort to understand connections between micro and macro involved going farther from the blocks. I visited Pennsylvania Station with Mudrick, who showed me the specific places where he had slept before the authorities had rid the station of unhoused persons. It was impossible to understand the migration to Sixth Avenue without understanding Amtrak's decision, so I spent a good deal of time interviewing Penn Station officials, and traveling to Washington, D.C., to interview attorneys who understood the lawsuit which had been filed against Amtrak. It was not enough to ask the men on the sidewalk about their movements. I needed a more rounded picture. In order to understand how the sale of written matter came about on New York's streets, I tracked down Edward Wallace, the former city councilman who had worked to pass a local law protecting a poet's rights. In order to understand how space had been cut in half on the blocks, leading to space wars between the vendors, I spent a great deal of time doing fieldwork at the Grand Central Partnership, a Business Improvement District that had used its influence to cut down on space for vendors throughout the city. In order to contextualize the occasional sale of stolen goods on Sixth Avenue, I undertook to examine the underside of the sale of written matter throughout New York City.

The most efficient way for me to understand these connections between micro and macro was through what the anthropologist George E. Marcus calls "multi-sited ethnography."[11] The key to what eventually became my extended place method was my own eventual recognition that the sidewalk was also "in" Pennsylvania Station, the City Council, the Farrar, Straus and Giroux lawsuit against the Strand, and the Business Improvement District, among many other places.

Checking Stuff

One of the ideas basic to my method was simply following my nose, going to great lengths to check stuff out and make sure there is a warrant for believing what I've been told. Here I was simply doing what any competent reporter would do, but something which ethnographers have not taken as seriously in their work. After all, the people I was writing about were not under oath. (And, as we know, even people under oath sometimes lie.) On points that were significant to developing the understandings that formed the basis of my book, I adopted the stance of the skeptic, often not accepting accounts at face value. Sometimes, as in the case of establishing the migration from Pennsylvania Station to Sixth Avenue, this involved asking many men to tell me their life stories. When the same events were told to me over and over again in the context of different individual lives, the stories were more convincing.

A number of vendors told me that, prior to living on Sixth Avenue, they had taken over a single train car of the Metropolitan Transit Authority. In order to find out whether this was possible, I ended up going on what seemed like a wild-goose chase until I met a Penn Station official who knew enough about this practice to tell me why this account was plausible. When Ron told me that he had given up his apartment voluntarily, I went with him to New Jersey to see if I could learn more about this story, which I knew some of my readers would find implausible. What I learned from the building's maintenance man on that day was highly illuminating, as shown in the chapter on book vendors.

When telling me part of his life story (see "The Men without Accounts"), Mudrick related his inability to read and write to the fact that he saw lynchings when he was a child. When I tried to get more information about lynchings in South Carolina during the time he was growing up, the story turned out to be implausible. Here was a case in which a story needed to be understood as a representation which told me something useful about the kind of man Mudrick is and the kind of life he has lived.[12]

In conducting this research, I benefited from developments in the humanities which emphasize the importance of stories and narrative, while not being so bound by those developments as to think that it is not legitimate and useful to look at stories for their factual value, depending on my purpose. I tried not to take people's accounts as history without doing some checking. Few people (housed or unhoused) are going to be completely honest with a researcher about the intimate details in their lives. And it's not always a matter of honesty. Poor memory, wishful thinking, and misinterpretation of the questions can lead to accounts I might characterize as less than useful.

There were some things which could be checked only gradually, and only after people had developed a great deal of trust in the researcher. Issues such as HIV status are private. Some people are also sensitive about their status as welfare dependents, and like to keep this information to themselves so far as is possible. Over time, different men showed me their welfare cards, or letters from the State indicating that their benefits had been or would be cut off. Other persons asked me for help in dealing with the welfare system. These incidents occurred gradually over the years, and were chiefly a consequence of my being there over time. Over time, I knew enough about each man's status with the welfare system to construct note 2 in the chapter on the magazine vendors.

At times, checking simply meant trying to track down people involved in passing interactions on the street to find out how they felt about them. It was one thing, for example, to see and hear Jerome's interactions with Hakim, another thing altogether to set up an interview off the blocks to find out what he thought about them.

The most difficult kind of checking occurred when I tried to speak with Carrie, the dog walker whose interactions form a basis of "Talking to Women." When Carrie's interaction with Keith occurred, my tape recorder was running. As I analyzed the tapes and determined that the recording of Carrie's interaction with Keith was technically good enough to produce a transcript, I realized that an interview with her might be illuminating.

By the following summer, I had completed a draft of that chapter (as well as a more technical paper with my colleague Harvey Molotch—who conveyed the Conversation Analysis technique), so I went back to New York with the idea of tracking Carrie down to ask what she thought of her social situation as a pedestrian.[13] On my first day back, I asked Keith if he had seen Daisy's owner (the woman's name was not on the tape) and he said she came by every morning at around 8:30. I asked him to let her know that I was hoping to interview her for the book, that one of his interactions with her and her dog had been of interest to me. "You gonna interview the dog, Mitch?" he asked. "That's deep."

During the next week, I arrived on the block every morning by 8:30. Keith Johnson had checked into a detox program, so I was there in his space by myself. I didn't remember what Carrie or the dog looked like, so every woman who passed by with a small dog got asked the same question day after day: Is your dog named Daisy? This was the only way I could locate the woman. After a few days, people must have thought the whole thing a bit strange. I certainly felt embarrassed asking strange women this question, and I couldn't figure out why Carrie, who supposedly had the same routine every morning, never walked by.

After a week of failed effort, I saw Keith and told him I had not found Carrie. He said he would keep his eye out, and the next day he informed me that I had just missed her when I left him. It turned out that she had been on vacation the week I had been there. Keith told her that she was going to be in a book. It was clear from his account that she was a bit skeptical, but she said she would be by the next day. When we met, Carrie was very pleasant. She took my phone number and said she would call me that day, which she did. When we finally got together, she provided illuminating information about her experience as a pedestrian and told me what she thought of my interpretations of what had gone on between her and Keith, as well as correcting my estimates of her monthly rent and her age.

In some cases, "checking stuff out" meant talking to family members, who were happy to cooperate, if surprised that their loved one was going to be the subject of a book. I spoke with Ron's brother-in-law and sister, Mudrick's daughter, son-in-law, and granddaughter, Grady's ex-wife, and Conrad, who was married to Butteroll's second cousin and had known Butteroll since he was a teenager. The stories the men had told me were consistent with what their relatives knew to have happened, and the relatives filled in striking details.

During the summer of 1998, Ishmael arranged for his mother, Joan Howard, to visit us on the block so that I could interview her. She lived a subway ride away in the Bronx, but she had never seen him working on Sixth Avenue. After she arrived, Ishmael introduced her to some of the other men, and proudly showed her how his business works. When we went to lunch, she asked me about the book, saying, "Who would buy a book about Ishmael? He's not Michael Jackson or Madonna!" She said that she had always wanted to tell her story and that it was worth telling. The next day, Ishmael told me that his mother's visit was an important moment in his life. He had hurt her a great deal before he went to jail, and he knew that it comforted her to see him turning his life around and making "an honest living."

Publishing Ethnography

The genre of books based on sociological fieldwork can be distinguished from many first-hand works by journalists by the way each genre deals with anonymity. Since the 1920s, American sociologists have generally used fictitious names for people and places they have written about, whereas most journalists make it a practice to identify their subjects by name. Sociologists say that they use pseudonyms to protect the privacy of the people they write about; journalists insist that they must name their subjects to give truthfulness to the accounts and assure the reader that these are not composite characters or made-up characters.

I have decided to follow the practice of the journalists rather than the sociologists. I have not found that the people I write about ask to have their identities disguised. Some seem to enjoy the prospect of being in a book, and they are already known to hundreds of New Yorkers anyway. Moreover, it seems to me that to disclose the place and names of the people I have written about holds me up to a higher standard of evidence. Scholars and journalists may speak with these people, visit the site I have studied, or replicate aspects of my study. So my professional reputation depends on competent description—which I define as description that others who were there or who go there recognize as plausibly accurate, even if it is not the way they would have done it.

Disclosing place names increases accountability. The pressure to "publish or perish" is a significant motivation for quick production in the academic world, and if a researcher does not make himself or herself accountable by disclosing a site, there is increased likelihood of misrepresentation. (Why should we informally assume that the academic world is immune from the kinds of problems that have been disclosed at many newspapers, where well-known journalists have lost their jobs for fabricating quotations?) At the same time, I recognize that there are sometimes good reasons for keeping a site or a person's name anonymous, especially when the account would be humiliating or embarrassing, or when people will speak only on condition of anonymity (as did some people from the book industry in this book). But in my own work, when I have asked myself whom I am protecting by refusing to disclose the names, the answer has always been me.

I did not believe that anyone could make an informed judgment about whether they would like their name and image to be in the book without knowing how they have been depicted. With this in mind, I brought the completed manuscript to a hotel room and tried to read it to every person whose life was mentioned. I gave each man a written release which described the arrangement whereby royalties of the book are shared with the persons who are in it. But I did not tell them that I would do so until the book was nearing completion.

It was not always easy to get people to sit and listen to the larger argument of the book and to pay attention to all the places where they were discussed. Most people were much more interested in how they looked in the photographs than in how they sounded or were depicted. I practically had to beg people to concentrate on what I was saying. It also did not help that they now knew they would share in the profits, a factor that sometimes made them feel less motivation to listen carefully, on the assumption that I could be trusted. The following conversation, while somewhat extreme, illustrates (among other things) that the effort to be respectful by showing the text to the person in it sometimes turns out not to seem very respectful at all. In this case, I end up insisting that the individual listen to me, and imposing my agenda on someone who seemed annoyed by my efforts. What follows is a transcription of a tape I made one Christmas Day, told in the third person:

Keith: Get on this. We got to talk about what life is about out here.

Mitch starts to read the release to Keith. When he gets to the end of the first line, Keith says, "Yo! It's all good, man. Far as I'm concerned, you're family. You came out here. You walked the walk with us, you talked the talk. It's all good. And you brought something to the attention of the people and let them know that it ain't easy. We not individuals lacksidasical. No way! For the simple fact that we work hard and we fight harder than your Wall Street executives. Okay? I'm keeping it real. You came out here. You bringing it to the attention of the world that we are the backbone of society because we work. We *actually* work. The rest of them people don't work. Sit and answer the phone? That's work? Go out and dig through the garbage and try to find some books to sell and take a chance of getting bit by a rat. They ain't working.

Mitch continues to read. He says, "As a scholar, my purpose has been to . . ."

Keith interrupts: "I hate this kind of shit. Put this in the movie. This is real."

Mitch: ". . . and the difficult urban problems our society must confront in the years to come."

Keith: Well, I'm gonna tell you like this. I don't think it's just in suburbia. It's a world-wide situation. And in New York there is no reason why anyone should have to suffer. You don't know how deep your book is, do you?

At this point, Keith has still not heard any of the book.

Mitch: "I hope that this study will . . ."

Keith: Talking to a friend on the corner. Crack the beer, Reg.

Mitch: Keith, listen.

Keith: I'm listening.

Mitch: "Though there is no way to anticipate the consequences of any work . . ."

Keith: It's cool!

Mitch: "I don't expect the book to make a lot of money."

Keith: Just give me the contract, Mitch. I told you. I'm signing. I'm just proud to be in the book. All this reading and everything is completely unnecessary 'cause I'm just proud to be in the book. Something to make my family proud.

Mitch: [Continues to read] "And I would like you to share in the profits."

Keith: Thank you very much and I'm gonna accept whatever's given to me 'cause it's paper. I love this!

Mitch continues reading.

Keith: Man, do me a favor. Open the beer.

Hakim: Let's do this. Let him just finish this for one second, then you can get on with your business.

Keith: I'm celebrating Christmas, man. Kwaanza. It's a done deal.

Mitch: [Continues reading] ". . . of a biographical nature." Do you understand what that means?

Keith: Yes. Now, can you tell me how I sound in the book?

Mitch: I'm gonna show you every part you're in.

Keith: It's all good with me. After this book, I intend to get like Montel. Get my own show. We gonna call it "Keeping It Real." Me and brother Hakim are gonna be like Johnny Carson and Ed McMahon. Yo! Don King? Cut your hair and step aside because there's some new big dogs in town. Understand this here, Mitch. There's something you don't understand. To me this is not a money thing. It's something good that I did. I had to suffer to prove to my family that I could make it out here. And I don't need that. When they kick you to the curb and when they help you, it's a bunch of fucking bullshit. Because once you up on your feet, they turn their nose up at you. Hello you all. Kiss my ass. I got something good out of something bad.

Mitch: "If you do not receive payment, and you do not contact me, the money for you will be put in an escrow bank account for two years."

Keith: That sounds okay, too. I'd rather not know about it. That way, in the two years I got something I can go pick up. That's better than welfare!

Mitch: "If I still have not heard from you at the end of two years, you will forfeit the money."

Keith: I ain't forfeiting nothing.

Mitch: If I don't hear from you in two years, that money becomes mine.

Keith: Well, you'll hear from me. As long as I'm breathing, you'll hear from me. Mitch, give me the damn paper and the damn pen and let me sign.

Mitch: First, you gotta hear what the book says.

Keith: Oh, my God. Open the beer, please. This is getting on my nerves.

Mitch: First we gotta finish our work.

Keith: Damn that! I'm not signing nothing without no beer.

Mitch: "I want you to know how honored I am to have worked on this project. Thank you for your cooperation."

Keith: It was a pleasure, man. Like I said, my grandma can go to her grave and say, "That's my baby in that book."

Mitch: Okay, now we gotta go through the book.

Keith: I just wanna hear what's said about *me*. Yo, Reg, get the beer, please.

Mitch: Reads Keith's entry on the map to him. It says, "Keith is a panhandler. He loves babies and dogs."

Keith: That sounds crazy.

Mitch: Does that sound crazy in a bad way?

Keith: No. It's like this here, man. A dog will stick by you one hundred percent. Family, your girl, everybody turn their back on you, a dog is still by your side. Children, they not only need to be taught by their family, with all the wickedness going on, they need to be protected.

Mitch continues to go through the pictures.

Keith: Where am I at? Damn with everybody else. I'm looking for me. [Laughing] I'll see all of them, too. But I want to see me. I see all of them every day. Shit!

Mitch: I'm getting to you.

Keith: I want to know about me. I hope this shit becomes a movie. You all have to excuse me on this tape because I am somewhat inebriated right now. It's Christmas. Merry Christmas to whoever listens to this tape. And what's up?

Mitch: Keith, if you're inebriated, we should do this at a time when you are not inebriated.

Keith: Put it like this. I ain't drunk. I just feel all right. I'm fully competent and aware of everything you said. And I know it's Christmas and that there's a lot of people who ain't got no Christmas.

Mitch: Here's a picture of Ron taking care of his aunt.

Keith: Oh, that's deep, man. Let me see what she looks like. God bless her. You got all deep and in-depth.

Mitch: Yeah. Now, this is you, standing by the door of the bank here and the lady is giving you some money.

Keith: I like this. This is funny.

Mitch reads Keith's statement on panhandling.

Keith: I remember that. True words.

Mitch reads more.

Keith: Yo! Those are my words! Verbatim. You got me good, Mitch. You got the realness out. Does it say "Fuck" in the book?

Mitch: Yes.

Keith: I like it.

Mitch reads more.

Keith: [Laughter] Oh my God! Oh my God. I've never been quoted before. My words is in print. That means it's law.

Mitch: The next chapter here is called "Talking to Women."

Keith laughs.

Mitch: Here's a section called "Keith and the Dog Walker." There are some pictures of you.

Keith: I want to see the pictures. Yo, I might just go buy me a dog today. Oh, that's my baby, Daisy.

Mitch: [Reading from manuscript] "Sometimes a man's efforts to gain conversation . . . In ordinary conversation, participants not only respond to cues."

Keith: Damn, I'm deep! I didn't know I was a philosopher until now. This is damn good.

Mitch: ". . . Entanglement is accompanied through a dog."

Keith: I'm deep! I'm in my own zone now. I gotta get into my zone to comprehend what is going on.

Mitch: "As evidenced in the following interaction. She is a graduate of college. She straightens her back. 'Hold on, I gotta go talk to my baby.' "

Keith: Yo, man. You make me sound like some kind of freak in this article. "Come on, kiss me." You make me sound like some kind of pervert or some shit. No! I just love dogs!

Mitch continues going through the dialogue.

Keith: [Laughs] This is funny shit.

Mitch: [Reading] " 'Drop the leash.' As events unfold, Keith uses the dog to bring the woman over to him."

Keith: [Laughter, hysterical laughter] The dog is leading the woman!

Mitch: [Reading] "Keith has the woman by the leash."

Keith: Oh, women are gonna hate me for shit like that, man. I'm ready to get on my tail and chill out. All the player haters out there. It's all good by me. I like this. You don't got to read no more, Mitch. I'd rather read the book when it comes out. It's cool. It's reality. Hardcore reality.

Keith signs the release. He picks up the microphone. "I'm in a book. I'm in a book. Yeah! Yeah! Yeah! Stan, I love you, man. Thank you for teaching me to be a man. That's my old uncle, the one in Denver. Mickey, thanks. And Nana, I love you. And I miss Papa. Merry Christmas."

Because Keith might have been drunk on this occasion, I had to go back and see him to go through the relevant parts of the manuscript a second and third time.

One of the most difficult aspects of reading people the sections they are in is the fear or nervousness I feel as I approach passages in the manuscript that they might interpret as negative or disrespectful. This might be one of the best arguments for making the people one writes about completely anonymous. Some observers may feel a greater license to tell the truth as they see it, even when it might be hurtful, if they never have to face the people they write about. But I have developed a rather thick skin when it comes to reading people passages they may not like. Ultimately, I believe I should never publish something about an identifiable person which I cannot look him or her in the eye and read.

As I read the book to the people depicted in it, I was often asked to correct specific dates or facts of a person's life. These changes would be noticeable only to the person and his/her family. In a few cases, the corrections would make a difference to people who knew the blocks or neighborhood. Yet it was absolutely essential that these aspects of the book be correct if the work was to have integrity to the persons in it.

As I went about representing others, I was aware of programmatic efforts in cultural anthropology[14] and feminist methods within sociology[15] to be more conscious of power relations between the author and the persons being written about. One approach is to ask the people in the book to respond in the footnotes, as did Elliot Liebow in his excellent last book, *Tell Them Who I Am: The Lives of Homeless Women.*[16] But I found that this particular experiment in Liebow's book made for tedious reading, so I thought it would be worthwhile to experiment with an alternative: asking Hakim to write an afterword. He and I knew that he couldn't speak for the other men on Sixth Avenue, and that some might object to the idea that he could represent them. There might have been good reasons for choosing to ask other men as well. But as the one person on these blocks who had read Jane Jacobs and knew Sixth Avenue, it seemed fitting that Hakim should have the last word. Yet Hakim and I both knew that, in the end, I was the author. Our experiment does not alter that fact and the responsibility it implies.

A Final Note on Social Position

For the past decade and a half I have been engaged in research on intergroup relations, race, and poverty in American cities. I regard myself as an urban sociologist working in the traditions of the Chicago School of Urban Sociology of the 1920s, as informed by contemporary developments in the social sciences and the humanities. The Chicago School was devoted mainly to studying local communities and social worlds at firsthand. My intellectual forebears include W.E.B. Du Bois, Robert E. Park, W. I. Thomas, Carolyn Ware, Charles Johnson, Everett Hughes, St. Clair Drake, William Foote Whyte, Horace Cayton, Robert and Helen Lynd, Howard S. Becker, Erving Goffman, Elliot Liebow, Gerald Suttles, Herbert Gans, and Elijah Anderson. My primary goal as a scholar is to carry on some of their traditions in order to illuminate issues of race and/or poverty as found in American cities in the current era.

As an upper-middle-class white male academic writing about poor black men and women, who are some of the most disadvantaged and stigmatized members of my own society, I have documented lives very different from my own.

How might this social position influence my work? I have already noted that in the United States, blacks and whites often speak differently when they are among people of their own race than when they are in the presence of members of another race. As a white person, it would be naïve for me to believe that the things blacks will say to me are the same as they would say to a black researcher. For this reason, I have relied upon the method of participant observation, rather than interviewing, to obtain the bulk of my data. Vendors would have urinated against the sides of buildings, for example, whether I was black or white, and whether I was there or not. I asked many questions, but rarely ones that assumed an honest dialogue about race. Sometimes, of course, as when Jerome told me about his experience buying black books, such discussions flowed from the context.

A second way that my social position can influence my work comes from the heightened sense on the part of the people I write about that I am "exploiting" them by appropriating their words and images for my own purposes and personal gain. I believe that this occurs intensely in some relations between white researchers and poor blacks because of the long history of whites' exploitation of blacks. I am always sensitive to this issue as I deal with the people I hope to write about, and I try to encourage discussion about it with them, which is sometimes a losing battle, given that it is difficult for us to always have honest dialogues, and some people simply don't want to offend me. Once the book was completed, I expressed my intention to the people in it that I would share my royalties with them. But even this cannot always eliminate the sense of exploitation, which grows out of the way a researcher's actions are interpreted in the context of a complex history.

A third way that my social position (or in this case the standpoint that emerges from my social position) can influence my work comes from the blindness I might have to the circumstances of people who are very different from me. During my first summer working as a magazine vendor with Marvin and Ron, for example, I routinely entered restaurants on the block to urinate and defecate. I would sometimes see vendors doing their bodily functions in public places, but I never thought twice about why they did so. I think the reason the issue didn't register on my radar is that my privileges made it a non-issue for me personally. Had the researcher been a poor black, he or she might have been excluded from local bathrooms enough times to say, "This is a process that needs to be understood."

Ultimately, I came to understand that such stigmatization and exclusion needed to be addressed. When I listened to tapes made on Sixth Avenue, I heard references to men's problems gaining access to rest rooms. I listened to these tapes while reviewing notes of interviews with local residents who complained about the tendency of some vendors to urinate in public. As a white male who took his bathroom privileges for granted, I might have looked at the people working the street as persons not unlike friends of mine who are white and rich and who urinate on the golf course because they don't want to bother going back to the clubhouse. But because I listened carefully to my tapes, I noted that the situation was more complex, and this led me to research it in some depth. Though I constantly obsess about the ways that my upper-middle-class whiteness influences what I see, I must emphasize my uncertainty about what I do not see and what I do not know I missed.

I have endeavored to trade on the disadvantage of being from a different social position from the people I write about by maximizing the advantages that come from being in that position. I try to use myself as a kind of control group, comparing the way I am treated in particular situations with the way people on the street are treated. When the dog walker responded immediately to me while delaying her reaction to Keith, I could see that our social positions and behavior led to the dog walker's differing response. When the police treated an educated white male professor differently from an unhoused vendor on Christmas Day, I was in a better position to speculate on the underlying dynamics. And when I realized how effortlessly I walked into public bathrooms, I could make a useful comparison in my chapter on that topic. In none of these cases are the inferences made from the comparisons clear-cut, but they are comparisons that I am able to make *because* of my privileged position.

In addition to benefiting from some of the advantages of my upper-middle-class white-ness, I try to overcome my disadvantages by consulting with black scholars and intellectu-als, some of whom grew up in poor families themselves. Sometimes their suggestions led me back to the field with new ideas and questions I had not thought to ask. In trying to un-derstand why black women don't get entangled to the same extent as white women by street harassment in encounters with poor black men, for example, I was helped by the sug-gestion of a black sociologist, Franklin D. Wilson. He thinks that because the black women share a racial history with the men on the street, they do not feel responsible or guilty for the men's plight and so are less willing to excuse the men's behavior toward them. Surely a white scholar could have had that insight, but none of those who read my chapter did. I suspect it comes out of Wilson's particular life experience, from situations and people he has known.

Another thing that has helped me has been my collaboration with the African–American photographer Ovie Carter, whose professional and life experiences enable him to give me good advice. Ovie is fifty-two years old, was born in Mississippi, and grew up in Chicago and St. Louis, before serving in the Air Force. He joined the *Chicago Tribune* at the age of twenty-three. He has worked in Africa as a photojournalist, but has spent most of his career covering poor neighborhoods in Chicago. Shortly before our work began on this book, his brother moved in with him from the streets as he made his way off crack. Conse-quently, Ovie has a deep appreciation for the anguish and problems associated with addic-tion. Ovie read and commented on all the chapters in *Sidewalk* as I wrote them, and the long hours we have spent together have helped me to understand aspects of life on Sixth Avenue that I would otherwise have been blind to.

All these circumstances have worked for me at times, but there is no simple way to overcome ingrained racial bias, inexperience, or others' suspicions. Perhaps the best start-ing point is to be aware that a different social position can have a serious effect on one's work, and these differences must be taken seriously.

Interventions

One of the most difficult issues faced by social scientists and journalists who do sociologi-cal fieldwork is the question of when it is appropriate to intervene in the lives of the people they write about. This is especially true when such persons are living in states of depriva-tion. Some journalists have given assistance back to the people they have written about, and they have found a way to do so that is consistent with their goals as researchers.[17] Pos-itivistic social scientists, who remain obsessed with securing unobtrusive measures of so-cial phenomena which are not of their own creation, tend to be more uneasy about such involvements.

In my early weeks working as a magazine vendor, I found it very hard to say no to re-quests for money, usually small change, which came from a certain group of panhandlers and table watchers. In the methodological appendix to *Tally's Corner*, Elliot Liebow (who, like me, was thirty-seven years old when he completed his book) recalls being confronted with a similar problem. Liebow says that some people "exploited" him, not as an outsider but rather as one who, as a rule, had more resources than they did. When one of them came up with the resources—money or a car, for example—he, too, was "exploited" in the same way.[18] Liebow "usually tried to limit money or other favors to what . . . each would have gotten from another friend had he the same resources" as the researcher.[19]

I tried to maintain a similar stance. But as time went on, panhandlers and a few magazine vendors asked me, more and more often. Nobody expected me to give any more money than they might get from another vendor who had a good day, but a number of panhandlers came to expect me to give something on a regular basis.

Hakim and Marvin said these men asked me for money on a regular basis because they thought that as a college professor, and a Jew, I was "rich" enough to afford the donations. The questions for me were: Could I show my deep appreciation for their struggles *and* gain their appreciation for my purposes as a sociologist without paying for some simulacrum of it? How could I communicate my purposes as a researcher without dollar bills and small change in my hand? Did the constant requests for money suggest that I had not shown or earned proper "respect" and was being paid back accordingly?

In the end, out of practical necessity, I needed to find a way to tell certain persons that I could hardly afford the tapes I was using to record the street life, and that as a professor I could afford to be in New York City only due to the goodwill of friends who were allowing me to sleep in their spare bedrooms or on their couches. Yet I could never bring myself to say even this. I knew that my salary (while not very high) was quite high compared to the going rate on the sidewalk. Furthermore, the spare bedroom I was sleeping in (on the Upper East Side) was more hospitable than the places many of them would stay in that night. But with time I did learn to say no, and to communicate the anguish I felt in giving such an answer.

The question of how to avoid intervening when one cannot or should not do so is different from the question of whether and how to help when one can and should. At times, I was asked to do things as simple as telling what I knew about the law, serving as a reference for a person on the sidewalk as he or she dealt with a landlord or potential landlord, helping someone with rent when he was about to be evicted, and on one occasion finding and paying for a lawyer. In these situations, I did everything I could to be helpful, but I never gave advice, opinions, or help beyond what was asked for.

At other times, the question was whether and how to make larger efforts to intervene. One such situation occurred at the close of the summer of 1997. After I had worked as a magazine vendor during two summers, I began having discussions about my research with Nolan Zail, an architect from Australia on the frontiers of designing innovative housing alternatives for unhoused persons in New York City. One of the issues we discussed concerned the difficulty some unhoused men like Ishmael had in moving their magazines and personal belongings around, as well as the complaint made by Business Improvement Districts and police officers that the presence of these vendors was unsightly and frustrating because their merchandise and belongings were strewn on the pavement under their tables. I asked Zail whether he could design a vending cart which might address some of these concerns.

Here was an opportunity for us to use what we knew to make a small but practical contribution to improving conditions on Sixth Avenue. Surely this was not the same as helping to transform the larger structural conditions which brought about these problems, but it might make a difference in Ishmael's day-to-day life. First, though, it was necessary to find out if Ishmael wanted such a cart, and how he would feel about such an effort on his behalf.

I could not ignore the fact that both Zail and I are white, and that Ishmael had described being treated in patronizing ways by many whites throughout his life.

Zail suggested that we meet with Ishmael to try to establish what kind of functional characteristics he was looking for in a vending cart. There on the sidewalk, Zail spent time with Ishmael trying to understand how his table functions within his business and life routine as an unhoused vendor.

Ishmael described his need for sufficient storage space to hold his merchandise and personal belongings safely. He also said that it would be useful if the design made provision for a separate lightweight carriage which he would use for his hunts and which could be attached to the vending cart.

After two weeks, Zail had designed a cart and presented drawings to Ishmael to get his input and reaction. Then he modified the designs to incorporate Ishmael's suggestions. In one meeting, Ishmael expressed his wish to pay back, in installments, the costs of manufacturing the cart. The cost had not yet come up (I knew it would, in due time), and we agreed that this would be a good way to do it. In the meantime, I received permission from Ishmael to try to raise the money to pay for the manufacture of the cart through donations.

When Ishmael felt satisfied with the cart's design, Zail and I scheduled an appointment with one of the large manufacturers of steel-and-aluminum food carts. He was already manufacturing a food cart which was pretty similar to the one we would ask him to make for us. His reaction to our ideas, and the difficulty we had in getting the cart built, became another kind of data for me, showing the nature of prejudice against the destitute and unhoused. It was yet another occasion when I was able to trade on the advantage of being white. Had I been black, I would likely never have heard the following:

"Okay, let's see what you got," he said as we began the meeting, which he gave me permission to record.

"This is what we have in mind," I said as Zail placed the architectural drawings in front of him.

"Did you show this to the head of Business Improvement District A?" (The head of BID A was a powerful man in New York real estate who, the manufacturer asserted, was an enemy of sidewalk vending.)

"No," I replied.

"Well, then, forget about it," he said.

"He doesn't have any say about what goes on in Greenwich Village," I said.

"Mitch, please! They own everything that's happening. The real-estate board controls New York City. They *are* the real-estate board. You're gonna show them this? Are you kidding? They want to get rid of these people!"

"Part of their argument for getting rid of these guys is that it looks so bad," I responded.

"It's not a question that we can't make something," he said. "It's the opposition. If we go out there with one of these carts, they would crucify us. They would nail me to the cross."

"Nail you?"

"Look! You know what started all this? Really simple. They want to get all the niggers off the street. They told me: 'We want them off. They're bad for business!' *You* want to put them on, *Mitch*! Why you making so much trouble, Mitch? You're spitting in their face with this!"

"What we are saying," Zail interjected, "is that this is what you can do to improve the image . . . It's actually not too dissimilar from the cart you have there."

"So how does this help?"

"Well, for several reasons," Zail continued. "One, it allows storage. Two is display. It can be displayed in a professional manner, rather than strewn all over."

"All we're asking is for you to make *one* of these for us on an experimental basis," I said. If it worked for Ishmael, we would likely order more.

"I'll make anything you want," the manufacturer replied. "If that's what you're telling me to do. But there is nothing that will change their appearance!"

"It will increase the aesthetic of this type of vending," I said.

"What about him, the homeless person?" he asked.

We seemed destined to go around in circles.

A few weeks later, Zail called to confirm a subsequent meeting with the manufacturer, but he said he had changed his mind. He wouldn't have any part of our project. He didn't want to do anything to make the "homeless" vendors look more like the food vendors, who constituted the real market for his carts. He said he was also concerned that he might antagonize the real-estate interests of the city, who he said were already trying to eliminate food vendors on sidewalks. (In fact, one year later, Mayor Giuliani tried to eliminate food vendors from hundreds of locations in lower Manhattan and midtown, but changed his mind in response to a public outpouring of support for the food vendors.)

When we told Ishmael of our trouble in getting the cart made, he was not surprised. After all, he had been dealing with such responses ever since he began working as a magazine vendor, seven years earlier.

In the end, despite my having given small change on some occasions and despite efforts to do more than that on others, the quality of my regard must be in the research work itself. To this day, I cannot say how much "acceptance," or "rapport," or "respect" I have on the sidewalk, or how much respect I have shown these men in our personal relations. But I would like to think that whatever respect I ultimately get will be based not on what I did or didn't give in the way of resources but on whether the people working and/or living on Sixth Avenue think the work I did has integrity, by whatever yardstick they use to take that measure.

Notes

Introduction

1. Jane Jacobs, *The Death and Life of Great American Cities* (New York: Vintage, 1961), p. 68.
2. Ibid., p. 47.
3. Ibid., p. 56.
4. For an excellent statement, see Stephen Steinberg, "The Urban Villagers: Thirty Years Later," remarks prepared for a plenary session at meeting of the Eastern Sociology Society, Boston, March 25, 1993.
5. For an excellent collection of ethnographies of the East Village, see Janet L. Abu-Lughod, *From Urban Village to "East Village": The Battle for New York's Lower East Side* (Cambridge: Blackwell, 1994); for an excellent ethnography of the political culture of Corona, with reference to quality-of-life discourse among working-class blacks in Queens, see Steven Gregory, *Black Corona: Race and the Politics of Place in an Urban Community* (Princeton, N.J.: Princeton University Press, 1988).
6. For a comprehensive analysis, see Lyn H. Lofland, *The Public Realm* (Hawthorne, N.Y.: Aldine De Gruyter, 1998).

The Book Vendor

1. See Patricia Williams, *The Alchemy of Race and Rights* (Cambridge, Mass.: Harvard University Press, 1991); Regina Austin, "Social Inequality, Physical Restraints on Mobility, and the Black Public Sphere," a paper presented at "*An American Dilemma* Revisited: Fiftieth Anniversary Conference," Harvard University, September 29, 1995; Regina Austin, "An Honest Living: Street Vendors, Municipal Regulation, and the Black Public Sphere," *Yale Law Journal* 10, no. 8 (June 1994).
2. See Joe R. Feagin, Hernan Vera, and Nikitah Imani, *The Agony of Education: Black Students at White Colleges and Universities* (New York: Routledge, 1996); Walter R. Allen, Edgar Epps, and Nesha Z. Haniff, *College in Black and White* (Albany: SUNY Press, 1991), p. 12. For some of the most influential popular books about the variety of expe-

riences of African Americans in the workplace, see Jill Nelson, *Volunteer Slavery: My Authentic Negro Experience* (Chicago: Noble Press, 1993); Nathan McCall, *Makes Me Wanna Holler* (New York: Simon & Schuster, 1993); Sara Lawrence Lightfoot, *I've Known Rivers* (New York: Addison Wesley, 1994); Brent Staples, *Parallel Time* (New York: Pantheon, 1994).

3. I have looked up his article in that magazine, "None Dare Call It Treason: Black Greeks," which won a 1982 Unity Award in Media, an award given annually by Lincoln University. The article argued that African Americans must cease their membership in all Greek-lettered fraternities and sororities.

4. Although I have never doubted any of the things Hakim told me about his life, in conducting this study I have looked upon it as my responsibility to check salient things people tell me about themselves before reporting them. (Usually my need to check things that I regarded as salient, of course, said something more about me than about them.) I wanted to make sure that he had attended Rutgers and worked for all those years in the formal economy. He thought this was reasonable in light of my project and agreed to request his college records as well as official employment information from the last firm he worked at. Everything checked out. I have seen Hakim's final transcript from Rutgers University, indicating that he completed his B.A. According to an official letter on firm stationery, he worked at Robinson, Silverman as a proofreader on the late-night shift, from 9:00 p.m. to 4:00 a.m., from April 25, 1988, through January 18, 1991. This letter to Hakim from the director of administrative services states that the firm will provide no information beyond verifying the dates and times of his employment.

5. See Houston Baker, *Rap, Black Studies, and the Academy* (Chicago: University of Chicago Press, 1993).

6. G. William Domhoff, *Blacks in the White Establishment: A Study of Race and Class in America* (New Haven: Yale University Press, 1991).

7. J. A. Rogers, *From Superman to Man* (Freeport, N.Y.: Books for Libraries Press, 1972).

8. Timothy Holt, *Catch a Fire: The Life of Bob Marley* (New York: Holt, Rinehart and Winston, 1983).

9. Booker T. Washington, *Up from Slavery* (New York: Dover Publications, 1995).

10. Ronald B. Mincy, *Nurturing Young Black Males: Challenges to Agencies, Programs, and Social Policy* (Washington, D.C.: Urban Institute, 1994), p. 12.

11. Ibid.

12. Judith Stacey, *In the Name of the Family: Rethinking Family Values in the Postmodern Age* (Boston: Beacon Press, 1996).

13. Sara McLanahan and Gary Sandefur, *Growing Up with a Single Parent* (Cambridge, Mass.: Harvard University Press, 1994).

14. Ibid., p. 3.

15. Ibid., p. 5.

16. Elijah Anderson, *Streetwise* (Chicago: University of Chicago Press, 1990), p. 69.

17. Max Weber, *Economy and Society*, Vol. 1 (Berkeley: University of California Press, 1978), p. 212.

18. Anderson, *Streetwise*, p. 72.

19. See William Julius Wilson, *When Work Disappears* (New York: Alfred A. Knopf, 1997).

The Magazine Vendors

1. In a careful study of this subject, Kathryn Edin and Laura Lein found evidence that few single women live on welfare alone (*Making Ends Meet: How Single Mothers Survive Welfare and Low-Wage Work* [New York: Russell Sage Foundation, 1997].) Additional support comes from boyfriends, the informal economy, fathers of their children, family members, etc.

2. Welfare laws have changed significantly in the years since I began this study. In August 1996, President Clinton signed the Personal Responsibility and Work Opportunity Reconciliation Act, which placed a five-year limit on federal public assistance and replaced Aid to Families with Dependent Children (AFDC) with Temporary Assistance for Needy Families (TANF). Under the new law, parents on welfare must be engaged in some type of work activity within twenty-four months after benefits begin. Under New York State's Welfare Reform Act, passed in August 1997, all adult recipients of public assistance must be engaged in work "as soon as practicable." New York has also begun screening welfare recipients for drug and alcohol abuse, and recipients who fail to comply with mandated treatment can be sanctioned off both public assistance and medical assistance.

   At the time of this writing, it is impossible to assess the significance of these changes on the sidewalks I have studied. At any given time, some people have lost their benefits after "willfully and without cause" (to use the language of the letters they have received) refusing workfare assignments. Most people on the blocks who were entitled to benefits were certified as unable to work due to various disabilities. These persons continued to receive benefits after the first wave of workfare requirements forced many welfare recipients to go to work. In the next wave of welfare changes, which is occurring at the time of this writing, some of these people have been notified that they, too, will have to take jobs in the formal economy.

   Often people who have lost benefits appeal the decision through a fair hearing or reapply for benefits after their sanction period has ended. Others have shown me papers indicating that they have been off public assistance for as long as a year. Although some people have shown me the notices discontinuing their benefits, in other cases I have seen no documentation when told of such experiences. On a subject of this kind, without documentation, a researcher would be irresponsible to make statements with confidence.

   What is very clear is that the life of these sidewalks in Greenwich Village does not exist in isolation from public assistance, medical assistance, or food-stamp benefits, though people's reliance on such benefits varies, depending on when they are surveyed. At any given time, the vending is supplementing public assistance for some people but not for others. And at different times, the same people may or may not be receiving public assistance, depending on where their cases are in the process of appeals and reapplication. It is worth noting that no man has left these blocks to take a workfare job. The choice is always to give up the benefits rather than leave one's job on the block.

3. In neighborhoods such as the one Ron comes from, where the poverty rate is over 40

percent, more than 50 percent of the residents are high-school dropouts. (Paul A. Jargowsky, *Poverty and Place: Ghettos, Barrios, and the American City* [New York: Russell Sage Foundation, 1997], p. 111. See also Gregg Duncan, "Families and Neighbors as Sources of Disadvantage in the Schooling Decisions of White and Black Adolescents," *American Journal of Education* 103 [November 1994]: 20–53.)

4. After Ron and I got to know one another better, I asked him to help me clarify the story about the apartment. We took a train from New York City to Newark, New Jersey, and then a bus to the very block in East Orange on which he said he had lived. (On the way he told me that, like Marvin, he is certified as unable to work because of a disability. He receives the same public assistance as Marvin, though he does not get money for an apartment, since he is officially homeless.)

The area in which Ron says he lived was a run-down black neighborhood populated mainly by West Indians. The building was at 50 Walnut Street, a rooming house with furnished rooms. Residents sitting on the front porch appeared down-and-out. None seemed to recognize Ron. They said that the superintendent, who, like them, was relatively new to the building, wouldn't be home until the evening. Ron told me which room he had lived in, and we met the current resident. Ron pointed to the bed and said he had situated it against the other wall. The only person present in an official capacity whom we met was Jimmy Carrol, who does maintenance work. When I told him why we were there, he turned to Ron and asked, "Were you behind on the rent?"

"Yes," admitted Ron.

"Most of the people who live here just leave everything when they go," said Carrol. "If they can't pay the rent, there is no place for them to go. They can't drag their stuff around. When they leave, we got to clean the whole apartment out: TVs, VCRs, furniture."

When added to Ron's story, Jimmy Carrol's response is illuminating. It suggests, first, that Ron's sense of having gone to the street voluntarily is not merely an artifact of his having been on the street for a long time, as is sometimes the case with such testimony. (See David Snow and Leon Anderson, *Down on Their Luck: The Lives of Homeless Street People* [Berkeley: University of California Press, 1993], p. 254.) From the account of Ron's landlord in East Orange, it seems that other people also leave all their belongings behind when they believe they cannot pay their rent, and men like Ron sometimes go to the street voluntarily, before they are evicted by the marshals. It is not clear that going to the street was the best possible alternative for Ron. According to his own memory, no eviction proceedings had begun against him. It would probably have been many months before he was actually forced out, though he might not have known that.

5. Some people's stories, then, would be examples of the phenomenon of "learned helplessness," whereby an outcome appears "beyond control"; the person gives up and "expects that no voluntary action can control the outcome." See Martin E. P. Seligman, *Helplessness* (New York: W. H. Freeman, 1992), p. xvii.

6. David Snow and Leon Anderson, *Down on their Luck* (Berkeley and Los Angeles: University of California Press, 1993).

7. Craig Reinarman, Dan Waldorf, Sheila B. Murphy, and Harry G. Levine, "The Contingent Call of the Pipe: Bingeing and Addiction Among Heavy Cocaine Smokers," in

Craig Reinarman and Harry G. Levine, eds., *Crack in America* (Berkeley: University of California Press, 1997), p. 79.

8. John P. Morgan and Lynn Zimmer, "The Social Pharmacology of Smokeable Cocaine: Not All It's Cracked Up to Be," ibid., p. 155.

9. Like Marvin's earlier account, the brief story Ishmael tells stresses this point: "I completed P.S.I. Computer School. I went hunting for a job. I was denied a job just by one point. There was ten of us, and out of ten there was three blacks and the rest white. None of the blacks got picked. Me and this one white guy, we had the same points. But I didn't get taken in. He was taken in. I got so frustrated with that. I said, 'Here you give society what they want and they still deny you for who you are. What makes him more better than I am? In that area, I give you what you want. Why can't I have that job?' It put me in the position to rob and steal. And after I did that I went to jail for five years, and then I came straight to Sixth Avenue."

The data of other ethnographies supports this view. In one study of women and the informal drug economy of Brooklyn, Lisa Maher shows her subjects as "likely candidate[s] for the informal economy even prior to . . . immersion in drug use." (Lisa Maher, *Sexed Work: Gender, Race, and Resistance in a Brooklyn Drug Market* [Oxford: Clarendon Press, 1997], p. 74.)

10. William H. James and Stephen L. Johnson, *Doin' Drugs: Patterns of African American Addiction* (Austin: University of Texas Press, 1996), p. 31.

11. I am grateful to Debby Carr for making this point to me.

12. For example, friendship ties that result in obligations that function as even greater constraints and lead to even fewer choices. This is a useful contribution of Gwendolyn A. Dordick, *Something Left to Lose: Personal Relations and Survival Among the Homeless* (Philadelphia: Temple University Press, 1997). She writes that we should not assume that, "in making choices, the homeless behave as isolated actors, unconstrained and unaffected by their relationships with others." I will suggest other constraints in a later chapter. For the study of social and institutional constraints, see Dalton Clark Conley, "Getting It Together," *Sociological Forum* 11, no. 1 (1996).

13. As Levine and Reinarman write, "Middle class people whose lives become too difficult often have psychiatrists who prescribe them antidepressants like Prozac. . . . By contrast, the inner-city poor and working class are far less often employed and more often live at the margins of the conventional order. When their lives become too difficult, they rarely have psychiatrists, but they sometimes self-medicate, escape, or seek moments of intense euphoria with what might be called anti-despondents, such as crack."

14. When a combination of cocaine and alcohol is used, there is good chemical evidence that it causes a depletion of neurotransmitters in the brain, which are the same neurotransmitters whose absence is responsible for depression in people who are not using drugs. Paul Casadonte, chief of addiction-therapy and substance-abuse programs at the VA Medical Center, explained this to me in an interview. He continued, "So these neurotransmitters become depleted and it becomes a mixed picture of alcohol-cocaine depression. You don't know what comes first or what comes second unless you have a very clear picture of a person's history. But the picture of depression you are describing is one that is very, very similar to that of a cocaine addict who stopped using cocaine and is feeling down or depressed, or an alcoholic who stopped using alcohol and is

feeling down or depressed. It becomes impossible to separate out the psychosocial factors from the biological factors in drug addiction, depression, and so forth." See also Morgan and Zimmer, pp. 131–70; and Ronald L. Akers, *Drugs, Alcohol, and Society* (Belmont, Calif.: Wadsworth Publishing Company, 1992), pp. 120–21.

15. For over half a century, American sociology has used a brilliant scheme to interpret the structural conditions that lead people to give up on culturally prescribed goals and means. In his seminal article, "Social Theory and Anomie," in *Social Theory and Social Structure*, rev. ed. (New York: Free Press, 1957), Robert K. Merton distinguished between five types of individual adaptation to the structural conditions of American society: *conformists*, who accept dominant cultural goals and dominant ways of achieving them; *innovators*, who accept the goals but reject the means; *ritualists*, who reject the goals, but go through the motions of accepting the means; *retreatists*, who reject both the goals and the means; and *rebels*, who try to overturn existing structures.

Where does a man who has said "Fuck it" fit in this scheme? He is not a conformist, because he does not accept the dominant goals or means of achieving them. He is not an innovator, because he has given up on trying. No longer going through the motions, he cannot be classified as a ritualist. And he is too lethargic and uncaring to be a rebel. These men are best classified as retreatists. According to Merton, "Defeatism, quietism, and resignation are manifested in escape mechanisms which ultimately lead him to 'escape' from the requirements of the society." In a later article, Merton argued that vagrants and tramps were retreatists. See Merton in Marshall Clinard, ed., *Anomie and Deviant Behavior: A Discussion and Critique* (New York: Free Press, 1964).

16. See W. Cochran and A. Tesser, "The 'What the Hell' Effect: Some Effects of Goal Proximity and Framing for Performance," in Leonard L. Martin and Abraham Tesser, eds., *Striving and Feeling: Interactions Among Goals, Affect and Self Regulation* (Mahwah, N.J.: Lawrence Erlbaum Associates, 1996).

17. Stanley Cohen, "Property Destruction: Motives and Meanings," in Colin Ward, ed., *Vandalism* (London: Architectural Press, 1973), pp. 41–49.

18. For an analysis of shame and embarrassment as *the* social emotions, see Thomas J. Scheff, *Microsociology* (Chicago: University of Chicago Press, 1994).

19. Alfred R. Lindesmith and John H. Gangnon, "Anomie and Drug Addiction," in Marshall Clinard, ed., *Anomie and Deviant Behavior*, pp. 158–88.

20. As Melvin L. Kohn and his associates have argued on the basis of much empirical study, job conditions "that facilitate or restrict the exercise of self-direction in work affect workers' values, orientations to self and society, and cognitive functioning primarily through a direct process of learning from the job and generalizing what has been learned to other realms of life." See Melvin L. Kohn and Kazimierz M. Slomczyski (with Karen A. Miller, Carrie Schoenback, and Ronald Schoenberg), *Social Structure and Self-Direction: A Comparative Analysis of the United States and Poland* (Cambridge, Mass: Basil Blackwell, 1990), p. 297. See also Melvin L. Kohn and Carmi Schooler, *Work and Personality: An Inquiry into the Impact of Social Stratification* (Norwood, N.J.: Ablex Publishing Corp., 1983).

21. See Kim Hopper, "Economics of Makeshifts," *Urban Anthropology* 14 (1985): 1–3. For an alternative interpretation of hustling as mainly illegal activity, see Loic Wacquant, "Inside the Zone," *Theory, Culture, and Society* 15, no. 2 (1998): 1–36.

22. The social psychologist Melvin Kohn argues in his classic work *Class and Conformity* (Chicago: University of Chicago Press, 1969): "People's positions in the social stratification hierarchy have profound effects on their personalities; these effects occur primarily because stratification position strongly affects more proximate conditions of life, particularly job conditions; and job conditions, in turn, profoundly affect personality. Specifically, a higher position in the stratification order affords greater opportunity to be self-directed in one's work—that is, to work at jobs that are substantively complex, are not subject to close supervision, and are not routinized. The experience of occupational self-direction leads in turn to a higher valuation of self-direction for oneself and for one's children, and to a more self-directed orientation to self and to society." See also Kohn's "Doing Social Research Under Conditions of Radical Social Change: The Biography of an Ongoing Research Project," *Social Psychology Quarterly* 56, no. 1 (1993): 6.

23. "Census data show salaried professionals and managers represented under 5% of New York City residents in the nineteenth century and early twentieth century; today they constitute 30% . . . [These high-income workers] have become a very visible part of city life through distinct consumption patterns, lifestyles . . ." Though their "earned income is too little to be investment capital, it is too much for the basically thrifty, savings-oriented middle class. These new high income earners emerge as primary candidates for new types of intermediate investments: arts, antiques, and luxury consumption." (Saskia Sassen, *The Global City* [Princeton: Princeton University Press, p. 335].)

24. Erik Olin Wright, *Class Counts* (Cambridge: Cambridge University Press, 1997), p. 203: "A rigid class structure in which people's lives are tightly bounded within particular class locations is not simply one in which there are few prospects for individual mobility but one in which social networks rarely cross class boundaries."

The Men without Accounts

1. In less developed countries, vendors have much more elaborate mechanisms for transferring public property. Hernando De Soto's research on the underground economy in Lima, Peru, for example, indicates that the extralegal control of vending space takes the form of excise taxes that the vendors pay to work in specific plots of land. Legally, he reports, the receipts from these taxes do not confer any rights of occupancy, but vendors understand them to confer such rights and act as if they do. See Hernando De Soto, *The Other Path: The Invisible Revolution in the Third World* (New York: Harper and Row, 1989, p. 68).

2. He continued, "When I was going to school in South Carolina, and I would see people hanging up in trees, I had to quit, because I'm not gonna get hanged up by a tree."

   Once, after hearing Mudrick's accounts, I went to the library to learn more about conditions in South Carolina when he grew up there. Much to my surprise, it was impossible to find any evidence of lynchings during that period. When I mentioned Mudrick's stories to Professor Walter B. Edgar, a leading expert on the history of the state at the University of South Carolina, he was surprised to hear that Mudrick regularly saw people hanging from trees in the 1940s, when he would have been in grade school. Professor Edgar referred me to I. A. Newby's 1973 treatise, *Black Carolinians*, which shows that lynching had "virtually disappeared" in South Carolina by 1940. (I. A. Newby, *Black Carolinians: A History of Blacks in South Carolina from 1895 to 1968* [Columbia: South Carolina Tricentennial Commission/University of South Carolina Press, 1973], p. 242.)

Yet there was horrible violence directed against blacks and there were some lynchings after 1940. It is possible that Mudrick saw a body hanging from a tree, or that such images were part of his consciousness as he grew up: if he was told stories about lynchings as a child, he could remember them as though he saw them. It is possible that he was afraid of being lynched and afraid to walk to school.

The powerful cultural symbol of the lynching is invested with meanings with which African Americans still live. In addition to telling me about something he may remember as a regular occurrence, Mudrick may have been trying to sum up a history of violence and threats for me, or tell me a story of the kind of racial violence suffered by his relatives and people like him. Perhaps the potent symbol was a literary device that this illiterate man was using. He couldn't read, but he sure could use the symbol.

A few months later, I tried to clarify the story Mudrick had told me to explain his illiteracy.

"I'd see a lot of black guys hanging by their necks in the swamp on my way to school," he said.

"Are you saying that they were lynched?"

"Lynched! By the Ku Klux Klan. By the white sheets and the horses. I didn't see it one day. I seed it a lot of days."

Another possible explanation is that Mudrick may be wrong about his age—though, according to Professor Edgar, if he were sixty-seven instead of fifty-seven, that would not have made much difference. There was more racial violence in the state during the 1930s, but not, after 1933, the kind of usual lynchings that would have made it likely for him to see people hanging regularly from trees. In fact, according to Professor Stewart Tolnay, co-author of the leading demographic study of Southern lynchings, even in those counties in which lynching took place often during a ten-year period, it wouldn't have been the kind of event that a child would regularly see evidence of on his way to school.

"When you were growing up, did you hear stories about this from your parents?" I asked Mudrick.

"Stories? This ain't no story. This is in real life! Not a story. The first man they hanged was a black guy accused to rape a white woman. Then, when they came to find out it was a white man, that they hanged the wrong man—it put too much fear in me, and I didn't go to school. How could I go? Get hanged like the rest of them? Get 'lectricuted? I used to hide. We used to see the fire coming and the people riding in the woods riding horseback. This is not a game I am talking about. This is real. And if my mama was living today, she would tell you."

Even though I note that Mudrick's explanation for his illiteracy is factually implausible to historians like Professor Edgar or demographers like Professor Tolnay, I see it as the kind of story that only a man who had lived a particular kind of life would have thought to tell me or even make up. As Professor Tolnay and E. M. Beck note in their book on lynchings, "As staggering as the lynching toll was, it vastly understates the total volume of violence aimed toward African American citizens of the south. Our lynching inventory does not count casualties of the urban race riots that erupted during those years, nor does it embrace victims of racially motivated murders by a single killer or pairs of assassins. Neither does it include the all too frequent beatings, whippings, verbal humiliations, threats, harangues and other countless indignities suffered by the south's black population during this period." (Stewart E. Tolnay and E. M. Beck, *A Festival of Violence: An Analysis of Southern Lynchings, 1882–1930* [Urbana, Il.: University of Illinois Press, 1995]).

What seems most important is the strong link between other historical conditions in South Carolina at that time and the life of this man on the streets of Greenwich Village today. What can be documented and requires no guessing, according to Professor Edgar, is that 62 percent of the adult black population of South Carolina was illiterate when Mudrick was growing up (compared with 18 percent of the white population). Mudrick's parents, grandparents, and adult neighbors likely did not read or write. Mudrick likely attended a one-room school, where the amount of money spent on education was minimal. "In 1915, South Carolina was spending an [annual] average of $23.76 on the education of each white child and $2.91 on that of each black child," writes Derrick Bell in *Race, Racism, and American Law* (Boston: Little, Brown, 1973). "As late as 1931, six Southern states (Alabama, Arkansas, Florida, Georgia, and North and South Carolina) spent less than a third as much for black children as for whites, and ten years later this figure had risen to only 44 percent. At the time of the 1954 decision in *Brown* v. *Board of Education*, the South as a whole was spending on the average $165 a year for a white pupil, and $115 for a black."

"When you were growing up, Mudrick, most of the adults in your town probably couldn't read or write."

"Right."

"Your parents probably couldn't read or write, either, right?"

"Well, my mother could read and write a little bit. She could read good enough to teach us when we couldn't go to school."

"What about your father?"

"I never seen my father one time in my life."

"Does your daughter know you can't read?"

"My daughter knows," he assured me.

"But you can read the dollar bills!" I said.

"I can read the dollar bills!" Mudrick yelled, laughing. "I can think good and I can read the dollar bills! I know what's going on! And I'm more qualified than a lot of motherfuckers in the street!"

How Sixth Avenue Became a Sustaining Habitat

1. Jacobs, *The Death and Life of Great American Cities*, p. 30.
2. Ibid., p. 36.
3. Ibid., p. 50.

4. Only three years after her book was published, for example, a young woman named Kitty Genovese was stabbed to death in New York City while thirty-eight people watched from their windows. Since that event, social pyschologists have taken a keen interest in the conditions that lead bystanders to be indifferent. One well-known study by Irving Piliavin, Judith Rodin, and Jane Piliavin showed that in 95 percent of cases bystanders will rush to the aid of stricken people in the subways, but the evidence on sidewalks is not nearly so encouraging. Whereas, in Jacobs's ideal city, the presence of eyes upon the street implies that people will be there "when the chips are down," when experimenters staged car burglaries in eighteen cities, fewer than one in ten passersby asked the burglars questions about their activity. Whereas in the subways people are face-to-face with the victim and share a common fate on a small train car, this is not the case on sidewalks. The influence of her work is such that Jacobs's ideas are still taught as basic assumptions for urban planning in the same universities that offer social-psychology courses that would raise serious questions about them.

Some of the most often quoted phrases from Jacobs's book illustrate the nature of her well-accepted but unverified argument: "A well used city street is apt to be a safe street. A deserted city street is apt to be unsafe" (p. 34). "The greater and more plentiful the range of all legitimate interests (in the strictly legal sense) that city streets and their enterprises can satisfy, the better for the streets and for the safety and civilization of the city" (p. 41). "The trust of a city street is formed over time from many, many little sidewalk contacts" (p. 56).

5. Data are for 1989 for Census Block Group 006500-1, which has 2,018 residents, 6.6 percent of whom are African American and 3.1 percent Hispanic. I thank Professor Lincoln Quillian for doing this demographic analysis for me.

6. See U.S. Bureau of the Census, "General Population Characteristics," Table 64, 1990 Census of Population (Washington, D.C.: Government Printing Office, 1990).

7. See Joanne Passaro, *The Unequal Homeless: Men on the Street, Women in Their Place* (New York: Routledge, 1996).

8. For state-of-the-art understanding of the impact of racial residential segregation, see Douglas Massey and Nancy Denton, *American Apartheid* (Cambridge, Mass.: Harvard University Press, 1993). For the latest data on job and housing discrimination, see Joe Feagin and Herman Vera, *White Racism* (New York: Routledge, 1996). See also Reynolds Farley, *Blacks and Whites: Narrowing the Gap* (Cambridge, Mass.: Harvard University Press, 1984).

9. See Farley, ibid.

10. For an understanding of the impact of spatial concentration of poverty and the disappearance of work, see Wilson, *When Work Disappears*. For an analysis of the extent and causes of the spatial concentration of poverty, see Paul Jargowsky, *Poverty and Place* (New York: Russell Sage Foundation, 1997).

11. For an account of the relationship between law and racial oppression, see A. Leon Higginbotham, Jr., *Shades of Freedom: Racial Politics and Presumptions of the American Legal Process* (New York: Alfred A. Knopf, 1996).

12. See Gerald Jaynes and Robin M. Williams, *A Common Destiny: Blacks and American Society* (Washington, D.C.: National Academy Press, 1989), and Richard Freeman, ed., *The Black Youth Labor Market Crisis* (Chicago: University of Chicago Press, 1986). See

also Rebecca Blank, *It Takes a Nation* (New York: Russell Sage Foundation; Princeton, N.J.: Princeton University Press, 1997).

13. For a study of "street criminals" who, unlike the men in this book, remain offenders, see Mark S. Fleisher, *Beggars and Thieves* (Madison: University of Wisconsin Press, 1995).

14. At least twenty-three men working out on Sixth Avenue have discussed serving time for crack possession or distribution; others, who have not wanted to discuss their records, have not denied that crack might have been involved in their offenses.

15. U.S. Sentencing Commission, "Special Report to Congress: Cocaine and Federal Sentencing Policy," April 1997 [referring to 1993 statistics]. See also Jerome G. Miller, *Search and Destroy: African American Males in the Criminal Justice System* (Cambridge: Cambridge University Press, 1996).

16. U.S. Sentencing Commission, "Cocaine and Federal Sentencing Policy."

17. A few of my white middle-class students who use powder cocaine end up in treatment, but none to my knowledge has served time for possession or sale, and none has been left broke and isolated by the criminal-justice system.

18. Christopher Jencks, *The Homeless* (Cambridge, Mass.: Harvard University Press, 1994), p. 53.

19. Roger Waldinger, *Still the Promised City? African-Americans and New Immigrants in Postindustrial New York* (Cambridge, Mass.: Harvard University Press, 1996), p. 173.

20. This focus makes the habitat as I discuss it different from the "natural area" as defined by Robert Park and the Chicago School. The natural area was conceived as a geographic area determined by unplanned, subcultural forces.

    My aspiration here is to engage in an exercise of micro-demographic ethnographic analysis, asking after the processes by which a small population of homeless men migrate and become distributed in a particular pattern in response to larger cultural, economic, and political forces.

    It seems to me that such an analysis was never undertaken by the Chicago fieldworkers, who, working within a framework of human ecology (in studies like *The Taxi-Dance Hall* and *The Gold Coast and the Slum*), mainly settled for maps of distributions and assumed functional complementarity. One additional thing an ethnographer can do, however, is to look for ways in which demographic, cultural, and political data can be complemented by studies of day-to-day life which *show*, rather than assume, *how* the system works. That is my goal for this chapter.

21. Ralph H. Turner and Lewis M. Killian, *Collective Behavior* (Englewood Cliffs, N.J.: Prentice-Hall, 1957), p. 58. The authors use these words to describe a common definition of "milling."

22. Jencks, *The Homeless*.

23. I got the idea of inquiring about this from reading Joel Siegel, "Wretch Rooms No Comfort: Addicts & Derelicts Turn Them into Rail Road Station Cesspools," *New York Daily News*, September 24, 1989, p. 47.

24. Michael Deutsch prepared the briefs for the Center for Constitutional Rights; Robert A. Solomon and Gerald P. Hauser prepared the brief for Jerome Frank Legal Services.

25. 875 F. Supp. 1055 (S.D.N.Y. 1995).

26. These design elements were of the same type as the "bum proof bench" described by Mike Davis in his treatise on Los Angeles's "socio-spatial" strategy against the poor and homeless (*City of Quartz* [New York: Vintage, 1990]).
27. Interview with clerk of the New York City Council.
28. Local Law 80 of 1996, "amending the administrative code of the city of New York in relation to a prohibition against certain forms of aggressive solicitation."
29. See *Graff* v. *City of Chicago*, 9 F.3d 1309 (7th Cir. 1993).
30. See Albert Cohen, Alfred Lindesmith, and Karl Schuessler, *The Sutherland Papers* (Bloomington: Indiana University Press, 1956); Donald R. Cressey, *Delinquency, Crime, and Differential Association* (The Hague: Martinus Nijhoff, 1964).
31. See James Q. Wilson and George Kelling, "Broken Windows," *Atlantic Monthly*, March 1982, pp. 29–38.
32. In fact, the Department of Sanitation maintains two enforcement bodies. Enforcement agents, like traffic police, have summons power only. The sanitation police have arrest powers as well, derived from state law, not unlike New York City and Port Authority police. They are, however, completely independent of and unrelated to the latter forces.
33. From a public policy point of view, the benefit of clean streets must be weighed against the city's economic interest in controlling the theft of cans from recycled waste. Cans are the only item of real value to recyclers. The tonnage price for cans is quite high, and the city loses money when scavengers take them.

Sidewalk Sleeping

1. Jacobs, *The Death and Life of Great American Cities*, pp. 131–32.
2. Wilson had done empirical research in the 1970s arguing that the crime rate goes down when police focus on minor crimes such as citing for moving violations. These results were confirmed with more sophisticated statistical techniques by Robert Sampson and Jacqueline Cohen, who concluded: "Proactive policing has been shown to have significant and relatively strong inverse effects on robbery, especially adult robbery by both blacks and whites. . . . Hence, on strict empirical grounds the results suggest that cities . . . with higher levels of proactive police strategies directed at public disorders also generate significantly lower robbery rates." (Robert J. Sampson and Jacqueline Cohen, "Deterrent Effects of the Police on Crime: A Replication and Theoretical Extension," *Law and Society Review* 22, no. 1 [1988]: 163–89, 184–85.)
3. See, for example, Philippe Bourgeois, *In Search of Respect* (Cambridge: Cambridge University Press, 1995).
4. Jencks, *The Homeless*, p. 44.
5. In considering the distinctiveness of these unhoused persons, I will pay attention to four concepts—population, (social) organization, environment, and technology, POET—the very concepts that Otis Dudley Duncan once described as essential to territorial demography or human ecology. (See Otis Dudley Duncan, "Human Ecology and Population Studies," in Philip M. Hauser and Otis Dudley Duncan, eds., *The Study of Population* [Chicago: University of Chicago Press, 1959], pp. 678–716.) This population has four characteristics that make it distinctive. First, its individuals constitute a population unit in a particular space with a character different from any of the men as indi-

viduals. This unit enables men who could not survive on their own to "make it" as a group. Second, the population unit exists in an environment and remains there by acting on the environment despite the environment's best efforts to act on it. Third, the population unit develops particular techniques and technologies in order to gain sustenance from the environment. And fourth, an intricate social organization arises from those sustenance-producing activities. In developing the framework, I am building on the earlier work of Kim Hopper, "Economies of Makeshift," *Urban Anthropology*, vol. 14 (1985): 1–3, which argued for the importance of understanding "the particular way homelessness meshes with other subsistence activities" (p. 214).

6. Morgan and Zimmer, "The Social Pharmacology of Smokeable Cocaine," p. 145.
7. Galen Cranz, *The Chair* (New York: W. W. Norton, 1998).
8. For a wider view, see Jim Baumohl, ed., *Homelessness in America* (Phoenix: Oryx Press, 1996).
9. In looking at Sixth Avenue, therefore, my purpose is not to make generalizations about homelessness that could be sustained only with different methods or with comparisons to populations I don't know, but to understand the uses to which the sidewalks of Greenwich Village are being put today. In the process, though, we may learn something about the types of questions that could be asked about other homeless street people—that is, what it is about a particular environment that makes it a sustainable habitat for this person or group of people. After all, we can only know if the choices made by other types of homeless individuals have a similar complexity if we continue to respond to pleas for more and better evidence.
10. See Jencks, *The Homeless*, p. 44.

When You Gotta Go

1. For a highly original analysis, see Marc Linder and Ingrid Nygaard, *Void Where Prohibited: Rest Breaks and the Right to Urinate on Company Time* (Ithaca: ILR Press, 1998).

Talking to Women

1. This chapter is closely based on Mitchell Duneier and Harvey Molotch, "Talking City Trouble: Interactional Vandalism, Social Inequality, and the 'Urban Interaction Problem,' " *American Journal of Sociology* 104, no. 5 (March 1998): pp. 1263–95.
2. Carol Brooks Gardner, *Passing By: Gender and Public Harassment* (Berkeley: University of California Press, 1995).
3. Anderson, *Streetwise.*
4. Jacobs, *The Death and Life of Great American Cities*, p. 56.
5. In addition, Jacobs was ahead of her time in her understanding that "there are immense variations in the degree of civilization and safety found among . . . [minority] groups and among the city areas where they live" (ibid., p. 39).
6. William H. Whyte, *City* (New York: Anchor Books, 1988).
7. See, for example, Gardner, *Passing By*; Daphne Spain, *Gendered Spaces* (Chapel Hill: University of North Carolina Press, 1992); Elizabeth Wilson, *The Sphinx in the City* (Berkeley: University of California Press, 1991).

8. This field has its beginnings in Harvey Sacks's collaboration with Emanuel Schegloff and Gail Jefferson. A more recent presentation by Schegloff (1996) has laid out a concise statement of CA's basic precepts and of how it contrasts with and at least potentially complements more traditional work in the discipline. He makes clear that the CA program consists of "noticings of initially unremarkable features" of talk and conduct, "unmotivated" by any political or theoretical goals of citizens or conventional sociology.

   Although I, too, make use of these noticings, in contrast to CA scholarship I *am* motivated by a set of substantive concerns: how, in the process of deploying the procedures described in CA, people make trouble in the streets. This is a kind of policy-oriented applied CA.

9. The findings of CA have been found to be sufficiently robust to hold even across diverse language and national groupings—besides the languages of Western Europe, Japanese (Gene Lerner and T. Takagi, "On the Place of Linguistic Resources in the Organization of Talk-in-Interaction: Aco-investigation of English and Japanese Grammatical Practices," *Journal of Pragmatics* 30 [1998]), as well as Farsi and six other Indo-European languages (Deirdre Boden, *The Business of Talk: Organization in Action* [Cambridge: Polity Press, 1994]). Given the diversity of the base, CA provides an appropriate template against which to look for distinctive attributes of the conversations I examine. I compare the technical properties of street conversations with CA findings of how talk ordinarily operates. I draw on only a few of the most replicated and straightforward findings from CA scholars to do this.

10. Harvey Sacks, Emanuel Schegloff, and Gail Jefferson, "A Simplest Systematics for the Organization of Turn-taking in Conversation," *Language* 50 (1974): 696–735.

11. Duneier and Molotch, "Talking City Trouble."

12. The timing of responses in a conversation can indicate a solution instead of a problem. For example, a silence before a negative is not a problem, but expected. Similarly, a two-second pause could be unnoticeable if somebody has said, "Think about this before you answer."

13. Michele Wakin suggested this phrase.

14. Harvey L. Molotch and Deirdre Boden, "Talking Social Structure," *American Sociological Review* 50, no. 3 (1985): 273–88; Don Zimmerman and Candace West, "Doing Gender," *Gender and Society* 1 (1977): 125–51.

15. Douglas Robins, Clinton Sanders, and Spencer Cahill, "Dogs and Their People: Pet-Facilitated Interaction in a Public Setting," *Journal of Contemporary Ethnography* 20 (1991): 3–25.

16. I thank Gene Lerner for pointing this out to me.

17. Emanuel Schegloff, "Discourse as an Interactional Achievement: Some Uses of 'Uh Huh' and Other Things That Come Between Sentences," in Deborah Tannen, ed., *Analyzing Discourse: Text and Talk* (proceedings of Georgetown University Roundtable on Language and Linguistics, Washington, D.C., 1981).

18. Gail Jefferson, "Notes on a Possible Metric Which Provides for a 'Standard Maximum Silence' of Approximately One Second in Conversation," in C. Roger and P. Bull, *Conversation: An Interdisciplinary Perspective* (Clevedon, U.K.: Multilingual Matters, 1989).

19. This is called "latching" in the Conversation Analysis lexicon (see Gail Jefferson, "A Case of Precision Timing in Ordinary Conversation: Overlapped Tag-Position Address Terms in Closing Sequences," *Semiotica* 9 (1973): 47–96).

20. See Gardner, *Passing By*.

Accusations

1. Gresham M. Sykes and David Matza, "Techniques of Neutralization: A Theory of Delinquency," *American Sociological Review* 22 (1957): 664–70.

2. Dianne Vaughan, *The Challenger Launch Decision* (Chicago: University of Chicago Press, 1997).

3. Jerome Skolnick, *Justice Without Trial* (New York: Wiley, 1966), pp. 45–48. According to Irving Piliavin and Scott Briar ("Police Encounters with Juveniles," *American Journal of Sociology* 70 [April 1966]): "Compared to other youths, [blacks] and boys whose appearance matched the delinquent stereotype were more frequently stopped and interrogated by patrolmen—often even in the absence of evidence that an offense had been committed—[and] usually were given more severe dispositions for the same offense." See also Robert Sampson, "Effects of Socioeconomic Context on Official Reaction to Juvenile Delinquency," *American Sociological Review* 51 (December 1986): 876–85.

The Space Wars

1. In his community study of Corona, Queens, Steven Gregory shows a similar reaction to unhoused persons in Astoria: "Residents were invited to articulate their interests, identities, and goals through place-bound notions of 'community' and 'quality of life' that emerge through practices of policing and surveilling space. In short, the state's readiness to respond to community problems through law enforcement practices incited activists to represent and indeed experience their concerns through the tactical logic of controlling community space." [Steven Gregory, *Black Corona* [Princeton: Princeton University Press, 1998], p. 232.

2. 34th Street Partnership, Inc., "Introductory Statement," in *Capital Improvement Bonds*, ser. 1993, p. 1.

3. See Heather MacDonald, "BIDs Really Work," *City Journal* 6, no. 2 (Spring 1996): 29–42.

4. Meanwhile, the City Council had, after a full year of official requests, not yet granted me access to documents that I was legally entitled to see under the Freedom of Information Act. In July 1997, I met with Councilman John Sabini and told him about my problems gaining access to basic documents. He personally intervened, and I was finally granted access to the Council's records, almost two years after my initial request was filed.

5. This is an instance of an elite coalition brought together by real-estate interests (the "growth machine") to achieve their goals, as delineated by John Logan and Harvey Molotch in their book *Urban Fortunes* (Berkeley and Los Angeles: University of California Press, 1997).

6. Ibid.

7. Ibid.

8. For the best ethnography of relations between official and unofficial law, see Bonaventura de Sousa Santos, *Toward a New Common Sense* (New York: Routledge, 1996). For an illuminating discussion of the scholarly literature on "extralegal" norms, see Robert Ellickson, *Order Without Law* (Cambridge, Mass.: Harvard University Press, 1991).

9. Anderson, *Streetwise*, pp. 70–71, citing a concept developed by St. Clair Drake and Horace Cayton in *Black Metropolis* (New York: Harcourt, Brace, 1945).

10. On the breadth and narrowness of disputes, see Max Gluckman, *The Judicial Process Among the Barotse of Northern Rhodesia* (Manchester: Manchester University Press, 1955); Santos, *Toward a New Common Sense*.

11. In order to mark their interpretation of the exact spaces vendors could occupy, officers of the Sixth Precinct spray-painted orange or yellow neon arrows on the curb of each block where a vendor could place a table. This was designed to make it clear to the vendor and beat officer where vending could take place. Anyone outside these lines—which mainly had meaning to the regular vendors on the block—was in apparent violation of the Municipal Code. In some cases, the marks were inaccurate (giving less space to vendors than required), but vendors never raised objections.

A Christmas on Sixth Avenue

1. For a complete description of this movement, see George L. Kelling and Catherine M. Coles, *Fixing Broken Windows* (New York: Free Press, 1996).

2. Local Law 80 of 1996 "to amend the administrative code of the city of New York in relation to a prohibition against certain forms of aggressive solicitation."

3. For an excellent discussion, see Paul Stoler, "Spaces, Places, and Fields," *American Anthropologist* 98, no. 4 (1996): 776–88.

4. See Kelling and Coles, *Fixing Broken Windows*.

5. This analysis is an attempt to build on the work of others who have noticed the phenomenon, such as Elijah Anderson, "The Code of the Streets," *Atlantic Monthly*, May 1994, pp. 81–94; Philippe Bourgeois, *In Search of Respect: Selling Crack in El Barrio* (New York: Cambridge University Press, 1995).

6. Ever since Goffman published *Interaction Ritual* (Chicago: Aldine, 1967), sociologists have been sensitive to the ways in which status inconsistency can sometimes be the basis of embarrassment, an emotion that derives from seeing oneself in a negative light through the eyes of others. And ever since the publication of Thomas J. Scheff's *Microsociology* (Chicago: University of Chicago Press, 1990), some social psychologists have increasingly seen embarrassment and humiliation as "*the* social emotions, arising as [they] do out of the monitoring of one's actions by viewing one's self from the standpoint of others."

7. Thomas J. Scheff, personal communication.

8. Anderson, *Streetwise*, p. 190.

9. It is, of course, possible that the officer was emphasizing that he always treats Ishmael respectfully because I was present. We cannot dismiss the possibility that he wanted to

impress me. But I have seen many examples of this kind of behavior in situations in which I was not a potential influence. In fact, some other interactions I have witnessed on the street have included some effort on the part of the police to get their way by emphasizing some measure of "respect."

10. This is consistent with the descriptions found in other ethnographic accounts. Egon Bittner writes: "The safe way of gaining the privilege [of expressive freedom] is to respond to the patrolman in ways that do not challenge his right to ask questions and issue commands." (*Aspects of Police Work* [Boston: Northeastern University Press, 1990], p. 45.) Indeed, Anderson states, "In the presence of police officers, who clearly have the upper hand, black youths check themselves. They defer to the police or try to avoid them."

11. Bittner, *Aspects of Police Work*, p. 159: "Community policing recognizes that organizational structures and administrative processes that treat officers like factory workers have failed. Police work, unlike factory work, is not simple and routine, but complex; it is usually conducted by one or two officers in the field, without direct oversight, who must use considerable discretion in handling problems. When officers confront complex life and death decisions, success depends not on direct supervision or rote application of specific rules, but on the application of general knowledge and skill, obtained through prolonged education and mentoring, to specific situations. Community policing aims to develop administrative techniques that recognize this complexity in the work of police officers. Sergeants, for example, become mentors and coaches, not overseers. Their focus is on assisting officers in solving neighborhood problems, not adherence to organizational rules."

12. Given the level of pressure that is placed on police by the local community board and the Business Improvement District to control the behavior of what they call street people, the officer thinks he is speaking for the community when he takes such action.

13. I am made sensitive to this possibility, and was inspired to look for evidence to support it, after reading David Garland's monumental book *Punishment and Modern Society* (Chicago: University of Chicago Press, 1990). See also Joel Feinberg, "The Expressive Function of Punishment," in *Doing and Deserving* (Princeton: Princeton University Press, 1970).

14. As Donald Black notes in a classic article ("Crime as Social Control," *American Sociological Review* 48 [1983]: pp. 34–45), "A great deal of the conduct labeled and processed as crime in modern societies resembles the modes of conflict management . . . that are found in traditional societies which have little or no law (in the sense of governmental social control)." By taking Black's observation about crime in modern society and applying it to the police, we can better understand the way in which the quality of life is regulated.

15. I believe it would be inconsistent with the argument of this chapter to name the police officer involved. To use his name would suggest that these incidents are the fault of a particular individual, rather than the pernicious result of a system of policing.

16. Indeed, directly across the street, there was a newsstand in operation. This was the first comparison to the newsstands that I had heard during my years on the block. Here, a homeless-rights organization might be on more solid factual ground in arguing in court

that singling out Ishmael's acts of selling on Christmas is irrational and fails equal-protection scrutiny. They also might argue that the police would confiscate Ishmael's magazines and belongings when he left his table unattended, but they would never confiscate the belongings of the newsstand when the attendant stepped out to use a washroom or went into McDonald's for a soda, which I have often seen him do. Both the newsstand attendant and Ishmael are using public land for the same purpose, distributing written matter, and an unattended table does not interfere with public use of the sidewalks any more than an unattended newsstand. The reason for treating Ishmael and the newsstand differently, it might be argued, is that seizing Ishmael's property achieves the purpose of punishing him for behavior that is disfavored by the community but not illegal. The behavior being punished is not that of distributing written matter, but the lifestyle of street homelessness. Punishing the lifestyle is certainly an illegitimate state objective. No doubt, the newsstand vendor would object to being compared to Ishmael on the grounds that he runs a licensed business, a permanent structure which cannot be built without the approval of five agencies.

17. I chose this periodical deliberately because at that time it was distributed through the mail (and not sold on newsstands), so it had no price marked on it. In the few months prior, officers of the Sixth Precinct had been routinely asking vendors to produce tax-identification numbers. When vendors could not, police told them to break down their tables. I had left my tax ID at home, because I hadn't expected to do any vending that day. I decided to put a sign on the table indicating that the magazines were free. It said, "Merry Christmas. Free Magazines. One per person."

18. Paul Chevigny, *Edge of the Knife: Police Violence in the Americas* (New York: New Press, 1995), p. 33.

19. Egon Bittner, "The Police on Skid Row: A Study of Peace Keeping," reprinted in Bittner, *Aspects of Police Work* (Boston: Northeastern University Press, 1990).

20. Ibid., p. 701.

21. Ibid., p. 708.

22. Ibid., p. 711.

23. Ibid., p. 715.

24. Scheff writes, "Mutual conformity and respect lead to pride and fellow feeling, which lead to further conformity, which leads to further positive feeling, and so on." *Microsociology*, p. 76.

25. Anderson, *Streetwise*, pp. 70–71, citing a concept developed by St. Clair Drake and Horace Cayton, in *Black Metropolis* (New York: Harcourt, Brace, 1945).

26. Kelling and Coles, *Fixing Broken Windows*, p. 15.

27. Ibid., p. 161.

28. Ibid.

29. They write: "Philip Zimbardo, a Stanford psychologist, reported in 1969 on some experiments testing the broken-windows theory. He arranged to have an automobile without license plates parked with its hood up on a street in the Bronx and a comparable automobile on a street in Palo Alto, California. The car in the Bronx was attacked by 'vandals' within ten minutes of its 'abandonment.' . . . The car in Palo Alto sat untouched for more than a week. Then Zimbardo smashed part of it with a sledgehammer.

Soon, passersby were joining in. Within a few hours, the car had been turned upside down and utterly destroyed. . . . Vandalism can occur anywhere once communal barriers—the sense of mutual regard and the obligations of civility—are lowered by actions that seem to signal that '*no one cares.*' " (Wilson and Kelling, "Broken Windows," reprinted in James Q. Wilson, *Thinking About Crime* [New York: Vintage, 1985], p. 78).

30. For an excellent study, see also Wesley Skogan, *Disorder and Decline* (Berkeley and Los Angeles: University of California Press, 1990), which focuses on solidly residential areas, unlike Sixth Avenue.

A Scene from Jane Street

1. Local Laws of the City of New York for the Year 1984, No. 17.
2. The altruism and helping behavior we see toward public characters like the Romps can be interpreted in terms of a long-standing set of findings within social psychology that consistently demonstrate that "people are more likely to help others who are similar to themselves than they are to help those who are dissimilar." (David A. Schroeder, Louis A. Penner, John F. Dovidio, and Jane A. Piliavin, *The Psychology of Helping and Altruism* [New York: McGraw-Hill, 1995], p. 48.)
3. Anderson, *Streetwise*.
4. Ibid.
5. It is, of course, possible that black residents of the Village would have found the black Romps less threatening. One black professor living in the neighborhood reported to me that she and her husband, also a black professor, invited Hakim and Alice to their New Year's Eve party. Hakim says he would have liked to go, but it was impossible to find child care for Alice's grandchildren.
6. For a penetrating analyses, see Jennifer L. Hochschild, *Facing Up to the American Dream* (Princeton: Princeton University Press, 1998); Bob Blauner, *Black Lives, White Lives* (Berkeley: University of California Press, 1992).
7. Schroeder et al., *Psychology of Helping*.
8. I am attempting here to add a dimension to the idea, already prominent in thinking about deviance, that deviant behavior is sometimes a response to the society's initial response to aberration, which makes it difficult to carry on as a normal person, so that the deviant looks worse than ever. The idea is that the response pushes the person even further into misbehaving. This is known as "secondary deviance," an outgrowth of labeling theories that argued that deviance is in the first place the product of definition, so that the same behavior is not always responded to in the same way. See Edwin Lemert, *Human Deviance, Social Problems, and Social Control* (Englewood Cliffs, N.J.: Prentice-Hall, 1972) and Howard S. Becker, *Outsiders* (New York: Free Press, 1963). According to labeling theory, the quality of deviance is not a feature of the deviant person but of the interactive and definitional process. By focusing on spatiality and temporality, we can provide a framework for seeing the variation in possible outcomes. By treating these things systematically, we can also add to the related idea that people can avoid the consequences of deviance and being labeled deviant by keeping the audiences for their behavior separate from one another, so that when they do "deviant

things" the people who would label them don't see them. The housed residents of New York City accomplish the segregation of audiences by manipulating space and/or by manipulating time, or by using them as resources.

9. John Hagan and Patricia Parker, "White Collar Crime and Punishment," *American Sociological Review* 50, no. 3 (June 1985): p. 312.

Appendix

1. Erving Goffman, "On Fieldwork," in Lyn H. Lofland, ed., *Journal of Contemporary Ethnography* 18, no. 2 (July 1969): 123–32. Goffman said he was repeating John Lofland's earlier remarks, in which, according to an editorial note, he commented that it was likely difficult for fieldworkers to "know" exactly what it is they do to generate their analyses.

2. Paul Laurence Dunbar, "We Wear the Mask," in *Lyrics of Lowly Life* (Seacaucus, N.J.: Citadel Press, 1997), p. 167. I thank Aldon Morris for bringing Dunbar's poem to my attention.

3. Some of Becker's other techniques are discussed in two other books which have been very helpful to me over the years: Howard S. Becker, *Tricks of the Trade: How to Think About Your Research While You're Doing It* (Chicago: University of Chicago Press, 1998); and his *Writing for Social Scientists* (Chicago: University of Chicago Press, 1986).

4. For a couple of excellent exceptions in the journals, see Bob Blauner, "Problems of Editing 'First Person' Sociology," *Qualitative Sociology* 10, no. 1 (Spring 1987); Marjorie DeVault, "Talking and Listening from a Woman's Standpoint: Feminist Strategies for Interviewing and Analysis," *Social Problems* 37, no. 1 (February 1990).

5. For an analysis of contemporary photojournalism which has influenced my thinking on these issues, see Dianne Hagaman, *How I Learned Not to Be a Photojournalist* (Lexington: University of Kentucky Press, 1996).

6. For a useful statement on why interviewing is sometimes not enough, see Paul Lichterman, *The Search for Political Community* (Cambridge: Cambridge University Press, 1996), pp. 237–42.

7. Karl R. Popper, *The Logic of Scientific Discovery* (New York: Harper and Row, 1968). As cited in Gary King, Robert O. Keohane, and Sidney Verba, *Designing Social Inquiry* (Princeton: Princeton University Press, 1994), p. 14.

8. Michael Burawoy et al., *Ethnography Unbound: Power and Resistance in the Modern Metropolis* (Berkeley: University of California Press, 1991).

9. Stephen Steinberg, "The Urban Villagers." Yvonne M. Lassalle and Maureen O'Dougherty, "In Search of Weeping Worlds: Economies of Agency and Politics of Representation in the Ethnography of Inequality," *Radical History Review* 69 (1997): 243–60. For important work emphasizing other aspects of this problem, see Avery Gordon, *Ghostly Matters* (Minneapolis: University of Minnesota Press, 1996), and George E. Marcus, "Contemporary Problems of Ethnography in the Modern World System," in James Clifford and George E. Marcus, *Writing Culture* (Berkeley, University of California Press, 1986), pp. 165–93.

10. Burawoy, *Ethnography Unbound*.

11. George E. Marcus, *Ethnography Through Thick and Thin* (Princeton: Princeton University Press, 1998). For a programmatic discussion of how important it is to explore the "relations of ruling," see Dorothy Smith, *The Everyday World As Problematic* (Boston: Northeastern University Press, 1988).

12. In thinking about these issues, I had been heavily influenced by the writings of Alessandro Portelli, including *The Battle of Valle Giulia: Oral History and the Art of Dialogue* (Madison: University of Wisconsin Press, 1997).

13. I was not trying to get her interpretation of this particular episode of conversation, or trying to substitute her opinion of it for the details of the actual conversation. Nor was it my purpose to use the interview to create conversational data.

14. See James Clifford and George Marcus, eds., *Writing Culture* (Berkeley: University of California Press, 1986); Ruth Behar and Deborah A. Gordon, *Women Writing Culture* (Berkeley: University of California Press, 1995). See also Norman Denzin, *Interpretive Ethnography* (Thousand Oaks, Calif.: Sage, 1996).

15. See, for example, Marjorie DeVault, *Liberating Method* (Philadephia: Temple University Press, 1999); Kum Kum Bhavnani, "Tracing the Contours: Feminist Research and Feminist Objectivity," *Woman's Studies International Forum* 16, no. 2 (1993): 95–104; Shulamit Reinharz, with the assistance of Lynn Davidman, *Feminist Methods in Social Research* (New York: Oxford University Press, 1992); Michelle Fine, *Disruptive Voices: The Possibilities of Feminist Research* (Ann Arbor: University of Michigan Press, 1992); Patricia Hill Collins, *Black Feminist Thought: Knowledge, Consciousness, and the Politics of Empowerment* (Boston: Unwin Hyman, 1990).

16. Elliot Liebow, *Tell Them Who I Am: The Lives of Homeless Women* (New York: Penguin, 1993).

17. See, for example, Alex Kotlowitz, *There Are No Children Here* (New York: Doubleday, 1991), and William Finnegan, *Cold New World* (New York: Random House, 1998).

18. Elliot Liebow, *Tally's Corner: A Study of Negro Streetcorner Men* (Boston: Little, Brown, 1968), p. 253.

19. Ibid.

Acknowledgments

As I began research on this book, Professor Edward Shils of the University of Chicago passed away. I hope that he would have looked kindly upon this effort to make use of some of what he tried to teach me.

My editors at Farrar, Straus and Giroux, Jonathan Galassi and Paul Elie, showed a monumental commitment to this project. Jonathan helped me conceive the project from its very beginning and was always there when I needed him. Paul Elie gave detailed advice that vastly improved the final manuscript. At FSG, I also thank Pete Miller, Frieda Duggan, Brian Blanchfield, Toleda Bennett, and Cynthia Krupat.

I continue to be enormously grateful to Howard S. Becker, who, while I was in college at Northwestern University, conveyed the method of participant observation and later advised me on all aspects of this book; to Gerald Suttles and Roger Michener from the University of Chicago and William Sampson and Christopher Jencks from Northwestern University; and to Mr. Davenport, Mr. Fleishacker, and Dr. Beyrer of Lynbrook High School—all teachers who cared.

During the past six years, I have had the honor of co-teaching a graduate seminar in ethnography with Harvey Molotch, the consummate urban sociologist. In addition to showing me the method of Conversation Analysis, and co-authoring an article with me upon which the section using Conversation Analysis is significantly based, he gave himself to this book no differently than if it had been his own. I would like to express the deep appreciation I feel.

I have no foundation grants or research staff to thank for making this book possible, but I do have the pleasure of expressing thanks to the people who let me sleep on their couches while I did my fieldwork: Josh Goldfein and Yvonne Brown, my roommates from the NYU School of Law, have always had a couch or bed for me. Without their support, none of this would have been possible. Jane, Robert, and Rachel Toll, and Elinor Snyder, put up with me in their spare bedrooms. In addition to being a source of important friendship, the Tolls have been a great inspiration to me with their "Say Yes to Education" program for inner-city youth in Philadelphia.

I also wish to express heartfelt thanks to a number of colleagues and students who bent over backwards to help me, reading anywhere from a few pages to individual chapters, or just commenting on a talk or idea discussed in the hallways: Erik Wright, Jane Piliavin, Bob Blauner, Stephen Steinberg, Bob Hauser, Franklin D. Wilson, Constance M. Penley, Phil Gorski, Adam Winkler, Karl Taeuber, Gene Lerner, Don Zimmerman, Deirdre Boden, Debby Carr, Doug Maynard, Hal Winsborough, Jack Sutton, Tom Scheff, Robert Bookman, Chas Camic, Adam Gamoran, Irv Piliavin, Bobbi Wolfe, Bob Haveman, Alex Jeffers, Larry Wu, Gary Sandefur, Tess Hauser, Boa Santos, Chuck Halaby, Morton Goldfein, John Foran, Noah Friedkin, Rob Mare, Hella Heydorn, Gay Seidman, Rich Appelbaum, Marino Bruce, Allen Hunter, Bert Adams, Bruce Straits, Kum Kum Bhavnani, Avery Gordon, Christopher Newfield, France Winddance Twine, Jonathan Warren, Regina Austin, Sarah Fenstermaker, Bill Sewell, Melissa Bomes, Nina Eliasoph, Lincoln Quillian, Jane Collins, Marino Bruce, Nora Schaeffer, Eve Darian-Smith, Pam Oliver, Jonathan Rosenbaum, Beth Le Poire, Gerald Marwell, Lisa Torres, Bill Bielby, Dick Flacks, Roger Friedland, Mardi Kidwell, Michele Wakin, Beth Schneider, Ed Donnerstein, John Mohr, Mark Suchman, Audrey Sprenger, Yumiko Kida, Christopher Kollmeyer, Janette Kawachi, Darcie Vandegraft, Mardi Kidwell, Eric Grodsky, Rachel Luft, Mika Lo, Ari Rosner, Neil Gross, Devah Pager, Thomas Macias, Leonard Nevarez, Christabel Garcia-Zamor, Clifford Westfall, Katherina Zippel, Alair MacLean, Kelly Musick, Darren Good, Alex Jeffers, and Ronnie Goldberg.

At the NYU School of Law, where I was a student in the early nineties, I continue to be grateful to the atmosphere for the study of the sociology of law that inspired me to undertake much that is in these pages. I am particularly grateful to James B. Jacobs, David Garland, and Peggy Cooper Davis as well as a long list of many other fine teachers in that great institution. Dean John Sexton and Vice Dean Oscar Chase have always been very supportive.

For further support in New York I thank Penny Hardy, Cressida Leyshon, Jenny Wolfe, Nolan Zail, Barry Alexander Brown, Scott Sillers, Sebastian Hardy, Jeff and Monica Cohen, Andrew White, Yodon Thonden, Elizabeth Wood, Alison Brooks, Sherman Douglas, Paul Zarowin, Amy Katz, Josh Leitner, William Powell, Mercedes Elam, Angelo Scotto and Jason Duterte of the Washington Square Hotel, Majec Williams and Jason Goldfarb of TSR Wireless, Francis Johnson, Amir Al-Islam, Donna Peters, Lamont Muhammad, Greg Thomas, Harriet Francis, Phyllis Vickers, Cathy Bowman, Mark Levine, and Stephen Dunn. In Washington, D.C., Maria Foscarinis, Robert Tier, David Weiner, and Sean Enright. In Chicago, Mary Knoblauch, Bob Roth, Cleo Wilson, Phyllis Johnson, Judy Marriot, Jonathan Segal, Doug Mitchell, Mr. London, Susan Allen, Spiros and Mary Argiris and all the regulars at Valois "See Your Food" Cafeteria, Andrea Ellington, Brenda Butler, Bill Mullen, Chris Brailey, Walter Kale, Steve Marino, Barbara Brotman, Erin Connolly, and Jack Cella at the Seminary Coop Bookstore and 57th Street Books. In Philadelphia, Dianne Weiss and Ellen Solms. In Santa Barbara, Glenn Wharton, Joan and Bill Murdoch, Karen Shapiro, Mickey Flacks, Chris Allen, Nancy Willstatter, Kim Summerfield, Marie Vierra, Linda Le Cam, Suzanne Labrucherie, Evely and Ron Shlensky, Lael Mohr, Suzanne Soule, Alexandra and Josh at Bread D'Angelo; Michael, Rob, Alice, Emilio, at Emilios's, Roy of Roy's and Tim, Max, Barbara, and Chad of the Montecito Del Mar Motel. In Madison, Ginny Rogers, Deanna Moore, Toni Schulze, Sandy Ramer, Barb Schwoerer, Janet Short, Ellen Jacobson, Carol Mooney, Janet Donlin, and Mark at Sunroom.

This book was very fortunate to have been represented by the consummate literary agent of my own generation, Cullen Stanley of Janklow and Nesbit. With boundless energy, lavish care, and wise counsel since the day it was a one-page proposal, she has done much to earn my gratitude. I also thank Tifanny Richards, Bennett Ashley, Kate Schaeffer, and Lynn Nesbit for their efforts. Thanks to Irwin and Margo Winkler for introducing me to Lynn.

I wish to express my gratitude to Hakim Hasan—intellectual and friend—for his generosity and moral gravity; to Alice, for everything she did to make this book possible; and to all the people working on Sixth Avenue who continue to give me the honor of letting me be part of their lives.

Ovie Carter read every draft of this manuscript and influenced every subsequent version with the photographs he made. He has taught me so much since we began our collaboration on *Slim's Table*. I look forward to many more years of work together.

I thank my parents, who after much begging bought me my first tape recorder, a Realistic from Radio Shack, when I was ten. Little did they or I know. For his love and support for everything I have ever tried to do, I thank my father. I also thank my sister, Candi Stamm, and her husband, Philip Stamm, and Gary King, and Muriel and Arthur King.

This book is dedicated to my mother, and to all the mothers of men who are on Sixth Avenue and other American sidewalks. With love.